Fireship

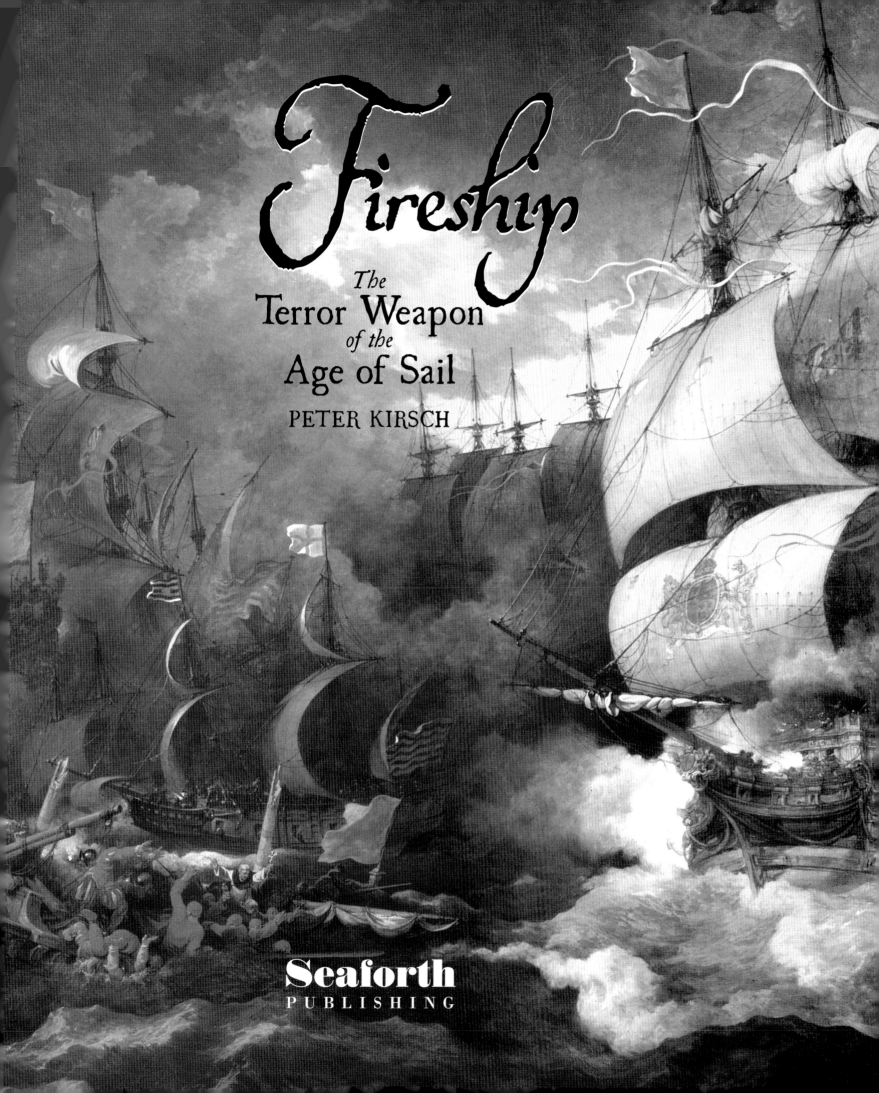

Fireship

The Terror Weapon of the Age of Sail

PETER KIRSCH

Seaforth

PUBLISHING

I wish to thank my dear wife Nina,
who has once again allowed me the time to write a book,
and also helped by undertaking the translations from Russian.

FRONTISPIECE:
A highly romanticised depiction of the English fireship attack on the Spanish Armada
off Gravelines in August 1588; oil painting by Philippe-Jacques de Loutherbourg, 1796.

[NATIONAL MARITIME MUSEUM BHC0264]

Translated from the German by John Harland

First published in Great Britain in 2009 by
Seaforth Publishing
An imprint of Pen & Sword Books Ltd
47 Church Street, Barnsley
S Yorkshire s70 2AS

www.seaforthpublishing.com
Email info@seaforthpublishing.com

British Library Cataloguing in Publication Data
A CIP data record for this book is available from the British Library

ISBN 978-1-84832-025-3

Typeset and designed by Roger Daniels
Printed and bound in Thailand

CONTENTS

INTRODUCTION

'They ought not to have been alarmed by your fireships, but fear deprived them of their senses, and they no longer knew how to act in their own defence.'

Napoleon describing the behaviour of the French captains
and their crews during the fireship attack at Basque Roads, 1809

'Fireship!' For centuries, on board any warship in the days of sail, this cry provoked horror and fear. At worst it meant serious injury or death for the whole crew, and many would rather jump overboard or surrender than fall victim to the flames. However, if the would-be victim could keep a cool head, there were many ways to avert the danger. It was a matter of remaining sufficiently single-minded, determined and cold-blooded.

What in fact was a fireship? It was not necessarily a specific ship type, and the term only defined its function. It could be nothing more than a vessel whose hold was filled with readily inflammable material – that was the usual type. But it might also be a ship crammed with a large amount of high explosive that could blow sky-high at any moment. There was no obvious visible difference, and this made every attempt to disarm a fireship a trial of courage.

Subject to wind, tide and wave action, sailing ships did not have complete freedom of movement like modern powered vessels, so, despite every effort, it was not always possible to avoid a fireship. To those on board the target, it often appeared to be fixed in the path of the approaching fireship.[1] Crews felt defenceless and were forced to watch helplessly as their doom approached – as in a nightmare where you are nailed to the spot. When the ship was first ignited, black smoke erupted from it, and soon afterwards bright flames engulfed the rigging and sails. At this point panic often set in, because every sailor was aware that he was standing on a giant bonfire of seasoned wood and tar, not to mention that a fully stored ship of the line had about thirty tons of gunpowder aboard.

To modern thinking, the fireship was one of the most appalling weapons of the days of sail, but it was seen quite differently by contemporary seamen. The hard-headed and pragmatic commanders of seventeenth-century fleets considered them extremely useful, indeed capable of determining the outcome of a sea-battle. But there were others who contemplated the poor rate of success in fireship attacks, and concluded that they were of little use. Given the expense and their lack of flexibility, they were simply not worth bothering with: '… like a log and [the] crew liable to be shot'. However, to most authors, the word 'fireship' was synonymous with 'frightful', a weapon 'not worthy of a civilized nation'. But, they might ask, what should one do when the other side has them too? Even if it was morally questionable, this principle was often enough to salve the conscience of good Christians. Using this gruesome weapon might make for a dirty war, but they engaged in it unhesitatingly.

By their very nature fireships were somewhat disreputable and dishonourable. Only if they looked like merchantmen, or tenders for the fleet, could they get close enough to their victim, so they reeked of subterfuge and the underhand. The Italians called them *maccina infernale* and the Dutch *helsche werktuig*, both of which might translate as 'instruments from hell', terms which expressed elegantly how they and their capabilities were esteemed. They were often given names which suggested deceit or the clandestine: in the French navy of 1671 there were fireships named *Le Caché* (The Hidden), *Le Déguisé* (The Disguised), *Le Trompeur* (The Deceiver) and *Le Perilleux* (The Dangerous).[2] On the other hand, the English preferred names more expressive of their ultimate end: *Firebrand, Incendiary, Infernal* and *Furnace*;[3] many a *Vesuvius, Stromboli* and *Etna* also sailed the seas, although volcanoes were also used to name bomb-vessels. The names of purpose-built fireships often reflected their nature, but many were converted, purchased or hired, and these ones retained what then became singularly inappropriate names which did not reflect their purpose.

Despite all moral considerations, at the time of its greatest deployment this disreputable weapon was an important factor in the war at sea. It did not command the same attention as ships of the line, and represented a far smaller investment. Nor could its success be guaranteed: it was largely dependent on the personal skill and courage of a small group of resolute men, and such men, overtly ready to risk their lives, were not in great supply. But when sufficiently motivated, they could turn the fireship into the deadliest weapon of the day.

Although big sailing warships, their decks crammed with guns and men, could shatter their peers with broadsides, decimate the crew and dismast the ship or force surrender by boarding, they rarely sent the enemy to the bottom, even after an artillery duel lasting for hours. On the other hand the fireship was the mortal foe of the wooden ship, capable of causing total destruction; it could take the most impressive and powerful warship and reduce it to ashes. Furthermore, a fireship with an assault crew of ten men could cause terror among hundreds of seamen and gunners, however well armed their ship. But fear existed on both sides, because a defensive broadside could destroy the oncoming fireship or set it on fire prematurely. In this respect, it resembled the nineteenth-century torpedo-boat, or possibly the modern sea-skimming missile – both later examples of a small, cheap weapon theoretically capable of sinking the largest opponent. This made the fireship something of an equaliser when two navies were of different strengths, leading the inferior side to conceive of it as 'the poor man's battleship'.

A fireship attack was never intended to be a fair, chivalrous cannon-against-cannon affair. An unpredictable force of nature was unleashed which could afflict friend or foe, as fortune determined. History suggests that the typical victim of the fireship was a stationary vessel, or one with severe battle-damage which had lost the ability to defend itself. In most circumstances, it was not the statistical probability of physical destruction, but the psychological impact of a fireship that made the impression. It was precisely the fear of fire which gripped people aboard a wooden ship that explained why admirals believed that fireships could be decisive. Their mere presence could cause disarray, disorder and chaos for the enemy. So the story of the fireship is also the story of the often exaggerated fear they inspired. The commanders of every fleet understood this.

The heyday of the fireship was undoubtedly the era of the Anglo-Dutch Wars, in the latter half of the seventeenth century. These battles were fought in coastal waters, within a fairly limited area, so the fleets, with their fireships, could scarcely avoid one other. The fleets were large in number, and by later standards they were ill-disciplined and followed rudimentary tactics, all of which favoured the use of fireships. In comparison with later naval wars under sail, it is surprising how much value flag officers of those days attached to these devilish weapons, but quite often the admiral's decision as to whether or not to engage depended on how many fireships he, or the enemy, possessed, and whether he was in a position to deploy his own favourably.

By the nineteenth century it was quite different: developments in ship design, their weaponry, battle tactics and the training of crews had fundamentally changed the nature of sea warfare. Experience had also shown how to deal with fireships more effectively, and panic became a less potent weapon. The theatres of conflict spread out from European waters to distant oceans, making it more difficult for fireships to keep up with the fleet on long and arduous cruises. Thus their glory days came to a close, much as sail was itself giving way to steam, although they did manage to register a few successes during the century.

A successful fireship attack often depended on the co-operation and efforts of lesser warships of the fleet, and their boats – all those nameless small craft which were involved at the lowest levels of any engagement. Fireships themselves usually played only a small part in the battle as a whole, and because of their dubious moral character, so to speak, writers tend to refer to them only begrudgingly. The fireship did a dirty job: delivering the *coup de grâce* to a shattered and defenceless straggler, or the final annihilation of an immobilised vessel and its helpless crew. It could hardly be glorified, so it was downplayed or ignored.

In this book I would like to highlight how this extraordinarily gruesome form of combat related to the general story of sea warfare in the age of sail, so as to assign the fireship the place in maritime history that it deserves. Naturally, a naval history told only from the perspective of fireships would offer an overly narrow view – the story of the fireship is hardly the history of warfare in the age of sail – but I hope this deliberate focus will give a clearer view of a weapon which was for a long time more significant than is generally recognised.

My intention has not been to offer comprehensive details of each sea-battle described, about which more may be found in other published works, including numerical data on fleet strengths, casualties and losses. There are rarely figures that all authorities accept, and in most cases the best that can be achieved is to offer an estimate. Likewise I can make no claim to completeness when it comes to documenting the actual number of significant fireship attacks. I have chosen just a few accounts from a multitude of similar ones. Some of them were spectacular and widely reported; others far less so.

Fireships were used defensively as well as in offence, but chronicles say even less about their use in deterrence than about active operations. In reality most fireship attacks did not succeed, but for a long time the thought of a possible success, like a jackpot lottery win, outweighed any hard-headed calculation of odds. If this chapter in the history of sea warfare demonstrates anything, it is that the readiness to deploy gruesome and inhuman weapons has always outweighed moral considerations. In the days of supposedly 'chivalrous' warfare, the same rationale was applied as nowadays is applied to cluster-bombs, anti-personnel mines or 'weapons of mass destruction'. Then as now, the argument ran: if the enemy have them, so must we.

CHAPTER ONE

FIREPOTS
AND
GREEK FIRE

'The man who makes use of fire in the attack, shows intelligence.'

Sun Tzu, *The Art of War,* c512

As soon as man discovered how to travel on water, using wood or other organic material for transport, he found that these materials could catch fire, causing the destruction of the vessel and loss of life among its crew. Man was not just inventive enough to find ways of making life simpler and more comfortable for himself, but also ingenious enough to make life more difficult for his rivals, and this included the ability to set something on fire against the will of its owner. Since history began, ships have been vulnerable to fire, and a vessel specifically designed to burn an enemy craft or maritime structure by colliding with it is known as a fireship. The rise and decline of the fireship as a weapon of war is the subject of this book.

Fire aboard ship engendered as much respect and fear in antiquity as it did in later times. Not for nothing were the cooking stoves of Roman ships isolated in the stern gallery and surrounded with bricks. Underwater archaeologists have discovered Roman wrecks that were destroyed by fire, and ancient historical writings abound with references to the use of fire as an anti-ship weapon.[1] An almost classic example of a fireship attack is found in an early report dating from August 413 BC. In the course of a skirmish between the Syracusans and the Athenians, the former loosed a fireship against some stranded Athenian ships. In this case it was an old merchant ship filled with pitch, brushwood and resinous timber, and the intention was that it would drift down with the wind on to the stationary Athenian vessels. However, the Greeks sent boats out to engage it and managed to throw it off course and even put out the fire.[2] This is a perfect instance of a fireship attack against a motionless target which failed to achieve its object, a pattern that would be repeated throughout history.

In antiquity warships were propelled by oars when in action, which made them independent of wind and tide, and hence often capable of evading a burning ship bearing down on them. For this reason the fireship remained a rather marginal factor in sea warfare at that time. Nevertheless, a great deal of ingenuity was displayed in using fire to destroy an enemy ship, as a few examples will demonstrate. Ramming an enemy galley and then setting it on fire required the attacker to come right up to his victim. The ram, the major ship-killing weapon of the time, had to be prevented from forcing its way so deeply into the hull of the adversary that it could not be disengaged quickly, before fire could spread back to the attacker. This could be accomplished by fitting a baulk of wood above the spur, but it was even better if the enemy could be set on fire from a distance. Besides flaming arrows and fiery darts, there was the fire-basket, as adopted by Admiral Pausistratos of Rhodes when he fought the Syrians in 190 BC at the battle of Panhormos. This was an iron container which swung from a chain at the end of a long pole and held burning charcoal or other inflammable material, which could be poured down on the deck of the enemy by manipulating the pole.[3]

In the Third Punic War (149–146 BC), the

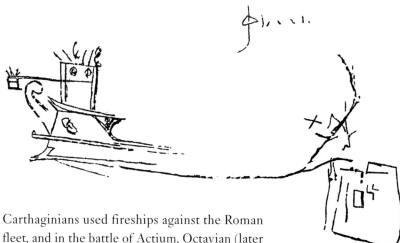

Carthaginians used fireships against the Roman fleet, and in the battle of Actium, Octavian (later the Emperor Augustus) successfully deployed fireships off north-western Greece to destroy the anchored fleet of Marcus Antonius and Cleopatra.

In late antiquity the Byzantines developed a new type of fire-weapon, the mysterious 'Greek Fire'.[4] Traditionally, this device is attributed to one Kallinikos, who worked for Emperor Constantine V (Copronymos) in AD 687. As first described by the Byzantine monk and chronicler Theophanes (752–c818) in his *Chronographia*, the emperor fitted out his warships with 'firepots' and 'siphons'. The primary weapon of these swift galleys was the ram, but these Dromons, as they were known, were also equipped with a movable 'siphon' under the bow platform. According to the account this was a long wooden pipe enclosed in brass. Through this an inflammable mixture was pumped, ignited and

This graffito from an Alexandrian tomb, dated to about 190–180 BC, shows a fire-basket fitted over the bow of a warship. Supposedly invented by Admiral Pausistratos of Rhodes, it consisted of an iron brazier suspended from a pole whose burning contents were poured down on the deck of an enemy ship after it had been rammed.

(FROM: VIERECK 1975)

One of the most impressive and influential naval weapons of Antiquity and the early Middle Ages was 'Greek Fire', first described by the Byzantine monk and chronicler Theophanes (752– c818). A heated inflammable mixture was forced through a pipe by an air-pump, making a primitive flame-thrower. It was said that the fire could not be extinguished by water, but could be stifled by smothering. Originally, it was probably a mixture of crude oil, sulphur and resin, which was set afire at the nozzle with unslaked lime, but in the Middle Ages people discovered that if phosphorus was added it would burn without oxygen. Greek Fire fell into disuse only after the introduction of cannon at sea, which allowed ships to engage at a greater range. This illustration is from a twelfth-century manuscript in the National Library of Spain in Madrid, a copy of the *Synopsis of Histories* by the late eleventh-century Byzantine historian Ioannes Skylitzes.

sprayed out on the enemy, making it the earliest flamethrower.

There were probably longer siphons, the Greek word meaning both 'pipe' and 'syringe', and this apparatus may have resembled a fire-hose. It would have needed a force-pump, like that invented by Ctesbius in the third century BC, and a pressure-vessel or boiler of some kind.

It is said that the fire could not be extinguished with water, only with urine or vinegar, and since it could be choked by sand, we can conclude that it needed oxygen for combustion. However, its exact ingredients were a state secret, and today there are many theories about them. One idea is that the flame burned coal-dust or an early form of gunpowder.[5] Against this is the fact that even if the Greeks knew about saltpetre, there was very little of it available.

Other scholars suspect that the key ingredients of Greek Fire might have been unslaked lime and naphtha, of which there were deposits near the Caspian Sea and in Georgia. When the unslaked lime made contact with water it released heat and ignited the fumes of the naphtha. As with the first idea, it seems doubtful that mixing these would have been very practical.

But what was the real secret of Greek Fire? As with the later fireships, one significant reason for its success was its psychological effect. The universal terror that this weapon evoked may have contributed to the fact that later, when quite different techniques and recipes were employed, it was still referred to as 'Greek Fire'. But was there an original recipe that was lost for ever with the downfall of the Byzantine Empire? There may never be a definitive answer to this, but an analysis of all the old accounts of the use of Greek Fire produces some consistent observations.

One is that the weapon could be deployed only by people experienced in its use. During the attack the noise of powerful bellows was to be heard, and thick smoke was seen to rise from the deck. That

A modern experimental reconstruction of Greek Fire by Professor John Haldon, using only the technology available at the time, produced a weapon capable of projecting a jet of fire up to fifteen metres and sustainable for several seconds at a time. It proved sufficient to destroy the wooden boat used as a target, and generated heat so intense that it would have killed the enemy crew or forced them to abandon ship; the temperatures generated required the operators themselves to be well protected. Indeed, there is some evidence of flame-resistant materials in use at the time: according to an account by a Greek from Alexandria, the head of the Egyptian arsenals invented 'something which was never before heard of. He took cotton and some mineral substances, he mixed them all together and smeared the ships of the fleet with the mixture, so that when the fire was thrown by the Greeks upon the ships, they did not burn. And this I saw with my own eyes: the ships were struck by Greek fire and did not burn but the fire was at once extinguished.' There were also fireproof garments: one recipe specified dipping a cloak in a mixture of talc, alum, ammonium, hematite, gypsum, stale urine and egg whites. Such garments were used to protect both soldiers and horses (Greek Fire was also employed on land), though whether they were used at sea is unknown.

(FROM: VASSILIOS 1998. PHOTOGRAPH BY COURTESY OF PROFESSOR JOHN HALDON, ANDREW LACEY AND COLIN HUGHES)

would fit in with the idea that Greek Fire was not a secret mixture but a heated-up form of flammable naphtha, perhaps mixed with a distillate like turpentine.

The material would be poured into a tightly sealed boiler and heated with a small, carefully shielded fire, which rendered the naphtha fluid less viscous and more readily ignitable. Then the pump came into action and increased the pressure in the boiler. A valve was then opened, and the hot oil rushed into the siphon and lit as it sprayed out. A long sinister tongue of flame reached out to the enemy ship, and the burning oil stuck to it. A similar principle was employed with the flame-throwers of the First and Second World Wars. The smoke that is mentioned in all the old reports came from a fire smouldering under the boiler, and the thunderous roar was caused by the bellows, which caused it to blaze up and raise the boiler temperature very rapidly. It also burned on the surface of the sea.

The most recent investigations into the possible nature of Greek Fire, carried out by Professor John Haldon and his associates Colin Hewes and Andrew Lacey, followed these broad principles.

They used a spectacular modern replica of the Byzantine apparatus, using a force-pump submerged in a cistern of pre-heated naphtha and ignited by a wad of burning tow. Dr Haldon believes that the Byzantines, because of a geological accident and good timing, happened to have fairly ready access to the right kind of oil deposit, and were able to make use of it to construct their flame-throwing weapon. In the later twelfth century they lost control of the areas where these deposits were found, a development which coincided with their apparent loss of the 'secret' of Greek Fire.[6]

Not surprisingly, the Byzantines installed the complicated apparatus only on stable ships that had sufficient deck space. They also knew that, if they wanted to deploy it successfully, experienced specialists were needed to control pressure, temperature and several other factors. Perhaps, therefore, the real secret of Greek Fire lay less in its special ingredients than in expertise in its use. A lot of experience was essential, and no doubt various practical tips and tricks were developed, which also were lost in the course of time.

Secret or not, there can be no doubting that in

its day Greek Fire was an extremely effective weapon, the only real counter being an attack on the specialist (and probably irreplaceable) fire crew with missiles and arrows from the enemy ship. However, the lethal mixture could also be hurled from a distance by a catapult as a firepot, and in this case it could simply consist of burning oil. Since unslaked lime could not be extinguished by water, it may also have played a part, since it caused panic and fear among superstitious men.

Greek Fire was always regarded as inherently fiendish, and anyone who knew how to use it enjoyed a big tactical advantage: whole crews are known to have jumped overboard when it was deployed against them. It helped the soldiers of the Eastern Roman Empire defend their capital, Constantinople, against the Arab fleets in 674–8 and 717–18, but eventually Byzantium lost its monopoly of fire weapons.

The Muslim powers seem to have inherited some of the expertise if not the exact technology after conquering Byzantine territory, and they later successfully employed their own methods and

Leonardo da Vinci's proposal of 1488 to use a fire-raft to destroy enemy vessels in harbour. The method of ignition that he sketched is rather fanciful – at the moment of collision, a pole fitted with barbed iron points was meant to cause burning cinders to ignite some priming-powder, which in turn would cause brushwood to catch fire.

(FROM: FELDHAUS 1914)

recipes. During the Crusade of 1249 by Louis IX, for instance, the Crusaders were attacked after the taking of Damietta by an Egyptian army, who used a huge catapult to hurl barrel-sized firepots at them, said to contain Greek Fire. An eyewitness to this affair was the author and chronicler Jean de Joinville (c1224–1317), who in his *History of Saint Louis* produced a famous description of it: 'Greek Fire came in containers as big as a barrel, and the fiery tail it emitted was about four paces in length. It made a noise like thunder, and it looked to me like a huge dragon flying in the air.'[7] Despite its name,

this was not the Greek Fire employed by the Byzantine navy.

In the centuries that followed the composition of the mixture altered, notably with the incorporation of phosphorus, which engendered a fire that erupted everywhere simultaneously and was especially difficult to extinguish, since it was not dependent on the presence of oxygen in the air.[8] This terror-inspiring weapon survived in the Mediterranean Sea area until the introduction of cannon and an era when ships fought at distances too great for the use of fire, which would flame out before it reached its target.

Greek Fire shot by siphons may have died out and been replaced by gunpowder and cannon, but it continued to haunt military thought. As late as the beginning of the fifteenth century, there is mention of flame-throwing in a treatise on sea warfare written for the edification of the young Emperor Charles V by a Burgundian nobleman at the court of the Emperor Maximilian, Filips van Kleef (of Cleves) 1456–1528:

Into an enemy ship you can hurl a sort of fire which cannot be extinguished, but this is an extremely dangerous weapon because it can well happen that you set your own vessel on fire, instead of that of the enemy. However, if you have at your disposal people who know how to use it, then it can be deployed. However, this can only be done before boarding, and if you are in lee of the enemy, so you can get out of the way if the enemy ship catches fire. Once you have boarded the enemy, fire cannot be used in any event.[9]

The composition of Filips van Kleef's inflammable material is only superficially comparable to the Greek Fire of antiquity. By his time there was access to saltpetre, with its ability to generate oxygen and its explosive nature, so it seems likely that his incendiary mixture consisted of saltpetre with resin, sulphur and other material.

Beside this offshoot of fire-raising at sea, there is the occasional account of the genuine fireship attack, as understood in this book – that is to say the firing and destruction of a vessel or other flammable structure by having a burning ship drift down upon it.

One such example was revealed by the wreck of a Viking ship discovered in 1953 on the site of the old Viking town of Haithabu, near Haddeby in the region of Schleswig-Flensburg, northern Germany. The find lay just outside a crescent-shaped wall which had surrounded the city. When in 1979 archaeologists began the excavation of the ship they called 'Haithabu 1', they found about four strakes of planking surviving, with everything above badly burned. On the basis of the evidence, it seems to have been a clinker-built vessel about 30m long and 2.7m wide, constructed of timber that may be dated to AD 985. It was a well-built sturdy ship, but it was old, and was used during a fireship attack on the town between AD 990 and 1010. It had been filled with hay and resin and allowed to drift against the wooden defensive wall of the town, where it had burned to the waterline before sinking, to be preserved in the mud.[10]

From the fourteenth century there is also the example of the two-day-long battle of Zierikzee at the entrance to the river Scheldt in the Netherlands. In August 1304 a Franco-Dutch fleet met one from Flanders and attacked the Flemish ships with fireships loaded with straw, pitch, resin and oil.

The idea of reaching and destroying the enemy with fire was of course a common tactic, but when planning its use a central question was how it could be employed to inflict the greatest possible damage. With the coming of the Renaissance, much abstract thought and invention was applied to many aspects of military science, including fire weapons. A fascinating example of this is offered by Leonardo da Vinci (1452–1519), who in 1488 designed a fireship in the form of a raft for use in a port against enemy shipping. Typical of Leonardo's inventions, it had a sophisticated if rather impractical method of ignition. For a fire attack it was important that the fireship could securely grapple the enemy ship and then have the flames roar up very quickly, to prevent their being extinguished. Da Vinci designed an iron pointed device which would hook fast to the enemy hull, at which point the shock of collision would displace a pole fitted with wires with burning fuzes. When it fell, the burning rags came in contact with a layer of gunpowder that was spread out under a layer of brushwood and firewood, causing the raft to burst rapidly into flames.[11] Like Leonardo's 'helicopter' and his armoured vehicles, this device was never given a practical trial in war.

THE
HELLBURNERS
OF
ANTWERP

'... a very useful engine of war.'

Lord John Montagu, Earl of Sandwich, 1778

AT THE BEGINNING OF JULY 1584[1] A besieging army appeared outside Antwerp, but the inhabitants were not too concerned because, although several towns in the region had already surrendered to the Spaniards, Antwerp was thought too tough a nut to crack. There was an eight-kilometre line of well-built forts surrounding the city, and because of the access provided by the river Scheldt, it was believed that men, material and supplies for the city could never be prevented from entering. So the inhabitants could weather any siege.

Antwerp was something special. Where else could one find more artists than bakers? Where else were there so many trading houses? What Stock Exchange handled more money? Where else, at least in the past, had such a liberal political climate reigned that merchants of whatever persuasion could pursue their business unhindered?

Antwerp lay in the northern provinces of the Netherlands, which in 1579, by signing the Union of Utrecht, had joined forces to throw off the oppressive rule of Spain. But the 'trading centre of the Christian world' was now taking on one of the toughest and most successful military leaders of the time – Alessandro Farnese (1545–1592), usually known in contemporary accounts by his later title, Duke of Parma. Descended from a family of Condottieri, the processional mercenary soldiers – a feature of Renaissance Italy – which had once fought for the Pope, he was the son of the Duke of Parma, a nephew of Charles V, Holy Roman Emperor, and since 1578 – when the King of Spain appointed him Vice-Regent and Supreme Commander of the Netherlands – he had recaptured one renegade city after the other. He rarely made direct attacks, preferring if possible to use the cheaper strategy of starving the citizens out. Then he negotiated with the besieged inhabitants, permitting the garrison to withdraw honourably, and by these means had brought the whole of Flanders back under Spanish rule. In 1583 Philip II of Spain had refilled his war chest with treasure brought by the Silver Fleet from America, and the campaign against the rebellious Netherlanders was given new impetus with the arrival of fresh troops from Spain and Italy. The recapture of Antwerp would crown the offensive.

As usual, Parma did not choose to make a direct onslaught. He estimated that with a big city, whose inhabitants were estimated to number between 90,000 and 100,000, it would be easy to cut off the substantial supplies normally brought by land, but Antwerp is also a port, and at night supply ships entered with the flood tide. A surprise attack managed to take Fort Leifkenshoek, on the left bank of the Scheldt about ten kilometres down river from the city, but there was still the Lillo fortress on the other side of the river. Parma's strategy was based on the idea that whoever controlled both strongpoints could make access very difficult for the supply ships, but the citizens knew what was at stake and defended Lillo fiercely. They broke the dyke, leaving the fortress completely surrounded by water, and at that point the Spaniards gave up, having lost 2,000 men.[2] But the Spanish general knew how to deal with the problem. His engineers surveyed the river and identified the ideal place for a barrage, in the area of Callo (Kallo) on the left bank and Ordam on the right bank, where the river is narrow and twisting, Parma had over 60,000 hardened and disciplined troops at his disposal, and now the besiegers set to work to force Antwerp to its knees. Every smith and carpenter in the region was rounded up, and building materials were brought in from all over the reconquered territories of Brabant and Flanders – baulks of timber, masts and many shallow-draught ships. A special canal was even built for the purpose. First of all, stout bastions were erected on either side of the Scheldt to cover the building work, and then the troops began to drive piles from both banks. These were hammered down into the sandy ground with specially constructed pile-drivers to a depth of fourteen metres, foundations strong enough to withstand the drifting ice that would form on the Scheldt in winter. Lastly Parma's soldiers pushed bridgework out into the stream. It was not just the ice they had to fear but also attacks from the citizens, so a gun platform was placed at the end of the bridgework to form a bastion in the stream. So many guns were mounted on the banks that any blockade-runner could expect a greeting of seventy or eighty rounds. But again and again, courageous skippers managed to slip through the opening with the tide at night, although many were sunk or taken by the Spaniards.[3] However, the citizens were not able to prevent the building materials from getting to the site, and the confident mood they had displayed at the beginning of the siege began to evaporate.

Winter arrived and brought campaigning to an end. The Scheldt iced over, but the bridgework withstood the strain, and scarcely had the ice melted in the spring than Parma pressed ahead

Alessandro Farnese, Duke of Parma (1545–1592), a nephew of the Emperor Charles V, was the Spanish ruler of the Netherlands and a highly respected soldier. He returned the southern provinces of the Netherlands to Spanish control, and the siege of Antwerp would be the final act of an offensive against the rebellious cities which had started in 1582. His blockade of the river Scheldt completed the encirclement of the port, although the fireship attack on the 'bridge' in 1585, shown in the background of the portrait, almost cost him his life. The city fell, and the southern Netherlands remained under Spanish rule. Less successfully, in 1586 the duke became one of the planners of Philip II's ambitious scheme to invade England with the Spanish Armada.

(DRAWING: AUTHOR AFTER P D GUNST AND ADRIAAN VAN DER WERFF)

once more. He staked everything on this structure, declaring that it would be either his grave or his highway into Antwerp.[4] And what no one had imagined possible was achieved: the open water between the bridgeheads was closed off with thirty-one flat-bottomed boats (*pleiten*).[5] These had been brought in over the flooded fields, and were now secured with two anchors at bow and stern. Each *pleit* had room for two cannons and a crew of about thirty. Over the *pleiten* were laid planks and masts, lashed together with chains, and on top of everything ran a gangway protected by barricades to

shelter the musketeers. Smaller ships were moored both upstream and downstream, with men-of-war at each end of the bridge, and iron-pointed stakes in the river faced anyone who might approach. The whole edifice was defended by 1,500 men and ninety-seven cannon.

How this structure looked to its contemporaries is graphically described by the great German writer Friedrich Schiller in his history of the siege of Antwerp. 'This frightful machine was so skilfully organised and elaborately fitted out with engines of death that it almost looked like a living being defending itself, which could, on command, spew flames and shoot ruin on all who approached it.'[6]

On 25 March 1585 the citizens of Antwerp heard the rattle of musketry and the thunder of cannon. The noise came from the direction of the bridge, which could not be seen from the city, and when the citizens realised that it was not the sound of an attack, it could only mean one thing – the enemy were celebrating what had looked impossible but was now reality. After six months' work the barrier was finished and Antwerp was completely cut off. At the same time came the bad news that Brussels had fallen. Its citizens had been starved into submission.

What were they to do? Food supplies for the great city were slowly becoming scarce, the besiegers were well dug in, and all efforts to drive them off had proved fruitless. Into the story at this point stepped a man who is inseparably connected with the events that followed. He was an Italian from Mantua, whose name is variously spelled Gianibelli or Jenebelli, and is given in latinised form as Fridericus Jenibellius in Emanuel van Meteren's history of the Spanish–Dutch War.[7] He had lived in Antwerp for a long time and knew a great deal about armaments; he was even paid a yearly stipend by Elizabeth I of England, who supported a number of prominent Dutch Protestants.

Gianibelli had already attempted to advise the Municipal Council (Magistrat) of Antwerp on several occasions. Before the city was surrounded, he had campaigned for provisions to be stored, but the merchants and grocers who sat on the governing body had turned deaf ears to his plea, reluctant to spend money on all but the most pressing needs. Nor was his cause helped by the nominal

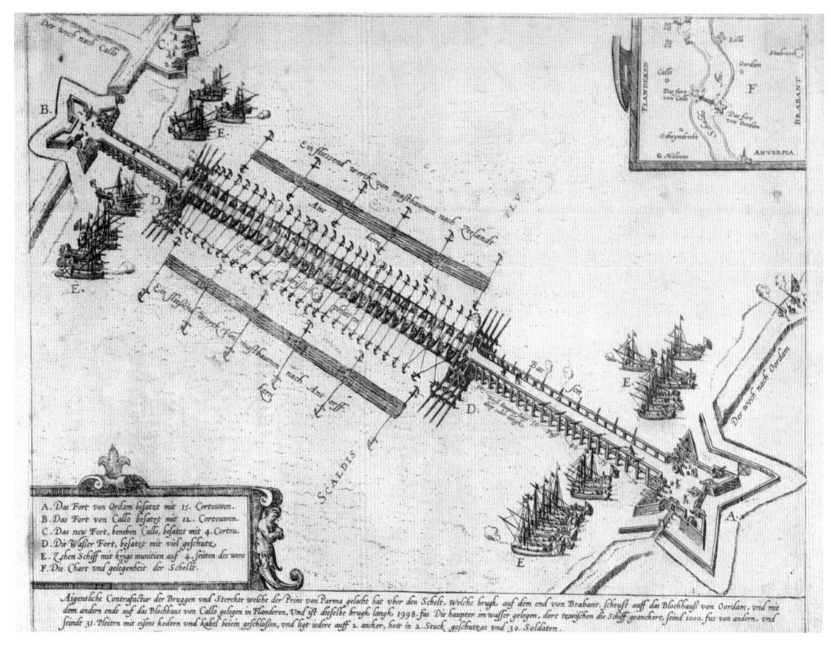

A. Das Fort von Ordam besatzt mit 15. Cortouwen.
B. Das Fort von Callo besatzt mit 12. Cortouwen.
C. Das new Fort, beneben Callo, besatzt mit 4. Cortou.
D. Die Waßer Fort, besatzt mit viel geschutz.
E. Zehen Schiff mit krigs munition auf 4. seiten des wers
F. Die Chart vnd gelegenheit der Schelt.

Aigentliche Contrafactur der Bruggen vnd Sterckte welche der Prins von Parma gelacht hat vber den Schelt, welche brugk auf dem end von Brabant, scheust auff das Blockhauß von Oordam, vnd mit dem andern ende auf das Blockhaus von Callo gelegen in Flanderen, Vnd ist dieselbe brugk langk 1998. fus Die haupter im waßer gelegen, dort tzwischen die Schiff geanckert, seind 1000. fus von andern. vnd seindt 31. Pleiten mit eisern kedten vnd kabel beiein geschloßen, vnd ligt iedere auff 2. ancker, hott in 2. Stuck geschutz es vnd 30. Soldaten.

An engraving published in 1616 showing the structure and elaborate defences of the barrier or 'bridge' that the Duke of Parma had built in 1585 as part of the siege-works around the city of Antwerp (the inset shows its position on the Scheldt).The multi-layer defensive system included boats and rafts equipped with poles which were supposed to fend off vessels drifting down towards the bridge. They were unable to prevent one of Gianibelli's explosion-vessels from reaching its target, and the infernal machine tore a hole in the bridge, but it was quickly repaired and the gap closed.

(NATIONAL MARITIME MUSEUM
PU4957)

leader of the city, the Burgomaster, Filip van Marnix, Lord of St Aldegonde (1540–1598). He was well educated, a man of letters and a theologian, but, lacking military authority, he found it difficult to govern a city where there were so many decision-making committees and factions from different denominational camps.[8]

It so happens that when the tide ebbs, the Scheldt runs very fast at the point where the barrage had been constructed, and on this basis Gianibelli developed a plan to destroy the bridge. He asked for ships and other materials, but initially the frugal citizens of Antwerp were dubious about the proposal: success could not be guaranteed, and valuable materials might just be wasted. Finally, after much deliberation, they agreed to at least some of his demands.[9]

For his first attack he tried floating down rafts made of empty wine-casks fixed together with wood and laden with tar-barrels and kegs of gunpowder, but these flamed out before they reached the bridge. In a second attempt he lashed together twenty barges laden with stones and powder-kegs and sent them down the river. The smouldering brushwood and straw on the rafts would have made it hard for the troops on the bridge to make out details, but the barges ran aground before they reached the target. Gianibelli next tried fitting the barges with poles pointing down into the water to prevent them from running into the shallows, but that was not entirely satisfactory.[10] However, he gathered valuable experience from these first miscarriages, and he put everything he had learned together in his next attempt.

The municipality of Antwerp had allotted him two small unrigged ships of about seventy to eighty tons each, which he christened *Fortuijn* (Luck) and *Hoop* (Hope) – the names of the two things that he needed above all else. He began the fitting-out by installing some of his long poles to prevent premature grounding. The rest of the work is described by Nicolaes Witsen in his *Architectura Navalis* of 1690:

> The holds of the ships were covered with stone blocks to a height of two feet, and over this was erected a wooden casing twenty feet long and four feet broad at the base. This tapered above, so that at the top it was just two feet across and filled with 18,000 pounds of gunpowder. In the cabin of the ship was a curved tin pipe pierced with holes. Running fore and aft, about midships, were four smaller pipes, connected to the bigger pipe which ran athwartship. These were filled with fine priming-powder, and they would carry the fire out to the edges of the powder load and ignite it almost simultaneously. On the casing were several pans filled with musket powder, and in these were twenty-four fuzes which had been soaked in turpentine. The casing was surrounded with ashlars and gravestones, altogether 400 wagonloads of stone apart from the mortar, lime and sand involved. On top of the stonework lay dry brushwood, and barrels of pitch and tar were placed fore and aft.[11]

The ships were not just intended to blow up the bridge. They were also loaded with nails, bolts, shackles and chunks of wood joined with chain,

The attack on the Duke of Parma's 'bridge' by explosion-vessels and fireships in April 1585 should have brought the siege of Antwerp to an end. This bird's eye view shows the attack of Gianibelli's two explosion-ships, and the 'harmless' fireships, which were intended to distract attention from them, a tactic which succeeded. The horrendous effect of the blast made such an impression on contemporaries that for a century afterwards, the approach of a burning ship summoned up fears that an explosion was imminent.

(FROM: RODRIGUEZ-SALGADO 1988)

Pontis Antuerpiani fractura.

A. *Pons* B. *Flotta ante pontem.* C. *Arx S. Mariæ.*
D. *Naues septendecim Antuerpia in pontem immissæ.*
E. *Quatuor ex his maiores ignem foris, intus cuniculos portantes.*
F. *Vna ex maioribus, extincto agua igniario, in fumum abit.*
G. *Altera, et tertia, ad ripam uento impulsæ, ruinam euomunt.*

H. *Quarta ponti impacta magnam pontis, atq, hominum stragem edit.*
I. *Pr.Parmensis, Caetanus, et Vastius humi strati, à relabentibus saxis, trabibusq,*
sauciantur. K. *Tuccius Centurio sublimi elatus, demissusq, ad ripam*
enatat. L. *Adolescens prætorianus ex medio ponte in alteram*
ripam uiolenter infertur.

which would work like chain-shot.[12] This suggests that Gianibelli was consciously aiming to maim or kill as many of the enemy as possible. One of the ships, the *Fortuijn*, had the fuzing arrangement described by Witsen, but the *Hoop* used a different means of ignition: a clockwork device driven by weights and equipped with a verge escapement and a form of wheel-lock, made by the Antwerp clockmaker Jean Bovy. At the desired moment a wheel was set in motion, striking a flint and causing sparks to fly into a powder-laden pan, which set the whole thing off.[13]

That Gianibelli had available such a sophisticated ignition device suggests that he was not working alone. Several master tradesmen were involved in the construction of what became known as the Hellburners, and they must have agreed to participate before he first presented his plans. He clearly knew of the devastating effect that a gunpowder explosion had when it occurred within a small space enclosed in masonry, as by this time

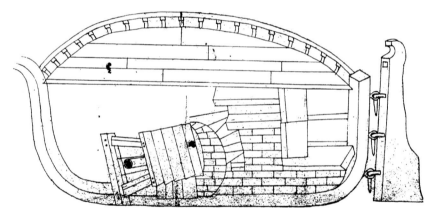

'The boat opened up showing the interior arrangements.' The Antwerp explosion-vessel made a huge impact on contemporary military thought. Count Johann of Nassau-Siegen (1562–1623), one of the most scholarly soldiers of his time, included a description and illustration of the 'Infernal Machine' in his book on warfare. Particularly interesting are the construction of the explosion-chamber and the method of constraining the powder-charge, described as a wooden chest buried in sand and stone.

(FROM: NASSAU-SIEGEN)

the use of 'mines' was a common stratagem of war. An evacuated fortress, for example, might have its vaults filled with powder to be set off at the appropriate moment following its triumphant occupation by the enemy. Likewise, the gates and walls of besieged cities could be brought down by driving a sap under them and exploding a mine. And everyone had heard tales of horrendous accidents involving gunpowder, a fairly recent example being the explosion of 25,000 Mass of powder stored in the governor's headquarters in Ragusa (now Dubrovnik), which caused frightful damage. The energy released by a powder explosion was again demonstrated in 1503, when a mine almost totally destroyed the Castel dell'Ovo near Naples, a

fortress previously considered impregnable.[14] It is reasonable to assume that Gianibelli knew from that sort of experience just how much powder was needed and the best means of igniting it. His innovation was to transfer the concept of an enclosed explosive chamber from land to water.

On the evening of 5April, the Spaniards heard from their spies that the citizens were up to something. Parma himself was on hand, and as a precaution he ordered the watch on the shore to be doubled and reliable troops to be stationed near the bridge. Just after darkness fell, the first burning vessel came in sight. Altogether more than thirty barges and *pleiten* came gliding down the river. Gianibelli hoped that his first group of fireships would destroy the outlying part of the barrage, and allow the succeeding ships to get closer to his real target. His plan was to have the two crucial vessels, *Fortuijn* and *Hoop*, drift downstream inconspicuously among the other craft. Brushwood piled up on the masonry would burn with a clear flame and deceive the enemy into thinking they were just ordinary fireships. In the course of the night, the enemy would become tired, drop their guard and expend their ammunition by shooting at the first arrivals.[15]

The Spanish camp went to high alert, and the bridge filled with men ready to try to fend off the fireships with poles. Schiller describes the scene in masterly fashion:

> Meanwhile the train of fireships came nearer and nearer, and the darkness of the night enhanced the extraordinary scene. As far as you could see upstream, everything was afire, with the fireships emitting such huge flames that you would have imagined that they themselves were on fire. Light lit up the water's surface, illuminating the causeways and bastions on the shore, and the banners, weapons and the armour of the soldiers who stood in parade order on the bridge glistened. With mixed feelings of dread and satisfaction, the soldiers watched the unusual spectacle, which in some ways resembled a celebration rather than a military affair. But they shuddered with emotion at the wonderful contrast between

outward appearance and inner feeling. As the burning fleet came within 2,000 paces of the bridge, the expedition leaders lit the fuzes, pushed the two mine-vessels right into the middle of the stream, and made off as fast as they could in the waiting dinghies, leaving the rest to the play of the waves.[16]

Fortuijn, the first fireship, ran aground despite its poles, but its explosion killed several Spaniards who were entrenched on the bank. The *Hoop* next drove against the bridge outworks and hung there, but the deception succeeded, for the burning mate-

rial persuaded the defenders that it was an ordinary fireship. Then the ship tore itself free and drove into the main part of the bridge, where the order was given to use poles to fend it off from the wooden structure.

The mechanical fuze went off at the predetermined time. This was the ultimate 'infernal machine'; Schiller tried to put into words what happened:

> It was as if the Earth had burst, and the vaults of Heaven had collapsed. The deepest waters of the Scheldt opened up with the impact of the Blazing Volcano, and a wall of water flooded over the surrounding dyke and spread out, putting the fortifications on the bank under several feet of water. The earth shook over a three-mile radius, and nearly all the scaffolding on the left side, to which the fireship had attached itself, besides part of the bridge of boats was blown up, along with everything which had been stationed there … masts, cannon and men all went sky-high.

The explosion of the *Hoop* tore a sixty-metre-long breach in the bridge. Parma survived this only by accident, but he lost 800 of his best men, and even some of his key commanders. The body of his captain-general, the Marquis de Roubaix, who had commanded the cavalry, was found in the rigging of a ship, and the remains of Caspar de Robles, Lord of Billy und Malepert (1527–1585), were found a month later hanging from a bridge-piling.[17] De Robles was a particularly valuable man, who as governor of Limburg had constructed a new dyke following the 1570 'Flood of All Saints', in which 25,000 people were drowned.

The citizens of Antwerp stood on the walls and listened to the violent explosions. Had the plan succeeded, and was the bridge really destroyed? No one knew. They should have sent boats right down the blockaded river to see how much damage had been done, but the men in the boats had lost heart, and when they were fired upon they turned around and reported that nothing had happened and the river was still blocked. It seems that

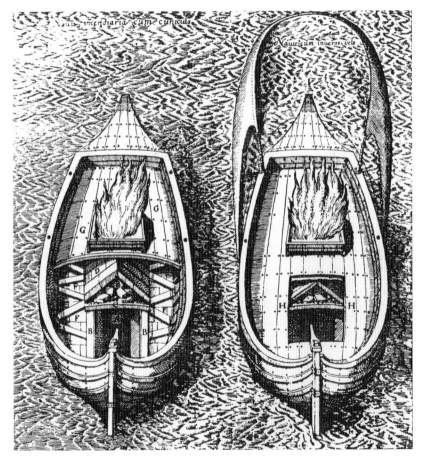

In his book about the War of Independence in the Netherlands, *De bello Belgico*, Pater Famiano Strada (1572–1649) published detailed illustrations of the Antwerp fireships and explosion-vessels.

(AUTHOR)

The keys read as follows:
A The bottom and sides of the hold that contained the powder were strewn with lime to make sure the space was really dry.
B Bulkheads resting on the bottom of the hull.
C Covering of large stones.
D Roof covering, similarly of stone.
E The chamber formed by the stones is filled with iron, marble round-shot, chains and millstones.
F Squared-off stone slabs form the sides of the hold.
G The deck of the ship with a fire placed there to make the ship look like a fireship.
H The hold below deck.
I A very large 'water-sail' or drogue is deployed from the bow of the ship and causes the vessel to be pulled along with the current.

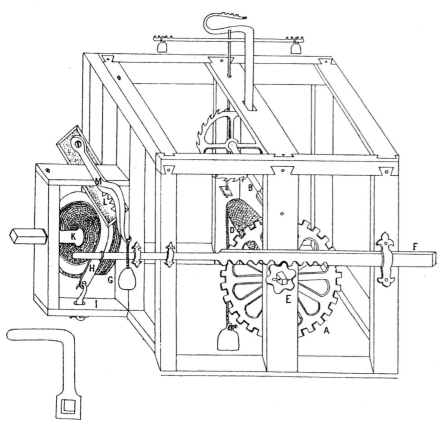

Besides its burning fuzes, one of the Antwerp explosion-ships was fitted with a clockwork detonator, constructed by the clockmaker Jean Bovy. The surviving plan shows that it was driven by weights and had a spindle escapement. The toothed rack (F) was driven by a pinion, so that after a predetermined time it would release the spring-driven toothed wheel (G), which struck sparks from a flint igniting the powder in the pan. It worked well enough – it was the explosion of this vessel which caused the destruction of the Duke of Parma's massive barrier across the river Scheldt.

(FROM: FELDHAUS 1914)

the citizens just could not grasp the potential of the vessels sent downriver, nor how destructive they had proved. In the city the rumour quickly spread that all the effort had been wasted. The people were incensed, believing that Gianibelli had failed, and his life was threatened. But finally a messenger reached the city. He had swum through the bridge in the darkness, and now he reported on the real state of Parma's obstacle – but it was too late to act.

So in the end the citizens failed to profit from the success. The bridge was demolished, but then nothing happened. A fleet from Zeeland was waiting at the mouth of the Scheldt, poised to break through after the assault on the barricade, but the signal never came. Slowly the Spaniards realised that no one was exploiting the situation, and Parma, who was beginning to recover from the shock, ordered an immediate start on repairs to the structure. The blockade was even improved by

arranging the central bridge of boats so that it could be opened to let an approaching fireship pass through without causing damage.[18]

Although it was now really a lost cause, Gianibelli was provided with new ships and materials, and he made several further attempts to destroy the bridge. However, the wind and tide were never again as favourable as the night of his triumph, and it became more and more difficult to find men brave enough to man the fireships. On land, the starving citizens carried on the fight, from the bastions of the city and the banks of the dykes, but after several setbacks morale sank everywhere. The Catholic population of the city, about a third of the total, began to press for an end to the siege, and on 6 June an emissary was sent to Parma; the city finally surrendered on 15 August.

Parma had achieved his aim, and Spain now controlled the area which later (from 1648) would mark the boundary between the Spanish Netherlands and the United Provinces of the Netherlands. A garrison of staunch Castilians from the heart of Spain was stationed in Antwerp, and all who did not profess the Catholic faith were obliged to sell up and flee the city. Nearly half the population, about 38,000 souls, left for the northern Netherlands in the next four years.[19] What Parma had begun with his bridge – cutting off the economic lifeblood to the city and its hinterland – was finished off by the northern Netherlands fleet, which blockaded the entrance to the Scheldt estuary, bringing to an end Antwerp's significance as a centre of world commerce.

Gianibelli's attempt to break the blockade at Antwerp with fireships and explosion-vessels was unique and was so influential that it was described in the technical literature for a hundred years to come. Its thunder echoed in the ears of seamen and soldiers for centuries. Every fireship that approached a warship made the crew wonder if it might blow up like the Antwerp Hellburner, and the sheer terror inspired by the thought was often more effective than the flames themselves.

CHAPTER THREE

JOHN HAWKINS
AND THE
SPANISH FIRESHIP

*'... a cruel substitute
for a manly engagement'*

Jack Nastyface, *Nautical Economy*, 1836

IN THE SECOND HALF OF THE SIXTEENTH century there was a fireship attack which marked the beginning of a series of increasingly belligerent encounters between England and Spain. The hostilities reached a climax with the creation of an enormous fleet – the Spanish Armada of 1588 – whose mission to invade England went up in the flames of an onslaught by fireships.

It began with a conflict of interest not involving England but between the seafaring nations of Spain and Portugal. Towards the end of the fifteenth century tension arose over competing claims to the newly discovered overseas territories, and in particular to rights in those areas which were as yet undiscovered. Since both Spain and Portugal were Catholic countries, the Pope was asked to arbitrate and decide where the demarcation boundary should lie. The resulting Treaty of Tordesillas (1494) divided the Atlantic in two along an imaginary north–south meridian 370 leagues west of the Cape Verde islands and east of the Antilles, giving everything east of this line to Portugal, and all west of it to Spain.

Other nations were not consulted and, so naturally, Protestant states like England and the Netherlands did not recognise the treaty. Furthermore, as their sea trade expanded, they began to operate a policy based on 'the freedom of the seas', even before that actual concept had been formulated by Dutch jurists.

———— • ————

During the reign of Elizabeth I the Hawkins family were one of the richest mercantile dynasties in England. They were not just merchants but also entrepreneurs, possessing a fleet of trading ships and enjoying excellent contacts with investors who were prepared to put up some of the capital required to fit out speculative voyages. As first-class seamen, they were not afraid to engage in relatively dangerous enterprises, provided there was promise of enough profit.

Sir John Hawkins (1532–1595) had extended his trading voyages as far as the Azores, where he heard about the Spanish colonies in the Caribbean and how the settlers there were completely dependent on the Spanish motherland. All the necessities of life were brought from Spain and were heavily taxed, with every aspect of trade being closely controlled by the Crown. The new lands were there only to be exploited, and no other free enterprises were encouraged. America produced more silver annually than all the silver mines in Europe combined, and each Silver Fleet brought home to Spain about 350 tons of silver, besides several tons of gold,

John Hawkins (1532–1595) was one of the most enterprising sea-merchants of the Elizabethan age. The Spanish felt challenged by his illegal trading expeditions to their colonies in Central America and the Caribbean, and in 1568 his ships were forced into a fight with the Spanish Silver Fleet in the Mexican harbour of San Juan de Ulua. The Spanish got the upper hand by using a fireship, but made bitter enemies of the English. Hawkins was later to have great influence on the English race-built galleon. He served as a vice admiral in the struggle against the Armada in 1588, and he was present when the decision to use fireships against the Spaniards was made.

(NATIONAL MARITIME MUSEUM BHC2755)

an influx which generated price inflation, not only in Europe but also in the colonies of Central and South America, where the colonists were unable to produce the goods that they themselves urgently needed. In an attempt to keep down costs, the cheapest possible labour force was employed – slaves. At that time, black Africans were not seen as human beings, so slave-dealing was not morally reprehensible: even kings and popes sanctioned the trade.

John Hawkins decided to get into this business, aware that African slaves were a prized commodity in Hispaniola (Haiti). They were costly, however, because the Spanish slave-dealers required an expensive licence from the Crown to import them, and Hawkins thought he could deliver them more cheaply. Naturally the King of Spain, Philip II, sought to protect his monopoly, but he also feared the spread of false doctrines that Protestant foreign traders might introduce into his domains. On these grounds anyone in Spanish-American waters flying a foreign flag was declared a pirate.[1]

Hawkins made his first slave-dealing voyage in 1562–3, and this was so successful that he repeated the enterprise in 1564. This time he had several business partners, including the queen, who put one of her ships at his disposal, since at this time the 'Navy Royal' was effectively the private property of the monarch. Upon Hawkins's return to England, the Spanish ambassador worriedly reported to Philip II that the investors had made a 60 per cent profit, which was bound to be an incentive to others to follow suit.[2] Hawkins's third voyage was the most complex.[3] The first stage was to obtain slaves on the Guinea coast, but then he intended to sell them to Spanish colonists in the West Indies. The enterprise was financed by a consortium, this time including the queen and several courtiers. For the venture, the queen put two of her ships at his disposal. One was that used on the first expedition, a 700-ton[4] carrack *Jesus of Lübeck* with a crew of 180 men and carrying twenty-two heavy cannon as well as forty-two smaller pieces on the decks of the high fore and after castles. It was an old and outmoded vessel which had been purchased from Lübeck by Elizabeth's father, Henry VIII. Next was the *Minion*, at about 350 tons roughly half the size of the *Jesus*, but there were also four even smaller craft, of from thirty-two to 150 tons, which belonged to the Hawkins family. Among them was the fifty-ton *Judith*, commanded by an ambitious young 'captain and master' called Francis Drake (c1540–1596). The whole squadron comprised 408 men, among them several of noble birth.

On 2 October 1567 the ships sailed out of Plymouth, laden primarily with beans, which were the standard sustenance for the hoped-for cargo of slaves. Besides their own provisions, the ships also carried items of clothing and textiles to trade with the Spanish-American settlers, and it was hoped that the cargo for the return voyage would be even lighter – some hides with 'gold, pearls and emeralds', as Hawkins wrote to the queen.[5]

As soon as he reached the Guinea coast, Hawkins noted that the Portuguese in their forts were less obliging than they had been during his earlier voyages, and the Spanish too were more reserved, not to say hostile. The Spanish king's trade embargo was making an impact. During November he sought for his 'trade goods' at the river mouths along the Guinea coast and was told that it had become more difficult to obtain slaves, so he turned to the capture of a Portuguese caravel and some Spanish ships in order to get hold of their human cargo. Then, in the region of modern Sierra Leone, a local chieftain offered him the opportunity of attacking an enemy town which, duly captured, brought his slave-haul up to 480.

In March 1568 the little fleet crossed the Atlantic and reached the Leeward Islands. At Dominica the trading began, and then Hawkins followed his time-tested route through the West Indies and to the Spanish Main at the coast of what is today Venezuela. Hawkins was in fact working in a grey area, somewhere between smuggling, armed robbery, privateering and piracy on the one hand and honest trade on the other. From the point of view of the Spanish colonial authorities, he was unequivocally a pirate, while he would have thought of himself as a worthy merchant, one with the interests of his queen at heart. He visited the islands of Margarita and Curaçao in the Leeward Islands (Dutch Antilles), and at the mouth of the Rio Magdalena (in modern Colombia), according to Hawkins, the inhabitants were happy to trade with him. The Spaniards paid with precious metals and gems, and in particular with hides. But things did not go so smoothly everywhere. When the local governor hesitated to give the interlopers water and provisions, they resorted to violence.

The sales of slaves proved sluggish, and at the end of July the ships still had fifty unsold slaves on board. It would soon be August, the beginning of the hurricane season in that area, and Hawkins decided to return to Europe. Perhaps he would be able to dispose of the remaining slaves on the way home. The proven route took him northwards, to the Straits of Yucatan, through the Florida Straits and then, by making use of the Florida Current, to the Gulf Stream. However, at the west coast of Cuba his ships were struck by a storm. The old *Jesus* in particular was severely damaged and started to leak, but Hawkins did not dare abandon her, for she was the property of the queen. So he looked for a harbour on the Florida coast where he could

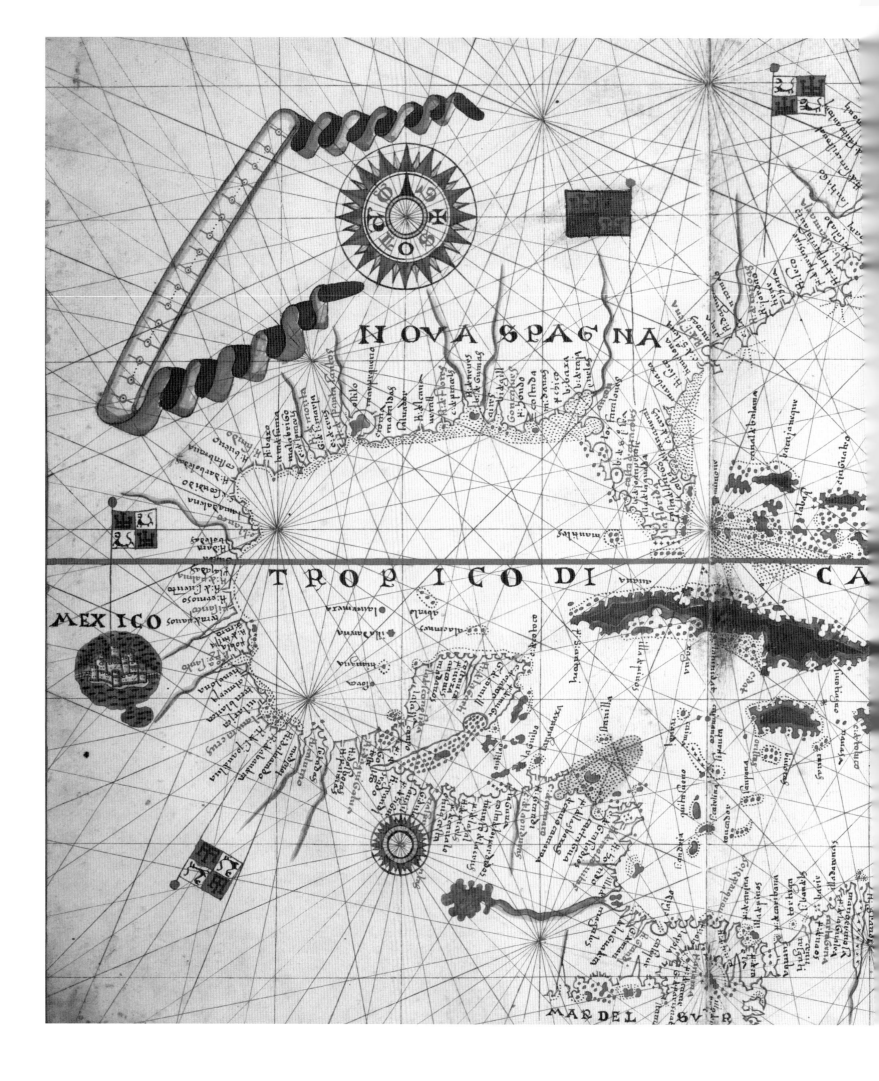

NOVA SPAGNA

MEXICO

TROPICO DI ... CA

MAR DEL SVR

make her seaworthy once more. The coastal waters there are very shallow, and there were few settlements. In September storms drove him ever further into the Gulf of Mexico, where he sailed along a lee shore that was subject to devastation by strong north winds and hurricanes. He learned that the only port here was San Juan de Ulúa, the port for Mexico City, about twenty-four kilometres south of the coastal city of Vera Cruz.

At that time San Juan de Ulúa was nothing more than a tiny settlement, with a sheltered roadstead where a small coral island lay at a distance of 300 metres from the shore. Nowhere was it more than 150 metres wide, but it protected ships adequately from storms coming from the north. On its landward side the coral had been cut away to form a quay. While Hawkins's ships lay before the port, they were initially taken to be Spanish, because the inhabitants were expecting part of the annual fleet of New Spain to arrive. Consequently there was consternation when the port authorities saw Englishmen on the decks of the newly arrived vessels.

Hawkins managed to calm the Spaniards by explaining that he would be on his way once he had purchased supplies and made some quick repairs. As proof of his friendly intentions he released a number of Spaniards who had been passengers on the captured ships. The port authorities agreed, and on 16 September, almost two months after he had decided to terminate the trading voyage, he finally brought his squadron to anchor in the harbour. Twelve Spanish ships were already moored there, and quickly a rumour spread that they had great treasure on board. But neither the English nor the Spaniards had calculated correctly, for the very next morning thirteen large vessels could be seen lying off San Juan de Ulúa – the New Spain fleet, which had arrived about two weeks early.

Hawkins was in a tight spot and wondered what to do. The harbour was so narrow that the ships had to lie close together, and he was sure that the Spaniards would feel threatened if they found English ships lying too close to their own vessels. With his cannon and 'with God's help' he was in position to prevent the Spanish ships from entering, but there was no other safe anchorage along

A chart of the Caribbean and Central America produced by Joan Martines in 1572. The production and dissemination of such information made it more difficult for the Spanish to keep interlopers out of their spheres of influence.

the entire coastline. As he later described his dilemma: 'If I had kept them out then had there been present shipwreck of all the fleet which amounted in value to six millions, which was in value of our money 1,800,000 pounds, which I considered I was not able to answer, fearing the Queen's Majesty's indignation in so weighty a matter.[6]

So he made a deal. Aboard the Spanish fleet, besides the ships' commanders, was the new Viceroy of Mexico, Don Martin Enriquez. The Spaniards, aware that they had to move quickly so long as their ships lay unprotected outside the harbour, responded with fair words to the demands of the English. They would allow them to buy supplies and pay for them with their goods. Hostages were exchanged, and Hawkins's men took possession of the coral island, upon which the Spanish had mounted eleven bronze cannon. With many gun salutes the fleet of New Spain sailed in, with the 'capitana' (or flagship), a powerfully armed galleon, in the lead. The ships now lay side by side,

in the shelter of the island, moored closely together with scarcely twenty metres separating the English and Spanish vessels. Accident and the fear of hurricanes had forced co-operation between two nationalities which, apart from the safe haven in which they lay, had absolutely nothing in common. So they pretended, bluffed and smiled, all the while loading their guns and sharpening their weapons.

Hawkins was right to be suspicious, as the Spaniards did not feel bound to keep any promise made to a pirate. They immediately began preparations for an attack on the English, distributing weapons, bringing troops from Vera Cruz, hauling cannon into threatening positions and cutting gunports in the sides of the merchantmen. Hawkins protested, and was unconvinced by the reassurance that was proffered. Eventually the English found that their Spanish hostages were carrying concealed daggers, and their intentions became obvious. At this point, the viceroy, Don Martin Enriquez, deciding that 'It was time to chasten the

The fort of El Mina on the Guinea coast (modern Ghana), built by the Portuguese in 1485, was the earliest European trading post established in the area. It soon became the centre of the west African slave trade, and this was where Hawkins came to acquire his human cargo, although this engraving was made about a century later.

(PUBLIC DOMAIN)

corsairs', threw off all pretence and declared open hostilities.

At 10am on Thursday 23 September a trumpet blast gave the signal to attack, and the Spanish soldiers and sailors fell upon the English from all sides. Their first object was the coral island, where they proceeded without mercy to slaughter Hawkins's men, only three of whom survived and got back to their ship. At the same time about 300 men from the ship lying next to the *Minion* attacked her. However, the English were ready for this and managed to shift the ship away from the quay so quickly that reinforcements were cut off, and the boarders repelled in a counter-attack. Besides these attempts at boarding, the cannoneers on both sides had begun their work. Firing at point-blank range, amid clouds of powder-smoke, a hail of splinters and the shrieks of the wounded, they tore each other apart with round-shot and grape. The *capitana* took several hits below the waterline with the first salvo, and began to sink. Later it was estimated

Henry VIII purchased the big carrack *Jesus of Lübeck* from the Hanseatic League about 1545, and later his daughter Elizabeth I put the ship at the disposal of John Hawkins for his Caribbean trade expedition. It was the principal victim of the Spanish fireship attack in the Mexican harbour of San Juan de Ulua.

(DRAWING: AUTHOR AFTER THE ANTHONY ANTHONY ROLL, 1545)

that sixty rounds had penetrated the hull. Aboard the vice admiral's galleon, canister-shot had set a powder-barrel on fire. This could not be contained, and soon the entire ship was burning fiercely. Meanwhile the *Minion* was still able to manoeuvre and, once clear, brought the vice admiral's burning ship under fire, the extent of the blaze putting much of her crew and the valuable cargo beyond rescue. Now the Spaniards turned their

attention to Hawkins's own ship. Boarding parties from three ships tried vainly to get a footing on the *Jesus*, and many more men lost their lives.

In the meantime, the Spaniards on the island had recovered their guns, and began to fire into the English with such great effect that not only did Hawkins lose some of his most experienced men – gun captains and petty officers – but the masts and rigging of the *Jesus* were so damaged that she was rendered totally unseaworthy. It was clearly time to retreat. Hawkins abandoned the carrack, leaving it to screen the *Minion* from gunfire from the island until evening, while at the same time salvaging anything of value from the stricken *Jesus* that he could find. What happened then is described by the second-in-command of the Spaniards, Juan de Ubilla, in a letter to Philip II:

> … the Englishmen placed launches between us and them so that we could not board them, so I gathered together some sailors and set fire to an old empty vessel, and sent it drifting down upon the enemy; when they saw our fireship approaching, their attack on our flagship and vice-flagship slackened. This fireship, by creating a diversion, contributed materially to our victory, as otherwise our fleet might have been sunk with everything it carried, its ships being overloaded, and those of the enemy light.[7]

The sight of the fireship bearing down on them had a far greater impact on the English than hours of Spanish cannonade. Panic broke out, discipline fell apart, and every man looked to his own safety. The brailed-up sails were cut loose and the English ship began to drift to leeward, leaving their comrades and the wounded in the lurch. Hawkins just managed to leap aboard the *Minion* before she gathered way. Some of those left behind tried to swim to the ship, while others followed in a boat. As for the other vessels, only Francis Drake in the *Judith* escaped the inferno, although both ships were still within range of the Spanish guns. There was nothing to do but to lie side by side through the night, until they could make their escape with the morning breeze. The Spaniards were too weak to pursue them, and it was later established that this brutal encounter at the closest possible range had cost them 450 men.

There were not sufficient supplies for the 200 men squeezed into the *Minion*. Soon all the rats and even the ship's cat had been eaten, followed by the parrots which sundry folk had hoped to bring back to Europe. About half of the men decided to go ashore somewhere along the coast of Mexico and trade for food, but they fell into the hands of the Inquisition and lost their lives anyway. Hawkins and the remaining men sailed through the Florida Straits, and in mid-November, in unfavourable weather, began the transatlantic crossing. Many of his men died of starvation, but finally he reached the bay of Vigo in northern Spain. In Vigo, using his commanding presence, he managed to intimidate the dealers into selling him provisions, and the astonished Spaniards let him continue on his way. When King Philip learned about this, he was furious.

Hawkins finally saw the Cornish coast again in January 1569, but the overall result of the voyage was catastrophic, with three-quarters of the original complement of 400 dead and the total investment lost. He never again tried to sell slaves in the West Indies. However, he brought home one important lesson from the experience: he now knew how it felt when a burning vessel bore down, how panic robbed all but the coolest heads of the power of thought and the will to resist; with his own eyes he had seen otherwise brave men so desperate to escape the wall of flames that they threw themselves into the water even though they could not swim.

———•———

The events in San Juan de Ulúa soured relations between England and Spain, initiating a 'cold war' which ten years later would develop into a real one. John Hawkins realised that trading enterprises of the sort he had carried out up to that time were no longer practicable. The future belonged to more reckless men like Francis Drake, who now commenced a series of exploratory voyages and raids, searching out the weak points of the Spanish Empire.

The career of John Hawkins took a different turn. As luck would have it, he had married the daughter of the Treasurer of the Navy, and he became an official in his department. In 1577 he took over as treasurer and thereby became one of the most influential members of the Navy Board, the committee responsible for the design and maintenance of the queen's ships and the manning of the fleet. Because of his experience he was able to make a decisive contribution to the development of what we nowadays call the Elizabethan race-built galleon.[8] These vessels were remarkably seaworthy, and their sailing characteristics and weaponry made them distinctly superior to the warships of other nations of the day.

By July 1588 the tensions which followed the events at San Juan de Ulúa had escalated to the point where Spain was driven to mount the biggest effort of her history to date – the invasion fleet known to the English as the Spanish Armada. Over the succeeding weeks English warships of the new design were to be put to their ultimate test. John Hawkins himself played a part, flying his vice admiral's flag on the galleon *Victory*, but it was the deployment of fireships that would prove the decisive turning point in the operation.

CHAPTER FOUR

THE INVINCIBLE ARMADA

*'There is a stratagem as old as the
invention of ships though the common
people attribute it to the wit of
Sir Francis Drake, at Calais,
in 1588, against the Spaniards...'*

Sir William Monson (1568–1643)

CONFLICT BETWEEN SPAIN AND ENGLAND had become inevitable, with the former determined to exclude all other seafaring nations from the New World, and the latter equally determined to increase its trade and sphere of influence and break the trade barriers that the Spanish wanted to erect. But it was not just on the far side of the Atlantic that Spanish influence threatened to prevail. Philip II, a deeply religious Catholic, was determined to use the enormous power at his disposal in Europe to resist the progress of the Protestant Reformation in the Netherlands, in Brittany and even in other parts of France, which he regarded as a dangerous heresy.

The Netherlands were in open revolt against Spanish rule, but by this time the rebels were in a parlous state, with their armies in retreat. This was very worrying for the English queen, Elizabeth I, since she dared not allow the independent Protestant Netherlands to fall to the Catholics. If the rebellion were suppressed, it would be too late to stave off a Spanish attack on England itself.

Over the years Elizabeth had calculated how to inflict damage on Spain without provoking open war. In 1572 Francis Drake, equipped with Letters of Marque from the queen, led an expedition to the West Indies and attacked the city of Nombre de Dios in Panama. Five years later he set off on his voyage of circumnavigation. Officially, this was intended to nurture trade relations, but in reality the object was to plunder the Pacific coast of South America.

When Drake returned home in 1580, the English public was thrilled, and he was knighted by the queen. The value of the treasure which he brought back was enormous: from just one captured Spanish ship he had taken twenty-six tons of silver. Five years later, in command of twenty-five ships, Drake again plundered and robbed the Spaniards in the Cape Verde Islands, Central America, the area that is today Florida and Haiti.[1] Philip II watched as Spanish trade with its own New World colonies came under increasing threat, and he feared for the security of the treasure fleet, with the steady flow of silver it brought, which was the economic lifeline of the Spanish state.

Every year Spain received 350 tons of silver and several tons of gold from the mines of America.

But despite this influx of treasure, Philip's financial troubles were increasing, and the successes of the daredevil Drake severely threatened Spain's prestige, making it more difficult to raise money to finance the war effort. However, Philip's ability to engage in sea warfare was substantially increased in 1580 when he took over the throne of Portugal, thereby putting its fleet at his disposal, and it was apparently at this time that he finally decided to take up arms against England.[2] Admiral Don Alvaro de Bazán, the Marquis of Santa Cruz (1526–1588), came up with a detailed proposal for the conquest of England, and in 1583, along with the Duke of Parma (with whom we are already familiar from the siege of Antwerp in Chapter 2), he began planning for the English campaign.

Three years later, in 1586, the plans for the 'punishment' of Elizabeth I, in whose name the English pirates sailed and who supported the rebellion in the Netherlands, were finally ready. In Parma's opinion the revolt would totally collapse once England was defeated. Santa Cruz began preparations for gathering the huge fleet which would later be known as the 'Spanish Armada'. Soldiers, sailors and ships were assembled in Lisbon and Cadiz, and everything needed for this complex one-of-a-kind operation, from bronze cannon to wooden tankards, was procured. Men, material and ships came from all over the Spanish Empire, and, as far as could be foreseen, every need was catered for. However, things did not always run smoothly. There were shortages of anchors and guns, and those guns that were collected were of widely varying calibres. Nor were these the greatest of the problems: in 1587 Francis Drake attacked the harbour at Cadiz with a large fleet, taking the Spaniards by surprise, and succeeded in setting many of the assembled ships and stores on fire, famously describing his exploit as 'singeing the king of Spain's beard'. Then in February 1588, just before preparations were complete, Santa Cruz, the designated captain-general of the operation, died. He had been one of the greatest and most experienced naval commanders of his day, and now the king had to find a new commander-in-chief for the Armada. To lead such a multifaceted operation, it was not just ability but also personal prestige that counted; such a commander would need the acceptance and approval of his officers. Philip's choice fell on Alonso Pérez de Guzmán, Duke of Medina-Sidonia (1550–1619), a very experienced man and heir to one of the greatest fortunes in Europe, who at the time was captain-general of the Andalusian coast. However, his previous military experience was in land warfare only, and he protested violently when he heard of his appointment – but the king would have his way.

On 25 April 1588 the Royal Standard was ceremoniously consecrated in the cathedral of Lisbon

At the time of Hawkins's third and last Caribbean slave-dealing voyage, Francis Drake (c1540–1596) was still just an ambitious young 'captain and master' who commanded a small fifty-ton vessel. However, the experience he gained during the Spanish fireship attack at San Juan de Ulua in 1568 was put to good use twenty years later during the Armada campaign.

(OIL PAINTING BY MARCUS GHEERAERTS THE YOUNGER, 1591. NATIONAL MARITIME MUSEUM BHC2662)

and, with thundering gun salutes, brought aboard the flagship. The Armada was ready to sail, and 7,000 seamen and galley-slaves, 17,000 soldiers and about 160 priests waited for the moment when all the planning and preparation ended and they came under the unpredictable rule of wind and weather. Philip knew that there were gaps and imponderables in his plans. The preparations had not been entirely completed, and there were not enough troops aboard the Armada to bring England to its knees. To achieve this, it would be necessary to steer the giant fleet of transports and warships to a predetermined point on the Dutch coast near Ostend, where they would link up with Parma, supreme commander in the Netherlands, and ferry his troops across to England. Everything depended on Medina-Sidonia's fleet and Parma's army being

ready at the same time.

However, at the point where the embarkation was to take place there was no sheltered harbour for big deep-draught ships: the success of the operation would be totally dependent on good weather, and for that the Spanish king firmly believed he could rely on God's help. In his view, this was a holy crusade that could be sure of divine and miraculous assistance. After all, it involved the Holy Church and the One True Faith.[3] However, in the event conditions were less favourable, and adverse winds and sluggish transports prevented the fleet from making good progress. On 19 June Medina-Sidonia reached La Coruña in north-western Spain,[4] where a severe storm damaged and destroyed some ships. There was already a shortage of drinking water and a need for repairs, and it was not until 22 July that the fleet finally left the Iberian Peninsula and set its course for England. Comprising 138 ships, armed with over 2,630 heavy cannon and carrying more than 24,000 men, the Armada was first sighted by English patrol vessels a week later at the latitude of the Lizard in south-western Cornwall.

The next day, 30 July, the ships of the Armada took up their sailing and fighting formation.[5] This was disposed more like a land army than a fleet. Scouts sailed ahead, and the main force followed, with the van or centre in front and wings to right and left. This was something of a tradition for the Spanish officers, many of whom had fought in the galleys when they defeated the Turks at the battle of Lepanto in 1571. The ships maintained a distance of about sixty-five metres apart and sailed in rows, each of which kept about seventy-five metres from the next one. The wings swept backwards, with individual ships *en échelon*, the mass of the fleet forming a giant crescent moon formation when viewed from above (contemporaries called it the 'eagle formation'). Altogether it spread out for five and a half kilometres, arranged so that no ship could be cut out, and if a ship was attacked from astern, the attacker would have to deal with the ships on the wings.

The English were ready. While their spies had watched the Armada being assembled in Spain, the English fleet had expanded, and Elizabeth I now had over 197 ships and more than 16,000 men at her

disposal, with some outstanding commanders who were among the most experienced seamen of the age. She had posted the squadrons on the south coast of England, and as soon as the Armada was sighted, the English warped their ships out of the harbour at Plymouth, with the tide and against the wind. At that time there were about thirty-five vessels under the command of the Lord High Admiral, Howard of Effingham, Duke of Nottingham (1536–1624); the vice admiral was Francis Drake. The following day (31 July) the English ships came up in the rear of the Spanish formation. In the early morning Medina-Sidonia ran up the royal ensign at the mainmast of his flagship, *San Martin*, as a sign that battle was to commence.

For about four hours, the English ships, fast and agile, attacked, firing their guns, tacking and withdrawing. This was in fact what the Spanish had expected. Philip's instructions were explicit, predicting that the nimble English ships with their long-range guns would remain at a distance, and would not attempt boarding. The answer to this tactic was the 'eagle formation', which was to be maintained with iron discipline. The task of the Spanish fleet was not to bring the English ships to battle, but to cover the transport of Parma's troops from Dunkirk and Nieuport to England.

Philip imagined that for the land campaign he would be able to deploy his army in Flanders, which numbered 30,000 men, and had estimated that the embarkation might take two days, with the crossing achieved in eight to twelve hours. The main thing was that at the end of the operation, his troops, well trained and battle-hardened, would be on English soil at Margate or the mouth of the Thames. The English had nothing comparable to stand up to them.

For four days, from 1 to 4 August, the mighty crescent of the Armada drove to the east, with Medina-Sidonia striving with every means at his disposal to maintain this defensive formation. He threatened his captains with instant death if they fell out of position – and with good reason, since every ship that did so was immediately attacked by the English. The Spanish were astonished at the manoeuvrability and advanced design of the English ships, something for which John Hawkins, in his capacity as Treasurer of the Navy, could take

Believed to be a design for a tapestry, this anonymous painting shows, in stylised form, the types of ship involved in the Armada battle. Prominent in the foreground is one of the big galleasses, an oar-and-sail hybrid developed by the Venetians. The four-masted English ship in the middle of the picture is typical of the race-built galleons with reduced superstructure whose development is usually attributed to John Hawkins.

(NATIONAL MARITIME MUSEUM BHC0262)

substantial credit. He had lost all respect for the Spanish at San Juan de Ulúa, and now, alongside Drake and other experienced 'sea-dogs' like Martin Frobisher, was one of the commanders doing their best to defeat them. However, the long-range English culverins inflicted relatively little damage, and there was no decisive outcome. The English were forced to realise that the Spanish ships were heavily armed, and that their large crews were thirsty for battle and anxious to make short work of their opponents – if only they would come near enough.

Again and again the English ships ran in to attack, and again and again the ships of the Armada held their trusted eagle formation. Of course the Spanish began to suffer losses, by accident or incompetence, but in the main the fleet remained intact and continued imperturbably on its course up the Channel. The artillery battle had now lasted for some days, with both sides expending large quantities of powder and shot, but whereas the English could replenish their munitions from local

bases, Medina-Sidonia would have to wait for the rendezvous with Parma.

On 6 August the Spaniards sighted the coast off Boulogne. The weather was unfavourable, with a south-west wind, rain-squalls and poor visibility. Medina-Sidonia convened a council of war, and the pilots unanimously agreed that in these conditions the fleet would be driven northwards well into the North Sea, from where it would then be very difficult to sail back against the wind to meet up with Parma. So the order was given to anchor, and by around seven in the evening the fleet lay at anchor not far from Calais on the French coast, the vessels close together in a round formation.[6] The admiral and his staff knew very well that the anchorage was dangerous, with the ships exposed to wind and weather. But the site of the planned meeting point with the army in Flanders was not far away, and that was the most important consideration. The admiral's secretary was dispatched to inform Parma of the situation of the fleet and determine his state of readiness.

The events played out in the Channel between Dover and Calais in August 1588 inspired not just the nations directly involved but also artists of other countries, especially the Netherlands, where the defeat of the Spanish was particularly welcome. This Dutch engraving, produced a decade later, shows the English fireships being loosed on the anchored Armada. In the left foreground are a high-charged Spanish galleon and oared galleasses, which are attacked by a lower-built English galleon to the right. In the centre of the picture a Spanish ship is using boats to haul it clear of the fireships drifting down on it.

(THE ARMADA IN THE STRAITS OF DOVER, DUTCH SCHOOL, C1600–10, NEDERLANDS HISTORISCH SCHEEPVAARTSMUSEUM, AMSTERDAM)

On the English side, an additional squadron, which had been waiting for the Armada further to the east, now joined the main force, and the English fleet, now numbering about 140 ships, anchored roughly a cannon-shot to windward of the Spaniards. At nine in the evening Admiral Howard convened a council of war on board his flagship, *Ark Royal*, at which those present included Hawkins, Drake, Frobisher and also William Wynter, who held high office in the Admiralty and commanded the newly arrived galleon *Vanguard*. Wynter reported the result of their deliberations to Walsingham, the Secretary of State, thus:

> having viewed myself the great and hugeness of the Spanish army, and did consider that it was not possible to remove them but by a device of firing of ships, which would make them to lose the only road [anchorage] which was apt and meetest to serve their purpose, as also an occasion to put many of them in danger of firing, and at the least to make them to lose their cables and anchors which could not be less than two for every ship …'[7]

Wynter claimed in his letter that the idea of deploying fireships was his inspiration alone, but we may assume that it occurred to other members of the council as well, and especially to John Hawkins. Wynter continued: 'His Lordship did like very well of it, and said the next day his Lordship would call a council and put the same in practice.'

The next morning, Sunday 7 August, both fleets still lay at anchor in the same position. At first light the flag at the mainmast head of the *Ark Royal* signalled another council, at which it was finally decided that a fireship attack was to be made that night. Suitable ships were not to be found in the English fleet, so Howard sent off one of his captains, Sir Henry Palmer, to seek out and requisition vessels and inflammable material. A little later, however, it dawned on the English that by the time Palmer returned it might be too late to make a fireship attack: the tide and wind were so favourable now that they simply had to seize the opportunity, making use of whatever was available.

Drake and Hawkins each offered one of their ships, and six more were designated for use in the attack, varying in size from ninety to 200 tons. All eight were privately owned vessels; subsequently the Treasurer of the Navy paid £5,111 in compensation, with an additional £416 10s added to the bill for the material consumed by fire. In fact the weapons were of a very improvisatory nature, ingeniously put together with whatever was to hand. The designated vessels were cleared, and were laden with pitch, fish-oil, tar, sulphur, brushwood and dry firewood.[8] The guns were primed and double-shotted so that their fire would be more destructive. Work went on deep into the night until the extemporised fireships were ready and could be brought out of the body of the fleet.

For Medina-Sidonia, the captain-general of the Armada, 7 August was a very bad day. He received the unwelcome news that his expended powder and shot would not be replaced; that the Duke of Parma, supreme commander of the army of Flanders, was still in Bruges; and that it would be two weeks before his boats and troops would be at the disposal of the invasion force. Parma had a hard winter behind him, and his emaciated soldiers were in sad shape and had not received their pay. Sickness raged through their ranks, and many had simply deserted. It was true that Parma had received reinforcements from Italy in April, but this had only brought his army's strength up to 17,000 men.[9] To make matters worse, it now turned out that his fleet of shallow-draught invasion craft had been blockaded by a squadron of Dutch warships, and was unable to move along the canal between Dunkirk and Bruges. Under these circumstances, Medina-Sidonia had no choice but to beg Parma to make haste, and meanwhile remain in his present dangerous anchorage, wait and pray.

Philip had already warned Medina-Sidonia that the English might well use fireships. To his mind, they were capable of anything, and it was only three years since the fireships and explosion-ships had blown 800 Spaniards sky-high in Antwerp. It was said that the fiendish engineer Federico Gianibelli was in England. As recently as April, a harmless-looking Dutch merchantman had been towed into the harbour at Dunkirk: suddenly, its crew made itself scarce and a large quantity of gunpowder on board blew up, causing widespread damage and fear.[10]

This anonymous sixteenth-century Dutch painting focuses on the English fireship attack on the Armada. As is usual in such works, events which occurred at different times are conflated; night is turned into day, and in the foreground a mighty Spanish galleon is being shown attacked at close quarters and boarded by the smaller English galleon (a situation that the English tried to avoid at any price, because Spanish ships were so strongly manned). As in other representations of the fireship attack, the fireships themselves seem to lack masts and spars (although the top-hamper was probably reduced to ashes before the hulls themselves were consumed).

(NATIONAL MARITIME MUSEUM BHC0263)

The English might well try something of the sort, and the supreme commander made preparations accordingly. To seaward of the anchored Armada he stationed a pinnace, outfitted with grappling-irons and a long iron chain, which would serve to tow a burning vessel clear of the fleet. He further ordered his captains to have boats in the water ready to tow their ships clear of a drifting fireship.[11] Should there be a fireship attack, if necessary they were to slip their cables and return to the anchorage when the danger was over. That was about all that could be done.

'Monday the 8th of the same month at two of the clock in the night we saw coming all afire eight ships of the English in very good order toward us, with the flood, which came very swift, the which caused us to let slip our cables to the end, and we were marvellously separated bearing from the banks of Flanders.' That was the curt description of what happened off Calais by the Spanish soldier Pedro Estrades in a letter to his brother. He was a sort of reserve officer aboard one of the ships of the Portuguese division of the fleet. Elsewhere he wrote: 'The English did accomplish their business well, but why they were allowed to do it, only God knows.'[12] But this was no ordinary affair for the English sailors either. On that remarkable night in August, Captain John Young was in command of the *Bark Yonge*, one of the vessels picked for conversion into fireships. Later he committed his experiences to paper, recalling 'the old days' when the English inflicted as much damage as they could upon the enemy: '... if extreme need should require, then by some policy in firing, if you have any such good provision aforehand, which will be very costly and some danger in the doing of this desperate service; for unskillful men it is not meet and cowards dare it not.'[13]

At eleven o'clock, a shot from a saker signalled the start of the fireship attack, and the eight ships set sail with about a hundred men aboard, advancing in line abreast.[14] The timing was perfect, with the current setting at about three-quarters of a knot towards the Spanish fleet adding to the flood tide at another two and three-quarters knots. Then sail was set, adding further momentum. Two of the ships were probably set on fire prematurely, so the Spanish lookouts saw first two fires, and soon after-

wards eight, all heading straight for the Armada. The crews jumped into their boats and fled the scene. Naturally, the Spaniards were increasingly alarmed. Perhaps these were not just fireships, but infernal machines – everyone knew the story of Antwerp!

In this situation Medina-Sidonia gave what turned out to be a calamitous order: the *San Martin* should move out of the path of the drifting fireships, and then re-anchor in the same place. Aboard the other ships the sailors watched with apprehension as the supreme commander got under way. Did the captain-general know something that they did not? Were the approaching vessels something like the Hellburners of Antwerp? Was Gianibelli with the English at this moment? That the *San Martin* immediately returned to her old anchorage was not noted by the panic-stricken watchers, and the iron discipline of the Armada, which had so far held, finally broke down.[15] Every captain just wanted to get away as fast as possible, and so began a series of dangerous night manoeuvres. Many captains, intending to save time, avoided the laborious process of weighing anchor, and just ordered their cables to be cut; it is thought that about 120 anchors were lost in this way, a loss which was to prove disastrous later. Immediately, the strong current carried the Spanish ships north-east towards Dunkirk, and it took so long to break out the reserve anchors from the holds that many had drifted far to leeward before they could re-anchor.

Amazingly, there were few accidents, but one big galleasse, the *San Lorenzo*, lost her rudder when it fouled the cable of another ship. After drifting ashore the next morning, she was boarded and taken by the English after bitter hand-to-hand fighting. For the Spaniards this was the first loss of a capital ship, for in the event all the fireships had drifted harmlessly by, without one Spanish ship being destroyed. But the fleet had lost its anchorage, and the whole plan for a combined land and sea operation lay in ruins.

At dawn the next morning Medina-Sidonia saw few ships of his once invincible Armada in the immediate vicinity, but he discerned that the English were weighing anchor and were preparing to attack him from windward. Gunshots from

the *San Martin* gave the signal to form battle-order, but most of the ships were too far away to react effectively, and the peerless eagle formation was in tatters. Thus, about eight o'clock in the morning, as what was to go down in the history books as the 'battle of Gravelines' began, Medina-Sidonia had very few ships to support his flagship, and the *San Martin* and Drake's *Revenge* fought it out at very short range, about 180 metres' distance, with every weapon they had. Drake was backed up by two more English galleons, and at the end of the day a Spanish officer in the *San Martin* counted 200 hits on his ship. Slowly the dispersed Spanish ships managed to reassemble in a half-moon formation. In the course of the day, they expended so much powder that they could respond to the English attack only with small-arms fire. As the Spanish cannon fell silent the English approached more and closely, but their light sakers and culverins did little decisive damage to the massive bulwarks of the Spaniards. The casualties were heavy, with about 1,000 killed and 800 wounded, and many of the Spanish ships had sustained some damage – but the main thing was that they were still afloat,

and as before, the English did not try boarding tactics. So, as the cannon and small-arms fire sputtered out, the longest and bloodiest day of the Armada campaign drew to a close.

By the evening the English had lost none of their own ships and could claim three Spanish ships sunk and two or three lost by running aground on sandbanks. This was the first sea-battle fought entirely by sailing ships and cannon, without the involvement of galleys and boarding. The Lord High Admiral, Charles Howard, sat at his table aboard the *Ark Royal* and wrote to Walsingham, Secretary of State: 'the Armada is still wonderful great and strong, but we are plucking their feathers by little and little'.[16] The Duke of Medina-Sidonia was a sturdy soldier, and was not about to surrender. He would fight on, doing everything in his power to hold his position, and convoy Parma's invasion craft to England; and the English had run out of ammunition and did not renew their attack. In the evening a strong north-west wind sprang up, driving the Spanish ships landwards. The pilots warned the senior officers about the dangerous sand-bars and told them that the only way to escape was to set

This Dutch etching of the Armada is not intended to represent any particular moment of the campaign, but centres on the fireship attack, as did most of the contemporary illustrations. A galleasse is shown trying to head off the fireships.

This is the ninth in a series of twelve charts produced in 1590 by Robert Adams, each depicting a stage in the Armada campaign, based on the account by Lord Howard of Effingham. It shows the moment when eight fireships were released into the mass of anchored Spanish ships off Calais. None of the enemy ships was set on fire, but the panic caused the Spaniards to abandon the anchorage, with the loss of many anchors and cables.

course for the North Sea. However, the duke continued to hesitate.

During the night and the early morning of 9 August, the Armada was driven ever nearer to the sands, and the duke offered battle to the English, but the latter had spent all their powder and feared getting into shoal water. Wind and tide forced the Spanish ships relentlessly toward the dangerous coast of Flanders, the lead showing a depth of six and a half fathoms (about twelve metres), and the men on the driving ships began to fear for their lives. Then something happened which the Spanish took for the long-desired Divine Miracle – the wind shifted suddenly to west-south-west, and the ships were blown clear of the coast.

But the joy over escape from certain destruction was mixed with the bitter realisation that although they had fought bravely, they had lost the battle. At a council of war aboard the 'capitana' (flagship), the captains of the fleet learned that there would be no return from their present course: wind and weather would not permit sailing back and renewing the attack. Fate had given them only one chance; Philip had taken a gigantic gamble and lost. At the beginning of the campaign, the instructions for the fleet read: 'Victory is a gift from God: He gives it or takes it away as He wills.'[17] And now it was the will of God that the duke should give the order to sail northwards to Scotland and round the Shetlands, before turning south along the western coasts of

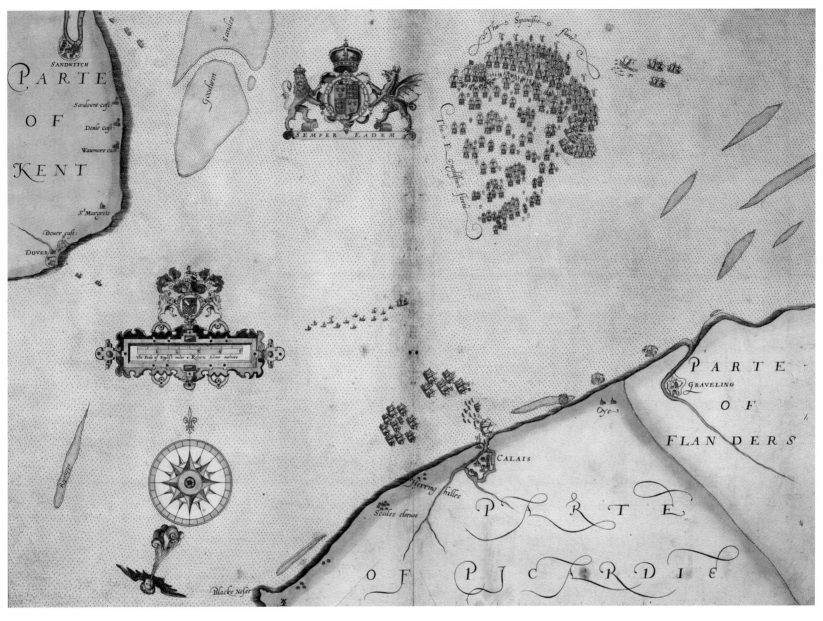

Scotland and Ireland and so back to Spain, where the ships would regroup at La Coruña.

The route followed by the battle-damaged ships took them into unknown waters. Powder-kegs and shot-racks were nearly empty, supplies of water disappearing, and provisions running short, so all available supplies were divided equally among the ships. Every man would receive a daily ration of only a half-pound of ship's biscuit, a pint of water and a pint of wine. The horses and mules were flung overboard.

The English fleet pursued the Armada as it sailed northwards, but there was no actual conflict between the opponents. On 12 August the pursuit was broken off, and the English sailed into the Firth of Forth, while the Armada, which no longer posed any threat, disappeared into the northern mists. But then came disaster for the English fleet, for an epidemic broke out. Historians disagree about whether it was typhus or just the result of rotten provisions. In the battle with the Armada the English had lost fewer than 100 men, but forty times as many died on land.[18]

The weather was cold and stormy, forcing the ships of the Armada to scatter. Many of them were designed for the Mediterranean and were too lightly built for the rough Atlantic. Some foundered or ran aground on the coasts of Scotland and Ireland. Fewer than half of the ships got back to Spain, and of the 24,000 men who had sailed off in

The tenth in the Robert Adams series depicts the battle off Gravelines that followed the dispersal of the Armada caused by the fireships. The main part of the English fleet continues to snap at the heels of the Spanish ships as they sail away northwards, while the boats of Howard's ships attack the stranded galleasse *San Lorenzo* while under fire from Calais. Between the two parts of the English fleet, a ship leads a flotilla of small craft.

(NATIONAL MARITIME MUSEUM F8048)

June, so confident of victory, about 11,000 never came back. The Duke of Medina-Sidonia returned to Spain a sick man. After his recovery, he placed himself again at the disposal of the king, who however never blamed him personally for the Armada catastrophe. His own courage was never in doubt and he remained in the king's service, but as the commander of a fleet his performance was no better than middling. He was later responsible for two further defeats – he failed to defend Cadiz against the attacking English in 1595, and then in 1607 his fleet succumbed to an attack off Gibraltar by the Dutch admiral Jacob van Heemskerk.

The destruction of the 'invincible Armada' did not mean that the war between Spain and England was automatically at an end. A number of skirmishes followed, most of them at sea, but a few minor ones on land. Elizabeth realised that Spain's naval power was far from beaten, and by late 1588 was already planning a 'counter-armada'.[19] This was to take the form of raids on the harbours of Santander, San Sebastian and La Coruña in the following year, in an attempt to annihilate the ships which had survived the Armada before they could be refitted and redeployed against England.

Elizabeth's orders to her captains were very specific: 'By burning of the King of Spain's ships of war in his havens before they should come forth to the seas, and therewith also destroying his magazines of victuals and his munitions for the arming of his navy.'[20] But this first counter-armada was badly planned. There was disagreement among the captains, and the undertaking miscarried, with most of the ships which had survived the Armada fiasco being left unharmed; these were subsequently rebuilt, and formed the core of a new fleet, directed against England.

For this first counter-armada strike the use of a particular type of fireship was discussed – the smoke-ship, which seems to have been one of Drake's ideas. With favourable wind and current, smoke-ships could be sent off towards the coastal batteries which defended a harbour entrance, and the gun crews would be so afraid that they might be explosion-vessels that they would fail to fire their heavy cannon accurately.[21] However, there is no report that such a plan was ever successfully put into effect.

As in 1589, every year there were more or less successful operations against Spain.[22] These were financed not only by the Crown, but also by merchants lured by the possibility of valuable loot. Almost every year, expeditions were mounted against Spanish and Portuguese harbours, and at the same time English ships cruised off the Azores in the hope of capturing Philip's treasure ships, ranging as far afield as Central America and the West Indies.

The rebuilding and refitting of a new fleet was thus continually hindered, but not completely halted. The most effective means of accomplishing the total destruction of ships lying in harbour was, of course, fire, and during this phase of the Anglo-Spanish conflict fireships were primarily planned with this role in mind. 'It were necessary to send six of Her Majesty's good ships together with a store of fireworks in some six old vessels resolutely conducted, into Santander, there to burn their 58 'armathoes'.[23] This is how Sir Roger Williams, author and military man, described the thinking during the planning of an attack on the harbour of Santander in 1589.

Likewise, in 1597, for the last of these operations, which was intended to destroy the Spanish ships in Ferrol, six 'double-flyboats' (flutes) were selected as fireships. These were relatively large vessels of more than 200 tons, and originally served as transports.[24] But the fleet hit bad weather and was driven back to Plymouth, and when it sailed again it was so late that the leaders abandoned the attack on Ferrol and headed straight for the Azores. They failed to catch the Spanish treasure fleet at sea, and it escaped into the safety of the harbour of the island of Terceira in the Azores, thwarting the attack – it made no sense to use fireships to attack ships carrying valuable cargo, because you could not plunder a ship that was incinerated.

By the end of the sixteenth century, it had become normal to have some vessels designated as fireships in the fleet-train of a naval operation directed against an enemy port. That was the beginning of the systematic use of fireships as a primary weapon, and in the course of following centuries they were to take on such great significance that many an admiral would express the wish that he had fewer warships and more fireships.

CHAPTER FIVE

THE
FIRESHIP JOINS
THE
BATTLEFLEET

'...a useful though horrid instrument'

Lord John Montagu, Earl of Sandwich, 1763

In the first decades of the seventeenth century the fireship gradually became a standard part of the order of battle in European navies. In fleet lists of the time there are smaller vessels designated not only as transports but also as fireships – that is, 'real' fireships, rather than those that were hastily fitted out as such just prior to their deployment. These were purpose-built or at least specifically fitted out for their final one-way journey, but were also capable of serving as transports in the interim.[1] Despite its adoption by many navies, the fireship as a weapon had both its advocates and its critics but, as always with any innovation, one great success was enough to wipe out the memory of all previous failures.

Let us suppose that we could ask a professional naval captain from the beginning of the seventeenth century to give his opinion about fireships. Actually, this is not as absurd as it sounds, because Nathaniel Boteler (or Butler) (c1577–c1643) was in the habit of seizing his pen and answering putative questions about basic maritime matters for landlubbers. Boteler was a captain in the English navy but, in the parlance of the age, more of a 'gentleman' than a 'tarpaulin', as the professional sailors who had worked their way up to this rank were known.[2] Boteler wrote not for his peers, but for those people who through favour, money or social connections found themselves quickly and unexpectedly on the quarterdeck of a warship. Surrounded by long-serving experienced sailors, it would be embarrassing for them to expose their lack of knowledge, and Boteler thought some sort of textbook would be useful for such folk. Boteler's contemporary Sir Henry Mainwaring (1587–1653), who started his career as a pirate and ended a vice admiral, had written a similar book, *The Seaman's Dictionary*.[3]

The particular usefulness of Boteler's text lies in the fact that his expertise was not just that of a ship captain, but also reflected his experience in civil administration. He had served in the government of the colony of Virginia and was later Governor of Santa Catalina, an island off the coast of Nicaragua. In 1625 he had command of the merchant ship *Jonathan* in the attack on Cadiz, and in 1628 he commanded the *Patient Adventure*, one of the vessels in the fleet sent to try and break the siege of La Rochelle.

Boteler formulated his lessons in the form of a conversation between an 'Admiral' and a 'Captain'. In this he weighs the pros and cons, limits and imponderables of warfare using fireships. He seems a little sceptical about the fireship attack on the Spanish Armada, remarking, 'For mine own part, I have no great opinion of them.'[4] He felt that the success of an attack depended on too many factors. The fireships had to sail down wind, have tide and currents favourable, and be provided with a strong screen of boats until they were very close to the enemy and could be set on fire. Besides, one had to reckon with the possibility that the enemy would send their own boats to try and tow the fireship out of the way of their own ships.

Boteler makes some interesting comments about 'Boat Warfare', something that developed in the shadow of the great sea-battles of that century. He thought it was all too easy for a target ship to cut or slip its cables, and sheer out of the path of the fireship. Therefore the most promising places for a fireship attack were canals and rivers, which were narrow enough to prevent a large ship from getting out of the way, or a boat from throwing a fireship off course. What he does not mention is the fact that, as was recognised later, ships moored or anchored closely together in a harbour are vulnerable, and of course the classic target was a ship disabled in battle, having lost her masts and rigging and lying motionless.

Another prerequisite of the successful fireship attack was surprising the foe, and an important aspect of this was camouflage. Boteler admitted that it was possible to trick out a fireship so that it just looked like an ordinary warship that had been given the order to attack and was thus able to close with the enemy without revealing its true purpose. It is known that this sort of thing was tried at the beginning of the First Anglo-Dutch War (1652). The Dutch certainly tried it: under the headline 'News from Holland', a report in an English newspaper of the time read: 'They [the Dutch] boast much of their fireships as carrying 24 and 30 guns, appearing like men-of-war, but indeed are no such things, having only two or three guns, and all the rest are painted, and so placed as they may best deceive the eye, and be less suspected when they come to service.'[5]

Later in the century, and long after Boteler's day, it seems that naval commanders no longer bothered with attempts at deception, or made any serious effort at disguise. As the fireship's fittings became more elaborate, it became easier to spot the typical marks of a 'hellship', with its hook-shaped irons at the yardarms, its grappling irons chained to the bowsprit and the boat in tow, ready for the crew to make their escape. Fleets employed dedicated lookouts whose job was to scan the enemy line for fireships. Smaller vessels in the screen were also given the special task of watching for fireships and their manoeuvres. The fireship could be effective before it ever caught fire, since just the fear of its presence caused many enemies to keep their distance. Not for nothing did the admirals of the seventeenth century keep their own 'personal fireships' close to their flagships. The threat of their use, especially if one were to windward, could give some respite if they were being pressed too closely by the enemy. However, when Nathaniel Boteler contemplated the success of the English fireships in the 'great business of '88' against the Spanish Armada, he came to the conclusion that these fireships had simply never achieved their primary aim – that of destroying an enemy warship. The Spanish had run aground, having possibly mistaken the burning ships for the Hellburners of Antwerp. In taking this view, Boteler underestimated their psychological effect. The experiences of the bitter sea-battles which would follow were different. Just the terror inspired by an ordinary fireship, the fear of almost certain death, could be quite enough to determine the behaviour and fate of the best-armed ship, and indeed whole fleets.

In Boteler's work the imaginary Admiral also raises the topic of a special form of fireship, the 'Explosion-Vessel' or 'Powder-Vessel'. The English referred to these ships as 'infernal machines', 'mine-vessels', 'machine-vessels' or sometimes simply 'machines'. Typically they would take the form of a small vessel, perhaps a fishing boat, in the bow of which was a charge of gunpowder. This was contained in a strongly constructed wooden chest or a copper boiler, which was in turn covered with stonework. In Boteler's dialogue the Admiral and the Captain are in agreement about the effectiveness of such an explosion in an enclosed space, but Boteler himself remained a bit sceptical. A vessel with a heavy load of stone would be inherently unstable, and how would one manoeuvre such a lumbering vessel into the desired position? And

In his *Architectura Navalis* of 1629 the architect and mathematician Joseph Furttenbach (1591–1667) shows a ship with a large number of fire-producing weapons, which could have fulfilled the purpose of a fireship without risking its own self-destruction. It was described as a 'caramuzzal' or 'karamusal', the name given to well-armed sailing ships that were used in the Mediterranean by the Turks and Barbary states. Like the later frigates, such ships served as patrol vessels, convoy escorts or privateers. The strong fore- and after-castles protected the crew, while the upper decks served as gun platforms for small-calibre cannon, making karamusals superior to the lower-built galleys. However, the most remarkable feature is the plethora of fire-making weaponry described by Furttenbach: grenades and fireworks fired from 'pipes' supported on forks, and some form of 'sticky fire' which was projected and combined to generate a 'rain of fire'. An inflammable material that was hard to extinguish is also mentioned, as well as hand-grenades and rockets intended to set the rigging of the enemy alight and create alarm and confusion. Inflammable material was also to be pumped through nozzles to spray the enemy. The karamusal seems to have been rigged with lateen sails, and Furttenbach describes how the peak of the long yard could be swung over the enemy's vessel in order to drop petards, bombs or inflammable material on its decks.

(AUTHOR)

again, how could you prevent the enemy extinguishing the burning fuze-cords, if they managed to get men aboard?

By way of an answer, Boteler's Captain offers a complicated scenario envisaging booby-trapping the explosion-ship, in case the enemy should board it and cut the fuze. The Admiral is to imagine a ship, with sails set and rudder wedged, coming out of the darkness and drifting towards her victim:

And because it is to be expected that the enemy, upon their first discovery, and the forsaking of them by their men, will adventure to board them, and by a speedy searching out for the trains that lead to the chamber of the vault where the powder is lodged, seek to prevent their firing; it is a safe course to cause many false trains to be laid in sundry places of those fireships; the which the enemy finding upon his

boarding, by removing them may be deluded upon a supposed prevention; and so give over from any farther search.

And as for the true trains, all such matches as are prepared for them are to be made fast to long twines or pack-threads; the other ends of which pack-threads are to be tied to the gears of two or three pistols, whose firelocks are to be ready bent; and the pistols being charged are to be so postured with their mouths, that being fired by the snatching up of the matches made fast to the pack-threads, tied by their other ends to their gears, they may shoot into the bed of powder laid within the vault and so fire it … by the one means or the other the wished effect of the blowing up the powder-ships, and the enemy by them, be accomplished.[6]

This was the ideal: in reality the difficulties in mak-

Among the most significant works of the great French graphic artist Jaques Callot (c1592–1635) are his large-format and highly detailed representations of the battle of the Île de Ré and the siege of La Rochelle (1625–8). This view depicts the first stage of the English campaign, the landings on the Île de Ré late in 1627. As long as the island was occupied in support of La Rochelle, the chances of a successful French siege of the city were minimal. However, the English failed to capture the forts on the island, which were continually resupplied by French blockade-runners, and eventually Buckingham's forces were driven off the island and the fleet sailed home in abject failure.

(NATIONAL MARITIME MUSEUM PU5047)

The French campaign against the besieged city of La Rochelle, the centre of Huguenot resistance, included a barrier built across the entrance of the city (seen at the top of the picture). The English tried to break the blockade and relieve the city using warships, fireships and explosion-vessels. In the middleground of this part of the picture Callot shows an English fireship attacking the French ships. It is already in flames, and all around a 'mosquito war' of small craft is in progress. The men in the boat are trying to force the fireship off course with long poles (numbered 81), and are being supported by other boats (80), while the boats at 101 are trying to prevent this. In the foreground of the picture is the main English fleet, with the fortified barrier in front of La Rochelle in the background.

(FROM: VICHOT 1971)

ing an attack with an explosion-ship were manifold.[7] At that time, it was not understood how to direct the explosive energy in a watercraft, and it was exerted in all directions, being dissipated upwards or through the ship's bottom. Because any suspicious ship, whether a fireship or explosion-ship, came under particularly heavy fire from the enemy, the fuze-trains (to which we will return later) had to be well protected to prevent premature ignition, which would cause the certain death of the crew. Powder had to be shielded from fire, shot and water. The hold of the ship had to be divided by several heavy bulkheads to prevent sinking when half a ton of iron shot hit the bulwarks.

On the other hand, one advantage of attacking with an explosion-ship was that the enemy did not know until the last minute what he was really dealing with, since in general the ship was not obviously on fire, and the explosion came suddenly and unexpectedly. However, the fuze could readily be extinguished as the flame reached the caulking where it entered the powder-keg, especially if the tar or pitch which had been used to seal the opening melted and put out the fire. It was said that the English preferred to set the whole ship on fire, and so be certain that the powder would go sky-high.[8]

The scepticism aired by the Captain in the dialogues reflects Boteler's own negative experiences with these special-purpose ships. In the spring and again in the autumn of 1628 he lay at anchor off La Rochelle. This heavily fortified city on the French Atlantic coast was the most important harbour and fortress of the Huguenots, the French Protestants, who under their leader, the Count of Rohan, enjoyed a degree of autonomy. They had long been tolerated by Louis XIII and his First Minister, the Cardinal and Duc de Richelieu (1585–1642), but now they had become embroiled in foreign policy and had allied themselves with Protestant England. Civil war threatened in France, and the forces of the French king laid siege to La Rochelle. The English king, Charles I, and his Lord High Admiral, the Duke of Buckingham, agreed to land on the Île de Ré, and this plan posed an intolerable threat to the security of France. The first English relief expedition reached La Rochelle in May 1628,[9] and lay off the city, trying to send in troops and supplies. To cut off this support from England, as well

as surrounding the city on the landward side, the besieging French forces needed to build a dam and a boom across the harbour entrance. They made the dam from stones and sunken ships, crowned with a wooden superstructure and reinforced it further with a line of ships, to prevent the English from reaching the city with their troop transports and deep-draught warships.

The English fleet comprised about sixty vessels, including ten large warships; one of the smaller ships was commanded by Nathaniel Boteler. Boteler was not optimistic about the chances of success. The English knew that it would not be possible to breach the defences with a direct attack on the heavy cannon-armed galleons, but if they had a flood tide and a sea-breeze, the conditions would be ideal for the new special-purpose ships. They commenced an attack with fireships, which was directed less against the dam itself than against the ships guarding it on the seaward side. However, the French were prepared, and a swarm of boats came out and tried to drag the fireships off course using long hooked poles.

However, one of the fireships spared them this dangerous task. According to numerous reports of the time, including that of Boteler himself, the fireship ignited prematurely. The vessel was laden with all kinds of fireworks and petards, and although the crew had just jumped into the boat in which to make their escape, the fire spread so quickly that they were incinerated along with the ship.[10] Then the wind changed, and the English ships had to withdraw to avoid being set on fire themselves. The attack had been a total fiasco.

But Charles I had promised to put pressure on the besiegers, and in September of the same year the English were back, bringing troops and fresh supplies to the beleaguered Huguenots. This time they had 122 ships, with ten designated as fireships, and since the big ships had not achieved much up to now, and the fighting spirit of the conventional forces in what they thought of as the king's business left something to be desired, the conflict developed into a war involving new-fangled special ships.[11]

The English attacked the dam and the ships lying before it with their fireships and 'machine-vessels', the latter devised by the Dutch engineer and inventor Cornelis Drebbel (1572–1631). This multi-talented man had worked on improving the microscope, probably constructed the first thermometer, and is credited with building the first workable submarine. He had lived for some years at the court of the English king, and repaid the hospitality by turning his attention to the king's current military problem. For the La Rochelle operation he rebuilt several busses – ships which were normally used in the herring-fishery – as explosion-vessels. Twelve of these were now deployed before the French port and sent with the flood tide against the barricade, where some exploded but without causing any decisive damage. Some were swept out to sea on the next ebb-tide and some were towed clear by the French. Next, the English tried sending in vessels laden with manure and set afire. It was hoped that these 'smoke-ships' would emit enough smoke to screen the fireships which followed them. But this operation too was a failure.

The French themselves struck back using their own fireships. Day after day, as the tide ebbed and flowed, it carried with it specially modified ships and boats of both sides, but without any decisive result. La Rochelle remained without relief and without hope, and in October it was starved out and the citizens surrendered. Richelieu destroyed the defensive installations around the city and removed the privileges of the remaining citizens, but they kept their lives and freedom of worship.

After the fall of La Rochelle, Richelieu and his army had to reckon with another threat, this time from the House of Habsburg and the Spanish Netherlands, which bordered on France. In addition, Spanish troops were putting pressure on France's allies in northern Italy, so in response Richelieu decided to ally France with the Dutch United Provinces, Sweden and the Protestant German states. In 1634, after the Swedish army was defeated by the Catholics at the battle of Nördlingen, there were fears that the Habsburgs would come to dominate Europe, and the cardinal felt so threatened that he took his country, which was predominantly Catholic, into the Thirty Years' War on the Protestant side and declared war against Spain. The French directed their operations principally at the Spanish supply-lines, which connected them to their possessions in Flanders and northern Italy.

The war on land is beyond the scope of this book, but there were significant operations at sea. In the Atlantic, Spanish privateers took Dutch and French prizes, and in the Mediterranean a Spanish fleet of galleys occupied the Lérin Islands, off Cannes on the coast of Provence, to secure the sea route to their Italian possessions. As the islands lay within gunshot of the mainland, this was something the French king simply could not tolerate. By dint of brilliant organisation and the technical help of the Dutch, Richelieu had begun to rebuild the French navy, and he now dispatched the *flotte de Ponant* (western, *ie* Atlantic, fleet) to the Mediterranean. At this time it included twelve transports and six dedicated fireships,[12] a number which was to increase over the next seven years to nineteen. The one thing lacking was experienced men.

The Franco-Spanish sea-war of 1635 to 1639 was fought out in the western Mediterranean and the Bay of Biscay. However, the big warships, with their rows of bronze cannon, were expensive objects of prestige, and during this war were rarely risked in serious encounters with the enemy. At that time the only way a ship of this type could be destroyed beyond repair was by falling victim to a fireship, and it is not surprising that the greatest successes of the war were achieved by fireships against vessels lying at anchor.

The first victory for French fireships was the destruction of a flagship from Naples off the coast of Friuli by a French fireship,[13] and the weapon had even greater success in the Atlantic. In 1638 the French western fleet, under the command of Henri de Sourdis, Bishop of Bordeaux, was supporting an invasion of the Basque country with forty-one warships besides transports and fireships. In August a Spanish squadron of twelve or fourteen galleons was sent to break the French blockade, a task for which it was not quite strong enough, but was forced to anchor off the village of Guéthary (Guetaria) between St Jean de Luz and Biarritz. The bishop's ships opened fire on it with only modest success, and then decided to send in their fireships. The venture succeeded, and the whole squadron fell victim to the flames with the loss of 4,000 men, while the French lost fewer than a hundred. This success established the importance of the fireship throughout all the European navies.[14] In the following year the number of fireships in the *flotte de Ponant* rose to nineteen.

The English fleet tried to break the siege of La Rochelle in a war of special-purpose vessels, fireships and explosion-ships, but failed. They were unable to destroy the boom or barrier (shown in the centre of this engraving) that cut off the city from the open sea, and in October 1628 the starving citizens surrendered. The victorious Cardinal Richelieu spared their lives and allowed them to retain their faith, but the fortifications were razed to the ground.

(NATIONAL MARITIME MUSEUM PU5053)

CHAPTER SIX

THE
MOTHER-AND-CHILD BOAT
AND OTHER
CHINESE SPECIALITIES

'...a fearful Danger ready to destroy us'

Peter Mundy, 1673

As we have seen, fireships were becoming increasingly popular in Europe by the beginning of the seventeenth century. But these destructive inventions were not limited to the West. Fireships were also used by the Imperial Chinese Navy in the seventeenth and eighteenth centuries, and their deployment and the deception of the enemy that went with them formed a well-understood part of the general Art of War.

In China, naval skirmishes occurred for the most part in rivers or in the mouths of estuaries, rather than on the open sea, for in these relatively calm waters it was possible to make use of favourable tides and currents, which were ideal for fireships. There are even descriptions of successful fireship attacks from Chinese antiquity, one example being the battle of the Red Cliffs, fought on the Yangtze-Kiang in 208 AD.[1] One side set alight a large number of boats laden with brushwood and oil, and these 'fireships' caused such panic among the enemy ships that they were run aground on the banks, with huge loss of life.

About 1553 there appeared a book written by Li Chao-Hsiang (Li Zhao-Xiang), the superintendent of a large and important installation near Nanking called the Dragon River Shipyard.[2] In this book, which is illustrated with woodcuts, he discusses historic vessels and events, from which it is clear that in China, just as in Europe, there were a number of specialised types of ship, and men of seemingly limitless inventiveness. As regards fireships, for the Chinese the most obvious problem was that of getting the ship within striking distance of an enemy without raising his suspicions. This was not regarded as purely a function of technology, but also a matter of psychology: how to exploit the enemy's wishes and expectations. For example, in the fourteenth century (by the Western calendar), there was an incident in which one of the warring parties managed to convince the other that some of its ships intended to defect, and as a result they were allowed to come near – too near, as it transpired, when it became clear that they were fireships and there was no way to avoid them.[3]

In his book, Li Chao-Hsiang discusses several technical tricks from the Chinese Art of War that could be used to disguise a fireship.[4] Prominent among these were various methods developed by the shipbuilders of constructing the hull in two parts, either in tandem or side by side. The original function of these 'two-part' junks was to divide on reaching shallow water, since each half drew less water than the whole ensemble. The fireship variation of the principle was built so that one part of the vessel – the inflammable 'business end', so

Chinese fire-rafts as illustrated in the *Wujing Zongyao*, a military treatise written in 1044 during the Song Dynasty. This demonstrates the antiquity of such devices.

(WIKIMEDIA COMMONS)

to speak – could be made fast to the enemy, while the crew used the other section to make their escape. The combination-vessel looked harmless enough as it approached, because one sure sign of a fireship was missing: a boat in tow, ready for the crew to make their escape. Li Chao-Hsiang described it as follows:

> A vessel of this type is about fourteen metres long, and from a distance looks just like an ordinary ship. But in reality, there are two parts to it, with the forward section making up about one third, and the after part two thirds of the length. These are bound together with hooks and rings, the forward part being loaded with explosives,

smoke-bombs, stones and other missiles, besides fire emitting toxic smoke. At the bow are dozens of barbed nails with their sharp tips pointing forward; above this are several blunderbusses, while the after part carries the crew and is equipped with oars. Should wind and current be favourable when they meet an enemy vessel, they set a collision course, ram the bow as hard as possible into the enemy's bulwarks, and at the same moment let go the fastenings between the two sections, and the after part heads back to its base.[5]

A variant of this vessel was the 'mother-and-child boat', a perfectly camouflaged fireship about twelve metres in length. The forward part was seven metres long and was built like a warship, while the after section, 5.25m long, consisted of a framework with what appeared from a distance to be the sides of the vessel separated only by a scaffolding, which supported the big balanced rudder and concealed the oar-propelled escape-boat. On either side of the bow there were 'wolf's-teeth nails' and sharp iron spikes to prevent boarding. The attack was made by ramming the enemy ship, which was then held fast with grapnels, and at the same time distracting the victim with a hail of arrows, stones and other missiles. The vessel was loaded with reeds, firewood and flax saturated with inflammable material and bound together with big black-powder fuzes. Once it had been ignited and the enemy was on fire, the daughter-boat was cut loose and the crew made their escape.

Europeans would encounter such weapons when their desire for commercial expansion brought them into conflict with the Chinese. The Portuguese first came to China about 1516, and by the following year an ambassador had visited the Chinese capital and obtained permission for merchants to establish themselves and transact business in the trading centre of Canton. For a long time the Portuguese were the only foreigners with this privilege, which they later tried to turn into a total monopoly of the export trade in the waters of southern China on the basis of their military strength. They expected to repeat the success they had enjoyed in India, but in 1521 and 1522 the Chinese decisively defeated them at sea, and when trade was resumed it was on Chinese and not Portuguese terms. The merchants switched to smuggling, and when the authorities found they could not stamp this out completely, in 1587 they permitted the Portuguese to set up a trading post on the island of Macao, at the mouth of the Pearl river. This was the foundation for the Portuguese monopoly of trade between China and Japan.[6]

For decades the Portuguese suffered no competition from other Europeans and made huge profits, but at the beginning of the seventeenth century the first Dutch fleets began to poach upon the preserves of their colonial empire. The sea power of the Dutch slowly increased after the foundation of the Dutch East India Company (VOC) in 1602; Molucca came under their sway, and the town of Batavia was established on Java, on the Sunda Strait. Apart from some minor setbacks, Dutch merchants enjoyed great success in Asia, but they could not get a toehold in China. They failed to establish a permanent trading post on the mainland, never winning the trust of Chinese high officials. In the Middle Kingdom the 'red barbarians' were considered cunning and greedy. The only notable thing about them was their powerful ships, with their double-planking and 'rigging like a spider's web'.[7]

In the year 1622 the Governor of the VOC in Batavia gathered enough courage to take his fleet on an offensive against the Portuguese in Macao, in an attempt to take over the China trade by force. However, the attack was repulsed and the Dutch proceeded to the Pescadore Islands in the Formosa Strait, where they began work on a fortified strongpoint. At the same time they tried to set up a permanent trading base in Amoy (Xiamen), but just as before, their negotiations with the mandarins went nowhere, and they failed.

The Dutch now decided to use a trade war and a blockade to force the Chinese government to trade with them. Thus in January 1623 a VOC fleet raided the coasts of Fukien and Kwantung in south China, destroying the huts of the farmers and reducing the trading junks in the little coastal ports to ashes.[8] This was a poverty-stricken part of the country, and the Chinese military were powerless to stop them ashore. At sea, the navy could not

子母舟圖

An illustration of a fireship from a book written about 1553 by the Chinese imperial official Li Chao-Hsiang, superintendent of the Dragon River Shipyard near Nanking. The Chinese devoted a great deal of ingenuity into making fireships look like ordinary warships. The main trick was to conceal the boat in which the crew would make their escape. In the 'mother-and-child' boat the escape-boat was completely concealed within the after part of the hull, and appeared only when the victim had been rammed and set on fire. To make the principle clearer, the escape-boat in the picture is more visible than it would have been in reality. At the bow we see the 'wolf's-teeth nails' which secured the fireship to its victim.

(FROM: SCHEURING 1987)

stand up to the heavily armed vessels of the Dutch, but there was one thing it could do: attack with fireships. The fireship was the one Chinese weapon that inspired fear in the Europeans.

As previously mentioned, Chinese fireships were normally deployed in rivers and estuary mouths, for the most part disguised as fishing boats, so the apparently innocent craft could drift down on the anchored Indiamen at all hours. However, the Dutch learned to moor their ships with two anchors, athwart the stream, so that if need be they could slip one, allowing the ship to swing round and avoid the attacker. The crews were kept on the alert, with the slow-match always burning and guns at the ready, so they could engage quickly; any suspicious vessel would be immediately brought under fire and sunk. Standing orders were nailed to the mainmast by the commandant of the fleet, with stiff penalties for disobedience: anyone absent from his post, or sleeping on watch, would be hauled up to the main yardarm and dropped into the water three times for the first offence; a second offence attracted fifty lashes; and if he further misbehaved, the ship's council might decide it was a capital matter, and he would be hanged.[9]

The VOC's war on the Chinese state did not have the desired effect and, apart from gaining a seasonal trading permit which they had to renew every year, the Dutch again failed to establish themselves on the mainland. The strongpoint in the Pescadores had to be abandoned, and only in 1624, after building a fort and trading post on Formosa, did they gain indirect access to the lucrative China trade.

It was not just the Dutch who had to face the Chinese fireships. Among others who had to deal with them on the Pearl river were three English East Indiamen under the command of Captain John Weddell. The English ships were observed with hostility and suspicion by their competitors, the Portuguese, as they sailed up the river, trying to get as close as possible to Canton, the trading *entrepôt* of the area. On board one of them was a remarkable man, Peter Mundy, a traveller who had roamed all over Europe and Asia recording his adventures and observations, and it is from his journal that we know what happened on the Pearl river on the dark night of 10 September 1637.[10]

The three ships, the *Anne*, the *Catherine* and the *Dragon*, lay at anchor astern of one another, and at two in the morning the water was flowing quickly, with the ebb-tide reinforcing the normal current. They were expecting goods to arrive from Canton and did not think too much about it when they saw some junks sailing towards them. The *Anne*, the smallest of the three, lay furthest upstream, and at first it looked as if the junks were just going to sail past, but then they altered course to bring themselves athwart the hawse of the bigger *Catherine*. The alarm was raised and the junk was fired on, alerting the other ships. The shot appeared to act as a signal to the junks, which all at once burst into flames – they were fireships!

The Chinese fireship represented here also derives from Li Chao-Hsiang's book about the Dragon River Shipyard. We can see it is a kind of combination-vessel, with the fastenings amidships working on the hook-and-eye principle. At the bow the 'wolf's-teeth nails' were rammed into the opponent's hull, the rockets and fire-missiles which are to be seen in the forward part of the hull were ignited, and the crew made their escape from aft. In this arrangement, too, the escape-boat for the fireship crew was invisible.

(FROM: SCHEURING 1987)

Immediately the English realised what was going on. The first two fireships were connected by chains, and then three more appeared, all steering for the English ships. However, they had no more time to observe, for they had to work flat out if they were to save their lives. Luckily it was almost the end of the ebb, and the current slackened somewhat, which gave them time to cut or slip their cables and make sail. Even more fortunately, just at that moment a light breeze sprang up, and having had the foresight to keep their boats in the water, they were quickly able to take the ships in tow. 'The fire was vehement. Balls of wild fire, rockets and fire arrows flew thick as they passed us, But God be praised, not one of us all was touched.'

The night was lit up by blinding flames, which illuminated the hills above the river bank. And the noise as the fireships drifted by was unnerving, the cries of the Chinese crews aboard them blending with the crackling of burning bamboo and the whistling and hissing of rocket and fireworks canisters. In the light of the flames, the English watched as the men on the burning junks jumped into the water and swam for the shore. One of the junks ran aground at the level of the Indiamen, while two more drifted out of sight downstream, and one junk seemed to have been set on fire prematurely and burned out harmlessly, before she reached the English ships. Now they awaited a second attack while it was still dark, but after two hours the fireworks were finally over.[11]

When day broke the English looked on the river banks for Chinese sailors who had abandoned the burning junks, but they found just one swimmer, who attempted to evade them by diving. Finally he was hooked with a pike and hauled aboard half-dead. Then behind an island they found the biggest of the fire-junks, which was still intact, having run aground before being set on fire. Peter Mundy learned about the appearance of this vessel from the crew of the boat:

> This being full off dry wood, sticks, heath, hay, etc, thick interlaid with long small bags of gunpowder and other combustible stuff, also cases and chests of fire-arrows dispersed here and there in abundance, being so laid that might strike into ships' hulls, masts, sails, etc, and to hang on shrouds, tackling, etc, having fastened to them small pieces of crooked wire to hitch and hang on any thing that should meet withal. Moreover, sundry booms on each side with 2 or 3 grapnels at each with iron chains; other also that hung down in the water to catch hold of cables, ground tackle, etc so that if they had but come to touch a ship, it were almost impossible but they catch and hold fast.[12]

The English salvaged the grapnels and chains from the junk and then set it alight. 'It burnt awhile so furiously that it consumed the grass on the side of the hill as far as a man could fling a stone; so that had they come within as they came without us, they had endangered us and at least driven us out.'

The Chinese sailor in the boat was patched up by the ship's surgeon and survived, and was put in irons. The English learned from him that the fireship attack had been instigated by the Portuguese at Macao, and that the intention had been to catch the ships just at change of tide, when they would swing broadside to the stream and present a bigger target. Captain Weddell and his men had been very lucky.

CHAPTER SEVEN

THE
BATTLE
OF
THE DOWNS

'...nothing can hinder the
Enemy's Destruction'

William Mountaine, 1756

ESPITE THE LOSS OF A WHOLE FLEET OF galleons to fireship attack at Guéthary, 1638 was not the worst year for the mighty Spanish fleet. Following a twelve-year armistice in the northern Netherlands, the war against the Dutch 'rebels' was renewed. However, resupplying the Spanish army in Flanders with men, money and material proved difficult. The land route (shipped from Spanish harbours to Genoa and then through Milan, Savoy, Lorraine, the Rhine valley to the Netherlands) had been under constant threat since 1631 from the French and Swedish armies, and this increased the importance of the alternative sea route – across the Bay of Biscay, along the French coast and into the English Channel, taking the convoys into Dunkirk, which was in Spanish hands. Every year the Spanish mounted a convoy operation, and every year the Dutch fleet tried to prevent it from getting through, but initially without much success. This situation began to change when three energetic newcomers took over direction of the Dutch navy: Maarten Harpertszoon Tromp (1598–1653), Witte Corneliszoon de With (1599–1651) and Cornelis Evertsen the Elder.[1]

In December 1637 a big Spanish convoy carrying fresh troops to Flanders succeeded once again in reaching Dunkirk, but Tromp, who had recently taken command of the Dutch fleet, had increased the number of ships available to establish a patrol-line in the Channel and keep a sharp lookout. Dunkirk was closely blockaded, with all passing merchant ships being examined, and the Dutch fleet remained at sea, under dreadful conditions, until March 1638. That year no Spanish fleet reached Dunkirk, but this was due less to the blockade there than to the series of French attacks on the ports in northern Spain. So it was widely expected that in 1639 there would be a renewed effort to reach Dunkirk with a big convoy.

And sure enough, at the behest of Philip IV of Spain, a large expedition assembled, with divisions at La Coruña, Cadiz, Cartagena and Naples, ready to enter the waters of the Channel when the opportunity arose. The supreme commander of this fleet – which was nearly as big the Armada of 1588 – was General-Admiral of the Seas Antonio de Oquendo, an experienced fighting seaman. His mission was to deliver two infantry divisions, over 10,000 men, safe to Dunkirk, but unlike the Duke of Medina-Sidonia in 1588 he had orders to bring the enemy fleet to battle should he meet them en route. As it turned out, his soldiers were not seasoned troops, but poor, half-starved, badly paid and poorly armed wretches, who had been brutally impressed and taken to the rendezvous point in chains, with their wives and children wailing at the loss of their only breadwinner.[2] Before long they would be ripped apart by Dutch cannonballs and burned to death by Dutch fireships.

The new Spanish Armada set sail from La Coruña on 27 August 1639 with about seventy ships, of which forty-five were warships. The rest consisted of hired vessels, prizes and merchantmen purchased from various countries. Even the warships included only three powerful fighting units, but they were the pride of the lands from which they came. Firstly there was the *Santa Teresa*, a big Portuguese galleon of more than 1,000 tons originally built for the East India trade. She was richly outfitted, with two galleries to her towering stern and sixty bronze cannon – the most splendid ship in the fleet. Then there was the *Santiago*, built of best Spanish oak, with her 60 guns, a 1,000-ton colossus with an 800-man crew, serving as Oquendo's flagship. Finally, the 56-gun flagship of the Neapolitan squadron was a sight to behold: '… a jewel made of massy gold & bronze, rich and rare, so ornamented and so strong was she'.[3]

In the preceding months Tromp had been getting ready for the Spaniards, tirelessly travelling around the country to cajole and browbeat the multiple admiralties of the United Provinces. His efforts produced some additional ships, and by July he was on patrol in the Channel. Then, in August, the blockade of Dunkirk was re-established. On 15 September, as he approached the Dutch coast, Oquendo received news from his scouts that only a few enemy ships were in sight. There was jubilation among the sailors and soldiers aboard the splendid galleons, who had expected more formidable opposition. What they did not know was that they had seen just part of Tromp's force. He had split his fleet into three divisions, one protecting the herring-fishery in the North Sea, one blockading Dunkirk and one patrolling the Channel.

The Dutch fleet forming up in a rough sea before attacking the Spanish fleet sheltering in the Downs off the Kent coast in October 1639. In the foreground the painter Reinier Nooms, known as 'Seaman', depicts the *Amelia*, flagship of the renowned Admiral Maarten Harpertszoon Tromp. Launched in 1632, the ship weighed 300 lasts (approximately 600 English tons), had fine lines, was a good sailer, and served as a prototype for many subsequent Dutch warships, despite having the disadvantage that the lower tier of gunports could not be opened in rough weather. The Spanish, not visible here, were at anchor off a lee shore, offering Tromp an ideal opportunity to using fireships.

The next day, the 16th, abreast Beachy Head at the entrance to the Straits of Dover, the fleets made visual contact. The Spaniards, joyfully expecting certain victory, were sailing in a state of disarray, in no particular order, not certain that the Dutch would even accept battle. At 8am Tromp on his flagship, the *Amelia*, had only seventeen ships available, sailing in a single line ahead. At that time such a formation was most unusual, but its advantages were obvious: as the line passed the enemy, each ship came into action successively, and could use its broadside firepower to maximum effect. An hour later the two fleets were only two ship's lengths apart, a deadly range for the heavy guns of that time. Immediately, Oquendo tried to board the *Amelia* from the *Santiago*, but the former sheered off. Broadside after broadside roared across the sea, and right at the onset of battle one of the foremost ships in the Dutch line blew up; then a powder-keg in the cabin of De With's flagship exploded, destroying much of the ship's upperworks. Not a good start! The Spaniards were jubilant, but Tromp's gun crews carried on calmly about their business.[4]

Later a Portuguese eyewitness, Dom Francisco Manuel, noted what he saw after the first exchange of broadsides between Tromp and Oquendo. Despite the explosion the tactical situation had not changed, but the Spanish flagship was recognisable only because she still occupied the same position. When the smoke cleared, the remains of her shot-riddled ensign still flew, but all the rigging was cut to pieces by chain-shot, and the remains of shrouds, halyards, braces and sails whipped in the breeze like streamers. On the overcrowded decks men lay dead, dismembered and wounded. But the sixty-six-year-old Oquendo fought on 'like a brave bull which is ferociously attacked by a pack of hounds'.[5]

In clouds of powder-smoke, the mis-matched fleets criss-crossed each other in a grimly determined fashion, and by three in the afternoon the ships lay just off the French coast. The Spaniards became more and more concerned about their masts and spars, and firing ceased as they fell back. Repairs were urgently needed, and Oquendo turned away to the north; by evening both fleets had anchored, but were still within sight of each other. In the afternoon, out of curiosity, the English ships under Vice-Admiral Sir Henry Mainwaring sailed past the Spaniards and noted that they had been 'shrewdly torn and beaten' by the seventeen Dutchmen.

Tromp seized the initiative. On the 17th, after replenishing his stores of powder and shot, he re-engaged the exhausted Spaniards in a night attack beginning at 11pm. Dom Manuel remembered the flashes of the heavy guns, and everywhere there was the rattle of musket-fire. The thunder of the guns rolled on through the night, and although the

Admiral Maarten Harpertszoon Tromp (1598–1653), like most of the Dutch fleet commanders, had learned his business from scratch and was a keen proponent of fireships. He was in command at the battle of the Downs, at which the Spanish were heavily defeated. By defying the English, he set off the First Anglo-Dutch War, and in the aftermath tried to compensate for the numerical inferiority of the Dutch fleet by using a large number of fireships. He was killed at the battle of Scheveningen in 1653, the victim of an English sharpshooter.

(FROM: DE JONGE 1858–62)

actual damage was not great, the Spaniards expended a lot of powder and shot.

On the morning of 18 September Tromp, now reinforced by a second squadron, held the weather gage, which gave him the initiative. Again the Dutch ships sailed in line to attack the Spanish, who formed up as they lay in rows four or five deep, getting in each other's way. The flagship *Santiago* received heavy punishment, but she was able to dish it out too, and after the battle it was established that the starboard broadside alone had fired 1,520 rounds – more than fifty per gun. After an artillery duel lasting for hours, the Spanish fire became weaker, and Tromp, having again run out of ammunition, broke off and withdrew in the direction of Calais. Oquendo had failed in his objective of landing the infantry reinforcements at Dunkirk and, fearing that his ships, with their rigging shot to ribbons, would be unable to stem the flood tide, led his fleet to the Downs, a sheltered anchorage off the coast of east Kent, in neutral English waters. Further out lay the protective banks of the Goodwin Sands.

The English coast promised more than a safe anchorage. The Spanish supreme commander also reckoned on some energetic help from Charles I, who was offered the massive sum of £15,000 to use his ships to prevent the Dutch entering his waters and engaging the Spanish. Despite treaty obligations to assist Spain, however, the king remained undecided, not wanting to compromise his relations with either party. So he provided very low-quality powder to the Spaniards at horrendous prices, and ordered the commander of the English fleet to make only threats if the Dutch crossed the Channel and anchored near the Spanish fleet, which of course they did. Antonio de Oquendo now fully realised the dire situation in which he now found himself at his anchorage. Despite his sixty-five ships, he could no longer hope to break through to Dunkirk with a fleet that had lost its confidence and fighting spirit. Week after week the Spanish would wait as though paralysed – but for what?

The three fleets lying off the coast, English Dutch and Spanish, were a rare spectacle, and during the weeks of September and October became a huge attraction on the coast of Kent. As would happen today, throngs of sightseers came to look at those splendid ships out at sea. One of the observers was that tireless traveller Peter Mundy, whose experiences in China concluded the previous chapter. As Mundy described it, 'The Dutch rode to the Southward, the Spaniards inward toward the North, and our King's ships rode between them both.'[6] He noted that the Dutch now blocked the Spaniards' path to the open sea, this being their reaction to a successful blockade-breaking operation by fourteen of the smaller Spanish ships which got into Dunkirk with some of the troops and supplies. After visiting the *Santiago* and sketching the huge vessel, he crossed to the *Santa Teresa* and described his impression of conditions in the Spanish fleet: 'They have abundance of Men in their Fleet, but most soldiers or sailors; all in general perplexed in this extremity, yet preparing

for the fight again, and repairing what hath been damaged by the Hollanders in the last skirmish … They have now a sickness amongst them, and many die, whose bodies being flung overboard, some of them are washed ashore along the beach. Both Hollander and Spaniard indifferently come ashore to buy provisions, refreshings, etc, in the market, one among the other as friends.' But replenishment ships were also coming from the Flemish coast at night, supplying the Spaniards with, among other things, 'straw-mattresses and women.'[7]

After visiting the English flagship, Mundy went aboard Tromp's *Amelia*, '…where I found them lusty, healthy and frolicky, encouraged by former good successes and this present fortunate opportunity witch they will hardly let go … having also in their fleet 8 to 10 fire ships fitted with chains, grapnels, etc. To say the truth, the Spaniard is become as it were a prey unto them, for I have heard themselves say, some that [it] is even a lost fleet.'[8]

Tromp and his fellow combatants De With and Evertsen were not content with their 'former good successes'. They knew that they had a unique opportunity to annihilate the Spanish fleet, and preparations for the final onslaught began. In a fever of activity, men were impressed and new ships fitted out. Even the West India and East India Companies permitted some of their vessels to be requisitioned, and fresh ships were added to the Dutch fleet almost daily. The anchored Spanish ships were an ideal target for fireships. Fireships! That was the magic solution, and the Dutch could not have enough of them. The master Maerten Claessen from Hoorn, who had delivered supplies in his flute, was summoned aboard the flagship. Tromp wrote in his diary: 'We asked for his ship as a fireship, which he was reluctant to consent to, but we took it as by force and gave him a certificate to that effect.' A captain was sent ashore to find combustible material for a fireship but came back empty-handed, so the flag officers made hurried efforts to buy 'firewood' in Dover. This was to be kept secret because 'since our Zeeland fireships were not yet ready, we would equip them in all haste; and the wind not being favourable, we would keep our secret for the present from the General Council of War until a fitter opportunity, to lessen the risk of its being discovered'.[9]

Tromp hoisted the white flag at the *Amelia*'s masthead on 11 October as a signal for a general council of war. By now he had 103 warships and about sixteen fireships altogether, the number of the latter indicating just how much importance he attached to this weapon. The huge success which de Sourdis had enjoyed off Guéthary was common knowledge in the relevant military circles. Tromp had secret orders to attack the Spaniards in any case, despite any protests the English might make.[10] What he did not know was that Oquendo had received similar orders to attack the Dutch in English waters or harbours, even if this were to lead to an open breach with England.[11] The Dutch now decided to launch their offensive at the first opportunity, which required a favourable wind and tide, and not too great a seaway, so that the gunports on the lower gun deck could be opened safely.

On the morning of 21 October 1639, at four in the morning, the English and Spanish sailors heard the roar of a signal gun from the Dutch fleet, which could mean only one thing – Tromp was on the move. The wind was from the north-north-west and it was foggy. At daybreak the Dutch had held prayers, and then manned the capstans. The messengers were set in motion, buntlines and clew-garnets loosed, and the ships proceeded to set sail. Aboard the *Amelia* the screens in the great cabin were dismantled and, together with Tromp's bedstead and dining-table, struck down into the hold for safety. Sir John Pennington ordered the English squadron to clear for action as well and got under sail. Aboard the flagship *Unicorn*, Peter White, a Navy Board official, tried to make sense of what was going on, and his eyewitness account of the battle is one of the most important sources for this event.[12]

A squadron of thirty Dutch warships and three fireships detached itself from the main force, the part of the fleet which the English had held in check. White noted that the Spanish got under sail later than anyone else, imagining until the last moment that the English would prevent an encounter from taking place in their home waters. When it became clear that the English were not going to defend them, they cut their cables. Now White was able to see through the mist that the

Spanish and Dutch flagships were very close to each other. A cannon shot was heard, and then another. The roar of a broadside came across the water, followed by another, and very quickly the individual salvos could not be distinguished. What would later be known as the battle of the Downs had begun.

A Dutch captain came aboard the English flagship from the *Amelia* and gave Admiral Pennington a long letter written in Dutch, claiming that the Spanish had fired first. Later the Spanish were to claim that the Dutch fireships came so close that they were forced to open fire. It is clear from this that use of a fireship could amount to a form of passive aggression.

In the haze and smoke of the cannon, White could no longer distinguish the ships of the two sides from each other. Visibility became so bad that the cannonade ceased for a while, but as the air cleared, heavy gunfire broke out once more. White watched a group of ships pour concentrated fire into a stranded Spanish ship. The English, whose sympathies were rather with the Dutch, began to fire at long range, and the Dutch withdrew. As Tromp wrote later in his official report: 'the English did little or nothing'.

About twenty-five Spanish ships turned away from the Dutch guns towards the Kent coast: a Dutch fireship was in their midst, and they fetched up off the village of Walmer in total disorder, with some hard aground. Among them was the 56-gun *San Agustin*, one of the finest ships in the fleet. Her commander had stranded the ship, but whether it was through a pilotage error or an attempt to avoid a fireship is impossible to say.

The core of the Spanish fleet behaved with great courage. It was around Oquendo's *Santiago* and the great galleon of Portugal, the *Santa Teresa*, that the powder-smoke was most dense and noise of battle loudest. The bowsprit of a Dutch pinnace fouled the lower stern gallery of the *Santa Teresa*, and the ships became so entangled with each other as to hinder rapid movement. This was the opportunity for which Tromp had been waiting, and at three in the afternoon he gave the fireships the order to attack. Five of them set course for the Portuguese flagship, and two of them reached their goal, grappling the port and starboard sides of the *Santa Teresa*.

An early portrait by Van de Velde the Elder of a Spanish ship identified on its stern as the *Santa Michael*. It was probably drawn in 1639 and may represent one of the smaller ships that ran the blockade into Dunkirk before the battle of the Downs in that year. The ship is pierced for 24 guns (but may have carried a few more on the forecastle) and resembles descriptions of the kind of ships favoured by the Dunkirk privateers of the time – ships that were to inspire the first frigates.

den 21. Octobris 1639. zů getragen, darinen die Hollander vnder dem Admir

Harperstromp die Victori erhalten.

Margat

The fire in their chimneys blazing aloft transformed the focal point of the battle into a huge bonfire. Once the fire reached her powder-magazine, the finest ship in the Spanish fleet exploded, with the loss of 800 of the 1,000 men aboard, including the captain, Don Lopez de Hoces. It was the beginning of the end for the Second Spanish Armada.

A week later Maarten Harpertszoon Tromp reported to the Dutch Estates-General that of the fifty-three enemy ships which had lain in the Downs on 21 October, forty were stranded, sunk or destroyed by fire, with the Spanish losses estimated to be 7,000, including 1,800 prisoners. In stark contrast, the Dutch had lost one ship and 100 dead. Admiral Oquendo's *Santiago*, with 1,700 shot-holes 'between wind and water', got back to Dunkirk accompanied by just thirteen battered and storm-tossed ships.

The battle of the Downs brought not just a material loss for Spain but also a psychological blow, confirming yet again how the mere presence of fireships could destroy the fighting spirit of a brave crew and adversely affect the behaviour of whole squadrons. For the Spaniards, the price paid at the Downs was simply too high, and they gave up trying to resupply the Flanders army by sea. Furthermore, the Dunkirk expedition turned out to be the last serious attempt by the Spanish to act like a great sea power. On the other side of the coin, the Dutch had unequivocally established themselves as the naval force to be reckoned with.[13]

However, Spanish ships did not disappear entirely from the seas. The Franco-Spanish naval campaigns of the Thirty Years' War were fought out with huge losses until the signing of the Treaty of Westphalia in 1648. In 1639, the year of the battle of the Downs, the French western fleet under Henri de Sourdis had over thirty-nine warships and nineteen fireships, the great number of the latter again reflecting the significance attached to this type of weapon. During the year there were some minor actions against small Spanish coastal towns, and with each season the number of fireships changed. In the course of 1642 for example, there were fourteen.[14]

On 30 June of that year a French fleet and a Spanish fleet met off Barcelona in a decisive encounter. This was the last occasion on which

Fireships played an important part in the battle of the Downs, preventing the Spanish fleet from making an organised and effective defence. Several Spaniards taking evasive action ended up aground on the coast, the most prominent loss being the Portuguese flagship the *Santa Teresa*. In the foreground the artist depicts the smoking remains of an expended fireship.

(NATIONAL MARITIME MUSEUM PU5058)

both fleets included both sailing warships, armed with broadside guns, and oared galleys. The conventional artillery duel that opened the affair did little damage to the ships, and the battle of Barcelona proved to be primarily a contest of ships' boats and fireships, with the former being used to tow the latter clear of their target. And it was the fireships which caused the painful losses of men and material. The French had over fourteen fireships and a bevy of small craft, while the Spaniards entered the fight with six fireships and thirty-five longboats.

On the first day of the battle two Spanish ships fell victim to the French fireships, and another surrendered in the face of a fireship attack. On the second day one of the French fireships attacked a heavily damaged Spanish galleon, but it was towed clear by boats. However, through misadventure another French fireship set fire to one of its own side, namely the splendidly appointed *Galion de Guise*, flagship of Admiral Hercule de Conigan de Cangé. The admiral was something of an old warhorse, and after giving his crew the order to abandon ship, he chose to remain aboard and go down with his burning ship. But the men who jumped into the water and swam to the enemy's boats had their hands mercilessly hacked off as they grabbed at the gunwales and drowned. Nor was that the end of the carnage: the *Magdalena*, a magnificent 66-gun ship with over 800 men aboard, also succumbed to one of the fireships.[15]

With a record of successes like these, by the mid-seventeenth century the fireship was accepted as the standard 'terror weapon' in major European fleets, without which, it was believed, no decisive victory over an enemy could be achieved. Having seen how fireships established themselves in the naval order of battle, we will now take a closer look at the construction of these vessels and how they were fitted out.

CHAPTER EIGHT

ACQUIRING
AND
FITTING OUT
FIRESHIPS

'...such truly destructive and hellish apparatus'

Charles Chambers describing the fireship *Prometheus*, 1807

THE SPECIFICATION FOR THE IDEAL fireship was fairly demanding. It had to be seaworthy and capable of keeping up with the fleet, and, if it was part of a squadron engaged in blockade duties, had to be capable of withstanding wind, weather and rough seas. Furthermore, it needed to be a speedy, handy and weatherly sailer, because otherwise it would have little chance of closing with an enemy fleet.

Although early examples were often improvised from the least valuable ships on hand, the dedicated fireship could not be a worthless old hulk, capable of merely staying afloat until it was set on fire. On this matter the interests of navy administrators and operational commanders were often at odds. The sea-commanders wanted successes, but the better outfitted and more expensive a fireship, the greater the financial consequences when it was 'expended', particularly if it had missed its target. In this respect it resembled the modern guided missile, a similarly costly and once-only weapon.

Some of the materials that were needed for outfitting fire-rooms were indeed expensive, and in September 1652 Admiral Witte de With, whom we have already met at the battle of the Downs, wrote to the Dutch Estates-General in the following terms: 'of my eight fireships, seven are missing. It makes no sense sending them with the fleet since they are such slow sailers, and poorly equipped. We need fireships which are fast, of at least 110–150 lasts, and able to keep the sea with us. If we continue in this manner, all the money will have been spent in vain.'[1] Later, he wrote demanding at least a dozen fireships and setting out his requirements: 'they should be two-deck flutes, of between 260 and 300 tons, fully equipped and capable of sailing in company with the fleet'.[2]

In addition, it was important that they looked like transports. If the enemy could spot a fireship at a distance, they would have time to take countermeasures and the element of surprise would be lost. On the other hand, this compromised the fireship's potential to instil fear – whole fleets had cut their cables when a fireship came within the danger zone, but the enemy could never tell with certainty whether ships that looked like ordinary transports were not camouflaged fireships. De With thought a fast flute of medium size was the best vessel to rebuild as a fireship, although the flutes' narrow upper decks were not really suitable for mounting defensive guns. Also favoured by the Dutch were galiots and pinnaces and, if they were available, English vessels taken as prizes, which they regarded as faster and more agile sailers than their own.[3] The key thing was a free space between orlop and upper deck, suitable for building the fire-room.

For the English, on the other hand, colliers were the preferred vessels for conversion. In times of war the need for these weapons skyrocketed, and the navy turned to hiring ships for refitting, paying the owner rent for as long as the ship was afloat, and compensation if it was expended. However, if funds were short, the ships were simply requisitioned; as we have seen, that was exactly what happened in the Netherlands before the battle of the Downs. In those cases, the owner often had to wait a long time for compensation.[4]

In the library of the famous English diarist and naval administrator Samuel Pepys there are fleet lists dating from 1660 to 1688 which include no fewer

After twenty-seven years' service as a 24-gun frigate, the Dutch *Postiljon* was converted to a fireship. The ship was typical of the type and size of vessel chosen for conversion, being a good sailer with two flush decks (one for the fire-room and a weather deck to cover it). There was no forecastle, which was an advantage since it meant that the flames from the fire-room would fly straight up into the rigging.

(DRAWING: AUTHOR AFTER WILLEM VAN DE VELDE THE ELDER, 1665)

An alternative to superannuated warships as a source for fireships: the converted merchantman *Thomas and Elizabeth* as represented by Willem van de Velde the Younger, 1690. It was purchased by the Royal Navy in 1688 and refitted, but was expended in 1692, the year of the battle of La Hogue, when there was a huge demand for fireships. It is however somewhat atypical for a fireship, with a forecastle and a half-deck. The ample waist would help the rapid spread of the fire, and the chimneys would have been found here. The fact that ten cannon are visible and that the port lids are hinged at their upper edge is likewise uncharacteristic, but the enlarged exit-port aft of the mainmast indicates the likely position of the bulkhead at the after end of the fireroom.

(DRAWING: AUTHOR AFTER WILLEM VAN DE VELDE THE YOUNGER)

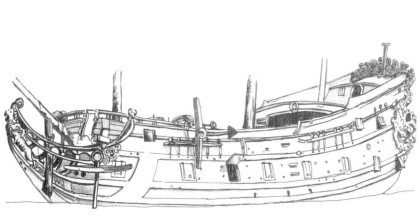

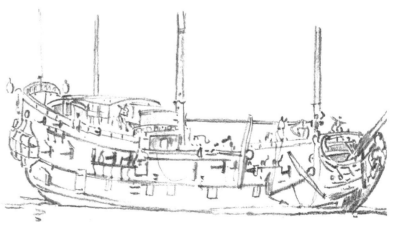

than 136 fireships. They were classed as Fifth or Sixth Rate warships, and many of them were rebuilt prizes, of Dutch or Algerian origin. As to size, they were far from uniform, with keel lengths between 15m and 28m and beams of between 5.5m and 8.5m. There are no records of the exact types of ship they were before conversion; where appropriate their fate is listed as 'Burnt in service', or occasionally 'Blown up by accident', 'Burnt by accident' or 'Sunk in the engagement'.[5]

Later, particularly in the eighteenth century, more attention had to be paid to the speed of the fireship, because the bigger ships of the fleet were becoming faster, so when the Royal Navy purchased merchantmen in wartime, only the fastest of them, with the sharpest lines, were designated as fireships.[6] The ultimate answer was to design purpose-built fireships, and from the late seventeenth century on some of the bigger navies followed this course; we will examine these vessels more closely in Chapter 16.

In converting a ship, the alterations were made for the most part in the interior, and only if an observer got quite close, and knew what to look for, would the secret be disclosed. For example, the hinges of the gunport lids were not on the top, as usually fitted, but on the lower edge, so that when the fire burned through the port tackle the lid fell downwards, fully opening the port and increasing the draught. A close inspection of the port would reveal no muzzle of a cannon, but perhaps a dummy, a 'bang-maker' as the Dutch called it, or a 'Quaker' in English terminology. There might be chimney-like structures on the deck, and more hatches than were the norm, while later fireships had a number of funnels to draw fire up to the sails and rigging. If one of the after gunports had been enlarged to form a sally-port, and a boat was secured close to this by a chain painter, then there was no longer any doubt. It was a fireship! Further clues as to its purpose included hooks or grapnels at the yardarms and the end of the bowsprit, but of course these were fitted only when the attack was imminent.

A prime requirement for a good fireship was not just that it reached its target, but that the fuzing system ignited the piles of combustibles in all parts of the ship simultaneously, and that this network was reliable. When it burst into flame, the fire was directed up various hatches and chimneys, so that the sails and rigging would catch fire and increase the chances of spreading the fire to its victim. However, sufficient time had to be allowed for the crew to get away. A row of broadside ports on the 'tweendeck supplied the fire with the necessary oxygen, but the pressure generated by expanding hot gases might cause the deck to buckle upwards, so extra hatches and chimneys were fitted to prevent this. The practical details of how to fit out a fireship scarcely changed in over two centuries of such warfare. The earliest description found by the author is that of Willem Claesz in his *Bosschieterye* (Marksmanship) of 1641, but the elements are very similar to those in Korth's *Schiffbaukunst* (The Art of Shipbuilding) of 1826, and what follows is a synthesis of information gleaned from sources over three centuries.[7]

The most important alterations in the outfitting

The earliest known original plan for outfitting a fireship is to be found in the Rigsarkivet (Danish National Archives) in Copenhagen. It is probably English and may represent one of the purpose-built fireships of the 1690s.

In profile view the ship has two continuous decks, between which the fire apparatus was installed at about the height of the undersides of the gunports. There are separating bulkheads, but not of full width, intended to act as protective firewalls around the masts and areas below the hatches. Wooden chimneys pierce the upper deck in order to conduct the fire up into the rigging. Also recognisable are the sally-ports aft and the gunport lids hinged on the lower side. In the upper part of the port aperture are the crossbeams supporting the iron-chambers, which would blow open the port lids at the appropriate time. At the main yardarms are the grapnels typical of a fireship. In plan view, the division between fire-room and crew's quarters is clear. Oblique troughs lead from the after bulkhead to the sally-port, through which the crew would leave just before setting the ship on fire.

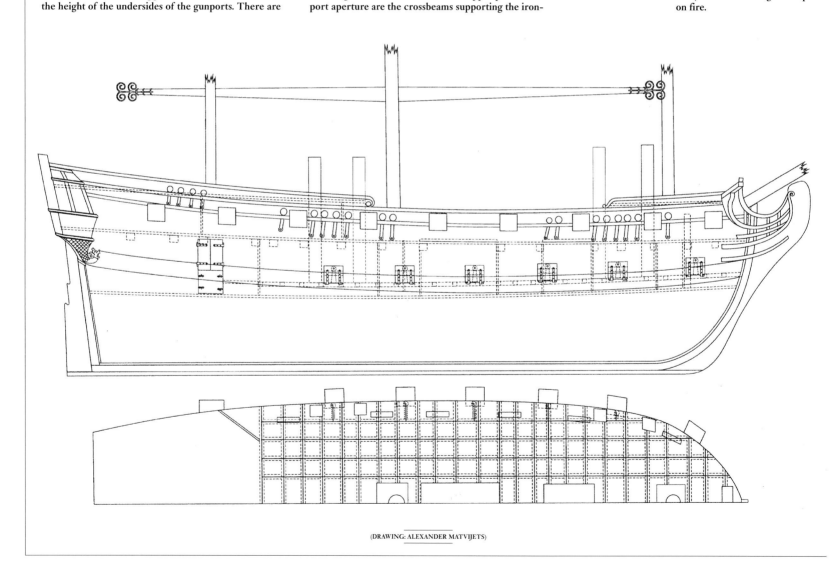

(DRAWING: ALEXANDER MATVIJETS)

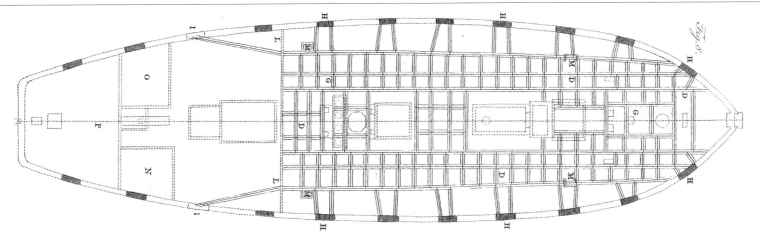

The fire-room of a fireship as depicted in Falconer's *Universal Dictionary of the Marine* of 1780 is similar in basic layout to that seen in the Rigsarkivet plan. The 'fire-apparatus' required two continuous decks. On the lower deck, a gridlike structure was built, designed to spread the fire as quickly as possible through the 'tween deck. This stretched from forward all the way back to a bulkhead just abaft the mainmast and consisted of a series of V-shaped gutters (D and G), which were placed on a framework or grid at about waist height. The gutters were filled with rapidly burning material, which would spread the conflagration through the fire-room and set off the piles of inflammable materials which were stacked between the gutters. Fire-spreader gutters ran to the gunports (H), so that these would be blown open as the fire took hold, supplying it with oxygen. Two of the gutters extended aft through the bulkhead, sloping towards the port and starboard sally-ports, where the captain, as the last man to leave the ship, would ignite the powder in the gutter. Falconer's fireship also featured four wooden chimneys (M) which led up through the deckhead of the fire-room on to the upper deck. Large fire-barrels filled with highly flammable materials were placed under the chimneys, so that the fire would roar up and set fire to the rigging of the fireship and that of its victim. Besides the chimneys, hatches were cut in the upper deck, which also would channel the fire up from the fire-room. About five minutes after ignition, the fire-apparatus would have successfully engulfed the whole ship in flames.

of a fireship occurred in the space between the orlop (or in larger ships the lower deck) and the upper deck. The space from bow to a bulkhead abaft the mainmast was designated the fire-room, and in it was installed what Röding called the 'fire apparatus'. The space abaft the bulkhead was kept as living space for officers and crew. The fitting-out of a vessel designated as a fireship took three to five days,[8] and was in the hands of specialists known as fireworkers. The first thing these specialists did was to build timber 'coffer dams' around the masts in the fire-room, so that the masts would not burn through too quickly and come down prematurely. After that, if there were no existing gunports, six or seven were cut in the sides (about 45cm by 30cm in size) and fitted with gunport lids that were hinged from the bottom, so that they opened downwards.

Behind the lids the fireworkers installed 'chamber-pieces'. These were iron pots of cylindrical shape, about 25cm deep and 10cm in diameter, similar to the separate chambers of breech-loading cannon of the Elizabethan era. They were filled with corned powder, and the aperture was closed by wedging in a wooden tompion with a hole bored for the fuze. This was secured in framework set up just behind the port lid, and the idea was for the fuzes to set off the charges in such a way that the port lids were all blown out simultaneously, and either crashed down or were completely blown away, opening the ports and ensuring that there was plenty of air to aid combustion.

Next the fireworkers turned their attention to the upper deck, cutting holes in it of the same size as the gunports to serve in exhausting the hot gases when the fire roared up. These had to be carefully covered with hatch covers and tarpaulins for the voyage, to prevent the ingress of water ruining all their work.

Between decks, the final fittings comprised a network of fire-troughs, which would ensure that the fire spread rapidly throughout the ship. Röding called them 'wildfires' (*Lauffeuer*) or 'fire-tubes' (*Brandröhren*). A lattice-work system of V-shaped gutters was constructed on trestles at about waist height. The gutters were made of wood or tin, and were about 9cm broad and 7cm deep, with three or four running fore and aft to port and starboard. Every 1.8m or so there were interconnecting athwartship branches running to the ship's sides, and just forward of the bulkhead was a transverse gutter that connected with all the fore-and-aft troughs. From this, two somewhat oblique gutters ran aft to the exit-ports, in some cases extending through them so that they could be ignited by the last man to leave the ship, allowing him to escape the hell that was about to erupt.

The inflammable materials had to be prepared beforehand, and an idea of the requirements is offered by a list of materials for a Dutch fireship dating from 1652:[9]

One of the oldest contemporary fireship models, preserved in the Henry Huddleston Rogers Collection at the US Naval Academy in Annapolis, Maryland. It almost certainly represents the English *Griffin* purpose-built in 1701 but depicted by the model as she appeared later in her long career in the 1730s. On the upper deck the wooden chimneys are conspicuous, and the gunports (hinged at the bottom) stand open, revealing in the upper third of the port the crossbeams that supported the chamber-pieces, which blew the port lids open. The aftermost port has been enlarged to make it easier for the crew to make their exit at the last moment as the train is ignited. The interior of the ship has the fire-room fitted with powder-trains.

The interior of the Annapolis model seen through a fibre-optic cable, showing the fire-train constructed off the deck and the support structure for the explosive 'chambers' in the gunport. To the left is the hole for the mast, which was protected by the bulkhead from burning through too rapidly; if the mast came down prematurely, the ship's speed and direction might be adversely affected.

Pine-resin (*Harpuis*) 3 oxheads (each of 234 litres). This material was a solid sticky, very inflammable material, skimmed off boiling resin and then mixed with cow-hair, sulphur and ground-glass

Pitch	8 tons (981 litres)
Tar	16 tons (1,963 litres)
Empty casks	50
Olive oil	1 aam (155.2 litres)
Camphor	6 pounds (3kg)
Sulphur	50 pounds (24.7kg)
Brushwood	1,500 bundles
Sailcloth	15 ells (the cloth was probably an Amsterdam ell in breadth (77.4cm), and impregnated with sulphur)

The inventory concludes with iron sheer-hooks for the yardarms, boarding-grapnels and more dry firewood. In a French inventory of 1787, there is mention of turpentine, flaxseed oil, saltpetre and fine priming-powder. All these materials became both harder to get and more expensive during the wars of the seventeenth century, which helps to explain why Admirals Witte de With and De Ruyter were concerned about the expense, and

The grapnels or boat-anchors attached to chains were the symbol of fireship warfare. With warping anchors of this sort the target was made fast to the attacker. Similar grappling-irons were used by small craft to hook the fireship and tow it clear of its victim.

(FROM: FALCONER 1780)

why they were so upset when the fireships supplied to their fleets could not keep up with the rest of the ships and had to be sent home again, having cost a lot and achieved nothing.

When all this material had been collected and the fireworkers were satisfied that it was thoroughly dry, they filled the fire-conducting gutters with a mixture of gunpowder, saltpetre, resin and sulphur, with some flaxseed oil added to make it more workable, though too much oil would make the mixture burn too slowly.[10] Once the gutters were full, they were covered with sulphur-impregnated sailcloth or cartridge paper. On top, and filling the space

between the trestles, went wood-shavings, brush-wood and dried heather.

In order to encourage the fire to race upwards and ignite the rigging of the fireship (and, it was hoped, its victim), special 'fire-barrels' were used. These were placed in the fire-room under a hatch on the upper deck, which was covered with a wooden chimney. The fire-barrels were big and heavy, stable and capable of burning for some time before they fell apart, in the meantime shooting their flames through the chimney and up into the rigging. At the bottom they were filled with reeds, and on top of that was a mixture of molten sulphur, pitch, tar and fat. While this was still warm, four holes were bored in the barrel, and a fifth hole down the centre, reaching to the bottom. Greased wooden plugs were inserted in this, and once everything had cooled and congealed, these were replaced with fine priming-powder, and each furnished with double-drilled fuze-cord.[11]

After the fireworkers had prepared the fire-barrels, they began to fill the spaces between the gutters with sheaves of reeds and brushwood, in bundles of various sizes. The bushy ends were soaked with an inflammable mixture of tar, sulphur, saltpetre, coarse gunpowder, resin and whale-oil, and laid against the trestles, arranged around the corners of the fire-room and close to the fire-barrels. Even that was not enough, however, and so fire-curtains were nailed to the beams and sides of the fire-room. According to Röding, these were made of sailcloth dipped in an inflammable mixture and sprinkled with mealed powder.

Now the whole arrangement of fire-barrels, chamber-pieces and fire-channels was connected up by a system of fuzes, and again the special expertise of the fireworkers was called into play. Double fuze-cords, intended to burn quickly, were made out of a three-strand cotton string, which was soaked in a boiling mixture of spirits of vinegar, saltpetre and fine powder and, once wet, dipped in a vat of priming-powder dampened with spirits of vinegar. After drying, it could be processed further.[12]

Finally, before the various hatches and openings into the fire-room were made watertight and caulked, melted rosin was poured on wood-shavings and the resulting mixture was painted on any

A detailed contemporary model of the *Firebrand*, which was purchased by the Royal Navy as the merchantman *Annapolis* in 1777 and, after brief service as the sloop *Porpoise*, converted into a fireship. Prominent features of the model are the tall chimneys close to the channels, which conduct the fire up into the rigging of the grappled victim, and the hatches in the gangways, designed to provide additional draught. Below deck are the grid of fire-troughs, which ensures rapid spread of the flames, and some strategically placed fire-barrels. The model also has bottom-hinged gunport lids, although they are not visible from this angle. *Firebrand* suffered the fate of many fireships, blowing up accidentally in 1781.

(NATIONAL MARITIME MUSEUM D4662)

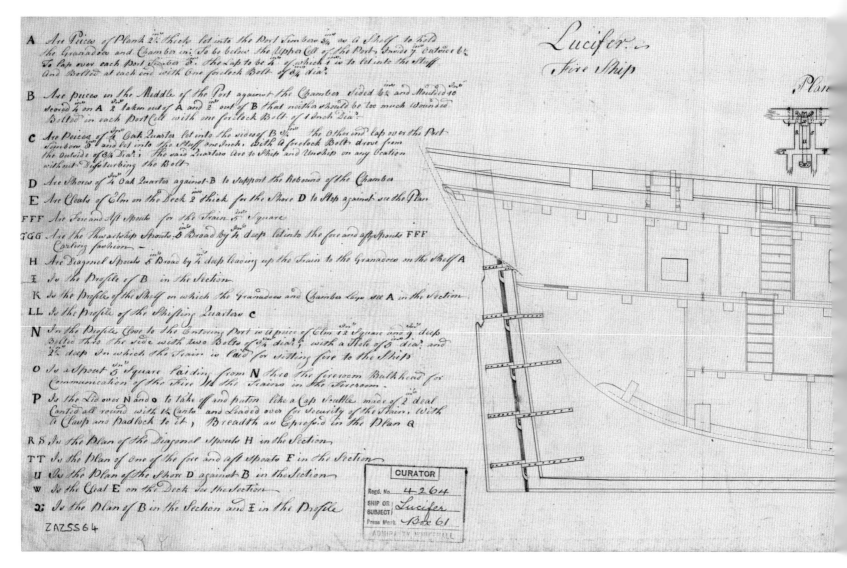

The *Lucifer* was a merchant ship purchased by the Royal Navy while under construction in 1778 and completed as a fireship. This draught was presumably intended to show an inexperienced merchant shipbuilder how to fit up the chamber-pieces that blew out the gunports. However, the unusual amount of attention devoted to the 'granadoes' suggests that these may have been a novelty; in normal military usage, they were hand-thrown explosive devices (the forerunners of modern grenades), but in this case they seem to have functioned as detonators for the chambers themselves. The annotation to the left of the draught is as follows:

KEY

A are pieces of plank 2½ins thick let into the port timbers ¾ins as a shelf to hold the granadoes and chamber in; to be below the upper cill of the port, inside 7ins outside 6½ins. To lap over each port timber 8ins the lap to be 4ins of which 1in is to set into the stuff and bolted at each end with one forelock bolt ¾ins diameter

B are pieces in the middle of the port against the chamber sided 6½ins and moulded 10ins scored 4ins on A; 2ins taken out of A and 2ins out of B that neither should be too much wounded. Bolted in each port cill with one forelock bolt of 1 inch diameter

C are pieces of 4ins oak quarter let into the sides of B ¾ins. The other end lap over the port limbers 8ins and let into the stuff one inch, with a forelock bolt drove from the outside of ¾ins diameter; the said quarters are to ship and unship on any location without disturbing the bolt

D are shores of 4ins oak quarter against B to support the rebound of the chamber

E are cleats of elm on the deck 2ins thick for the shore D to stop against. See the plan

FFF are fore and aft spouts for the train 5ins square

GGG are the thwartship spouts 5ins broad by 4ins deep set into the fore and aft spouts FFF carling fashion

H are diagonal spouts 5ins broad by 4ins deep leading up the train to the granadoes on the shelf A

I is the profile of B in the section

K is the profile of the shelf on which the granadoes and chamber lays. See A in the section

LL is the profile of the shifting quarters C

N in the profile close to the entering port is a piece of elm 12ins square and 9ins deep bolted thro' the side with two bolts of ¾ins diam; with a hole of 5ins diameter and 2½ins deep in which the train is laid for setting fire to the ship

O is a spout 5ins square leading from N thro' the fireroom bulkhead for communication of the fire to the trains in the fireroom

P is the lid over N and O to take off and put on like a cap scuttle made of 2in deal canted all round with 1½ cants and leaded over for security of the train with a clasp and padlock to it; breadth as expressed in the plan Q

RS is the plan of the diagonal spouts H in the section

TT is the plan of one of the fore and aft spouts F in the section

U is the plan of the shore D against B in the section

W is the cleat E on deck. See the section

X is the plan of B in the section and I in the profile

Enlarged detail from the *Lucifer* draught showing the fitting of the 'granadoes'. The annotation to these is as follows:

1&2 in the profile is the grenadoes let down 1½ins in the shelf A 3ins from the port timbers. See in the plan 4 and 5 granadoes ¾ins diameter

3 is the chamber let down on the shelf A ¾ins at the inner end and off at the outer end of the chamber to keep it steady. See 6 in the plan. Chamber long 5¼ins, diameter at the inner end 5¼ins, at the outer end 4¼ins and touch hole from inner end 1¼ins

NB The ticked lines in the plan is the train leading to the granadoes and chamber broad 1½ins deep ¾ins

The trains in the spouts are taken out of a triangular form broad 3½ins deep 2¾ins

The bolts appertaining to the port are drove from the outside and forelocked within as expressed by the profile and section

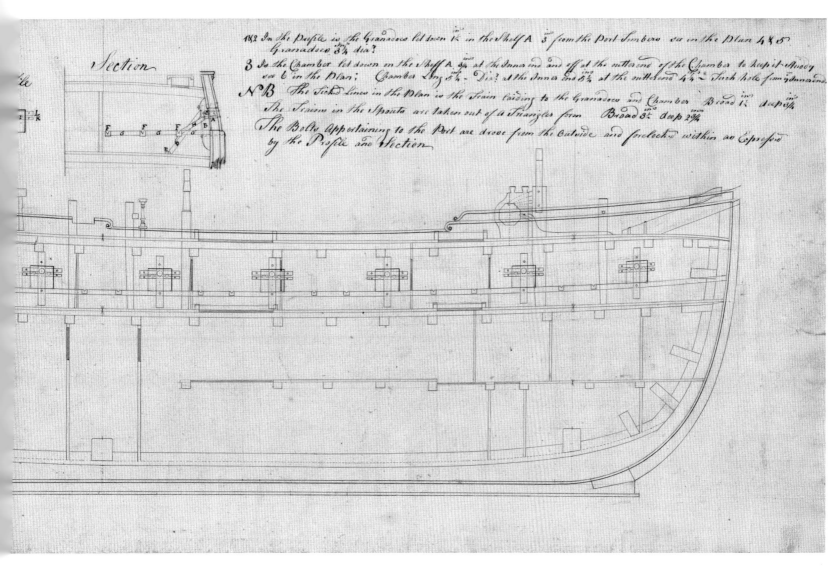

1&2 In the Profile is the Granadoes let down 1¼ in the Shelf A ⁵⁄₈ from the Port Timbers see in the Plan 4 & 5 Granadoes 3¾ dia?

3 So the Chamber let down on the Shelf A ¾ at the Inner end and off at the outter end of the Chamber to keep it steady see 6 in the Plan; Chamber long 5¼ — Dia? at the Inner end 6¼ at the outter end 4¼ — Such hole from ⁷⁄₈ Inner end.

N B The Pickd Lines in the Plan is the Seam leading to the Granadoes and Chamber Broad 1½ deep ⁵⁄₈
The Seams in the Spouts are taken out of a Triangler form Broad 3½ deep 2¾

The Bolts Appertaining to the Port are drove from the Outside and forelockd within as Expressd by the Profile and Section

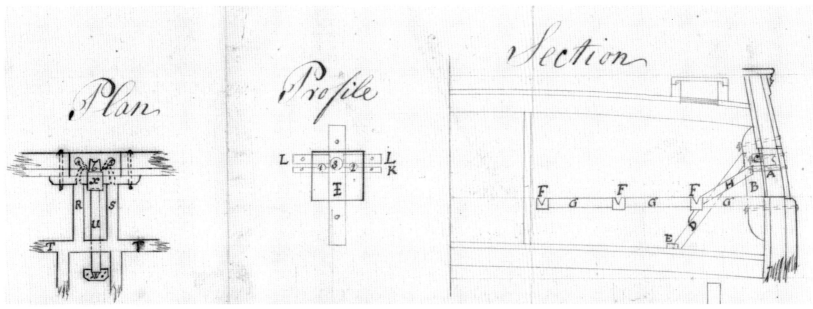

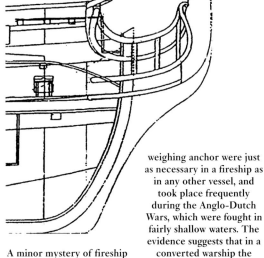

A minor mystery of fireship warfare is the question of how the fireships' ground-tackle was handled, particularly in two-decked ships whose gun deck was converted into the fire-room. This was the space ordinarily dedicated to handling the cables, and outfitted with bitts, capstan and stoppers. Dropping and weighing anchor were just as necessary in a fireship as in any other vessel, and took place frequently during the Anglo-Dutch Wars, which were fought in fairly shallow waters. The evidence suggests that in a converted warship the cables were handled on the upper deck. Many of them had a windlass of merchantman pattern fitted forward, but some of them acquired an additional capstan amidships. This was not of the common pattern with two capstans sharing a common spindle, one on the upper deck and the lower one on the gun deck, since there was no way of working a lower one. The cables were no doubt still stowed and handled in the cable-flat, and presumably bulkheads were built to allow ready access to the orlop from the upper deck. The hawse-holes often remained at the level of the gun deck, and some draughts and models suggest that there was some sort of ramp leading from hawse-holes to the upper deck, or else the deck itself curved down – as demonstrated by this X-ray photograph of the Annapolis *Griffin* model and the matching section of the draught. The cable would have been bitted to the cheeks of the windlass, and extra eye-bolts installed on the upper deck for stoppering the cable or messenger.

exposed wooden surfaces. Then the fireship captain personally nailed wooden covers over the openings through the after bulkhead, and secured them with padlocks. On many occasions an overturned candlestick or naked flame of some kind had set a fireship on fire unintentionally, and this was intended to minimise the risk.[13]

The fire-room was also carefully sealed off and protected against the ingress of water, but there was no way of avoiding the hellish stink of pitch and sulphur that it emitted. If you did not recognise a fireship when you saw it, the smell was unmistakable if you were downwind of it. And if that was the case, you were too close altogether. Even the crews themselves never became totally inured to the smell. Charles Chambers, ship's surgeon of the fireship *Prometheus*, talked of the bad headaches and lassitude among his shipmates engendered by the baneful dust and sulphurous smell.[14] In fact, the stink and dense fumes that were emitted once the fuzes had been lit contributed to the fearsome effect of the fireship. This was especially true of the Dutch fireships. Prior to an actual flame becoming visible, they produced a lot of impenetrable and evil-smelling smoke that spread to leeward and blew in the faces of the defenders.[15] It then became difficult for the enemy to locate exactly where the grapnels had hooked, or where the chains binding the ships together were. That could be determined only by climbing on board the fireship, and very few men had the courage to do that.

The first and best line of defence was the target ship's boats, and if employed resolutely in the early stages of the attack, they could be most useful in towing the fireship clear. The fireship itself would be very lightly armed, having only a few light cannon – usually 'sakers' of 5- or 6-pound calibre in the late seventeenth century – and anti-personnel weapons for its own defence. For example, in September 1666, at the time of the Second Anglo-Dutch War, the crews of the English fireships *White Boar* and *Milkmaid* were issued with two sakers, with carriages and appurtenances, fireworks, six bandoliers, three pairs of pistols, six daggers, and six half-pikes.[16] A heavy broadside from a threatened warship might be able to forestall or cause premature ignition of the fireship.

CHAPTER NINE

THE
CAPTAIN
AND
HIS CREW

'...every man taken on such an expedition
by the enemy, is liable to be dealt with in a similar
manner as a spy, and put to death'

Lord John Montagu, Earl of Sandwich, 1778

WE CANNOT BE CERTAIN WHAT associations the word 'fireship' aroused in the minds of people in past ages, but besides 'danger', 'courage' and 'heroism', there must have been a number of negative connotations – the feeling that even as a means of warfare, there was something unchristian and frightful about it. As if to emphasise the underlying aura of danger and unhealthiness that clung to the word, among sailors 'fireship' was a colloquial term for a prostitute, likely to 'burn' him with a venereal disease.[1]

The crew of a fireship comprised between thirty-five and fifty men, and as far as we can tell from contemporary sources, the men had a reputation for exceptional courage, cold-bloodedness and boldness. A few may have been motivated by patriotic feelings, but the main attraction was the money. It was a perilous occupation, likely to end in a near-suicidal mission, and on a day-to-day basis every fireshipman knew that the slightest carelessness with naked flames could result in the total conflagration of his floating home. The instructions about fire-prevention aboard fireships that we know of from surviving records were extremely stringent; as late as 1807 the purser's steward of one of the last such English ships received two dozen lashes because he left a candle burning in his workspace in the cockpit.[2] Candles were supposed to be lit only when safely enclosed within a lantern.

Officers, of course, were expected to set a good example, not like a carousing captain who so unnerved the commissioner at Portsmouth, who complained in February 1689:

> Here is the Commander of the *Rowbuck* Fireship puts me in fear of doing some mischief, he fireing so many Guns severall times, once with some Scandalous Women on board, and once at another time till eight a Clock at Night, and if he should sett fire of his Ship God knows what damage he may do, indeed Commanders of fireships should be sober Men, and Men of understanding, and if they did good Service should be well gratified and encouraged.[3]

However, a fireship captain who dared to sail that sort of dangerous vessel into a battleship's field of fire would not necessarily need sobriety and understanding as his principal attributes. Every fireship sailor knew that the enemy would make every effort to set the fire off prematurely, or try by one means or another to force it to abandon the mission. His vessel would draw the concentrated fire of every enemy ship in range, while the crews of any small craft on the water would also be bent on boarding and destroying it. Moreover, the danger was not past once they had grappled the enemy and had managed to get clear in their boat, because all guns would then be directed at the escape-craft. The captain also knew that if captured he might be treated like a spy,[4] not as a normal prisoner-of-war, and would face execution even if he surrendered.[5] Prior to the attack a wary fireship crewman always prepared a 'cover-story', to the effect that he was a survivor of a transport which had sunk earlier, or some such tale, knowing that he might face a firing-squad if his story was not believed.[6]

On the other hand there seem to have been some fireshipmen who were motivated by patriotism. Many men volunteered for fireship duty, and this was especially the case with ambitious young officers during the Napoleonic Wars.[7] At the funeral of Admiral Sir Christopher Myngs, fatally wounded during the Four Days' Battle in 1666, a dozen seamen approached Sir William Coventry of the Admiralty Board and asked him if the king would provide them with a fireship to attack the enemy, so that they could exact revenge for his death.[8]

There were some privileges. A fireshipman could claim compensation for possessions lost in an attack, and there were premiums for success. In 1652 Simon Orton, captain of the inappropriately named fireship *Charity*, and his surviving crew asked for compensation for the clothing lost when their vessel was destroyed during an attack.[9] At a time when the navy was undermanned and captains would go to any lengths to collect up a crew, fireship crews carried 'tickets' when ashore to ensure that they were not picked up by press-gangs and dragged aboard some other ship.[10] (Tickets were also issued when cash was short, and the promised bonuses were not paid immediately.) However, impressed men were also to be found aboard fire-

A detail from Willem van de Velde the Elder's large grisaille of the battle of Scheveningen (10 August 1653) showing the attack by the Dutch fireship *Fortuijn* (identified by the goddess Fortuna painted on the stern). As the *Fortuijn* goes up in flames, the crew of the English target vessel are jumping overboard in panic. Van de Velde later asserted that he himself had observed and sketched this event from life. The *Fortuijn*'s captain, Cornelis van Schonvelt, believed that he had sunk the English vessel, and arranged for Van de Velde and other witnesses to confirm this. However, the 56-gun *Andrew*, flagship of the English rear division, with its 360-man crew was not in fact lost, but survived the encounter, albeit badly damaged.

ships, for their commanders spared no efforts to round them up; indeed, fireship captains enjoyed a reputation for particular success in this respect.[11]

The most frequent motive persuading men to sail in a fireship was the prospect of a rich premium if the attack succeeded. Although fireships were among the smaller ships in the fleet, the crew were paid like those on the big ships, and moreover if a ship pulled off a successful attack, captain and crew were paid a bonus. The Royal Navy awarded members of a crew from 10s to £10, in addition to compensation for burned clothing (40s); £10 was more than eight times the monthly pay for an ordinary seaman.[12] The seventeenth-century fleet commanders knew what they were doing, and were insistent that their fireship captains and crews should be fully and promptly paid.[13]

Some idea of what was expected of an English fireship captain, and some of the privileges accorded him, can be found in a document drafted by James, Duke of York (1633–1701), and signed and dated on board the *Royal Charles* on 20 April 1665. James was the brother of Charles II, and as Lord High Admiral was influential in the remoulding of the Navy after the Restoration. What became known as the *Fighting Instructions* feature a section

entitled 'Encouragement for the captains and crews of fireships, small frigates and ketches'.[14] This notes that 'all persons employed in his majesty's fleet [have a duty] even to the utmost hazard of their lives to endeavour to destroy his majesty's enemies', and then goes on to specify the bonuses to be paid to fireship captains and crews: 'Every person remaining in the fireship till the service be performed shall receive on board the admiral, immediately after the service done, ten pounds as a reward for that service over and above his pay due to him.'

If a sailor did not survive the action, the sum was to be paid to the executor of his estate or to his nearest living relative, and captains who achieved a success were to be given a gold medal 'as a token of honour to him and his posterity'; additionally, they were to be favoured with a new command. Subordinate officers received £10 each, and their promotion to better ships usually followed. If an enemy flagship was successfully set on fire, the premiums were to be doubled and the officers' privileges correspondingly increased. The document next addresses other ships involved in a fireship action. If a frigate captain or commander of a smaller vessel should, by boarding an attacking fireship or by some other means, tow it clear

Getting a fireship ready for ignition, as depicted in a series of lively and detailed drawings by Richard Schlecht.

In the foreground one of the crew takes the caps off the chimneys, and canvas coverings have been removed from the hatches and gratings. Another man is watching the flagship with a glass, so the ship will respond promptly when the signal to attack is made. At the lower edge of the sketch the other crew members are busy strewing the decks with inflammable materials.

Meanwhile, below decks in the fire-room two men are busy filling the grid of fire-gutters with a mixture of powder, saltpetre, resin and sulphur to which some linseed oil has been added. Afterwards they will cover it with brushwood and bundles of dried heather. In the background a man is busy nailing the fire-curtains (sailcloth smeared with inflammable substances) to the deck-beams.

of one of the fleet's bigger ships, then every member of that crew (or his heirs) was to be paid £40, and if the service was especially remarkable, even more. The officers could expect special considerations also.

Accordingly, the letters and diaries of fleet commanders mention the prompt payment of bonuses to successful fireship captains. For instance, Henry Brown, captain of the *Richard*, who had 'massacred' a fleet of Dutch merchantmen in the area between Fly and Terschelling on 10 August 1666, received the handsome sum of £100 in recognition of good service. Captain Burstow, commanding the *Young Prince*, had 'fired her with good success' and collected £60, while his officers were given £10 each.[15] This system of payment remained in force in the Royal Navy until 1815, after which date there were no more gold chains, money or promises of advancement; successful commanders, however, were offered the prospect of becoming Knight Commanders of the Bath.[16]

If there was doubt about the performance of a captain or crew, the matter might be settled by the Board of Admiralty. For instance, on 5 December 1674 it was established that Joseph Harris, captain of the fireship *Ann and Judith*, really did get alongside De Ruyter's flagship, grappled it securely

and set his ship ablaze. However, the enemy were lucky and managed to free themselves, but it was decided that Harris had done all that was possible in the operational circumstances, and was therefore entitled to the full premium.[17]

Even where a fireship had not been successfully deployed, it was worthwhile for the captain to appeal. Most of the French ships burned at La Hogue in 1692 were not directly fired by the action of the fireships, but Captain Edward Littleton of the *Thomas and Elizabeth* took his case to the Admiralty, and Vice-Admiral Rooke certified:

that on May 23 the boats being repulsed in their attempt of burning the French ships at La Hogue, Littleton went in with his ship on board two of the enemy, but finding they had quitted their ships and that the boats had got on board them he put off again. He was again sent in next day to burn five other French ships, but they being set on fire by boats before the fireships got up to them the vice-admiral ordered him into the river to endeavour burning the ships of transportation, at which service he pushed fairly but, the harbour being shoal, unfortunately ran aground, and his ship

A specialist fire-worker is in the process of leading the quick-burning fuzes to the iron-chambers, which will blow open the port lids and ensure an ample supply of oxygen to spread the conflagration in the fire-room. This would be one of the last tasks to be carried out, to make sure that the fuzes had no time to get damp. The man is ensuring that the fire will spread rapidly and simultaneously between fuzes and fire-gutters.

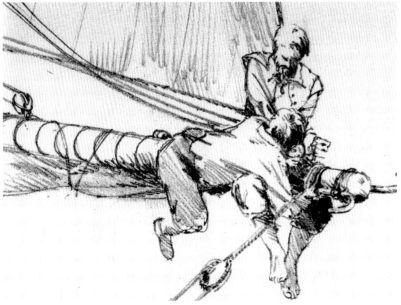

Lashing the iron grapnels to the fore and main yardarms was one of the last tasks prior to attack, because the hooks would indicate clearly to a potential target that a fireship was present. The yardarm grapnels were the first thing to engage the victim, tangling in its rigging, followed immediately by grappling irons and chains dropping on to the hull to make it fast.

being much disabled by the enemy's shot he, by the vice-admiral's order, set her on fire, himself and several of his men wounded.

His petition was annotated: 'To have the reward as if burnt.'[18]

Sometimes success itself was deceptive. The fireship captain Robert Washborne received a bonus of £200 for destroying a Dutch warship during the battle of the Texel (August 1673), the last major battle of the Third Anglo-Dutch War, but ten years later the Admiralty discovered that the alleged victim had safely reached the harbour of Helvoetsluis a few days after the battle.[19]

It is easy to understand why it was so difficult to be certain that a fireship attack had succeeded.

During a sea-battle an overall picture of everything that was happening was out of the question. Various phases of the battle might be played out many kilometres apart, and with light winds and clouds of smoke from gunfire and burning vessels, it became almost impossible to see what was going on beyond one's immediate vicinity. Ships might also alter course frequently, their position ever changing, so that no observer could keep them in sight for very long. Damaged ships dropped out of formation, often lacking the ability to manoeuvre, and in shallow waters they might even anchor; either way, at this point they were relatively defenceless. This was the ideal opportunity for the fireship captain, but even then how could he be sure which ship he had attacked? Before the later eighteenth century warships did not have their

Two views of the teeming decks of a Dutch man-of-war from around the middle of the seventeenth century. This is the *Eendracht*, the flagship of Admiral Jacob van Wassenaer, Lord of Obdam, which blew up on 13 June 1665 during the battle of Lowestoft. The ship was 43m long between perpendiculars, with a beam of 10.7m, and would have carried a crew of about 500 men, who not served only as seamen and musketeers on deck, but also worked the lower deck cannon. When threatened with fireship attack, everyone knew that their lives were in immediate peril, because if the ship caught fire the chances of rescue were slight. One of the ship's boats is made fast

under the main channels, but these craft were not intended for life-saving, and in any case the total capacity of all the ship's boats fell far short of crew numbers. Furthermore, many sailors could not swim, so it is not surprising that the mere threat of a fireship could cause panic to break out on the decks, leaving a handful of officers trying to control hundreds of sailors and marines in fear for their lives. In the history of sea warfare, there are many stories of battle-worthy warships which surrendered to the enemy when faced with the threat of a fireship.

(DETAILS FROM A GRISAILLE BY WILLEM VAN DE VELDE THE ELDER, IN THE MARITIME MUSEUM, ROTTERDAM. PHOTO: AUTHOR)

names prominently painted up, and in any case a fireship captain had to make off in his boat as fast as possible, and was in no position to hang around for confirmation of success.

To settle these issues, in an ideal world one would interview many eyewitnesses of the event and then obtain notarised statements from them, but before the days of war reporters there were no impartial and experienced observers, so this kind of evidence is almost non-existent. However, there is one remarkable exception, in the form of the work of two marine artists whom we would nowadays consider 'war artists', Willem van de Velde, father and son. Their finely detailed paintings and drawings are preserved in many museums, and their liveliness and precision are still a delight. Willem van de Velde the Elder (1611–1693) may be

considered one of the first professional naval war artists. When he put to sea in his galliot on the afternoon of 8 August 1653, he carried on board a large quantity of drawing paper and some letters for Admiral Tromp, who had given his captains written instructions that the galliot was to be left in peace, and had granted the artist permission to go anywhere he wanted in order to record what happened. Two days later, on Sunday 10 August, Van de Velde was close enough to record for posterity an encounter that became known to the English as the battle of Scheveningen, and to their Dutch opponents as the battle of Ter Heide.[20] He sat on deck with his sketchpad on his knee and made many panoramic drawings of the action, which formed the basis for paintings and engravings made in the studio later on.

Three years later, on 25 April 1656, along with several Dutch captains, Van de Velde swore before a notary in Amsterdam that he had seen the fire-ship *Fortuijn*, under Captain Cornelis van Schonvelt, attack an English flagship.[21] The captains did not know the name of the ship, but it was a big vessel of rather old-fashioned appearance carrying about 60 guns, and flew the white flag of a rear admiral. Van de Velde had seen the ship emitting smoke and men jumping overboard. Then he had been obliged to get clear in his galliot, but other eyewitnesses had assured him that the ship had sunk later.

But even a careful observer does not always get it quite right, and we know today that the artist ordered the master of his galliot to leave the scene a little too quickly, because the stricken ship, with 360 men aboard, was the 56-gun *Andrew*, flagship of Rear Admiral Thomas Graves, who did not survive the battle. However, the ship itself was in fact salvaged in a half-burned condition, and was not completely lost as he had imagined.[22] On one of the sketches that he made on that occasion, Van de Velde noted that the *Fortuijn* was on fire and had successfully grappled the Admiral of the White. The sketches became the basis for a painting of the battle, and a splendid grisaille on the same theme is still to be seen at the National Maritime Museum in Greenwich, showing the engagement between the *Fortuijn* and the *Andrew*.

The status of the fireship captain was the lowest of all commanding officers in the fleet. Often it was his first command, and fireship captains tended to be 'tarpaulins', that is to say practical sailors who had worked their way up rather than officers whose commission was the consequence of social status or political influence. In the English navy the commanding officer was accorded the rank of Captain in the early years, but towards the end of the seventeenth century, as seniority became more codified, this was downgraded to Master and Commander, the same rank held by those commanding other 'unrated' vessels, that is sloops and the like, below the six formal Rates of fighting ships proper. The rank lay between Lieutenant and Captain.[23]

A young captain would usually serve aboard a fireship for at least a year, but it was not an espe-

Willem van de Velde the Elder (1611–1693) liked to include burned-out expended fireships in the foreground of his grisailles of great sea-battles, to enhance the sense of perspective. This is a detail from a grisaille depicting the battle of the Sound, which was fought between the Swedish and a combined Danish-Dutch fleet in November 1658. There were three fireship attacks, but none of them was successful. The fireship on the right has burned practically to the waterline, and the shot-holes sustained during the attack are clearly visible on what remains of the hull; the water pouring into the sinking wreck is creating clouds of steam. All around, the boats are busy rescuing men from sinking ships.

(NATIONAL MARITIME MUSEUM BHC0280)

cially risky start to an officer's career, since on average only a quarter of fireships were used in anger (and only seven fireship captains were ever killed in action). For many the post was the first step up the career ladder: twenty-eight fireship captains became Members of Parliament, eighty-seven reached flag rank, and one, Sir Hyde Parker, even became First Sea Lord.[24]

In the French Marine, *capitaines de brûlot* were considered equal in rank to the captains of light frigates and flutes until 1669, when they were reduced to below the rank of *capitaine de frégate*, in 1676 they were again downgraded to the equivalent of a *lieutenant de port*, and in 1689 to that of a *lieutenant de marine*.[25] In the Netherlands the rank for fireship captains translates as 'commandor of small vessels', below the *commandeur* rank applied to captains of larger warships. They were recruited from experienced lieutenants or were drawn from the *gereformeerde kapiteinen*, who were members of the privileged Calvinist Reformed Church.[26]

There were both heroes and cowards among fireship captains. High up in the first category was Jan van Brakel, who eventually rose to flag rank before he was slain in a sea-battle in 1690. In August 1665, at the age of twenty-two, he was a fireship captain in the fleet sent to convoy the returning East Indies fleet in to Bergen, Norway. In the following year he was promoted to command a small fighting ship, which was shot to pieces in the Four Days' Battle with the English (June 1666). He and his men escaped in the boat and used the opportunity to tow away an English fireship, which had grappled a Dutch ship of the line. The next year he commanded a fireship in the Dutch force which sailed up the Medway and reduced a great part of the English fleet to ashes. He was also present with a ship of the line, the *Groot Hollandia*, at the battle of Sole Bay (1672), which he laid aboard the *Royal James*, flying the flag of the English admiral John Montagu, Earl of Sandwich, thereby opening the way for one of the most famous fireship attacks in maritime history.[27]

On the English side, there was Commander Callis, captain of the fireship *Duke*, one of the ships in a squadron which in June 1742 had pursued five Spanish galleys into the harbour at St Tropez, where they lay in hopeless disarray, an ideal target for a fireship. He sailed in, disregarding the gunfire from the galleys, and grappled one of them before setting his ship on fire and making his escape. As his crew sat in the boat they realised that the powder-train had not properly ignited, and without hesitation Callis leaped back on board and made sure that things were well alight. He got back into the boat dishevelled and badly burned, but the attack was hugely successful, with fire destroying all the enemy vessels and with '… no other loss than two men having their heads shot off'.[28]

A captain who had no great desire to be a hero and stand upon the burning deck sometimes adopted the expedient of setting his ship afire prematurely, well before it was within gunshot of the target. However, this might be obvious under the eyes of the rest of the fleet, so it carried the risk of punishment, ranging from being cashiered to a death sentence. At the battles off La Rochelle in 1628, at least seven English fireship captains were court-martialled for this offence.[29]

In 1667, when the Dutch came up the Medway and threatened to sail further up river, the English had at least ten fireships available for defence, but it seems that their commanders did not behave aggressively enough: several of them ignited their powder-trains too early, and some failed to attack the Dutch at all. The humiliation was hard to bear, and the navy's reaction was heavy-handed. William Howe of the *Virgin* was sentenced to death by firing-squad, and was executed two weeks later. Three captains suffered dishonourable discharge, with the court's verdict specifying the ritual that was to be observed. Each of them had a noose placed round his neck as a sign that he had narrowly escaped the death penalty; then a wooden sword was broken over his head; and finally he was towed behind a boat to the dock at Deptford, where he was declared 'incapable in future of any command'.[30]

Just one got away lightly. The fireship captain John Votier was charged with failing to follow the orders of the Lord High Admiral, and his defence was that he was unable to do so because he could neither read nor write. He was admonished and told to master these skills, and charges were dropped.[31]

CHAPTER TEN

THE FIRST
ANGLO-DUTCH WAR

*'...had we had the fire-ships with us
that were to leeward we could, with God's help,
have given the enemy a thorough drubbing.'*

Michiel Adriaanszoon de Ruyter, 1652

After the Spanish were expelled from the northern Netherlands in 1574, Antwerp's importance as a trading centre declined, but that of the independent Dutch ports, particularly Amsterdam, increased rapidly. The Dutch came to control the lucrative herring-fishery in the North Sea, and after the Dutch East India Company was founded in 1602, Dutch traders replaced the Portuguese in much of the Far East and established themselves almost everywhere on the globe. The end of the Thirty Years' War in 1648 marked the start of a Golden Age in the Netherlands. Spanish Jews and French Huguenots were welcomed, and cultural activities, science and the economy all underwent a huge expansion.

Dutch merchants competed (largely successfully) with those of Denmark and the Hanseatic cities of northern Germany, but particularly with the English.

By the middle of the seventeenth century the seaborne commerce of the United Netherlands had far outdistanced all other competing nations, with many profitable branches of trade virtually monopolised by the Dutch. At least that was how the merchants of the big English trading companies saw it. In planning any new enterprise, they had to reckon with the omnipresent Dutch – fleets of Dutch herring-busses shot their nets just off the English coast; the English colonists in the West Indies were supplied by the Dutch; even wool,

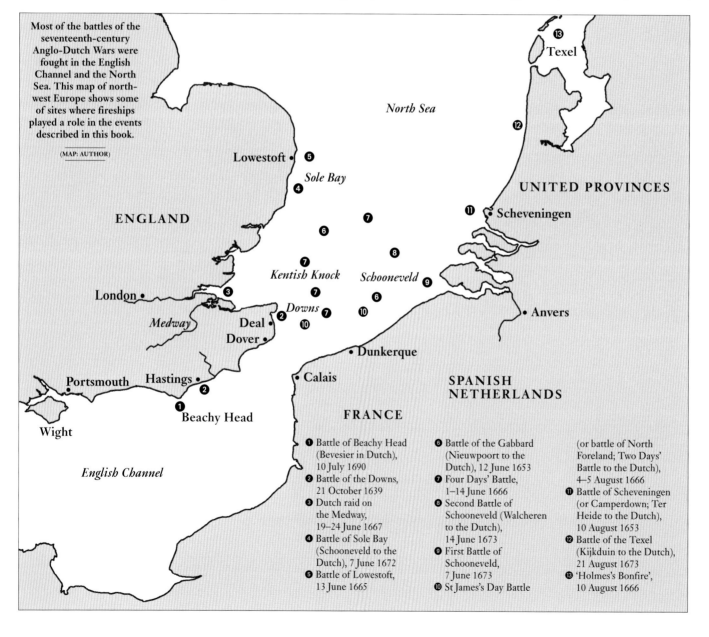

Most of the battles of the seventeenth-century Anglo-Dutch Wars were fought in the English Channel and the North Sea. This map of north-west Europe shows some of sites where fireships played a role in the events described in this book.

(MAP: AUTHOR)

❶ Battle of Beachy Head (Bevesier in Dutch), 10 July 1690
❷ Battle of the Downs, 21 October 1639
❸ Dutch raid on the Medway, 19–24 June 1667
❹ Battle of Sole Bay (Schooneveld to the Dutch), 7 June 1672
❺ Battle of Lowestoft, 13 June 1665
❻ Battle of the Gabbard (Nieuwpoort to the Dutch), 12 June 1653
❼ Four Days' Battle, 1–14 June 1666
❽ Second Battle of Schooneveld (Walcheren to the Dutch), 14 June 1673
❾ First Battle of Schooneveld, 7 June 1673
❿ St James's Day Battle
(or battle of North Foreland; Two Days' Battle to the Dutch), 4–5 August 1666
⓫ Battle of Scheveningen (or Camperdown; Ter Heide to the Dutch), 10 August 1653
⓬ Battle of the Texel (Kijkduin to the Dutch), 21 August 1673
⓭ 'Holmes's Bonfire', 10 August 1666

England's best product, was exported in Dutch ships. Between 50 and 70 per cent of the cargo vessels that passed through the Sound between Sweden and Denmark, the passage to the Baltic ports, were Dutch. The giant fleets of the Dutch western trade (*Westvaart*) sailed to Spain and Portugal and beyond through the Straits of Gibraltar (*Straatvaart*) to the Levant (*Levantvaart*). Dutch whalers sailed to Greenland and Spitzbergen and competed vigorously with the English in the Caribbean and the Guinea coast of west Africa, and Dutch East Indiamen were found from the waters of the Persian Gulf to the Sea of Japan.

The United Provinces consisted of the seven northern provinces of what had once been the

The modern understanding and image of sea-battles during the Anglo-Dutch Wars owe much to Willem van de Velde the Elder (*c*1611–1689), who went to sea as a young man, and later became an outstanding draughtsman and marine painter. Working long before the Impressionists, he took his inspiration from direct observations made at sea and on the coast. He was official artist of the Dutch Navy for many years and enjoyed the privilege of sailing unhindered among the fleets, even during battle. Together with his son Willem the Younger (1633–1707), he moved in 1672 to England, where he was able to draw the ships of Charles II's fleet. The creative period of the Van de Veldes coincided with the heyday of the fireship, and the artists used the fire, smoke and charred remains so characteristic of that type of warfare to accent their battle pictures.

(NATIONAL MARITIME MUSEUM PU 2659)

Spanish Netherlands. The prime mover in overthrowing the Spanish overlords was William the Silent, Prince of Orange-Nassau, who held the title of *Stadthouder* (state holder) and was in effect a sort of king. When his descendant William II died in 1650, republican sentiment and desire for more independence among the individual provinces resulted in the formation of a loose federation, with a president, or 'grand pensionary' as he was called. Jan de Witt filled this office for the next twenty years, but in 1672 he was murdered and the Prince of Orange, later William III of England, became the *Stadthouder*. During the First Anglo-Dutch War, the provinces jealously guarded their independence, and there were no fewer than five

admiralties. The Dutch population was about half the size of that of England, but it was urbanised to a much greater degree and economically more productive. Nevertheless, it is an indicator of the economic power of both states – and one of the most remarkable aspects of the Anglo-Dutch Wars – that both sides could so rapidly refit their fleets, even after devastating losses.

In 1609 the Dutch jurist Hugo de Groot, in giving his professional legal opinion to the VOC (United East India Company), had argued that the open sea does not belong solely to any one state, and that the ships of all nations should be able to sail freely thereon (in *Mare liberum, sive de iure quod Batavis competit ad Indicana commercia dissertatio*, or *The Open Sea: A Treatise on the Rights of the Dutch and the East India Trade*). By the middle of the seventeenth century the Dutch possessed about 10,000 ships, more than all other European nations put together,[1] so the concept of the 'freedom of the seas' was in their particular interest.

By contrast, English foreign trade was more constrained, and the heavily manned ships of the English merchant fleet could not compete on equal terms with the economical Dutch flute, a ship type that combined high capacity and low running costs. However, the English had a legal concept of their own to set against the 'freedom of the seas' – the traditional notion of English rule over the waters around the British Isles. This was not as well defined as modern 'territorial waters' but was nevertheless a firmly held belief. The enforcers of this power were the warships representing the English Crown (or Parliament during the Interregnum), and these had to be ritually saluted by all other vessels, which would dip their flags in recognition of England's control of the waters. However the limits of 'English waters' might be defined, Dutch vessels had to sail through them; as Admiral Sir William Monson (1568–1643) explained the practice, the flag salute applied not only to single vessels but also to ships sailing in a fleet, and a foreign vessel always had to pass the English warship on the lee side (among other considerations, this would obviate the danger of attack by a fireship).[2] The foreigner was never to fly his flag at the mainmast head, and every English warship, even the smallest, was obliged to fire upon any vessel which failed to salute and to pursue and arrest any stubborn captain who failed to follow the ritual, requiring him to pay the cost of powder and shot expended in the effort. During the reign of Charles I (1625–1649) the demand for the proper flag salute was pursued more and more aggressively and further afield, even off foreign ports like the Texel (a Dutch possession) and Boulogne – it was not insignificant that Charles I named his greatest ship *Sovereign of the Seas*. For a long time the Dutch had gone along with this exasperating tradition – after all, business was business – but as more and more ocean trade came to be carried in Dutch vessels, their warships became more and more reluctant to submit.[3]

Another convention that irritated the Dutch was the Prize Laws, which allowed the English to search all merchantmen that they found in 'English waters' and confiscate all goods being transported to or from an enemy nation, even by a ship flying a neutral flag. The Dutch did not construe this law so broadly and felt that the notion of 'contraband' should apply only to weapons of war.[4]

As befitted a trading nation, the warships of the United Provinces were primarily intended as convoy escorts, with more emphasis on seaworthiness than on firepower. For the English, however, the navy was primarily a battlefleet, designed to control its home waters by defeating any force sent against it. The deepwater ports of Britain allowed the English to accommodate bigger, more heavily armed warships than could the Dutch in their shallower waters, which were suitable only for vessels of relatively light draught. After the Civil War and the trial and execution of Charles I in 1649, Parliamentary control of taxation allowed a regular flow of revenue for rebuilding and expanding the fleet. The result was the biggest and strongest permanent navy that England had ever possessed.

Parliament also acted to promote the economy, following the principles of mercantilism, a concept which flourished everywhere in the middle of the seventeenth century. This was a national economic policy according to which the State attempted to control prices and measures, promote home-grown industries, import raw materials and export finished products, while exploiting to the maximum the resources of colonies abroad. It was predicated on the notion that the total amount of wealth was fixed, so one nation could increase its trade only at the expense of another – a 'zero-sum game' as we would say today. An important reflection of this idea as it applied in England was seen in the Acts of Trade and Navigation, passed by Parliament in October 1651. The Navigation Acts required that imported goods, whether from Europe or from the colonies, could be brought to England only in English ships. This law had wide-ranging consequences for the United Provinces – Dutch fishermen could no longer land their catch in England; the coastal trade, which was mainly in Dutch ships, declined sharply; and Dutch imports from the Baltic, the Mediterranean and English colonies in North America and the Caribbean could not be brought in Dutch vessels. The Navigation Acts broke new legal ground, and placed England irrevocably upon the road that would lead to command of the sea, but threatened the trade of everyone else. The newly created fleet would be big enough to enforce this ambition, but it also made war with the Dutch inevitable.[5]

On every ocean a relentless trade war against Dutch shipping began under the pretext of the new protectionist laws. In the year 1651 a total of 140 Dutch ships were forced into English harbours; in January 1652 alone there were thirty detentions, and in February a further twenty-four. The damage to Dutch trade was severe, and the commercial survival of the Netherlands was in such doubt that full-scale war could be postponed no longer.[6] The Dutch, who were more interested in business than in fighting, tried to settle things by negotiation, but while delegations met and talked in The Hague and London, both countries were preparing for war.

On a fine spring day, 12 May 1652, off Start Point, just south of Dartmouth, three English warships accidentally encountered a convoy of seven Dutch ships bound for the Mediterranean, accompanied by three warships. The English were under the command of Captain Anthony Young in the *President*. Normally they would have tried to avoid having to force foreign ships to dip the flag, but Captain Young had imagined that ships sailing so near to his coast would be English. Now that he was so close he was forced to demand a salute, and although the Dutch were under orders not to comply, the commander of the Dutch fleet, in the interest of peace and good business, struck his flag and fired a salute. But one of his captains, a true patriot, did not submit and challenged the British to board his ship and haul down the flag themselves, which left Young no option but to answer with a broadside. Naturally, the Dutch answered in the same fashion, and the battle that developed lasted ninety minutes, leaving one dead and four wounded on board the *President*, before the Dutch, in their damaged ships, deemed it expedient to give the salute. Young's aggressive behaviour was later approved by the authorities.[7]

The next act of the drama unfolded a few days later, on 19 May, and again accident played a part. In the Downs, off the east coast of Kent, a fleet of thirteen English warships lay at anchor, and a further nine lay in the distance, behind the Goodwin Sands. The main force was led by Admiral Robert Blake (1599–1657), who had command of the English Channel fleet.

A hard north-easter had been blowing in the Channel, causing a groundswell (hollow sea), and this weather system had driven a fleet of forty-one Dutch warships to seek refuge in a dangerous anchorage between Dunkirk and Nieuport. Cables had parted and anchors had been lost, with many ships being damaged, so the commander, Admiral Maarten Harpertszoon Tromp (1598–1653), was forced to weigh anchor and sail across the Channel to find shelter on the English coast off Dover.[8] His primary task was to protect Dutch merchantmen from seizure by the English, who were searching all vessels for contraband (mostly goods destined for France). Tromp was an old hand at the game and did not want to provoke the English, and so when he saw their fleet he sent two captains aboard the English flagship to explain the reason for his presence.

Blake was cautious. He was not sure what to make of the Dutch warships. Could he trust them? Might they be planning to attack him? So in the first morning light of 19 May he sent his ships tacking towards them. The weather improved sufficiently for Tromp to leave English waters, and at noon he weighed and made sail for the French coast. At this point he met a damaged Dutch war-

ship which had been at sea since the skirmish off Start Point, and learned that a convoy of seventeen valuable Mediterranean merchantmen was close to the English coast. Would the English capture this valuable prize? He altered course for the point where the convoy was anchored, and this took him into the vicinity of Blake's ship. The admiral could not figure out what the Dutch were doing, and as they came closer he felt threatened and provoked. He ordered his men to battle stations, and his fleet adopted a tactically favourable position against Tromp.

At around 3.30 in the afternoon the flagships of both fleets were only a musket shot (140–180 metres) apart, but as in so many similar situations there are contradictory versions of what happened next. Tromp, having been instructed to avoid aggression, later explained that his intention was only to pass the English fleet to reach the merchant convoy. But on the other hand, he had strict orders that he was on no account to dip his flag to the English, so when Blake's fleet demanded the ritual submissive salute by firing a gun, Tromp did not respond. He was a proud man and had no intention of saluting the English 'King-Killers' (Charles I had been tried and executed by Parliament in 1649). He was in command of a powerful fleet, and it was precisely in these waters, here off the Downs, that he had annihilated the Spanish. A second signal-gun was disregarded, and the third was not a signal but a round-shot fired at Tromp's ship *Brederode* that tore off a seaman's arm. This was answered by a thundering broadside from the *Brederode*, by Dutch standards a colossus of 54 guns. That was the English version of the story, but Tromp said later that the English fired the first broadside at his rigging.[9] Whatever the truth, everyone in both fleets now opened fire, and for the next five hours, until dusk set in, broadsides roared, men died, and the wood of masts and hulls was splintered. Only with the onset of darkness did the fleets slowly drift apart. The First Anglo-Dutch War (1652–4) had begun.

At the end of that day, as the smoke cleared, two Dutch ships with rigging destroyed by shot remained on the scene and were captured by the English. One of them had taken so many shots below the waterline that she sank, while the English had not lost any of their ships. As it turned out, this skirmish accurately presaged how almost all the encounters of this war would turn out, for the English ships were generally superior in size and firepower to those of the Dutch.[10]

What had happened to the once victorious and supposedly invincible Dutch navy? In the years following the victory over the Spaniards in the battle of the Downs of October 1639, it had been run down by the miserly lords of the Dutch admiralties; they had even sold Tromp's flagship, the 600-ton and 57-gun *Amelia*. At the beginning of the new war the Dutch could muster only seventy-nine ships, most of them old and many of them ex-merchantmen. By contrast, the fleet of the English navy was large, and included fourteen warships that were bigger and more heavily armed than the strongest in the Dutch fleet. At that time a gun had to be at least a 24-pounder if it were to be capable of inflicting serious damage; the Dutch ships were armed primarily with 12-pounders and carried correspondingly smaller crews.[11]

Powerfully armed and strongly built, the big English warships were designed to fight and win gunnery duels in home waters. It was here that they sought to end the Dutch domination of seaborne commerce and the fisheries. Dutch warships on the other hand were intended to protect valuable convoys in distant waters, including the West Indies and the Indian Ocean, and tended to be lighter in both armament and structure.[12] It was a battle-fleet strategy versus one ruled by commerce protection, and in almost every one of the fierce battles of 1652 and 1653, the Dutch fleet was thrashed and withdrew with heavy losses in ships and men. Several times it was only the shallows off the Flanders coast that saved it from annihilation.

The 1650s were the beginning of a period of rapid technical change and tactical innovation, but many of the characteristic aspects of later sea warfare did not as yet exist. In the course of this war the fleets became bigger – some formations could stretch out over sixteen kilometres or more – and more unmanageable. At first there was no line of battle, nor formal fleet tactics of any kind. Most captains drew their experience from the merchant service and few had any familiarity with fleet manoeuvres. Almost no one had professional train-

ing as a naval officer, as yet no Articles of War had been published, and *Sailing and Fighting Instructions* were still rudimentary. Discipline was correspondingly lax, with everyone doing what seemed best at the time.[13]

The overall commander split these giant fleets into three divisions: the van, commanded by his vice admiral; the centre, his own station; and the rear, commanded, naturally, by the rear admiral. These were distinguished by the colours of their ensigns as White, Red and Blue respectively, and in the Royal Navy of the 1660s each division was further split into three squadrons, van, centre and rear, under the control of their own flag officers, making nine admirals in total. The ships in these groups sailed in close company with their flagship, and it was difficult for them not to get in each other's way. The key mission for the flagship was to set a courageous example, leading the attack in a group from windward to try and separate enemy ships from their companions and weaken them by gunfire. Reports of the time speak of ships 'charging' the enemy, like slow-motion cavalry. In order to engage all guns, after firing a broadside a ship tacked so that it could fire those on the opposite side. This manoeuvre contributed to the general chaos. Besides, every captain was obliged to show determination in coming to the aid of any ship of his squadron that was hard pressed by the enemy,[14] especially if it was grappled by a fireship. No direct order from the admiral was needed, and once the captain had done this, he looked for the next enemy ship to attack. After the first exchange of broadsides, boarding was often the next tactical move in ship-to-ship action.

Once battle was joined, it made no sense to make more signals. Flags were no longer visible because of the smoke, and the admiral had practically no control. Unlike a general on land, he could not stand on a hill with a good view of the battle. Whether he took up position on the quarterdeck or went back and forth through the ship encouraging the men, he was in the thick of the gunsmoke, at close quarters with an enemy that might be 200 metres or less away. After a brave and resolute attack by the flagships of the admiral and vice admirals, which were heavily armed and well manned, , the rest was up to the other ships in the fleet, and now came the 'mêlée', a disorderly battle without central control.[15]

At the beginning of the First Anglo-Dutch War fireships were not a prominent part of either navy: in June 1652 there were just five in De Ruyter's fleet, and two with the English squadron in the Downs, but in the course of the year more and more were added. By July the Dutch had sixteen, split among different squadrons.[16] At this time Dutch commanders had no formal doctrine on how fireships should be employed, nor anything in writing on the tactics to be used in defence against them.

In the English fleet, on the other hand, there were already printed instructions. By 1650 captains and commanders had received the first collection of *Instructions for the Better Ordering and Managing of the Fleet*, with a section relating to fireships which read:

> It is the duty of our smaller frigates, ketches and smacks to recognize which ships of the enemy fleet are fireships. They are to observe their manoeuvres and launch boats to cut them out. If possible, they are to board, set them on fire and destroy them. That it is the duty of the commanders and masters of all the small frigates, ketches and smacks belonging to the fleet to know the fireships that belong to the enemy, and accordingly by observing their motion to do their utmost to cut off their boats (if possible), or if opportunity serve that they lay them on board, fire and destroy them; and to this purpose they are to keep to windward of the fleet in time of service. But in case they cannot prevent the fireships from coming on board us by coming between us and them, which by all means possible they are to endeavour, that then, in such a case, they show themselves in such a critical situation, and sheer aboard them, and with their boats, grapnels, and other means, clear them from us and destroy them; which service, if honourably done, according to its merit shall be rewarded, and the neglect thereof strictly and severely called to account. That the fireships belonging to the fleet endeavour to keep the wind, and they with the small

frigates to be as near the great ships as they can, and to attend the signal from the commander-in-chief and to act accordingly.[17]

What was expected of the captain of a Dutch fireship in battle is outlined in an order of August 1652:

> Admiral de Ruyter orders Cornelis Beeke of Amsterdam, captain of the fire ship *Goude Saele*, to be prepared to keep his ship and crew ready for action with the Admiral's squadron, and when nearing the enemy make every effort to get alongside the largest enemy ship and set it in flames. Like every good captain, a good [fireship] captain, having commenced such an undertaking, must do all in his power to carry it through; and if he should not succeed, must do all in his power to assist his squadron by doing all the mischief he can to the enemy.[18]

Similar orders were issued to the other fireship captain in the squadron.

But it all came to nothing. Several Dutch fireships were bad sailers, or were too small to keep up with the fleet. They had no success in the battle at Kentish Knock on 18 October 1652, or on 10 December off Dungeness, where for once the English came off worse. On one occasion, the fireships were separated from the fleet, and on another they were in the wrong position, or were set on fire to no purpose.[19] De Ruyter wrote in a letter to the Admiralty: 'had we had the fireships with us that were to leeward, we could, with God's help, have given the enemy a thorough drubbing'.[20]

It was not easy to keep a sufficient number of fireships in close company with the fleet, but Admiral Tromp had great hopes for them. Although aware that his ships were smaller and weaker than those of the English, he trusted that his fireships would reduce the odds. The decisive role he envisaged for them is hinted at in a letter to the Estates-General written in May 1653, prior to the battle of the Gabbard. It is primarily concerned with the fitting-out of a sufficient number of usable fireships:

Although outside the main theatre of combat, the battle off the port of Leghorn (Livorno) provided the most significant fireship success of the First Anglo-Dutch War. The total defeat of a numerically inferior English squadron in March 1653 led to Dutch dominance of the Mediterranean and the crippling of English trade with the Levant. This painting by Willem Hermanszoon van Dies shows the crucial moment in the battle when the English *Sampson*, attacked from leeward by the Dutch *Maan*, was set ablaze by the Dutch fireship on its weather side. The *Sampson* eventually blew up with the loss of all but forty-two of her crew of 180.

(NATIONAL MARITIME MUSEUM BHC0275)

On 10 August 1653 Willem van de Velde the Elder was underway in his ketch in the waters close to Scheveningen to observe and sketch the battle between the Dutch and English fleets. He witnessed an attack by the Dutch fireship *Fortuijn* (identifiable by the painting of the goddess Fortuna on her stern) on an English ship whose name he did not know at that time. As the English ship began to burn and many men jumped overboard, the artist became convinced that the ship was destined to sink and sailed on. Van de Velde used this event as basis for several of his later dramatic engravings and paintings, including this fine example. In the right foreground are the smouldering remains of an expended fireship. Later, it turned out that the victim of the fireship was the *Andrew*, which was damaged but not destroyed by the attack.

(THE WALLACE COLLECTION, LONDON)

Our fleet consists at present of ninety-two warships, five fireships and six small vessels … but it is very vexatious to us, and possibly not less so to their Lordships, that our oft-repeated requests and the Government's resolutions produce so little result, especially with regard to the fitting out of a good number of suitable fireships; because we are all of opinion that the expected effect of these fireships, and the terror with which they fill the enemy, would enable us to win the battle; and if we are not provided with them, we may very probably lose it.[21]

And so it transpired. In June 1653, at the south end of the Gabbard shoal, east of Harwich, the opposing fleets met and fought for two days. The Dutch were poorly equipped to withstand the heavy English broadsides. Tromp, commanding one squadron, sent a sloop round his fleet in a vain attempt to tell his captains how to meet this threat. His flagship, the big *Brederode*, the only two-decker in the Dutch fleet, was nearly taken by the English, but, although badly damaged by wind and water, managed to withdraw to the shallow waters at the mouth of the Scheldt. The few fireships, however, the hope of the Dutch admirals, had set themselves alight before they had even reached the enemy.[22]

There was another reason for the success of the English. They had learned from previous battles, and the experience of Admirals Robert Blake, Richard Deane (1610–1653) and George Monck (1608–1670) was reflected in the new *Instructions for the Better Ordering of the Fleet in Fighting* issued in March 1653.[23] While the Dutch still wanted to engage in a mêlée at the battle of the Gabbard, the English managed for the first time to fight in line ahead, one ship behind the other.[24] Broadside gunfire was optimised by having the captains sail in what came to be called the line of battle: as the Dutch found when they tried to close for boarding, a solid wall of fire was almost impossible to approach head-on. The line could engage more ships simultaneously, and hard-pressed captains in the line could support each other more easily. This innovation marked the beginning of new epoch in naval tactics, a theme to be taken up in later chapters.

By the middle of 1653 both sides were approaching exhaustion, but still they persisted in inflicting as much damage on each other as they could. The English blockaded the Dutch coast and took numerous prizes. The departing East Indiamen of the VOC were in danger of capture, as were the richly laden ships returning to port. The herring fleet could not go to sea, and nearly 500 merchant ships were blockaded in the shallow inlet known as the Zuiderzee. The vulnerability of the Dutch economy, and its dependence on unfettered overseas trade, was now obvious. Unemployment and social unrest increased across the Netherlands.

Nor did the English escape unscathed, although in terms of overseas trade the price was not so high for them. The Navigation Acts had also brought them some disadvantages: certain products that had once been brought in by Dutch ships had become more expensive, and in particular the cost of shipbuilding had gone up by a third. The fishery had declined, and, except in home waters, there were not sufficient warships to protect English convoys. Overseas, the English were inferior to the Dutch, who had blockaded the Sound, brought the Baltic trade to a standstill, and severely impaired the trade to the Levant.[25]

Gradually it became clear that peace negotiations must begin, but to strengthen their bargaining positions both sides first sought a decisive victory, and they scratched together their last reserves of ships, guns and men. The manning of such a large number of ships had become very difficult in both countries. In the Netherlands, with its liberal laws, a man could not be forced to serve in a warship. In the south of England, by contrast, press-gangs combed the streets, taverns and jails, and as one witness wrote, 'They pressed whole Church-fulls'; but in spite of using all available means, it remained difficult to gather up the necessary crews.

The opposing fleets in the Channel manoeuvred to take up the best starting position for the final slaughter: Admiral Monck on one side, and Admirals Tromp and De With on the other. The Dutch had 107 warships and about nine fireships, the English 104 ships and probably five fireships.[26] On 10 August 1653 the fleets met off Scheveningen (the battle of Scheveningen is also known as the battle of Camperdown, or Ter Heide). Three times

A detail from Willem van de Velde the Elder's large grisaille of the battle of Scheveningen, 10 August 1653. Despite being an eyewitness to the battle, the artist did not get all the details correct. For example, the sinking English ship to the left is fictional, as the only major vessel lost in this battle, the *Oak*, came to a fiery end after succumbing to a Dutch fireship.

(NATIONAL MARITIME MUSEUM BHC0277, DETAIL)

The last and bloodiest battle of the First Anglo-Dutch War, the battle of Scheveningen, 10 August 1653. In the centre of the picture, the artist, Jan Abrahamszoon Beerstraaten, shows Tromp's flagship, the *Brederode*, surrounded by English warships. To the right two burning ships are visible, probably the *Andrew* and the *Triumph*, which had been attacked from the weather side by Dutch fireships. With great effort both ships managed to extinguish the fires and were saved. Not illustrated here is a third English ship, the *Oak*, which was also attacked by fireships, but its crew panicked and abandoned the vessel, making her the only loss of an English ship in this battle.

the English fleet sailed through the Dutch ships, tacked, and repeated the manoeuvre. It was a fierce, desperate battle, the bloodiest of the war. All sorts of missiles were used besides regular round-shot – bar- and chain-shot, langridge (scrap iron) and fiery missiles, besides hand-grenades and pots filled with unslaked lime.[27] In the end, the heavier guns of the English again tipped the scales. Towards evening, what remained of the Dutch fleet withdrew to the shallow waters of the Texel. Many ships were dismasted, and between fifteen and twenty were total losses, with 3,000 men dead or wounded.[28] Fishermen sailing over the site of the gruesome battle the next day were horrified to find corpses and wreckage with blood, guts, bits of skull and hair matted in the rigging.[29] And perhaps worst of all, Admiral Tromp was killed, having taken a fatal musket bullet in the chest from an English sharpshooter. His flag was kept flying so that the Dutch fleet would not be discouraged, but this was a dreadful loss for the Dutch. In the words of Joost van den Vondel:

> He's carved himself an image in the hearts
> of all
> more lasting than grave's splendour and
> its marble stone.

On this occasion the Dutch fireships were successfully positioned to windward, but they were not in communication with a flag officer, so there was no co-ordination between fireships and supporting vessels; however, some of them attacked on their own initiative.[30] The large number of enemy ships enhanced their chances of success,

and they concentrated their effort against the English flagships, attacking three of them. The *Triumph*, of 62 guns with a crew of 350 men, flying the flag of Vice Admiral James Peacock, was attacked by two fireships, which hooked themselves to the ship and set it afire. As the fire spread the ship was in great danger, and the crew were already in a panic when a third fireship approached. However, Admiral Peacock, who was an excellent commander, kept a cool head. He managed to keep his men at the guns, and they brought the third fireship under heavy fire. In desperation, they managed to cast off the boarding-grapnels of the second fireship and free the ship, and then got the fire under control. Among the wounded was the admiral, who expired later from his burns.[31]

The *Andrew*, of 56 guns, with a crew of 360 men, was attacked by Dutch fireships, among them the *Fortuijn*, and was badly fire-damaged, Rear Admiral Thomas Graves and several of his men being killed before assistance arrived (this was the action witnessed by Van de Velde the Elder, noted in Chapter 9). But for the *Oak*, a ship of 400 tons and 32 guns commanded by Captain John Edwin, help came too late. As her rigging caught fire, the panic-stricken crew jumped overboard, and she became the only English total loss to a Dutch fireship of all these great Channel battles.[32]

After this last explosion of bellicosity, the English and Dutch delegations finally sat down at the negotiating table, and in April the First Peace of Westminster was negotiated. The terms chiefly concerned Dutch compensation for hindering English overseas trade. The Dutch accepted the Navigation Acts and promised from now on to dip the flag.

CHAPTER ELEVEN

THE SECOND
ANGLO-DUTCH WAR:
THE PINNACLE OF
FIRESHIP SUCCESS

'...for as without meat there is no living,
so without fireships there is now no naval fighting.'

Anonymous, *c*1660–70

THE FIRST ANGLO-DUTCH WAR HAD BEEN the bitterest naval conflict ever fought, and the English felt they were the clear victors. With their powerful fleet, they had come out ahead in nearly all the sea-battles, destroying many enemy warships and capturing between 1,000 and 1,700 Dutch merchant vessels, and they now dominated the waters surrounding the British Isles. However, English merchants and investors were disappointed with the long-term results of the war, for it was not long before Dutch trade expanded rapidly again.

It seemed that the Dutch were only reluctantly complying with the conditions of the Peace of Westminster, and if anything their trade policies were even more aggressive than before. They still controlled the international markets, disputing with the right of the English to trade in west Africa, the Caribbean or the East Indies, and impeding

Cornelis Tromp (1629–1691), son of Maarten Tromp, was a knowledgeable seaman and gifted tactician who took part in many of the big sea-battles of his day. He was considered aggressive, and indeed a little foolhardy. From time to time he forgot discipline and thereby brought whole fleets into danger. This always infuriated De Ruyter, but the two men were eventually reconciled in 1672. After De Ruyter's death, Tromp rose to overall command of the Dutch fleet.

(AUTHOR)

English trade and the passage of English ships. However, there were regions where the Dutch ships still ruled the seas. The Dutch East India Company was in the process of annexing the former overseas empire of the Portuguese, and had founded a Dutch settlement at the Cape of Good Hope in 1652. In home waters the Dutch demanded the 'right of free passage', while in trade with west Africa and the East Indies they operated a 'closed sea'

policy, excluding traders from other nations.

In 1660 a major domestic political upheaval in Britain had seen the restoration of the monarchy in the person of Charles II, but there was no change of attitude to the Dutch. Even before the First Anglo-Dutch War, competition had often resulted in localised violence, and eventually many concluded that it could be settled only by force. The 'War Party', centred on the court, promoted the advantages of outright hostilities, and its most prominent member was no less a figure than the Duke of York (1633–1701), younger brother of the king and heir to the throne. Young and ambitious, he had close connections with several overseas trading ventures.[1] His brother made him Lord High Admiral, and he would go on to command the strongest and most up-to-date battlefleet in the world.

In the course of 1664 the situation became critical. Charles II could not make a unilateral declaration of war, because he needed the approval of Parliament in order to raise the money, so he looked for a solid *casus belli* to justify any such declaration: '… in honour to begin a war', as Samuel Pepys saw it from his position inside the naval administration. A certain Robert Holmes (1622–1692) added fuel to the smouldering trade war when, as commander of a small squadron of English warships on the west coast of Africa, he occupied several Dutch trading posts, and then sailed across the Atlantic, took the Dutch settlement on the island of Manhattan, and changed its name from Nieuw Amsterdam to New York. He was to be a major player in the war that followed.

In December Holmes encountered a flotilla of Dutch ships consisting of thirty merchantmen and four frigates – the 'Smyrna Fleet' as it was known – on its way home from the Mediterranean. In a surprise attack his squadron took several prizes, and Pieter van Brakel, the convoy commandant, lost his life.[2] At the same time Admiral de Ruyter made a retaliatory foray into the Mediterranean, having made prizes of several English merchantmen on the west African coast and in the West Indies. That was the last straw.

During the winter both sides rearmed vigorously. Additional ships were hired, and men recruited or pressed, and in January 1665 the United

One of a series of situation sketches by Willem van de Velde the Elder of the battle of Lowestoft in June 1665. The opening battle of the Second Anglo-Dutch War, it developed in the old style with squadrons engaged in a mêlée, in which individual ships fought each other as best they could. The picture shows the situation after the explosion of the *Eendracht*, with the scene of the catastrophe, where the burning remains of the Dutch flagship are still afloat, in the centre. The dark smoke to the right of centre is coming from three Dutch warships entangled with each other, which have been attacked by an English fireship. After the explosion and the loss of their commander, the demoralised Dutch fleet began to disintegrate.

(NATIONAL MARITIME MUSEUM PY3901)

James, Duke of York (1633–1688), was the younger brother of the King of England, Charles II, and was himself later crowned as James II. He was a leading member of the 'War Party', which was anxious to reduce the power of the Dutch fleet and thereby Dutch overseas trade. In the Second Anglo-Dutch War (1665–7), as an ambitious young man, he commanded the strongest and most modern navy in the world. He fought in the battle of Lowestoft in 1665, and in the battle of Sole Bay in the Third Anglo-Dutch War in 1672, encounters which marked the highpoints of fireship warfare at sea.

(NATIONAL PORTRAIT GALLERY, LONDON, NPG D11515)

The great English victory in the Second Anglo-Dutch War was celebrated by a series of portraits known as the 'Flagmen of Lowestoft' by the court painter Sir Peter Lely (1618–1680). All the senior officers were included. This portrait shows Edward Montagu, First Earl of Sandwich, who commanded the *Prince* during the battle and successfully used a fireship attack to defend his flagship.

(NATIONAL MARITIME MUSEUM BHC3007)

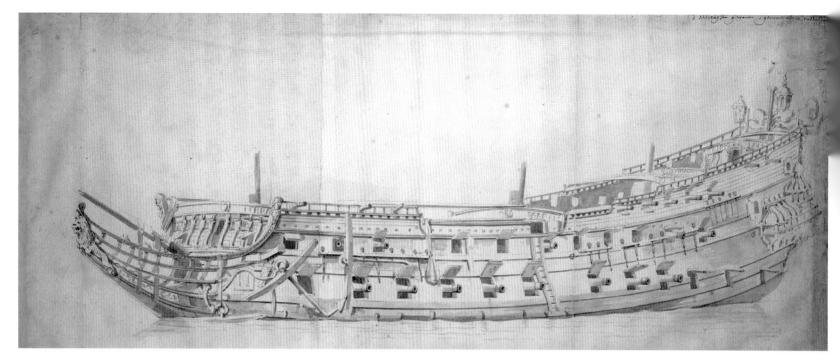

Portrait of the Dutch *Eendracht* (one of several ships so named) by Willem van de Velde the Younger. The ship was part of a thirty-strong building programme that the Dutch admiralties hoped would allow them to engage the stronger English ships on more equal terms. Characteristics of the new ships included the reduced sheer of the gun decks, and lower-deck gunports further from the waterline, achieved by greater beam and draught. The *Eendracht* was built in 1653 and had about 70 guns, and a length of 43m (152 Amsterdam feet) between perpendiculars. At the battle of Lowestoft in 1665 she was the flagship of Lieutenant General Jakob van Wassenaer, Lord of Obdam (1610–1665). During a fight with the *Royal Charles*, commanded by the Duke of York, the *Eendracht* caught fire (in this case not from a fireship) and exploded unexpectedly. Of the four or five hundred men in the crew, only five escaped. The cause of the catastrophe was never established, but was probably related to carelessness in the powder-magazine. A new and bigger *Eendracht* was built in 1666, this time with 80 guns.

(NATIONAL MARITIME MUSEUM PT2434)

Provinces declared war on England; a month later England responded with its own formal declaration of war. As far as numbers went, the fleets were of roughly equal strength, the English having about 109 ships suitable for the line of battle, including heavily armed three-deckers, besides smaller vessels and sixteen fireships. In total the fleet had about 4,200 guns of various calibres, with about 21,000 men. The Dutch had a similar number of ships, namely 103, including eleven fireships, carrying 4,870 guns and 21,600 men, many of whom were motivated by a desire for revenge.[3]

These gigantic war machines, with thousands of tons of gunpowder, and thousands of guns served by thousands of men, had just one aim – to inflict the greatest possible damage on the merchants and investors of the competing economy. They were not concerned with seizing territories or possessions. The key function of the Dutch navy was protecting the Dutch merchant ships, and thus the best means for England to hit the mercantile interests of the United Provinces would be to destroy the war-fleet: the Dutch trade routes which passed so close to the English coast would become vulnerable, and the herring-boats conducting the lucrative fishery could be easily driven off their fishing-grounds. Destroy the warships, and Dutch trade would be quickly brought to a standstill; Amsterdam would be finished as a trade centre,

and with it the whole of the United Provinces.

In contrast to the naval forces, European land armies of this era were not capable of achieving a quick and decisive victory. The giant armies moved like locusts from one area to another, exerting political pressure by their mere presence or by laying siege to cities. They lived off the land, and the economic havoc that they caused was part of their *raison d'être*. Decisive battles were the exception rather than the rule.

Things were quite different at sea. A big warship could operate only in a relatively restricted area, and a refit was often needed after a fairly short period at sea. Once water, provisions and powder were exhausted, the fighting capacity of the ship was nullified, so if anything was to be achieved by a battlefleet, prompt action was required. The principal aim of the Dutch was to defend their trade against English attack, but as aggressively as possible. To achieve this they hoped to engage the English fleet quickly and to defeat it heavily enough to make it withdraw from the high seas. If a damaged and dispersed English fleet could be confined to port, the seaways would once again be open, and the Dutch merchant ships could go about their business.[4]

The English supreme commander was the Lord High Admiral, the Duke of York, no mere figurehead, but a competent, capable soldier and military leader. A keen and enthusiastic yachtsman, he was also well versed in many of the technical aspects of his navy. On the other side, following the death of Maarten Harpertszoon Tromp, the Dutch were forced by political circumstances to give the command to Jakob van Wassenaer, Lord of Obdam (1610–1665), a venerable gout-stricken military man with little naval experience.

In the second week of June 1665 the fleets were ready for a trial of strength. The English were at sea in the hope of threatening a Dutch merchant convoy, and hence luring the Dutch fleet out of their home waters. On Saturday 12 June, just before sundown, the two vast fleets hove in sight of each other. They were somewhere off the coast of Suffolk, about the latitude of Lowestoft. It was too late in the day for a real passage of arms, but the English got an inkling of the concentrated destruc-

Prince Rupert, Duke of Cumberland and Count Palatine of the Rhine (1619–1682), in an oil portrait by Sir Peter Lely. 'Rupert of the Rhine', as he was known, was the son of Elizabeth Stuart, daughter of King James I. A cavalry general during the Civil War, and later admiral of the exiled Royalist fleet, he was appointed to overall command of the English fleet after the Restoration. He fought in the Second and Third Anglo-Dutch Wars, the heyday of sea warfare with fireships.

(NATIONAL MARITIME MUSEUM BHC2989)

tiveness to come as they watched the blaze on a Dutch fireship, set on fire prematurely by a drunken captain, which burned itself out for the rest of the night.[5] They saw this as a good omen.

At first light on the 13th the English realised that they were to windward of the Dutch, the favourable position. Obdam hesitated, and failed to attack right away or tack quickly enough to get to windward of the English.[6] That meant that the Dutch could not close to implement their favoured tactic, which was to cripple the enemy ship by firing

high to cut up its rigging and then, at the right moment, take it by boarding. Nor were the eleven Dutch fireships, which were kept ready on the side away from the enemy, well positioned: in fact they were useless.

The skies were still grey, with the sun below the horizon, when at 4am the first salvoes of the battle of Lowestoft roared across the sea. The two fleets, on parallel courses, passed by each other, and these movements developed into a running battle that lasted for hours. The English tried to make use of the new tactic of forming a line, with vanguard, centre and rearguard. As noted earlier, this had the advantage of bringing more ships into action quickly, and any vessel could withdraw behind the line and carry out repairs, rather than helplessly falling victim to an enemy fireship. The designated fireships could remain behind the line in proximity to the flagship until given the order to attack. One other novelty in this battle was that the admiral attempted to give his orders by flag-signals for the first time.[7]

Opposing the English lay the disorderly mass of the Dutch, and they suffered an early blow during the first pass of the fleets. On the stroke of five in the morning, Vice Admiral Egbert Meussen Cortenaer, an important adviser to the supreme commander, was struck by a cannonball aboard his flagship *Groot Hollandia* and mortally wounded. The captain, who would have been next in command, was not aboard the vessel, and it was the first lieutenant who now found himself in command, but in the confusion the admiral's flag was left flying.

The Dutch made strenuous efforts to work up to the English line to windward, and at one point the flagships of Admirals Cornelis Tromp (son of Maarten Harpertszoon Tromp) and Cornelis Evertsen the Elder were so close that the marines were able to exchange musket-fire with the *Prince*, the flagship of Admiral Edward Montagu, First Earl of Sandwich. To extricate himself from this tight spot, Sandwich decided to use the tried and true method and ordered his 'own' fireship to attack. The targets were particularly powerful ships, which made it a near-suicidal mission. However, Richard Cotton, the captain of the fireship *Bryar*, could not disobey orders, and the helmsman put the tiller over and changed course. The minute the ships' intention became clear to the enemy, they drew fire from all the Dutch vessels, and as they came within a ship's length of the Dutch flagship, the *Bryar*'s main topmast went by the board; five members of the crew lay dead or wounded on the deck, and the hull was badly shattered, but she still floated. Then the helmsman was fatally wounded

and it was over; the fireship sheered off course and missed her target. The English fireship attack had failed, but Sandwich survived.[8]

Towards midday, and after hours of pounding, Sandwich realised that a gap had opened up in the Dutch centre, and for a daredevil this was an open invitation. The admiral took his ships through the breach, splitting the Dutch fleet and bringing on

a mêlée. 'It was total chaos,' said an eyewitness later, 'and we pressed against each other like a herd of sheep in a pen. We could scarcely fire at the enemy without hitting our own ships.'[9]

Despite the line of battle, it was still common for the flagship of one fleet to seek out the enemy admiral and slug it out broadside to broadside, and about one o'clock in the afternoon just such a glad-

iatorial single combat began between the Duke of York in the *Royal Charles* and Obdam in the *Eendracht*. For two hours the ships let loose at each other with every gun that would bear. Immediately next to the duke, two young noblemen were ripped apart, and the heir to the throne was splattered by blood and body parts. Obdam tried to board but was repulsed, and then about three o'clock it hap-

After the battle of Lowestoft an English squadron tried to capture the richly laden 'Spice Fleet' of the Dutch East India Company, which took refuge in the neutral port of Bergen but was attacked there in August 1665. This view by Willem van de Velde the Younger, seen from the harbour looking out, shows the Dutch defensive position with the English ships obscured by the gunsmoke. The heavily armed East Indiamen lie broadside to the harbour entrance and are defending themselves successfully. As the gunsmoke indicates, there was an offshore wind, which prevented a fireship attack by the English. Had this not been the case, the Dutch merchants would have sustained the loss of one of the richest East Indies fleets.

(NATIONAL MARITIME MUSEUM BHC0698)

pened: the *Eendracht* blew sky-high in a huge cloud of smoke. The Dutch force had lost their supreme commander, and of the 400 men aboard his flagship, only four were rescued. No one was left who could explain what had caused the catastrophe.

Naturally the English were jubilant, while on the other side the Dutch became disheartened and lost their will to fight. Slowly the distance between the enemy fleets increased and they broke off the fight and withdrew. Leading the retreat was the *Groot Hollandia*, still flying the admiral's flag, and a host of ships that did not realise that Vice Admiral Cortenaer was dead followed her example. During the retreat one group of four Dutch ships had become entangled and separated from the main body of the fleet. Hundreds of men struggled feverishly to cut away spars and rigging and set the ships free, but it was too late. This was a classic opportunity for a fireship attack, and the Duke of York seized it. One of the fireships of his squadron was given the order, and in favourable conditions John Gethings in the *Fame* achieved a textbook success. Just one Dutch ship, even though on fire, managed to drift clear, and extinguish its flames. The other three became a gigantic crackling bonfire, their hulls torn apart by exploding powder-kegs. About 1,000 men died horribly in an inferno of burning tar, wood and sailcloth. Only a hundred or so were fished out of the water by passing English ships.

Horrid as it was, this was a great success for the fireship, but an incident elsewhere in the battle shows that there were moral boundaries to its employment. Another group of three ships, including the East Indiaman *Marsseveen*, the biggest ship in the Dutch fleet, had collided in the confusion of the retreat, and with yards and rigging entangled lay almost motionless side by side. Every English ship fired into the struggling mass as it passed, and after a heavy cannonade from the English rear under Lord Sandwich, the Dutch ships struck their flags. However, as Sandwich wrote in his diary:

> one Gregory in a fireship of Prince Rupert's squadron went and set fire on them … and they were all destroyed but 100 saved in a boat and some few taken up out of the water. This cruel fact was much

detested by us as not beseeming Christians and his Royal Highness ordered the Judge Advocate to examine the matter, in order to have the judgment of Court Martial thereupon.[10]

So while Captain Gethings, in the *Fame*, was awarded a gold medal, William Gregory commanding the *Dolphin*, fearing the fate that awaited him, took flight and was never seen again.[11] It is remarkable, in an age when magnanimity on the part of the victor was far from the norm, that Sandwich clearly considered the incineration of the surrendered ships to be against the rules of war.

During the Dutch retreat the English had managed to inflict a lot more damage, but they did not pursue the Dutch forcefully enough (they had probably expended all their fireships), and allowed the defeated ships to withdraw into the shallower waters behind Texel, where the deeper-draught English ships could not follow. That Sunday in June 1665 had cost the Dutch Republic 5,000 men and seventeen ships, including three flagships.

The victorious English fleet anchored at Sole Bay (Southwold Bay) off the coast of Suffolk, and started to make repairs, but it became apparent that it was in fact too weak to impose a successful and sustained blockade of the Dutch coast. In August the 'Spice Fleet' of the Dutch East India Company (VOC), with its richly laden vessels, reached European waters. The ships could not sail directly up the Channel and into the Zuiderzee, but were forced to take the northern route round Scotland, and then seek sanctuary in the neutral port of Bergen in Norway. There they were attacked by an English squadron. Being heavily armed, the East Indiamen were able to repel this, and the English sustained serious losses. Conditions were unfavourable for a fireship attack, with the wind blowing steadily offshore, and a squadron of Dutch ships sailed to the help of the East Indiamen, obviating any further opportunity for fireship attack. If this had been better managed the consequences would have been disastrous for the Dutch, and in the event the English, fresh from their recent victory, had allowed one of the richest-ever East Indies fleet to escape their clutches.[12] The total value of the cargo was estimated at eleven million guilders, a sum which could have ended the English financial crisis, with correspondingly disastrous consequences for Dutch shipping.

At the beginning of 1666 the splendid ships of the English fleet were to be seen lying at anchor in the Thames, but they were far from battle-ready because the king lacked the resources to pay for a war. Unlike the financially sophisticated Netherlands, England did not have at its disposal a flourishing money-market and an adequate system of credit.[13] The king frantically endeavoured to obtain credit, but in the short term there was no cash to pay the sailors and soldiers, leaving thousands of them starving. At the same time the corrupt naval administration could not obtain supplies for the ships, and refitting came to a standstill in the dockyards. Offshore in the Channel the 'defeated' Dutch under Admirals de With and de Ruyter proceeded to blockade the Thames. Undisturbed, they surveyed its waters and charted the whole estuary. Then, at last, Parliament approved the expenditure – the substantial sum of £1,250,000 – and the dockyards and ships came to life again.

At the end of May the English felt able to renew the fight, the fleet being led by two experienced warriors, George Monck, Duke of Albemarle (1608–1670), and Prince Rupert of the Rhine, Duke of Cumberland (1619–1682). Monck, like most of the senior officers at that time, was not bred to the sea, his military experience having been gained mainly as a soldier, but he was considered to be a tough enterprising man, who did not lose his head when under fire. As a former artillerist he was a firm believer in heavy close-quarter broadside gunnery. Prince Rupert was the son of Elizabeth of Bohemia, Electress of Palatine and daughter of King James I, known as the 'Winter Queen'. He had begun his military career as a cavalry officer, but during the Civil War he commanded the small fleet of Charles I, and afterwards continued as a privateer captain, so he had plenty of sea-going experience. Following the Restoration of 1660, as the cousin of the king, he enjoyed rapid advancement, and in 1666 he was co-commander of the fleet with Monck.

In January of that year, France and Denmark allied themselves with the Netherlands, so that the English now had to reckon with the fleet of Louis XIV, and in May the rumour spread round the English fleet that the French had sailed from Toulon with the intention of reaching the Channel and uniting with the Dutch fleet, thus altering the balance of naval power in favour of the Dutch. On the basis of this rumour, a calamitous decision was made: the English fleet was split into two divisions, with the greater part, under George Monck, left anchored inside the Gunfleet shoal (off the Essex coast), while Rupert's squadron, consisting of about twenty ships and five fireships, sailed in the direction of Plymouth on 29 May. His intention was to engage the French fleet, about which he had only unconfirmed intelligence, but in fact Louis XIV had decided not to risk his untried ships in any battle with experienced opponents, and the threat was completely imaginary.

The other part of the fleet, consisting of about fifty-four ships and nine fireships, remained at anchor. To judge by the events in the spring, it would be more than adequate to take on the weak Dutch ships. Besides, nothing indicated that the Dutch would put to sea – at least that was the opinion of the English strategists, and first and foremost that of the king himself. It was not yet clear to the officials of the Admiralty that the Dutch fleet in the past twelve-month had been refitting and rearming just as vigorously as the English. About thirty new heavily armed two-deckers had been put into service, stiffening the weaker Dutch line of battle.[14]

So Admiral Monck, aboard his flagship the *Royal Charles*, was completely taken by surprise when at dawn on 11 June the scout *Bristol* let her fore topgallant sheets fly and fired three guns in succession to signal 'Enemy in sight'![15] The admiral was fully aware that he was significantly outgunned and, because the seas were rough, he knew that his ships would not be able to open the gunports on the lower batteries – the English vessels were relatively crank (top-heavy) and heeled over too readily. But Monck was under enormous political and personal pressure to succeed. After the previous English victories, he would be reckoned a coward if he failed to accept battle this time, whatever the tactical disadvantages. At 7am when his captains came aboard the *Royal Charles* for a Council of War, his pride would allow only one decision: Attack!

CHAPTER TWELVE

THE
FOUR DAYS'
BATTLE

'...they may do as much mischief
to a friend as to an enemy'

Captain John Smith, *Sea Grammar,* 1627

ONTRARY TO ALL EXPECTATIONS OF THE English, the Dutch fleet had put to sea. Its most important task was the protection of Dutch shipping, and this time it was a matter of ensuring the security of the home-bound 'Spice Fleet' of the Dutch East India Company (VOC). Once again the richly laden ships from Batavia could not risk the Channel route, but sailed north around Scotland and then to the Dutch coast. They would have to do their utmost to prevent the English from intercepting this vital cargo.

Admiral Michiel Adriaanszoon de Ruyter (1607–1676) was the greatest of a generation of Dutch admirals who had been bred to the sea. A fierce patriot and a man of clear analytical understanding, he made very few mistakes during a professional life that ranged from successful merchant-captain to outstanding fleet commander. He was revered and trusted throughout the fleet, and played a leading part in all three Anglo-Dutch Wars, but his greatest triumphs were at the Four Days' Battle (1666) and the raid on the Medway (1667). He was a keen advocate of fireships and believed they were essential to achieve a resounding victory at sea.

(FROM: DE JONGE 1858–62)

Michiel Adriaanszoon de Ruyter (1607–1676), a lieutenant-general of the United Provinces, had command of about ninety warships and nine fireships. After an early career as a successful merchant captain, whaler, privateer and naval commander, his own preference was to seek retirement, but his reputation as a tactician and strategist led the Zeeland admiralty to give him more and more responsibility. He was trusted by the other officers and extremely popular with the men, who nicknamed him 'Grandfather', and this credibility was crucial because the commanders of Dutch warships at that time were rugged individualists who, seeing themselves as free citizens, showed little deference to established hierarchies. They were often reckless, with a tendency to overestimate their own capabilities; nor was there yet a codified set of rules or fighting instructions that they were expected to follow. Only a man like De Ruyter possessed the ability to reconcile different personalities, interests, needs and constraints; and these men were united only by their admiration and trust of De Ruyter himself.[1] In De Ruyter's fleet, Cornelis Evertsen the Elder (1610–1666) was Admiral of the Van, and Admiral Cornelis Tromp (1629–1691), son of Maarten Harpertszoon Tromp, commanded the rear.

On Friday 10 June 1666, about thirty miles from Ostend, De Ruyter had ordered his fleet to anchor at 7am, and he could scarcely believe his eyes when he saw the English ships heave into sight three hours later. There were fewer than seventy of them, and he noted the small number of ships of the line; having also observed that the sea was too high to allow their lower batteries to be run out, he concluded that the English were not likely to attack, and allowed his ships to remain at anchor. But he had underestimated George Monck, whose ships came on without hesitation. At the foremast head of the *Royal Charles* flew the 'bloody' red flag, the traditional signal to 'Engage the Enemy', and De Ruyter realised at this point that the English were serious. Now, when it was almost too late to prepare for battle, he ordered his ships to buoy their anchors and cut their cables. There was no time to form the line of battle, as by 2pm the English were within cannon-shot. The events that followed that first broadside developed into the bloodiest and

George Monck, First Duke of Albemarle (1608–1670), was a colleague of Prince Rupert and Edward Montagu. As a professional soldier he initially fought on the Parliamentary side in the Civil War, and was later a general-at-sea in the First Anglo-Dutch War. After Cromwell's death, he transferred his allegiance to the king and was ennobled at the Restoration, leading squadrons in the Second Anglo-Dutch War alongside Prince Rupert and the Duke of York. Oil painting by Sir Peter Lely.

(WIKIMEDIA COMMONS)

most bitter sea-battle that the world had ever seen. It came to be known as the Four Days' Battle.

For hours the fleets sailed on parallel courses, keeping their distance. The English were to windward, and as the ships heeled to leeward (towards the enemy), their lowest tier of gunports could not be opened without the risk of flooding the gun deck. The leeward Dutch, heeling away from the English, tended to fire high, hitting spars and rigging rather than the hulls of their opponents. Furthermore, from that position they could not use fireships. However, as the hours passed more and more Dutch ships managed to come within range of the English, as the Dutch squadrons tried to weather the enemy line so as to engage individual ships more closely.

Fire, the greatest enemy of the sailing ship in that era, was not just a threat from fireships. About five o'clock the Dutch saw with dismay that two of their own ships were ablaze, and fireships were not involved. First the *Hof van Zeeland* caught fire, and almost the entire crew of 278 men were lost. Then the smaller *Duivenvoorde*, which had also caught fire, collided with three other ships and set them ablaze, although their crews managed to put their fires out. Everyone who saw this drama play out wondered what had caused the fires. It was known that the wad used to secure the shot in a cannon could catch fire and then be blown back by the wind to set one's own ship or a neighbour on fire.[2] But some witnesses claimed to have seen red-coloured shot fired from the English cannon, and some sources indicate that something called 'brass fire shot' was indeed used to cause fires which were hard to extinguish.[3]

The numerical superiority of the Dutch now began to have its impact on the English ships. At various places in the battle area, ships drifted apart and anchored in order to look after their wounded, plug shot-holes in the hull, or repair the spars and rigging. Late in the afternoon, at various places along the long dispersed battle-line, individual ships engaged in desperate ship-to-ship battles, and only as darkness fell did the cannon-fire slacken off. The English had not had a good day, having lost three capital ships to cannon-fire or boarding, and as evening approached more and more of their ships sustained damage to the rig-

ging that was beyond repair. Now was the moment for the Dutch fireships.

Typical of the victims was the *Rainbow*, an old ship built originally about the time of the Spanish Armada, which had been so badly battered that she lagged badly behind. At seven in the evening a Dutch fireship attacked, 'but it pleased God that she did not stay so well as to take the wind of us, but came a little to leeward & left us, but I conceive not without some damage.', as John Hart, the captain, wrote later in his report.[4]

It was late, about ten o'clock, when, somewhere in the gloom, the English saw the flashes of a broadside and heard cannon-fire followed by the crackle of musketry. Then they saw a fire flicker up and realised that some of their stragglers were fighting for their lives. The *Henry* was a great ship of the Second Rate with 440 men aboard, and armed with 80 guns, most of which were bronze; but many of her masts and spars had been shot away and she was unable to defend herself against Dutch fire. In the twilight she had decided to anchor and bend fresh sails, and between nine and ten o'clock Vice Admiral John Harman (1630–1673) gave the order to get under sail. He was an experienced 'tarpaulin' captain and protégé of the Duke of York, promoted to flag rank after the battle of Lowestoft, and was now endeavouring to regain contact with his own squadron. However, instead he found himself surrounded by Dutch ships. He thought he could shoot his way through by exchanging broadsides with De Ruyter's powerful flagship, *Zeven Provinciën*, but then more Dutch ships crossed his bow and raked him with heavy cannon-fire, and although the *Henry* fought back with all her guns, the men on her decks sustained heavy losses, and her rigging was damaged further. Eventually she was so disabled that Admiral Cornelis Evertsen, leader of the Dutch van, decided that she looked ready for the coup de grâce, and at his mizzen he ran up the signal ordering the Dutch fireship *Vrijheid* to stand by to attack.

This was just what Engel Adrianszoon, captain of the *Vrijheid*, had been waiting for. His crew raced up the rigging to attach the boarding-hooks to the yardarms, something that was always done at the last minute in readying the ship, so that her role would not be betrayed. Iron chains and grapnels

Sir John Harman (1630–1673) was an experienced seaman and commander who demonstrated his ability in three wars with the Dutch. In the Four Days' Battle he commanded the *Henry* as vice admiral, and after the ship sustained severe battle damage he anchored in order to send new sails aloft. This made the *Henry* a sitting target for several Dutch ships, and finally Admiral Cornelis Evertsen gave the order to make a fireship attack. Harman maintained discipline in his ship and prevented the men from panicking, so although the *Henry* caught fire, he managed to ward off the attacks, extinguish the flames and retire from the battle.

were secured to yards and bowsprit, and at the same time other men began bringing inflammable material up from the hold and distributing it around the decks (it was stowed away in the hold to keep it dry, so that it would burn easily). After everything was ready and all the men were off the deck, the planks were covered with pitch and oil. Any remaining powder was taken into the boat – an important detail, because exploding powder could suck the oxygen out of the air, and hinder the course of the conflagration. Finally, Captain Adriaanszoon hoisted the signal indicating that his ship was armed and ready.[5]

In the meantime, Admiral Evertsen had hailed the *Henry*, advising that he intended to attack with a fireship and demanding that Harman surrender. In the past many proud ships in such a situation had struck their flags – but not John Harman in the *Henry*. His answer, which was later much lauded by his countrymen, was a defiant 'It hasn't come to that yet!', followed by a broadside. His ship could still bite.[6] Now Evertsen gave the order for the *Vrijheid* to attack, and under cover of darkness Adriaanszoon set course for the *Henry*. At first it was hard for the crew of the *Henry* to see the *Vrijheid* clearly, but once they did so, they opened fire with all guns. About this time Adriaanszoon realised that he had competition – a second Dutch fireship was heading for the *Henry*, and it later transpired that De Ruyter had not seen Evertsen's signal, but had independently spotted what looked like a very promising situation and sent in one of his own fireships, the *Gouden Ruiter* under Captain Jan Broerszoon Vermeulen. At this juncture it was closer to the *Henry* than the *Vrijheid*, and the crew of the latter began to mutter: if the other ship was successful, there went their bonus payment!

The second attacker now reached the *Henry* and grappled her with hooks and grapnels, and Adriaanszoon watched as a cloud of brown smoke rose up from the *Gouden Ruiter*, encompassing the scene in a foul-smelling haze. The dense smoke made it almost impossible for the English to determine exactly where the hooks and grapnels were entangled in their rigging, but it also prevented Adriaanszoon from seeing the daring action of Lieutenant Thomas Lamming of the *Henry*, who kept a cool head and jumped down on the deck of the blazing fireship, found the chains securing her to his own ship and managed to cast them loose. Then, wheezing and coughing, he clambered back aboard his ship, where men with fire-poles and oars managed to push the fireship clear and escape the worst.

At this moment of confusion and uproar, Adriaanszoon reached the other side of the English ship. The *Vrijheid*, sailing before the wind, was going at a good clip when she smacked into the mizzen channel of the *Henry*, her yardarm hooks caught in the rigging, and the grapnels and chains fell from bowsprit and yards, catching the rails of the Englishman. With that, the *Vrijheid*'s crew had done their job, and they now had to make their escape. They gathered abaft the fire-room bulkhead. Just before the collision Captain Adriaanszoon had lit his portfire, a stick which was soaked in potassium nitrate,[7] and by its flickering light he watched his men exit like shadows through the sally-port one after the other and leap into the boat that was tied up on the disengaged side of the fireship. There they waited, laying on their oars, for their captain, who was the last man to leave.

They had almost reached the target, and the only task left was the most important one: transforming the ship into a roaring hellfire of total destruction. But that was not easy. Adriaanszoon had to choose exactly the right moment. Too early, and the enemy would have time to engage in countermeasures, or the fireship's sails might burn, causing her to lose way, come under heavy enemy fire, and fail to reach her objective. On the other hand, if he waited for too long, the flames would not get a good hold, and it would be too easy to push or tow the ship clear. Finally Adriaanszoon opened the curtain and removed the wooden lid protecting the hole through the bulkhead to the fire-room. Near the sally-port the mouths of the fire-troughs protruded from the ship's side, and he dipped his torch into the inflammable mixture, sending the flame hissing its way along the trough and into the fire-room. In a well-prepared fireship, it would be only five minutes before the whole thing was transformed into a blazing bonfire. Down in the boat, he unlocked the padlock securing the chain-painter to the ship, and the relieved crew had only one thought on their minds – getting away!

As they bent to the oars, they saw that the *Vrijheid*'s attack had apparently been successful, and the stern-gallery of the *Henry* was ablaze. The artillery duel of the last few hours and the assaults of the two fireships had stretched the men on the beleaguered ship to the limit of their endurance and courage. Discipline began to crumble, and panic broke out. The marines, who had been standing with loaded muskets on the quarterdeck and at the hatchway ladders, left their posts. The first to flee was the ship's chaplain, who, completely out of his mind, jumped overboard; after him went forty men who, seeing no other way out, leaped into the dark water in the light of the flames. The Dutch fished some of them out, while the others drowned. Just as some men on board the *Henry* were struggling to lower the longboat and make their escape, Captain Harman's moment came. Drawing his dagger, he threatened to kill anyone

who came near the rails, and then he drove the men back to their posts, where they managed with poles and oars to shove the burning fireship clear, and began to extinguish the fire in the stern. Then a yard crashed down from aloft on the quarterdeck and crushed his ankle.

When Admiral Evertsen realised that both fireship attacks had failed, he gave orders for a third fireship to make an assault. It was the turn of the *Hoop*, a ship from Zeeland captained by Willem Meerman. Even in the face of this new threat, Harman managed to maintain discipline on board his ship. He ordered whatever sail that still remained to be set, and tried to outrun the fireship. For about an hour the latter was within a stone's throw of the English ship, but the crew managed to bring the four culverins in the stern-gallery into action, and chain-shot hit the main yard of

A scene from the Four Days' Battle in June 1666, the highpoint of the Second Anglo-Dutch War. This is by the Amsterdam painter Pieter Corneliszoon van Soest and shows groups of ships engaged in a mêlée, the lines of battle having broken down. In the middleground and foreground, burning and sinking ships, the victims of fireship attack, can be seen drifting. The painter has accurately shown how all the ships that can still manoeuvre keep a respectful distance from the burning vessels. The small number of boats and the many sailors fighting for their lives in the water underline the paucity of life-saving measures available to the hundreds of men who crewed these vessels.

the *Hoop*, bringing it down. This caused the fire-ship to drop back, and the disappointed Captain Meerman could only watch as the *Henry* slowly disappeared into the dusk.

Harman now had another stroke of luck: during the fireship attacks the Dutch ships had kept their distance, and he was now able to sail off into the darkness as if slipping up a deserted alley. One of his last shots hit the quarterdeck of the *Walcheren*, flagship of Cornelis Evertsen, and this Parthian shot slew the Dutch admiral. At that moment, none of the Dutchmen imagined that the English ship would reach port. But they were mistaken: Harman not only got his scorched vessel into Aldeburgh Bay near Harwich, but made repairs and reinforced his crew, so that the *Henry* was reported to have taken part in the battle again the following day.

In England Harman's heroic deed was later regarded as a 'victory' although it was more correctly a very lucky escape. He was knighted, but was never able to enjoy the fruits of success because his injured leg failed to heal properly, and aboard his subsequent commands he had to give orders from a chair on the quarterdeck. The gallant Thomas Lamming did not go unrewarded either, being promoted and given command of the *Ruby*, a Fourth Rate.

———•———

Saturday 12 June would have been a very promising summer day in the Channel, had it not been the second day of a bitterly fought sea-battle. The wind had slackened and was blowing from the south-west, and the sea had become calmer. During the night the two fleets lay at anchor within a few miles of each other. At break of day the fleet commanders tried to assess the situation and determine which ships were present, and where van, centre and rear were positioned. As the junior admirals headed for the flagship in their barges, it was already clear that the battle was to continue, and that Monck's determination was still unbroken. His captains scarcely had time to take up their prescribed positions in the line before at the mainmast head of the *Royal Charles* broke out the flag signal for 'General Pursuit', and it was just 7.30 when the first broadsides thundered across the sea.[8] The first aim of both sides was to try and get into the favourable position to windward of the enemy, and at the beginning of the day the English fleet were lucky in this regard, managing to keep to windward and avoid being outmanoeuvred by the enemy.

What then followed was a series of running battles. Again and again, sections of the fleets sailed on opposite but parallel courses towards each other and blazed away broadside to broadside. The hell of battle was somewhat different from that of the day before, because the wind was too weak to disperse the cannon-smoke from the disordered field of battle, and it was only rarely that a glint of sunshine broke through, allowing the men at the gunports of the mighty warships a glimpse of the enemy. Through the fog they saw the muzzle-flashes of the enemy, and the cannon roared again.

With each passage, the ships were exposed anew to enemy cannon-fire, the number of dead increased, and more damage to hull and rigging was sustained. In the course of the morning, Admiral de Ruyter in the *Zeven Provinciën* managed to get part of his fleet to windward of the English, but scarcely had he hoisted the signal for 'General Attack' than it became apparent that a squadron under Admiral van Tromp had been cut off by the English. De Ruyter had to break off the attack in order to go to his vice admiral's aid, but he was so far away that the English used the opportunity to pour concentrated fire mercilessly into Tromp's isolated group of ships.

Those vessels that were not totally pounded into wreckage had at the very least lost their mast and spars, and thus became an inviting target for the English fireships. First of all came the *Spread Eagle*

under Captain William Seale, and then the *Young Prince* commanded by William Bustow. The *Spread Eagle* reached her goal first, setting a Dutch vice admiral's ship on fire. However, the crew managed to free themselves from the attacker and extinguish the fire. Less fortunate was *De Liefde*, ship of 68 guns, which was set on fire by the *Young Prince*: the men panicked and leaped into the sea, with 280 drowning and just thirty-nine surviving.

De Ruyter had been obliged to break off the manoeuvre which had given him the windward gage in order to come to the aid of Tromp's isolated squadron, but the English were unable to take full advantage of this because they had only two fireships left. In the meantime the battle continued its course. Again and again, the fleets sailed past each other, hammering each other with punishing broadsides. Early in the afternoon of the second day, after an unparalleled battle of attrition, both sides were at the end of their tether. The crews were exhausted, and there had been heavy loss of life. Powder and shot were low, and more and more ships that had been totally ruined by gunfire had to slip out of the line and head for their own coasts. Eventually, Monck had only thirty-four ships capable of staying at sea. In the last glimmer of daylight, they sighted twelve Dutch ships heading in their direction. These were fresh reinforcements coming to De Ruyter's aid. That was the last straw, 'breaking their hearts' as a contemporary report put it, and Monck ordered the most seriously damaged of his ships to withdraw in the direction of the Gunfleet sandbank. Discipline in the English ships remained intact, and the *Royal Charles* and thirteen ships formed a defensive line, behind which the others managed to make their retreat.

With the onset of darkness, the distance between the enemy ships increased, the wind abated, and fighting fizzled out. During the night the ships lay almost motionless, the only signs of activity being the boats and ketches flitting from one dark shadow to another, picking up the badly wounded from these lamed giants so that they could be sent ashore. As the ships bobbed quietly up and down, men continued to die in their holds under the light of iron and horn lanterns; the decks, slippery with blood, were hosed down with buckets and pumps,

Detail from a grisaille by Willem van de Velde the Elder showing the episode on the third day of the Four Days' Battle when the *Royal Prince*, flagship of Admiral Sir George Ayscue, ran on to the Galloper sandbank. Stuck fast, unsupported by his own ships and threatened by two Dutch fireships, Ayscue was forced by his own men to surrender his almost intact ship to the Dutch captain Isaac Sweers, whose ship the *Gouda* is to be seen on the right of the picture. This section depicts the moment when the Dutch prize crew went on board. The white flag at the *Prince*'s mainmast head (distinguishing the Admiral of the Van, or White squadron), the English ensign on its staff at the stern and the main topsail yard are being struck as signs of surrender. The panic engendered by the sight of a fireship has caused some of the English crew to attempt escape by jumping over the bulwarks or through the gunports. Because they could not get the ship off the sandbank, the Dutch were eventually forced to burn this splendid vessel.

(STAATLICHE KUNSTHALLE, KARLSRUHE, INV. NO 2772).

A more painterly representation, by Willem Van de Velde the Younger, of the surrender of the *Royal Prince* on 13 June 1666. Although seen from the other quarter, the details of the ship accord closely with his father's grisaille. The original oil painting is in the Rijksmuseum, Amsterdam.

and the bloody effluent poured in streams out of the scuppers and into the black water.

Throughout the night the noise of axes and hammers could be heard as the boatswains, the carpenters and their crews did their work. Masts were fished, and standing rigging spliced. Below deck in the magazine, the gunners and their assistants prepared for the next day, opening up powder-barrels and using wooden scoops to pour the black-powder into paper cartridges.

At 3am a light breeze sprang up; it was now Sunday June 13, the third day of the battle. Again the flag officers rowed over to the flagship for the morning council of war. Monck's officers agreed with him that they should maintain the defensive line that their stoutest ships had established the night before, and have the rest of the fleet withdraw to the north-west behind it.[9] On the other side, De Ruyter gave the order for his swiftest ships to chase the retreating English. Again the rumble of cannon was heard as the English used their stern-chasers to keep their pursuers at bay with long-range fire.

During the morning the lookouts in the smaller warships on the fringes of the fleet spotted numerous masts on the horizon. But were they friend or foe? By noon it became clear that it was Prince Rupert's squadron returning from their wild-goose chase down-Channel. This influx of fresh warships put new heart into the downcast English, and of course Monck wanted to reunite his part of the fleet with Prince Rupert's ships, so the flags ran up to order the heavy ships to alter course once more. But all the cruising back and forth and frequent changes of course had made the English navigators uncertain of their exact position. It was about five o'clock when the English fleet ran into the shallows close to the Galloper, a long stretch of sandbank in the mouth of the Thames, off what

next flood tide could lift the ship off, and this was time they no longer had. The Dutch ships, of smaller size and lesser draught, began to circle the stranded giant, among them the flagships of Tromp and Van Nes. This was the opportunity that every fireship captain prayed for: the captains of Tromp's two fireships set all available sail to reach a striking position, and even as they came up from astern to get abreast the *Prince* they were still out of range

The Dutch captain Isaac Sweers (1622–1673) of the *Gouda* took the surrender of the *Royal Prince*. Sweers reported that Ayscue was calm and polite, handing over the key to the strong-box that held his personal silver service, which now resides in the Amsterdam Maritime Museum

(FROM: DE JONGE 1858–62)

today is Clacton-on-Sea. The smaller ships got safely over it, but the big ones grounded fast. With the incoming flood tide, most managed to get off again – all but one, the big three-decker *Royal Prince*, flagship of the English rear under the command of Sir George Ayscue.

Ayscue was an experienced man, veteran of many battles, but here he was stuck fast, with ninety-two bronze guns, 620 men and all their provisions pressing his ship deeper into the water than any other ship in the fleet. None of the English ships were prepared to tack among the unseen shoals and try to protect him, and the distance between him and his consorts increased. Although challenged to battle by the Dutch, even the ships of Prince Rupert's squadron refused to risk the navigational hazards.

Soundings with the lead showed that the *Royal Prince* had four fathoms on one side and only two on the other, indicating that she was sitting on a sloping sandbank. It would be hours before the

of the English cannon.

What actually transpired aboard the *Prince* at that moment will never be known. The hundreds of men crowding the decks seemed in danger of a certain and painful death; fear overtook officers and men indiscriminately, and all discipline broke down. On the quarterdeck, men crowded round the admiral crying and begging him to give in, to save their lives by surrendering. Ayscue of course angrily refused, saying that he would rather fire the ship himself (or at least this claim was made later). But he had little time left to make a deal, and while he struggled to make a decision and remain in control of the situation, some despairing men had already gone aloft and hauled down the admiral's flag and were calling to the Dutch asking for quarter. But it was almost too late; Tromp's fireships were fully ready to go and on the point of igniting the powder-trains, after which there would be no turning back.

Then, at the last moment, the fireships were

given the order to pause. One of the fireship captains came alongside the motionless ship and asked if they really had surrendered, and was told that there was no doubting it. A little later Captain Isaac Sweers of the *Gouda* went aboard to accept surrender officially. At the same time, on the disengaged side, about eighty men got away in boats and headed for their own ships. Ayscue remained on board with the remaining men and handed over his powerful flagship, almost undamaged yet helpless, to the enemy. The *Prince* had exchanged very few shots with the enemy in the earlier stages of the battle, not replying with fire even when surrounded by Dutch ships. The admiral was calm and considerate, and even handed over the keys of the chest containing the ship's silver tableware. (A memento of the occasion is on display at the Nederlands Scheepvaartmuseum in Amsterdam – two candle-sticks, a couple of lids and a sugar-bowl, now emblazoned with the crest of the Sweers family.) Then Dutch sailors boarded the ship and took 500 men prisoner. Among them was Admiral George Ayscue, the highest-ranking English officer ever to have surrendered his ship.[10]

The Dutch now made every effort to free the

ship from the Galloper, but De Ruyter, who had in the meantime been following the English ships, decided that she could not be saved, and gave the order for Captain Rein Pieterszoon Mars of the fireship *Fortuijn* to fire the *Prince* – which Tromp estimated to be worth the immense sum of 470,230 guilders.[11] The ship burned, the flames visible from

nearly touched, and they fired chain- and bar-shot at each other's rigging and raked each other's sterns. Case-shot and musket-fire swept the crowded decks, and the crews had no cover. There were examples of death-defying courage. Admiral Sir Christopher Myngs, commanding the English van in the *Victory*, was struck in the cheek by a musket-ball, but held the wound together with his own hands and refused to leave his post. Only when a second ball struck him in the neck and lodged in his shoulder did he allow himself, still protesting, to be taken below deck.[13] He would not survive the day, and as recounted earlier (see Chapter 9), after his funeral some of his men asked that a fireship be put at their disposal so that they could exact revenge on the Dutch.

The first fireship attack occurred quite early in the day. Prince Rupert expended his first fireship when he observed the heavily damaged flagship *Ridderschap* drifting helplessly. The fireship managed to ram it successfully, but two Dutch frigates came to its aid, and one of them towed the fireship clear before it could do much damage. At the same time the Dutch sent one of their own fireships against the English fireship, and, hooked together, they both burned to the waterline, allowing the flagship to be towed away without further damage.

Almost simultaneously something very similar happened on the other side. A Dutch fireship went for the heavily damaged *Royal James*, Prince Rupert's flagship, and success was prevented only when an English fireship edged itself between the two vessels and fended off the attacker. In the meantime Prince Rupert had seized the weather gage, providing a second chance for the English fireships. The *Hound* under Captain James Coleman managed to attack two Dutch ships which were entangled. One of them, the *Landman* with 46 guns and a crew of 230, caught fire and exploded, with only 180 survivors. The other just got away by the skin of its teeth.

In the late morning, after hours of strenuous manoeuvring and bitter fighting, the squadrons of both fleets were in total disarray, and there was a pause in the battle, reflecting the universal exhaustion, while the captains tried to restore some sort of order and close up the gaps in their divisions. From midday until early afternoon there was a

afar, until her magazine exploded, and at midnight she sank.

After the grounding of the *Prince*, the two fleets under Monck and Rupert managed to unite, bringing the total number of ships and fireships to parity with that of the Dutch. At a council of war in the evening the English decided to carry out the most urgent repairs, reorganise the fleet, and be ready to take up the battle the following morning. Everyone knew that the next day would be decisive.

———————•———————

Monday 14 June, the fourth day of the great battle, dawned damp and misty, with the seas not very high.[12] At first light the commanders-in-chief summoned their captains aboard their respective flagships, and encouraged them to do their utmost in the coming hours. The two fleets were now about equal in numbers, and either side had a chance of achieving a decisive victory. The first manoeuvres were aimed at trying to get the weather gage, as each fleet tried to sail across the bow of the other at the closest possible distance. Sometimes the ships came so near to each other that their yardarms

series of long-range passage fights. The Dutch had the weather gage but continued firing into the masts and rigging of the English. About three o'clock the various groups of ships tried to get into close formation with the intention of forcing a decision, and the English continued to repel attacks with vigorous broadsides from their heavy guns. The fortunes of battle see-sawed to and fro, but gradually the English ships had emptied their magazines of powder and shot. Monck once more tried a fireship attack, pitting the *Happy Entrance*, commanded by Captain Andrew Ball, against the 70-gun *Eendracht*. The latter only just escaped.

Towards four in the afternoon the Dutch ships had closed ranks, and De Ruyter decided to gamble everything on the turn of a card. At the masthead of the *Zeven Provenciën* he hoisted the red flag as the signal to pursue and engage the enemy more closely.[14] Several English captains who had thought that victory was within their grasp, and that the Dutch would break off, now lost their nerve. The Dutch broke through the English defensive line and engaged some of the English ships from both sides, and at this critical moment the masts and rigging of Prince Rupert's flagship, the *Royal James*, finally collapsed. Down came the main topmast and mizzenmast, and the main and mizzen yards. The Dutch gunners' concentration on the masts and rigging of the English ships had finally taken effect. Many of the other English vessels were in little better shape, with their captains so uncertain about the state of their masts that they were afraid to tack, and so could no longer manoeuvre properly to offer each other mutual support. Now the Dutch resorted to their favoured boarding tactics.

Prince Rupert made the mistake of not transferring his flag to another less damaged ship, but decided to remain aboard the crippled *Royal James*, which limped away, followed obediently by several of his captains. As the famed ability of the English to hold the line fell apart, and they made off with all powder and shot expended, the Dutch came storming after them, capturing four or five of the stragglers. About seven in the evening a fog descended, described as 'the work of God the Almighty' by a relieved De Ruyter, who could now give the order to break off pursuit.[15] The next day

not a single English ship was to be seen. Far and wide the waters were clear, and the Dutch merchant fleets could now get under way to sail freely in large convoys in the home waters of the King of England.[16]

The Four Days' Battle had cost England around 1,000 dead, 1,450 wounded and 1,800 taken prisoner. The king's navy had lost about ten warships, not counting those reduced to floating piles of splintered timber which could no longer keep up with the fleet and had been set on fire by their own crews to escape capture. Other ships made port, only to be written off as total losses and beyond economic repair. Several senior flag officers were dead, fatally wounded or in captivity.[17] Six fireships had been expended, and the captains and crews of those vessels whose attacks had been successful now demanded their reward.[18]

The Dutch navy's defence of the 'freedom of the seas' had cost it more than 1,550 dead and about 1,330 wounded, a high proportion of the fatalities occurring on the burning ships. Some flag officers and several captains were among the casualties, and as on the English side, many vessels were now little more than masses of shattered timber, no longer sea- or battle-worthy.[19]

After a sea-battle it was very difficult to make a realistic assessment of the outcome, since eyewitnesses' reports of both their own and enemy losses were often unreliable. It was often impossible to decide whether a burning or dismasted ship, seen through a haze of cannon-smoke and perhaps at a considerable distance, was the same vessel seen by a separate witness at a different distance and from another viewpoint. Even if a ship of the line was seen to be grappled by a fireship, it was not always possible to determine whether it was destroyed, was damaged or had escaped. Not even a flag officer, let alone the Admiral of the Fleet, was always in a position to see what his own units were doing. Too many things were going on at once, with the fleets sometimes spread over great distances.

So there were widespread exaggerated reports about enemy losses, and the Dutch concluded that the English casualties exceeded 11,000 men and thirty ships. All that was needed, it seemed, was a little push to finish off the Royal Navy; but as it turned out, this was a very dubious assessment.[20]

CHAPTER THIRTEEN

FIRESHIP AGAINST FIRESHIP:
THE SECOND ANGLO-DUTCH
WAR CONTINUES

*'...we are very sorry to find we are not like
to have so sudden a supply of fireships from you [...]
which will render us very inadequate to the enemy...'*

Prince Rupert, 1666

AFTER THE FOUR DAYS BATTLE, BOTH SIDES made great efforts to repair their damaged ships. In England the press-gangs made life on the coast very uneasy, sweeping up and hauling out of their homes anyone who had anything to do with boats (and some who did not), and the lack of ships and seamen threatened the collapse of London's vital waterborne supply routes. In the dockyards everybody worked feverishly, and each capital ship was dispatched to the fleet as soon as it was ready.

At the beginning of August 1666 the English fleet was again at sea, where the Dutch were waiting. Each side had about fifty-nine ships of the line. The English command was divided between George Monck, the Duke of Albemarle and Prince Rupert, who between them had available at least sixteen fireships. The Dutch side was commanded by Michiel de Ruyter, who had between eighteen and twenty fireships on hand. The high numbers are an indication of the significance that each side attached to this weapon. At daybreak on August 1666 the two fleets met, and thus commenced another bitter, hard-fought battle.[1] According to the English liturgical calendar, it was St James's Day, which in English history books gave its name to the ensuing fight, although it was also known as the battle of the North Foreland, and to the Dutch as the Two Days' Battle.

At the highpoint of the struggle the opposing flagships *Royal Charles* and *Zeven Provinciën* lay about half a musket-shot apart and blazed away at each other with all guns. The thick smoke laid a dense haze over the scene and camouflaged the first attempts to use fireships. First a Dutch fireship went for the *Royal Charles*, and the English had no choice but to send one of their own fireships to counter the Dutch effort, deflecting it successfully. Later, an English fireship, the *Land of Promise*, attacked *Zeven Provinciën*, which had lost its main topmast. The crews of the Dutch small craft reacted in the time-honoured manner, attempting to board the fireship or prevent the escape of its crew, but as it came closer De Ruyter's ship opened fire on it, and a lucky shot (or 'unlucky shot' as an English observer described it) caused the *Land of Promise* to catch fire prematurely and burn out, with her crew escaping by the skin of their teeth.[2]

On the other side, a Dutch fireship managed to reduce to ashes the 58-gun *Resolution* with 300 men aboard. In this case the crew were taken off by various small vessels, and did not perish with the ship. In the further course of the battle, another English fireship attacked a heavily damaged Dutch ship of the line, which was saved only when a Dutch fireship was towed into the way of the Englishman. Another Dutch ship of the line escaped destruction by quickly dropping anchor and allowing an English fireship to be swept harmlessly past by wind and tide.

The battle lasted until darkness fell on 4 August, and then at first light the next morning the cannonade opened up once more. By afternoon the Dutch had been driven from the field and withdrawn into the shallows, behind the protection of some sandbanks. Their failure to judge accurately the size of the English fleet, and the quality of its ordnance, had led to defeat.

Both sides began with great expectations for their fireships, but as it appeared they had been too optimistic. It was not fireships but heavy artillery which had decided the battle. Many fireships had been expended without success (six alone on the English side); others had been fended off or damaged, and for the English especially, the lack of Fifth Rates had proved crucial. These had the task of escorting the fireships until they were close enough to their victim to avoid being boarded from small craft or enemy frigates and towed out of the way. The light winds had not been favourable to fireship attack, because the approach to the target took too long a time, an interval during which they were exposed to enemy gunfire, requiring the crews to remain aboard these floating bonfires and delay their escape. The inevitable consequence was that many crews made their exit too quickly.[3]

The result of the St James's Day Battle was the withdrawal of the Dutch warships which should have protected their merchantmen, and no Dutch trader now dared to leave the supposedly safe waters of the Zuiderzee or approach the coast from the open sea. The English possessed complete mastery of the Channel, albeit briefly. At first they lay unchallenged off Vlissingen (Flushing) in Zeeland, and then they moved to the north. At that moment Monck and Prince Rupert were informed by a

'Holmes's Bonfire' at its height: behind the islands of Vlie and Terschelling over a hundred ships of a large Dutch merchant convoy and its escorts burn furiously after the attack by English fireships and boat crews under the command of Sir Robert Holmes in August 1666. In the left background the village of West Terschelling is on fire, and in the foreground English boats are landing on the Vlie.

(PUBLIC DOMAIN)

treacherous Dutch captain that a big fleet of merchantmen was sheltering behind the islands of Vlieland and Terschelling, protected by a very small number of warships. It was a tempting situation, and one that if exploited would result in heavy damage to the enemy's trade.

The choice of commander for the expedition against the almost defenceless merchantmen fell on Vice Admiral Sir Robert Holmes, whose involvement in operations against Dutch shipping since the beginning of the Anglo-Dutch wars has been described in Chapter II.[4] He had a force of between 11,000 and 12,000 men, five small frigates, five fireships and a large number of ketches and boats, all capable of manoeuvring in the relatively shallow waters. On the morning of 10 August, with the help of the Dutch traitor, they sailed into the channel between Vlieland and Terschelling and got their first glimpse of the enemy merchant fleet lying at anchor with its very feeble escort. There were so many ships that it was almost impossible to count them – estimates varied from 160 to 170 – and everywhere boat-loads of the crews from the anchored vessels were to be seen in headlong flight for the land. It was an ideal situation for fireships, but first of all Holmes decided to concentrate on the escorts.

The two anchored warships were unable to resist for long. Both were attacked by English fireships. One of the fireships, the *Richard*, grappled its victim relentlessly and soon destroyed it, the captain, Henry Brown, being rewarded with £100 for his good service. The captain of the other English fireship thought he was close enough to his target to light the powder-train, but at the crucial moment he grounded on a sand-bar, just a few feet short of his target. On board the Dutchman, the fearful sight of the approaching fireship had the usual effect, and the crew fled in panic, but when they realised that the loss of the ship was not inevitable, they turned back with the intention of reboarding. On seeing this, the fireship crew bent to their oars with all their might, with such good effect that they won the race to the Dutch ship. Once on board, they readied the stern-chasers, opened fire on the Dutch, and held them off for long enough to set the ship on fire.

When the crews of the merchantmen saw that

both convoy ships were out of the fight, all thought of resistance faded and countless boats headed off towards Amsterdam. Now Holmes's remaining fireships and flotilla of small craft could set to work unhindered. The fireships were reserved for the bigger merchantmen, and naturally attacking an undefended ship did not require the same courage as attacking a warship. Nonetheless, Captain John Elliott of the fireship *Fox* received £60 as a reward, with each of his twelve-man crew receiving £10 each.[5] One after another the merchantmen went up in flames – those that had been waiting to sail together with returned East Indiamen, those from Guinea, from the Mediterranean, from Danzig and Russia, Persia and the West Indies. Their valuable cargoes were sunk with them, and Holmes felt he had 'expended his fireships very profitably'.

The next day Holmes and eleven companies of infantry went ashore on Terschelling to plunder and burn the town of West Terschelling and its warehouses. In the evening of this successful stage of the war, 'after a great and memorable action', the boats slid out with the ebb-tide between Vlieland and Terschelling, their pockets 'well lined with ducats and other rich spoil'.

The English withdrew to their own coast. They had not had enough fireships, and Prince Rupert, who felt somewhat insecure, asked for replacements, specifying 'as many fireships as may be'.

The carpenters and shipwrights were sent off to look at prizes and other suitable vessels with a view to selecting those that could be converted into fireships in the shortest order.[6]

This hugely successful expedition had inflicted immeasurable damage on the Dutch trading fleet, and went down in history as 'Holmes's Bonfire'. However, the weaknesses of the victorious British fleet became apparent all too soon: supplies ran low and the ships were forced to abandon the blockade of the Dutch coast and make for port. The defeated Dutch, on the other hand, set to work feverishly to repair their damaged ships, and by 25 August they once again had eighty-one warships and no fewer than thirteen fireships at sea. They were tasked with attacking the English in their harbours, and to keep in contact with the French fleet. This brought the English fleet of ninety-three warships and ten fireships into the arena, but in the end storms and sickness temporarily diminished the fighting spirit on both sides and there was no further confrontation that year.

Two catastrophes, unrelated to the war at sea, had brought England to a crisis situation: first the Great Plague, which in 1665 had cost the lives of about 75,000 Londoners, and then the Great Fire, which raged from 2 to 5 September 1666 and reduced four-fifths of the City of London to ashes. Naturally the Dutch saw these as retribution for what the English had done a few weeks before on Terschelling. The two disasters reduced English tax revenues so severely that the fleet was now paralysed by lack of funds.

Charles II, also under financial pressure, had probably diverted some of the money voted by Parliament for the upkeep of the fleet to other purposes. As a result, many unpaid sailors mutinied, and starving and freezing dockyard workers were thrown out of work: the fleet was in no shape to undertake the campaign season of 1667.

The capital ships, the core of the Royal Navy, were decommissioned[7] and laid up at their usual winter moorings in a section of the Medway below the dockyard at Chatham. It was a narrow, winding river, but sufficiently deep for the purpose, and easy to close off to attack – or at least so it was thought. Just a tiny squadron remained at sea, to harass the Dutch merchant fleet.

The English, anxious about the financial situation and the threat of social unrest, resumed peace negotiations, but their diplomats were arrogant and disinclined to compromise, believing that the Dutch would not deploy their fleet aggressively during the discussions. This was a mistake: in fact the Dutch, who were still able to raise money through taxation, had the resources to continue hostilities, and they decided to demonstrate their military strength to reinforce their negotiating position.[8]

Besides, they had not forgotten Holmes's Bonfire and the plundering on Terschelling, and so on 26 May 1667 Admiral de Ruyter and his fleet left their anchorage near Texel with orders to blockade the Thames estuary and make a foray into the Medway. He had available fifty warships, ten frigates and armed yachts and innumerable galliots and boats, including as many as fourteen or fifteen fireships. The number of fireships again indicated De Ruyter's high opinion of them; the conditions of the planned attack were ideal.

The English were well informed about the enemy's intentions: they knew that troops had been embarked in the ships, and that De Ruyter, with renegade pilots and watermen in his service, would have no problem in finding his way through the estuaries of the Thames and Medway. However, the defensive preparations on the English side were inadequate. Money was short, the morale of the unpaid seamen and dockyard workers was abysmal, and nobody really felt obliged to support the king.

The English understood perfectly well the threat posed by enemy fireships, the classic weapon against ships lying in confined waters. To fend them off, they installed a strong iron chain across the Medway at Gillingham, supported at intervals by pontoons so that it did not hang too deeply. They also had about thirty pinnaces and longboats, fitted with fire-poles, grapnels and chains, which would be used to tow attacking fireships clear. Two warships anchored abreast the chain, their cannon threatening any enemy vessel that might come this far upstream. This, together with some fortifications on shore, would form the only line of defence should the Dutch manage to get this far upriver. Were the boom to be broken, the vessels laid up above it would be to all intents and purposes unprotected.

On 7 June the Dutch force was in King's Channel, one of the entrances to the Thames, and here De Ruyter remained with his biggest warships. A small force of boats, armed yachts and frigates and nearly all the available fireships pressed on to the mouth of the Medway. On the 11th they took the fort at Sheerness on the Isle of Sheppey, the operation beginning with a fireship attack on an English frigate which was supporting the guns of the fort. The Dutch made a determined approach and the defenders offered little resistance, withdrawing upstream and leaving the fairway clear.

During the next day the Dutch ships worked their way slowly forward, and at the last minute George Monck, the Duke of Albemarle and Prince Rupert received orders from the king to improvise a defence. A bastion with cannon was hastily thrown together close to the chain at Gillingham, and feverish attempts were made to find vessels that could be converted to serve as fireships. Shipowners who hesitated to offer their vessels for this purpose were branded as unpatriotic scoundrels, and ships were sunk in the channel to act as barriers.

The big former flagships *Royal Charles* and *Royal James*, their rigging half-dismantled and most of their cannon removed, were to be towed further upstream as a security measure, and despite general command confusion and muddle, a large proportion of this work was accomplished. However, there were not enough men and small craft available to shift the *Royal Charles*.

On Wednesday 12 June the Dutch force, consisting of two warships and five or six fireships, pressed forward and reached the town of Gillingham and its chain. The fairway is narrow at this point, and the ships had to approach in single line ahead, which restricted the field of fire of their guns. As they advanced on the chain, they were exposed to fire from the shore and the anchored English warships, and were forced to halt. It was a critical moment, and the question for the Dutch was whether it was best to back off or go all out for victory. Was there a daredevil captain and crew who would risk the hail of bullets and shot and proceed against the chain and the guardships?

Now arrived the moment of glory for Captain Jan van Brakel (1618–1690), whose exploits were briefly covered in Chapter 9. He came from a military and naval family; his father, Pieter van Brakel, had commanded a convoy escort in the Mediterranean and been killed by English round-shot in December 1664, just before the declaration of hostilities that began the Second Anglo-Dutch War.[9] Now he had advanced to the rank of captain,

De Ruyter's warships in the river Medway: oil by Willem Schellings, *c*1667. This view is from the Dutch perspective, looking upriver from roughly Sheerness to Upnor Castle (upper right, surrounded by gunfire and burning ships in the river), with the spire of Rochester Cathedral in the middle distance. Following a convention of the time, the painting combines events which were actually separated in time. To the left side of the panorama are the blockships sunk to impede the progress of the Dutch; they are lying just below the great chain barrier, which the Dutch broke through. To the right of the burning ships, in the centre of the picture, lies the English flagship *Royal Charles*, which could not be moved upriver to safety in time. The ship was captured by the Dutch and taken downriver to the Netherlands in triumph.

(RIJKSMUSEUM AMSTERDAM, SK-A-1393)

commanding the *Vrede*, a 40-gun ship crewed by 125 men. His reputation for aggression had accelerated his promotion, but at this particular moment he was in disgrace. After the capture of the fort at Sheerness, his crew had engaged in some looting, disobeying De Ruyter's orders. This breach of discipline had resulted in Van Brakel being put under arrest, and now to redeem themselves he and the crew of the *Vrede* volunteered for the dan-

gerous task of attacking the chain and the guardships. Admiral Willem Joseph van Ghent, commander of the Medway squadron, accepted the offer, and a furious struggle began.

Followed by two fireships, the *Vrede* sailed imperturbably up the narrow fairway, avoiding the ships sunk in the channel by the English and coming under heavy fire from the land batteries on either bank and from the guardships. Van Brakel held his fire, until he was within musket-shot (140–180 metres) of the English ship *Unity*, which was just downstream of the chain. First he let loose a broadside, and then almost immediately boarded the Englishman, whose crew took to their heels. In defence of the honour of the Royal Navy it has to be pointed out that the *Unity*'s crew consisted almost entirely of poorly motivated Thames watermen who had been brought in haste from London, as an experienced naval crew had not been available.

One of the fireships sailed over the barrier, but was unable to break the chain, and then unintentionally burst into flames and burned out without influencing events further. The second, the somewhat bigger and heavier *Pro Patria*, rammed the chain and managed to break it; then, firing the powder-train, she grappled the second English guardship, the *Matthias* of 52 guns, and successfully ignited it. This fire could not be extinguished and burned until the ship exploded. A third fireship, the *Delft*, made for another English ship, the 54-gun *Charles V*, but was sunk by a cannonade from the intended victim. However, she was attacked by one more fireship, and at the same time Van Brakel came alongside and boarded the ship with a handful of men. That was too much for her crew, who fled in boats or jumped overboard. As a result of this deed Van Brakel became a famous man; he was rewarded with a gold chain and honoured with a commemorative medal, besides being given command of a big ship of the line. In addition, he was awarded 12,000 guilders as prize money for the captured *Unity*.[10] He would go on to play a starring role in the history of fireship warfare.

On the English side, George Monck lamented in his report on the calamity: '... if we had had but five or six Boats, to cut off the boats of the fireship, we had prevented the burning of these ships'.[11] The way upstream was now clear, and the Dutch easily reached the *Royal Charles*, which was half-rigged with only a few of her guns on board. This uniquely famous ship of almost 1,229 tons, pierced for 100 guns, had been put into service by Cromwell as the *Naseby*, and then following the Restoration renamed the *Royal Charles*.[12] Now she was boarded unchallenged by a few Dutch sailors, who set about making her ready for towing down the river to the

coast. After that she would be sailed across the Channel and brought home in triumph to the Netherlands.

On 13 June the Dutch overpowered the forts on shore and moved further upriver with a favourable wind and tide. The crews of a number of the ships which had originally sheltered behind the boom now saw that there was no chance of saving them, so they were unmoored and allowed to run ashore on the banks of the Medway. Their bottom planks were smashed and they settled down in the mud, the pride of the Royal Navy sinking with them: in all there were sixteen ships, among them such famous names as *Royal Oak*, *Royal James* and *Loyal London*. Only a few terrified soldiers, who had been hurriedly deployed, remained to protect the remains of this once-splendid fleet.

In this situation the attacker needed more fireships, and De Ruyter sailed up the Medway with five new ones. With a vanguard of frigates and yachts shooting their way up the river, the ships advanced upstream under heavy fire from shore batteries. Fireships were towed over with boats and attached to each of the big ships of the line. De Ruyter could not spare a second fireship for any ship that did not catch fire properly, so not all the potential targets were burned, but, even so, by two in the afternoon, on this most bitter day for the English, three of their largest ships were entirely destroyed. Everything was enveloped in smoke and haze from the burning ships, and the normally peaceful Medway was like a scene from Hell, with countless ships and boats on the river, the interminable thunder of cannon-fire, the rattle of musketry and the yells of triumph from the ship and boat crews.

Late in the afternoon of 14 June De Ruyter broke off the attack. All but two of his fireships had been expended, and ten Dutch fireship captains would be able to claim premiums of at least 5,000 to 6,000 guilders.[13] The fleet withdrew downriver, with *Royal Charles* and *Unity* as prizes. But further humiliation was in store for the English. On 2 August, just as the Dutch main force was heading for home, Admiral Aert Janszoon van Nes (1626–1693) entered the Thames with five frigates and twelve fireships. The Thames was an ideal location for using fireships, because the limited manoeuvring room in the navigational channels made it difficult to dodge

The Dutch in the Medway: the English perspective, looking downriver from Rochester. Again events from different days are conflated, with the beached *Royal Oak*, *Royal James* and *Loyal London* on fire at Upnor, while other ships are seen on fire around the boom at Gillingham.

(BEVERLEY R ROBINSON COLLECTION, ANNAPOLIS)

The estuary of the Medway and the Thames, after a sketch by Samuel Pepys's friend and fellow diarist John Evelyn. In 1667 Charles II had laid up his capital ships in the Medway, just below Chatham, on account of shortage of funds, and in June they became the target of an attack by a Dutch fleet under Admiral de Ruyter. About fifteen fireships were involved in this successful raid. This plan shows the chain barriers in the Medway, just below Gillingham. Shortly afterwards, in the northern entrance to the Thames estuary, the Dutch admiral Aert van Nes led his squadron consisting mainly of fireships in an assault on Gravesend, where they engaged numerous English fireships. In the ensuing battle it was fireship against fireship.

(FROM: DE JONGE 1858–62)

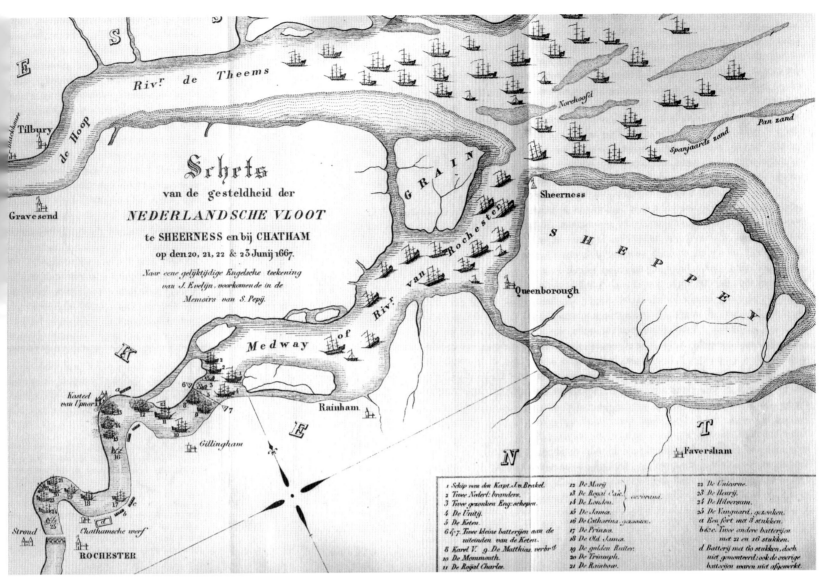

Schets van de gesteldheid der NEDERLANDSCHE VLOOT te SHEERNESS en bij CHATHAM op den 20, 21, 22 & 23 Junij 1667.

Naar eene gelijktijdige Engelsche teekening van J. Eveljin, voorkomende in de Memoirs van S. Pepij.

1 Schip van den Kapt. J. v. Brakel.	12 De Marij.	22 De Unicorne.
2 Twee Nederl: branders.	13 De Royal Oak, verbrand.	23 De Heurij.
3 Twee gezonken Eng: schepen.	14 De London.	24 De Hilversum.
4 De Unitij.	15 De James.	25 De Vanguard, gezonken.
5 De Keten.	16 De Catharina, gezonken.	a Een fort met 8 stukken.
6 & 7 Twee kleine batterijen aan de	17 De Prinses.	b & c Twee andere batterijen
uiteinden van de Keten.	18 De Old James.	met 21 en 16 stukken.
8 Karel V. 9 De Matthias, verbrd	19 De golden Ruiter.	d Batterij met 60 stukken, doch
10 De Monmouth.	20 De Triumph.	niet gemonteerd; ook de overige
11 De Royal Charles.	21 De Rainbow.	batterijen waren niet afgewerkt.

Afbeeldingh van de STADT en REVIER van ROCHESTER, CHETHAM, etc. Aerdigh na 't leven geteeckent door W. Schellinks van de Zuydt-West Syde, waer in klaer vertoont wert de Victorieuse Uytwerckingh van de Oorlochs vloot der Hooghmogende de H.r Staten Generael der Vereenighde Nederlanden voorgevallen op den 19, 20, 21, 22, en 23 Iunii A°. 1667. uytgegeven by J. Ottens tot Amsterdam.

an oncoming attacker,[14] but Van Nes, who had his eye on Gravesend, had run into a squadron of five frigates and seventeen fireships commanded by Admiral Sir Edward Spragge (*c*1629–1673), and these now lay at anchor blocking the way.

Although the relatively minor skirmish that followed is unimportant in the broad sweep of maritime history, it may be considered the zenith of fireship warfare. On both sides there were more fireships than conventional warships. The self-confident Van Nes, known to his countrymen as 'the second De Ruyter', sent eight fireships against the enemy. These refused battle, cut their cables and withdrew to the protection of the heavy guns on Spragge's flagship. But in the narrow waters of the Thames they could retreat no further, and had to turn and fight. Four English fireships were sent to attack those of the Dutch, and as the whole lot went up in flames, it looked as if the river itself was on fire. Seven more English fireships fell victim to Dutch cannon-fire and either sank or were prematurely ignited and abandoned by their own crews, forcing Spragge to withdraw and seek shelter under the guns of Gravesend. Then the wind dropped and no one could manoeuvre.

Van Nes, who had already spent eleven of his twelve fireships, felt that he had been robbed of his most valuable weapon and began an orderly retreat towards the mouth of the Thames.[15] There he anchored and, expecting a counter-attack from Spragge's fireships, adopted a fresh defensive measure. His ships anchored with a spring – that is to say, they secured a hawser to the cable – or else dropped a second anchor from the stern, so that when attacked, by veering and hauling on the two cables, they would be able to turn and take evasive action as the fireship made its approach.[16] In this way the frigate *Harderwijk* under Captain Nicolaas Naelhoudt successfully evaded an attack. However, the task required considerable cool-headedness, and not everyone kept his head: seventy sailors from the *Harderwijk* leaped overboard, uncertain that the expedient would succeed. Another anchored Dutch ship used its rudder to sheer aside, allowing the fireship to sweep harmlessly past. An ad hoc method of dealing with a fireship is described by an anonymous eyewitness of this event. A Dutch vessel had an English fireship across

Another representation of De Ruyter's fleet in the Thames estuary in 1667. The artist, Pieter van de Velde, strove for a realistic depiction of the Dutch fireships, which are correctly shown as small flutes (or flyboats as the English termed them). The internal glow shining through the sally-port and the rudder aperture is an authentic touch. However, in the middle of the picture, the portrait of the three-decker *Royal Charles* – the greatest prize of the expedition – is far less accurate, which is surprising since the ship could have been inspected by any Dutch artist until she was broken up in 1673.

(RIJKSMUSEUM AMSTERDAM, SK-A-307)

its bow, and a boat crew sent to tow it clear had to give up when the towrope burned through. Another was hastily improvised from the chain of a cooking-pot which hung in the ship's galley (this was apparently the only available chain on board). It was made fast to the fireship and used by the boat crew to pull the fireship clear at the last possible moment.[17]

The attacking English fireships either burned out uselessly or drove between the anchored Dutchmen. Sir Edward Spragge had expected great

Aert van Nes (1626–1693), Admiral of Holland and Westfriesland, gained his experience during the First and Second Anglo-Dutch Wars, and rose to be De Ruyter's deputy. After the latter's raid on Chatham in June 1667, Van Nes led a squadron of five frigates and twelve fireships deep into the Thames estuary. His target was the town of Gravesend, but he ran into a squadron under the command of Admiral Sir Edward Spragge (c1629–1673), who had five frigates and seventeen fireships at his disposal. The battle that followed may be considered the zenith of fireship warfare: it was fireship against fireship. As so often, the weapon proved a disappointment, and in the end each of the opposing squadrons had to withdraw, with neither side having scored a decisive victory.

(FROM: DE JONGE 1858–62)

A ship anchored with a spring on the cable. This illustration from Röding shows a ship at anchor with a line (a–a) led from aft and secured to the anchor cable (b). If the spring is hauled in with a tackle or capstan, it causes the pull of the anchor cable to be applied further aft, and thus allows the ship to turn on its anchor like a weather-vane. This method was more commonly used to allow an anchored vessel to bring its broadside to bear more favourably on a target, but it is clear how it would also allow a vessel anchored in the stream to swing itself clear of a fireship bearing down on it.

(FROM: RÖDING 1793)

success with his fireships, but at least ten of them were expended in vain without having inflicted the least damage on the Dutch invaders. Several of his commanders had set off their fuzes too early in an effort to guarantee their escape,[18] an error which in the eyes of the commanding officer demanded harsh disciplinary measures. One of the fireship captains was condemned to death by a court-martial, the sentence being carried out two weeks later, and three more were dishonourably discharged from the service.[19] The ritual that attended this penalty has been described in Chapter 9.

The Dutch victory in the Thames estuary forced the English negotiators to take a much more conciliatory line. The two sides, exhausted by this brutal war of attrition, signed the Treaty of Breda on 31 July. Despite the gigantic expenditure of men and material, and the human suffering, death and material loss they had endured, the terms of the agreement were quite restrained. The English, despite all their victories, agreed to moderation in enforcing the Navigation Acts, and Dutch and German goods would now be allowed into English ports aboard Dutch ships. On the other hand, they came to an understanding with the Dutch about their colonial possessions, and that led, among other things, to the English keeping the territory they had captured on the island of Manhattan, including Nieuw Amsterdam, which was henceforth called New York.

A Dutch frigate of the second half of the seventeenth century – like the *Harderwijk*, which evaded Spragge's fireship attack. Ships of this size were used to a more active role in fireship warfare. They were employed in the defence of capital ships by counter-attacking fireships; by using their boats to tow the fireship off course; and by threatening the enemy's escape-boats, in the hope that they would abandon the fireship too soon to hit the target. In offence, they escorted the fireship as closely as possible and then rescued its crew.

(DRAWING: AUTHOR AFTER WILLEM VAN DE VELDE THE YOUNGER)

CHAPTER FOURTEEN

COUNTERMEASURES:
CHANGING TACTICS AND
FIRESHIP WARFARE

'It is necessary that the manoeuvre to approach and grapple the enemy is made with much coolness, intelligence, commitment and speed.'

Diderot and d'Alembert, *Encyclopédie méthodique*, 1803

THE EXPERIENCES OF THE SECOND Anglo-Dutch War had shown very clearly the uncertain worth of the fireship. A trusty, reliable weapon it was not. The English had expended six of them in one battle, without a single success,[1] and in fact the history of sea warfare contains far more fireship failures than victories. Most of them were simply expended in vain, because the ideal conditions for an attack were many and various, and rarely occurred at the same time and in the same place. Of overriding importance was the position of the fleets in relation to the wind. In reality, fireships could only be deployed down-wind, so the commander not holding the weather gage (that is to say, not being to windward of his opponent) could not use his fireships. The struggle to attain this favourable position was largely responsible for the lengthy and wearisome manoeuvring prior to a seventeenth-century battle. Even with the advantage of the weather gage, there were few instances, if any, where a fireship destroyed an undamaged vessel that was capable of manoeuvring and defending itself. The classic victim was a ship at anchor in a roadstead, river or port; or during a battle, one straggling behind a fleet, with masts and rigging shot away and no longer able to depend on the support of its fellows.

As the Four Days' Battle demonstrated, the fireship's value lay not just in its potential for total destruction but in its ability to cause panic and disorder. The history of the fireship is largely the story of the terror it could induce. Often the threat posed by an approaching fireship was more psychological than real, but as late as the nineteenth century the fear engendered by a fireship could cause the total breakdown of discipline in a fleet.

This was something known and understood by all who used fireships. In 1652 Admiral Maarten Harpertszoon Tromp wrote in a letter to the Estates-General that fireships 'are very urgently needed in the fleet, the more especially as the English are so afraid of them that they will never lie at anchor with their fleet where they can come at them'.[2] Jean Baptiste Colbert (1619–1683), Louis XIV's Minister of the Marine, held even more extreme views:

consider firstly if it would not greatly strengthen the maritime forces of His Majesty for each ship of the line, if possible, to have one or two fireships that would serve so to speak to protect it and which would prove, to my mind, a great terror to the English. It seems to me that twenty good vessels, each accompanied by two fireships, would be better than forty large vessels.[3]

If Colbert's ideas had been followed literally, his men-of-war would have been impossible to see for all the fireships, but in practice each flagship had one or two fireships 'of its own'. The Dutch called them 'bijstanders', that is to say vessels that 'stood by' the flagship, and their captains were always specially picked for their reliability. With the flagship leading the attack and always in the thick of the action, the threat of fireships close at hand might keep the most aggressive enemy at a prudent distance. They could also prove useful in defence, fending off the enemy's own fireships, as occurred in the Four Days' Battle.

The terror that fireships induced was a manifestation of the seaman's deeply ingrained fear of fire aboard ship. It needed very little imagination for any sailor to comprehend that the edifice aboard which he lived and laboured was potentially a huge bonfire. Apart from its seasoned timber structure, it was stocked with inflammable materials: in every seam there was pitch and oakum, and above him fathoms of tarred rope and canvas sails, all of which would burn like a torch; below decks were dozens of powder-kegs, which would blow sky-high with the least spark. All in all, even a small fire could result in a catastrophe.

This fear was reflected in the very strict fire precautions observed aboard ship. There was a prohibition against open fires or lights except in a few protected locations. Smoking was not allowed below deck, only on the forecastle or on the upper deck, with a water-filled tub close by, and only when the 'smoking lantern' was lit. Candles had to be enclosed in a lantern, and not in an open candle-stick. After prayers at night, lights were forbidden, other than the lanterns carried by officers making the rounds, and these were kept in a single place so that they could always be accounted

DE L'ORDRE DE BATAILLE.

Les Vaiseaux, combattent par les cotés, parce que leur artillerie y est egalement partagée, et se tiennent dessous voiles afin d'avoir le mouvement necessaire pour agir, dans le combat, leur ordre de Bataille, se forme, sur une des lignes A B, ou C D, dont on verra la definition, dans la planche suivante; la distance qu'on laisse entre chaque V.ᵃᵘ depend de la force du vent, et de l'étendüe que le General juge necessaire de donner a l'armée, pour combattre avec plus d'avantage. On peut voir a ce sujet la planche 49

Les fregates E, marchent a portée de recevoir les ordres qu'on peut leur donner. Les brulots, sont en dehors des fregates a une grande portée de canon; des V.ᵃᵘˣ les batimᵗˢ de charge, marchent en dehors des brulots. On est dans l'usage, de nommer avant. garde, les cadre qui marche a la tête de la ligne, et ariere garde, celle qui forme la queüe, s'il y a une 3ᵉᵐᵉ division, on nomme celle du centre, Corps de Bataille, c'est la place du Gén.ᵃˡ quand la disposition de l'en.ᵐⁱ ou des raisons particulieres, ne l'obligent point de se placer ailleurs. Les V.ᵃᵘˣ a, b, c, representent les 3. divisions de l'arm.ᵉᵉ on combat aussi par Escadres, c'est a dire, que les divisiᵒⁿˢ agissent chaquune de leurs cotés, ce genre de combat est plus vif que le 1.ᵉʳ parce que les petits corps ont plus d'activᵗᵉ que les grᵈˢ et peuvent serrer da= vantage l'enne.ᵐⁱ mais une fois l'action engagée il est tres difficile de se reunir.

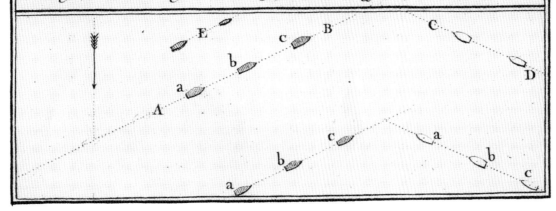

By the end of the seventeenth century the line of battle had become the conventional formation for warships during a fleet engagement, and in most cases the obligatory one. The opposing ships of the line sailed in two lines, each in the wake of the one ahead. Nicolas Ozanne in his treatise *Marine Militaire* of 1762 illustrates how this would have looked to an observer (ignoring the coastal landscape in the foreground, which would be an unusual scenario for a fleet battle). The line formation complicated the conditions for a fireship attack. The frigates, which are designated E in the lower part of the picture, were stationed on the disengaged side, and even further from the line, where they were unlikely to be hit by stray cannon-shot, were the fireships. For a successful attack perfect co-operation between frigates, small craft and the fireship was necessary if the latter was to reach its target intact. It is small wonder that after the introduction of the line, successful fireship attacks on the high seas became ever rarer.

(FROM: OZANNE 1762, PLATE 25)

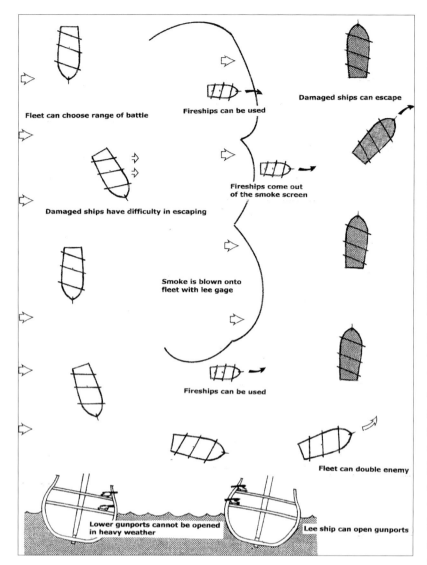

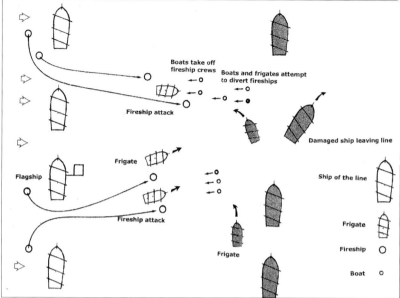

THE IMPORTANCE OF
THE WEATHER GAGE,
PARTICULARLY AS
APPLIED TO FIRESHIPS
After the introduction of line-
of-battle tactics, the advantage
of the weather gage was
considered paramount by
aggressive admirals, who might
spend days manoeuvring to
obtain this position before
giving battle. If properly
formed, the line resisted easy
penetration, so the mêlée
developed less frequently, which
itself diminished the
opportunities for fireship
attacks. In the leeward line, the
prime target – damaged and
unmanoeuvrable ships – tended
to be protected by falling away
behind their line, beyond the
reach of fireships. In the
weather line, damaged ships
tended to drift towards the
enemy, but the fireships of the
leeward fleet could not work up
to windward to attack them.

(DRAWING: AUTHOR)

for. Only in an officer's cabin was a lantern permitted, and even then only by permission of the
captain or master of the vessel.[4] The importance
that De Ruyter attached to fire precautions can be
seen in a list of orders he issued to his captains
in March 1676. Although the text is quite short,
there is a detailed section on avoidance of fire.
During a battle, particular attention was to be paid
to dealing with burning wads (either from one's
own or enemy fire) which landed on deck. They
were to be extinguished expeditiously with swabs
and buckets kept ready for that purpose.[5]

If a ship caught fire in battle, it was a matter of
urgency for a fire-fighting party, swinging axes and
crowbars, to smash through decks or bulkheads to
get at the source of the fire. Open gunports
increased the draught, fanning the fire, so ports,
hatches and companionways were closed off. If the

fire was confined to one side, if necessary the ship
would go about to bring the blaze on to the lee side,
which would direct it away and prevent it from
spreading. Flames were beaten out with clothes
and caps, and human chains passed water buckets or other containers from their normal stations.
Casks sawn in half, cans, pots and so forth had to
be within easy reach; even a boat stowed on deck
could contain water. The crew also had to reckon
with the enemy pouring tar-pots or firing other
inflammable or incendiary material on to the deck,
and for these tubs were kept ready filled with urine
or vinegar (which was thought to be particularly
effective in extinguishing fires that otherwise could
not be put out).[6] Fresh hides, if available, were kept
in readiness, and could be hung in vulnerable
places.

The one thing that ships do not seem to have
had – at least not during the Anglo-Dutch Wars –
was a pump that could spray water under pressure,
although there are a few later references to 'fire-
engines' on board ship. This is curious, since a
portable fire-fighting force pump, using lengths of
leather hose which could be coupled together, was
developed by a Dutchman, Jan van der Heyden
(1637–1712), in 1672. A pump of this type is illustrated
in Diderot and d'Alembert's *Encyclopédie méthodique*.

For centuries the approach of a burning fireship
would have prompted the officers and crew to at
least consider the question: surrender or die? The
mere threat of a fireship was occasionally enough

THE TACTICS OF
FIRESHIP WARFARE
From the second half of the
seventeenth century, line
tactics brought fireship
attacks in fleet battles ever
closer to suicide missions.
For a fireship to have any
chance of success, from the
moment it emerged from
behind the line it had to co-
operate closely with the
small craft and frigates that
escorted it towards the
enemy and offered covering
fire. The minute the enemy
realised that they were
dealing with a fireship, they
would concentrate their fire
on it; and they would also
launch their own counter-
attack with small craft. The
last time a fireship attacked
an enemy ship of the line at
sea was probably during the
battle of Toulon in 1744.

(DRAWING: AUTHOR)

regatte de 28. Canone
tane a Canone
Chabere la fait. fina

English (A), Dutch (B) and French (C) frigates from the second half of the seventeenth century. It was frigates of this type, along with small craft, that were used to set up a defensive anti-fireship screen. But frigates were also used to escort the fireship, drawing fire as it made its approach, when the fireship became the target for every enemy ship within firing range. They also had the job of rescuing the crew of the fireship as they made their escape. In defence, men in the frigates' boats would try to tow the fireship off course with grapnels, and frigates were expected to interpose themselves between an enemy fireship and their own capital ships and if possible to board the fireship.

(A, B: DRAWINGS AUTHOR AFTER WILLEM VAN DE VELDE THE YOUNGER; C: DRAWING AFTER CHABERT, JR)

to force an enemy to surrender, so it is conceivable that a commander who struck his flag in these circumstances did not run the same risk of dishonour and loss of reputation as one who failed to defend his ship to the utmost in conventional combat. There may have been a silent consensus that blindly submitting to certain and painful death was not required, so the extremity of the threat justified surrender. In the case of Sir George Ayscue, who surrendered the *Royal Prince* at the Four Days' Battle when faced with two fireships, the loss of his ship does not seem to have been held against him. There was of course an official cover-story, that he had been forced to surrender by his crew, but when he returned to England at the end of hostilities, he was received with honour by the king and continued to serve at sea as a vice admiral.[7]

From this and other incidents it seems clear that a warship commander threatened with a fireship might surrender honourably, without inevitably being branded a coward. Diderot and d'Alembert's *Encyclopédie méthodique* (1803), the inimitable collection of knowledge of the day, has this to say about fireships: 'Now that nations … no longer make war on the Turks and Moors, fireships appear to be used only as a threat … against vessels which obstinately refuse to surrender despite having no chance to save themselves.'[8] In fact, death at the hands of a fireship was by no means inevitable, provided that officers and men kept their heads and dealt with it in a disciplined and determined fashion. Even if a ship was set on fire, it would be lost only if the flames were allowed to spread out of control. As a direct contrast to the behaviour of Sir George Ayscue, the Four Days' Battle provides the example of Vice Admiral John Harman, who demonstrated that certain death could be averted by surviving not just one fireship attack but two.

The chances of resisting a fireship offensive were greatly improved by the introduction of the line of battle, with each ship sailing in the wake of the ship ahead of it.[9] It came into use gradually during the Anglo-Dutch Wars, the first clearly identifiable example being Monck's tactics at the

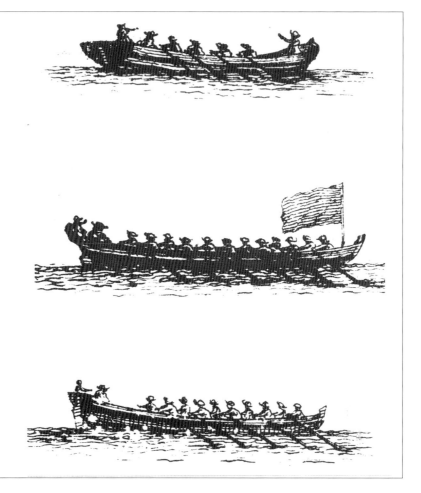

Small craft and boats played an important part in fireship warfare. Typical ships' boats of the early eighteenth century are illustrated in Blanckley's *A Naval Expositor* (published in 1750 but representing earlier practice). The launch (top) or longboat would be typical of the craft used by the fireship's crew in making their escape. Without a boat like this they were lost, and would have to break off the attack, so the enemy always tried to capture, cut away or sink the boat. The enemy would also use their own boats in defence, for instance by towing the fireship off course or boarding it. Longer, narrower and faster boats like barges (centre) or pinnaces (bottom) might be given the task of countering the enemy's own boats, and often a separate 'mosquito war' among the small craft developed within the larger battle. In normal service, barges were reserved for the use of flag officers, and pinnaces for captains.

(FROM: BLANCKLEY 1750)

VAISSEAUX EMBOSSÉS

Embosser des Vaisseaux A, *c'est les amarer (bb) près l'un de l'autre, dans le dessein d'empêcher l'ennemi de passer entre eux, pour forcer l'endroit qu'ils défendent; on embosse ordinairement les Vaisseaux, par des ancres jettées à l'avant et à l'ariere, ou par des amarages etablies à terre; mais si les courants, ou d'autres raisons, ne permettent pas d'embosser les Vaisseaux dans le passage, comme ici; on les amare, selon la disposition du lieu, sur les cotés* B, C, *d'où ils puissent canoner l'ennemi avec avantage, s'il tentoit de passer; on profite selon les occurrences, des postes avancés* D, *pour y cacher des brulots, que l'on tient toujours prets à agir, lorsque l'occasion le demande: on place encore pendant la nuit, des Chaloupes bien armées, en dehors des Vaisseaux, pour les garentir des brulots que l'ennemi pourroit envoier.*

This plate from Nicolas Ozanne's treatise *Marine Militaire* of 1762 shows how fireships could be utilised as a defensive weapon. Several ships are lying close together at anchor in a bay, forming an unbreachable line. At a distance lies the concealed protective fireship (D), which is held ready to counter-attack should an enemy approach from the open sea.

(FROM: OZANNE 1762, PLATE 42)

battle of the Gabbard in 1653, and was adopted by the Dutch within a few years. Prior to its introduction, the ships clustered round the admiral, and the idea was to get as close to any enemy ship as possible, and destroy it by gunfire or take by boarding in a general mêlée. The ideal situation was across the bow or stern of an enemy, firing a broadside into vulnerable parts of the ship where few guns could fire in retaliation.

The old style of fighting was often like a slow-motion cavalry charge, whereas the new tactics presented the enemy with something more akin to a solid wall of infantry. By forming into a line, the ships could fire broadsides without danger of hitting other ships of their own fleet, and could support one another, making it difficult for an enemy to get in a position to rake. Mutual support made for more cohesion, and a properly formed line was a difficult formation to break up. The admiral was now in the centre, supported by ships ahead and astern of him, which gave him more control. However, individual ships were no longer free to seek out opponents, which placed smaller ships at a disadvantage because they might find themselves facing a far more powerful ship. Over time this drove the lower rates out of the main battle, restricting the concept of the 'ship of the line' to the largest vessels (the term 'line of battle ship' was later shortened to the modern 'battleship'). Frigates, smaller craft and fireships now kept to the disengaged side, although the fireships remained close to the admiral, ready to attack when ordered.[10]

This imposed a degree of unaccustomed discipline on captains, who were no longer expected to demonstrate individual enterprise and aggression; on the contrary, they had to maintain the line and abide by the admiral's overall battle plan or follow his subsequent signals. With ships of varying size and sailing qualities, the line was a more difficult formation to achieve and preserve than it might be thought. De Ruyter thought it necessary to train his captains in forming a line of battle, at a time when such exercises were unusual in the extreme. However, training of this sort was invaluable because many of the ships were commanded by 'gentlemen' rather than true seamen with a lifetime's experience of ship-handling. The heavy

ships were difficult to manoeuvre, even in ideal conditions, and it could take a long time – sometimes days – before a fleet that stretched out for miles could form a line. At the same time the commander-in-chief would be struggling for the all-important weather gage, which would give him the initiative in the coming battle, and during this formative phase individual ships remained vulnerable.

Although these ideal lines of battle were aspired to, refined and formalised over the next 150 years, they were seldom achieved. The theoretical basis for the order of battle had been laid out and explained by the French Jesuit mathematician Paul Hoste (1652–1700) in a treatise published in 1697 and was subsequently adopted by the captains of all the nations involved in sea warfare. Ideally, to maximise its effectiveness, the line was made up of ships of roughly similar armament, distributing firepower uniformly along its whole length to avoid weak points. Independent action by squadrons, which would entail leaving the line, was forbid-

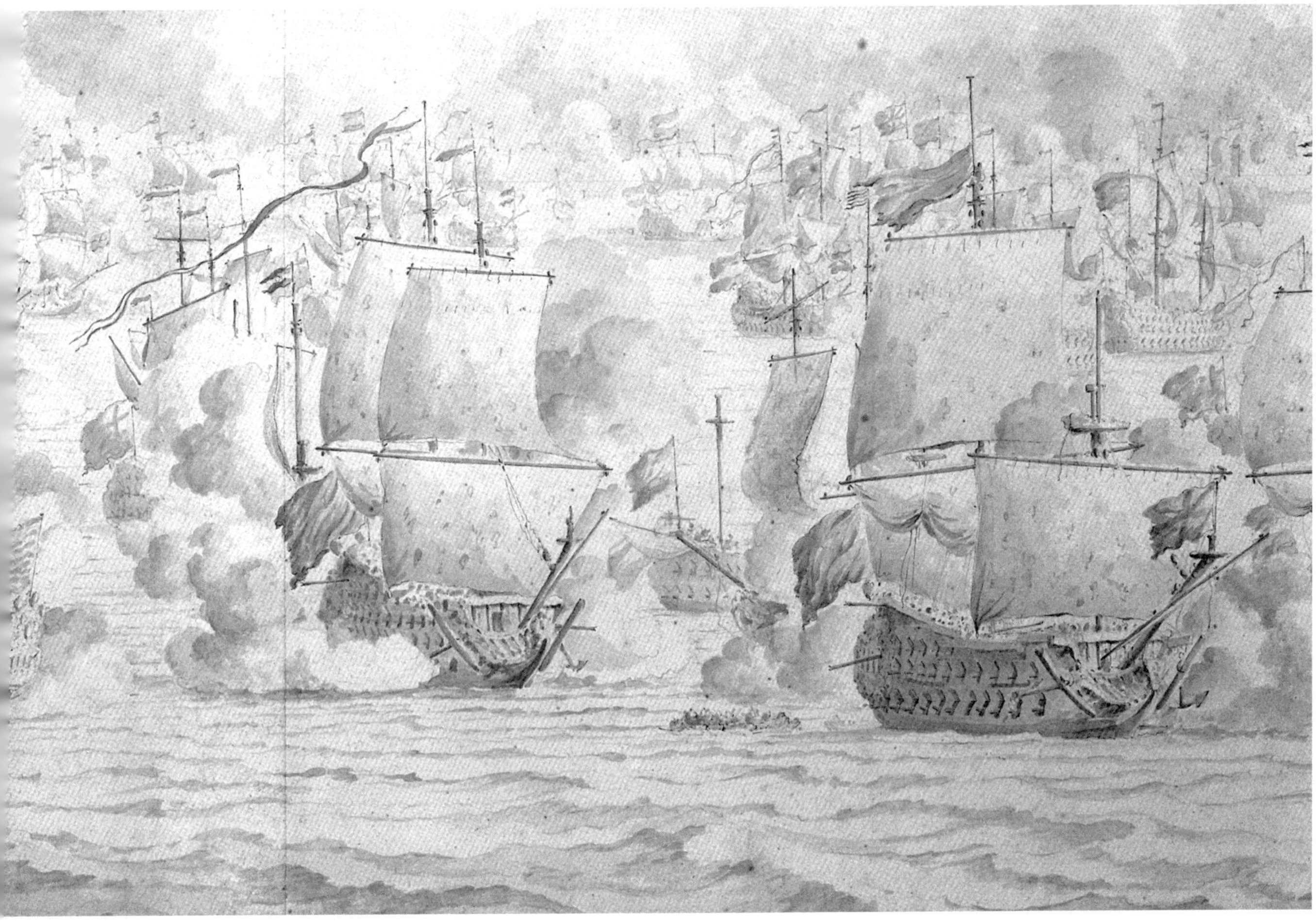

Typical of the Van de Veldes' obsession with accurate detail, this drawing of the battle of the Texel (1673) by Willem van de Velde the Elder shows a number of fire-booms deployed by English warships as the standard defence against fireships. In the right foreground the *St George* has two on her lee quarter, while in the left foreground the *Royal Prince* has two stepped on the poop, and two right forward protruding from middle-deck gunports, with another just visible on the lee bow. Fire-booms were about the length of the lower studdingsail booms, and were fitted at one end with an iron fork and at the other with an iron hook.

(NATIONAL MARITIME MUSEUM PT2525)

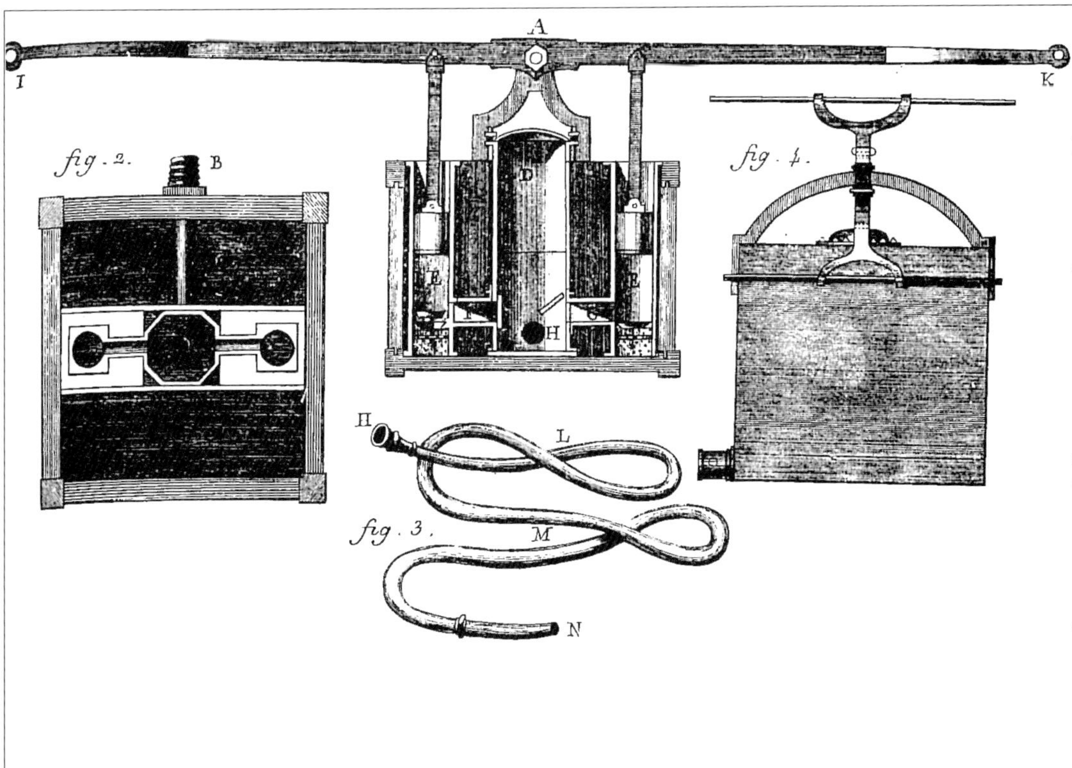

Although the evidence for their use in battle is scant, pumps suitable for fire fighting did exist from the late seventeenth century. In 1672, during the heyday of the fireship, Jan van der Heyden of Amsterdam manufactured the first modern fire-fighting pump, similar in principle to that shown here (from Diderot and d'Alembert's *Encyclopédie méthodique*). It was fitted with a leather hose, and its cistern was kept filled by buckets. A more sophisticated version, a combination suction- and force-pump, which was more practical for shipboard use, was developed later. Such fire-engines were certainly carried in both English and Dutch East Indiamen. One example was recovered from the *Hollandia*, which sank in 1743.

(BY COURTESY OF JOEL SANBORN)

den, so it now became difficult for divisions of the fleet to mass fire on a particular part of an enemy fleet or individual ship. Even breaking the enemy line was prohibited except in very special circumstances.[11]

Holding the weather gage now became an even greater advantage. From the windward position, the smoke of battle rolled towards the enemy, allowing signals flown from the flagship to be seen more easily. The admiral thus had a better chance to control his ships through signals referring to the *Fighting Instructions*. And, of course, it also allowed him to send fireships in to attack if he judged the situation favourable. However, the lee gage also had some advantages. As a ship heeled to the wind, the lower gunports were raised from the water level, allowing the use of the most powerful guns in the lower battery even when the sea was rough enough to prevent the enemy doing likewise. A severely damaged ship could drop out to leeward of the line, the ships ahead and astern closing the gap and reducing the risk of the lame duck being finished off by a fireship. But by the same token, from the leeward position it was difficult to launch an effective fireship attack of one's own.

The smaller ships, frigates, fireships and boats were now deployed on the disengaged side of the line, under the protection of the battleships, and it became harder for the enemy to pick out the fireships. They became recognisable only as they dodged out from behind the line and emerged from the powder-smoke, already on course for their targets. When this happened, the enemy ceased firing at the big ships, and the line formation allowed many ships to turn their guns on the fireship. For this reason the introduction of line tactics made the task of the fireship crew more of a suicide mission than it had been before. On the other hand, the warships of the line-of-battle era were more powerful than their predecessors, with an unprecedented weight of broadside, so the close-quarter artillery duels increased the chances of crippling individual enemy ships. Disabled vessels, incapable of manoeuvring or unable to keep up with the fleet, increased the potential targets for fireships.[12]

Line tactics meant new doctrine for the employment of fireships and the orders and instructions that formalised it. Admiral Cornelis Evertsen issued

a Fleet Order in 1688 in which he laid out the duties of a fireship backing up the line, and did not hesitate to describe the corporal punishment which would result from failure to follow orders.[13] Detailed instructions were also written about a century later by Admiral Lord Howe (1726–1799), a zealous proponent of the fireship. By this time, the role of the fireship had shrunk considerably, but it is clear that when battles were to be fought in line some sort of special instructions were needed for the use of fireships.[14]

By the end of the seventeenth century, a fireship attack was less of a risky individualistic effort and more of a co-ordinated operation involving several different vessels. Now it was not just the fireship that made the attack, but also the supporting frigates and the boats of the surrounding warships which had been detailed for fireship duty. Often the fireships and their supporting forces fought an almost separate battle, outside that in which the big ships were engaged.

In preparation, when battle was imminent, the ship's boats were put in the water on the disengaged side, armed and manned. They had manifold tasks: to come to the aid of a warship if it was threatened by an enemy fireship; to support their own fireship in making a strike or when its crew were making their escape; and to engage the enemy boats so as to prevent them carrying out similar tasks. The presence of a flotilla of such vessels in the water could dramatically influence the success or failure of the fireship. Men equipped with grappling-irons and chains could hook on to the fireship and push or tow it off its course and clear of its target. Even more risky, men could scramble on board the fireship, reach the tiller, and alter its course. Witsen (1690) suggested this expedient as the most useful of countermeasures, but it required someone with nerves of steel to manage it. [15] Alternatively, the men might be able to cut away or sink the escape-boat. A crew who could not escape were unlikely to fire their own vessel. Likewise, small craft could discourage the attempts of other boats to throw the fireship off course, and support the fireship crew as they made their escape.

The light frigates also had several tasks. If an enemy fireship approached a large warship, they were to engage it and, if it was not already on fire,

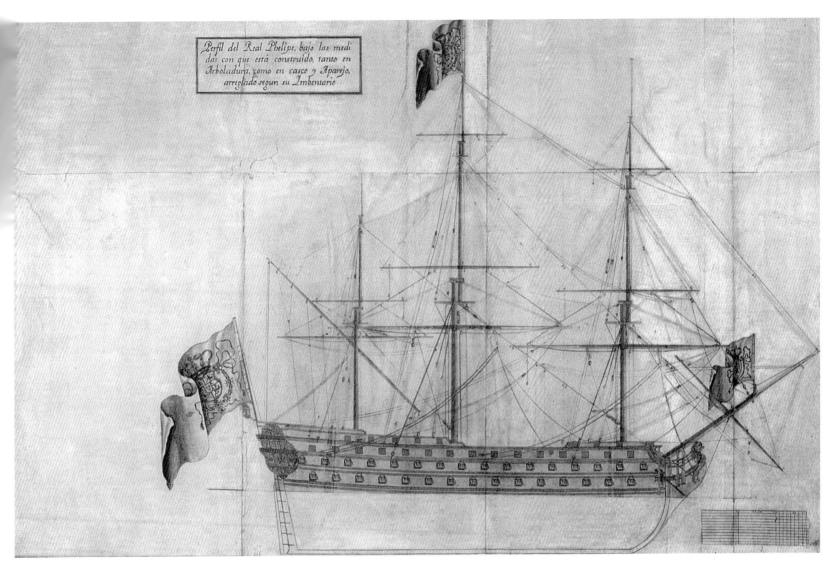

Perfil del Real Phelipe, başo las medi
das con que esta construido, tanto en
Arboladura, como en casco y Aparejo,
arreglado segun su Imbentario

prevent this from happening by boarding or fending it off. Likewise, they accompanied their own fireships as they set course for the enemy, offering covering fire and protecting them against boarding. If the fireship successfully grappled its victim, and captain and crew made their escape, it was the frigate's job to pick them up.[16] In the 1690s the English even designed a special class of oared vessel that they called a brigantine, whose principal role was 'to attend the fleet for towing off ships and cutting off fireships in battles'. This specification encompassed both defensive use – towing damaged ships out of the paths of fireships – and the offensive interception of fireships, where they would act in concert with the frigates and boats.[17]

When the admiral gave the signal to prepare for battle, it applied equally to the fireships. Boarding-grapnels and chains were got up and grappling-hooks secured at the yardarms. Once the enemy were in sight, and there was a stronger possibility of an engagement, the crew had to ready everything and 'arm' the fireship. When all was ready, the captain ran up a signal to so inform the admiral. At the time of Lord Howe, in 1778, the signal was a red flag at the maintop. If it were seen, the fireship might well attract enemy fire, but the line of battle offered the advantage that the armed and ready fireship, kept abreast the admiral on the disengaged side, remained more or less invisible to the enemy except through the short intervals between the big ships.

An order by the admiral for a fireship was promptly acknowledged, and the fireship, obscured by gunsmoke and covered by fire from neighbouring ships, broke out of the line and headed for its victim. This was the most dangerous phase of

The Spanish three-decker *Real Felipe*, a colossus of 114 guns built in 1732, was the target of a fireship attack at the battle of Toulon (also known as the battle of Cap Sicié) on 22 February 1744 – possibly the last such attack in a fleet engagement. The description of this event by an eyewitness in the *Real Felipe* is one of the few surviving accounts of a fireship attack from the target's perspective. The attack miscarried, but the Spanish ship was so heavily damaged by British gunfire that it had to be towed out of range.

(MUSEO NAVAL, MADRID)

the mission, with every enemy boat and frigate in the area setting course to intercept. The few small guns carried by the fireship were not of much use in this situation, and every enemy ship within range brought the fireship under heavy fire. This could damage the rigging, or cause a premature ignition of its fiery cargo. If possible the fireship sailed to windward and slightly ahead of an accompanying frigate; upon getting close, it braced its yards so that they would press heavily against the grappled target. Then, at the very last minute, the fireship luffed with the intention of striking the enemy abreast the fore shrouds, swinging alongside and grappling firmly.

From the target's point of view, if gunfire and the defensive flotilla failed and a burning fireship got very close, there were instances of cool-headed captains, familiar with local tides and soundings, unexpectedly dropping anchor and allowing the attacker to slide past and burn out harmlessly (this occurred during the St James's Day Battle). When all else failed, and the enemy fireship was on a collision course, there was one final line of defence: one's own fireships could be sent to intercept it. This was tried during the Four Days' Battle when Prince Rupert's flagship was attacked by two fireships. A counterattack by the flagship's 'own' fireship was launched 'and bravely burnt the bold assailants'.[18] Again, during the attack on the Medway, there were further examples of fireship pitted against fireship.

Even when a drifting fireship had already made contact with its victim, it could still be pushed or towed away by a disciplined and determined crew, even if had hooked fast. In this case grapplng-irons and their chains came into play. Every ship of the line was supposed to have four of these on board, and a small ship two.[19] Simultaneously 'fire-booms', which were as long as studdingsail booms, were thrust out through the lower gunports. These were armed with a fork at one end and a hook at the other, and could be used to push a fireship clear.[20] If all countermeasures failed, the crew invariably leaped into the water, where if they were lucky they might be picked up by a boat; few seamen could swim, but death by drowning was better than being incinerated.

In general, however, forewarning was the best defence. When ships were in open water, patrol vessels spread out from the main fleet to act as 'fire-guards', as the Dutch called them, tasked with sighting and keeping track of an enemy fleet, and if possible identifying fireships. This was a major task for the smaller Dutch and English vessels like Fifth Rates, where manoeuvrability and speed were more important than firepower. In more confined circumstances, precautions had to be instituted in advance. A harbour entrance or river mouth could be closed by a 'boom' made of chain, and if the enemy sent a fireship to break it, this could be countered by using another fireship. If a vessel was anchored in the stream, and captain and crew kept their heads, a spring could be secured to the cable in such way that the ship's position could be changed by heaving in on the spring and evading the attacker. Another similar trick, used during the Dutch attack in the Medway, was to sheer the vessel with the helm when at single anchor.[21]

———•———

A combination of line tactics and increasing confidence in countermeasures greatly reduced the effectiveness of fireships in fleet engagements. They did not disappear from the order of battle, but the opportunities for their use declined, and their successes were now confined to particularly favourable circumstances – where targets were effectively trapped or incapable of manoeuvring. As an example of the changed prospects for fireships in conventional warfare, it is instructive to look at the last recorded example of such a deployment in a fleet battle at sea, off Toulon in February 1744. This encounter took place during the War of the Austrian Succession (1740–8), another balance-of-power struggle masquerading as a dynastic dispute, which pitted France, Spain, Bavaria and Saxony (an alliance of those refusing to recognise Maria Theresa as Empress of Austria) against Britain, the Netherlands and the Austrians themselves.

Early in 1742 a Spanish squadron transporting troops to Italy to fight Austria took refuge in the harbour of Toulon. The commander of the British Mediterranean fleet, Thomas Mathews (1676–1751), closely blockaded the port for over two years, and it was not until 1744 that the French and Spanish

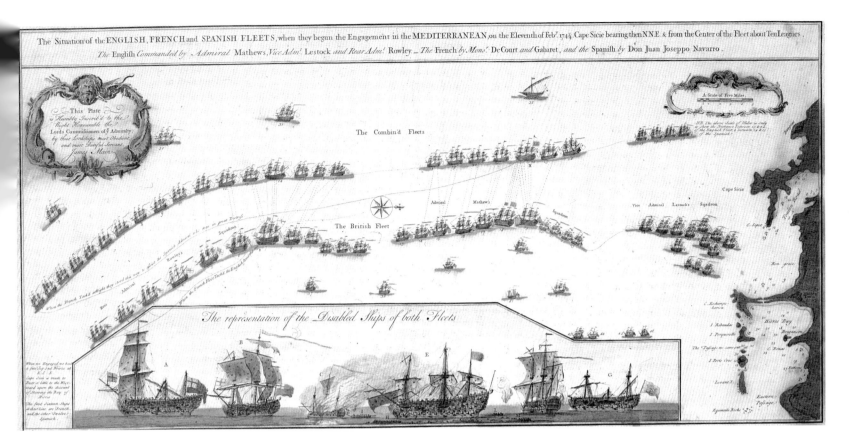

The Situation of the ENGLISH, FRENCH and SPANISH FLEETS, when they begun the Engagement in the MEDITERRANEAN, on the Eleventh of Feb.ʸ 1743/4. Cape Sicie bearing then N.N.E. & from the Center of the Fleet about Ten Leagues.

The English Commanded by Admiral Mathews, Vice Adm.ˡ Lestock and Rear Adm.ˡ Rowley.— The French by Mons.ʳ De Court and Gabaret, and the Spanish by Don Juan Joseppo Navarro.

A pictorial representation of disposition of the fleets at the battle of Toulon in February 1744, with the Franco-Spanish fleet at the top. Neither line is properly formed, with some miles between the British centre squadron under Admiral Sir Thomas Mathews and the rear under Vice Admiral Lestock. The French van was also separated from the Spanish centre, and Mathews concentrated his attack on the latter, and particularly on the *Real Felipe*, flagship of Admiral Don Juan José Navarro, who led the Spanish contingent. In the course of the battle, Mathews ordered a fireship, the *Anne Galley*, to attack the beleaguered Spaniard, but despite heroic efforts by the crew, the attack failed.

(BEVERLEY R ROBINSON COLLECTION, ANNAPOLIS)

made an effort to break out. Of course the British moved to prevent this.[22] At the centre of the Franco-Spanish squadron was the *Real Felipe*, a colossal three-decker carrying 114 guns and a crew of 1,350 men, the flagship of Admiral Don Juan José Navarro (1687–1771). He was assisted by two captains, one of whom was the Chevalier de Lage de Cueilly, commanding the *Real Felipe*'s forecastle. Cueilly was something of an adventurer who had made a fortune in the South Seas, and then purchased a captain's commission in the Spanish navy.[23]

Cueilly's importance to history is that during the campaign of 1744 he kept a diary, which was published in Amsterdam two years later. Like many diaries, it was intended principally to show its author in the best light, but it is nevertheless fascinating for its vivid picture of the situation aboard a ship of the line when it came under attack from a fireship. Cueilly's first-hand account touches on many of the issues, of both attack and defence, and would apply with only minor modification to much of the history of fireship warfare.

At the beginning of the skirmish, on Saturday 22 February 1744, Admiral Mathews tried to build a

line of battle, strictly by the book. Although this was not completely successful, he laid his flagship the *Namur* on a parallel course to that of the Spaniards. He had the weather gage, and the three squadrons (the French and Spanish sailing separately) were south-eastwards from Toulon, abreast Cap Sicié; a strong Mediterranean swell was running. Just prior to the battle, the tompions had been removed from the muzzles of the great guns behind the threatening open ports, and all was silent as everyone waited expectantly for what would come next.[24] The lines were just a pistol-shot apart – a deadly range. No shot had yet been fired and the tension was almost unbearable, but everyone knew that at any moment the broadsides would explode with a deafening roar, and tons of round-shot, bar-shot and

Detail from the previous illustration of the *Anne Galley* (C), which is already well alight while the remaining crew take to the boat (I). The state of the *Real Felipe* at the time of the attack is depicted by (E), with the boat that the Spaniards sent to intercept the fireship at H.

(BEVERLEY R ROBINSON COLLECTION, ANNAPOLIS)

Vista de la disposion en que estaba el Navio el R.ᵗ Felipe comandante Espa
Josè Nabarro, guando el Namùr comandante Inglès mandado por el Almirante Mathews cona
del dia 22 de Febrero de 1744. dada à 4. Leguas d Tolòn enla costa de Provenza, en

andado por el Gefe d Esquadra D.ⁿ Juan
Brulote para incendiar al Real en la Batalla Naval
dó el Mar de Batalla por los Españoles.

f. Moraleda 1783

chain-shot would howl over the decks and through the rigging. In the *Real Felipe* the men stood on deck, bare-headed, listening to the endless sermonising of one of the ship's three chaplains. He promised absolution of their sins if they fought bravely. De Lage, who wanted his men to take their posts on the forecastle, rose from his seat on the bench beside the chaplain and shouted, 'Long live the King! My Lads, the chaplain absolves us for all that we have done.' Then he directed the godly priest to go below deck, and sent his men to their stations.

The breathless silence lasted only a moment. The *Namur* fired three shots in quick succession as the signal for attack, and the Spaniards answered with a broadside followed by a volley of musketry. The mighty warships heeled at each broadside, and the *Real Felipe* became the focus of the action, because the British had concentrated their fire especially on the Spanish squadron. The *Real Felipe*, almost surrounded by the enemy, took heavy punishment, but she could also hand it out and managed to dismast one British ship. The rigging was so badly damaged that she became virtually impossible to manoeuvre, and after two hours of bitter fighting De Lage was summoned to the quarterdeck from his post on the forecastle. 'I thought I should there receive some orders from Don Navarro but he was not on deck; he was below on the cockpit.' According to De Lage, the admiral had received a wound and taken to his bed.

I saw only the captain, M. Gerardin, bathed in blood which was streaming from a large wound in his forehead. On the point of death, he was taken down to the cockpit where there were already a great number of wounded. The quarterdeck was covered with dead piled up on top of one another; the guns could no longer be served; everyone had been killed or wounded. I only found there alive Casamara, a Genoese, Capitaine de Frégate; Don Ignocio de St Just, the Chief of the Staff; Don Antoin Saleta, lieutenant of grenadiers, a cadet and a pilot. Don François Morales, Captain in the Seville Regiment of Grenadiers, was killed while talking to me, and several other persons were struck down. Such was the state of the *Royal Philippe* [*Real*

A dramatic portrayal of the attack on the 114-gun Spanish three-decker *Real Felipe* by the English fireship *Anne Galley* at the battle of Toulon (or Cap Sicié) on 22 February 1744. The attack failed, and may well have been the last attempt of its kind in a fleet engagement at sea.

(INK SKETCH BY F MORALEDA [1783]. MUSEO NAVAL, MADRID)

Felipe] from the time I took over the command till the end of the fight.

The three-decker continued to take fire from several British ships, and was obliged to divide her own fire among them. As the wind dropped, she lost steerage way because of damage to her top-hamper, and the British concentrated relentless fire on the stern gallery, wrecking the upperworks. There were many dead, and about 3.30 Admiral Mathews gave the order to cease firing; aboard the *Real Felipe* they began to clear up the wreckage and throw the dead overboard.

It seemed that Mathews was of the opinion that the Spanish ship, faced with such superiority in guns, had no choice but to surrender. De Lage climbed on to a gun and had a look at the scene of battle over the screens. A boat was under way from the flagship to a frigate nearby. At the same time, the flagship hoisted a yellow flag at the mizzen top. De Lage got the message that a British frigate was coming up towards the stern of his ship, but on climbing on to the poop he soon realised that the approaching frigate was a fireship. The reaction on the Spanish quarterdeck, as described by De Lage, epitomises the dilemma that so many officers must have faced in similar circumstances:

> I got up on the poop and recognized the frigate to which Mr. Mathews had sent his boat. Judging her to be a fireship, I had some guns on the starboard side made ready to receive her, and then, so that I could watch her, mounted on a gun on the same side. It is not possible to look outboard from Spanish ships without getting up to some considerable height, because they build their upper works very high so as to afford protection against musketry and grape-shot. While I was considering the best means of saving the *Real Felipe* from this fireship, I heard a voice three paces away from me saying: 'Gentlemen, we are assembled here to decide on what steps are to be taken; there is not a moment to lose; my advice is to haul down the flag and surrender ourselves: it is the only way to save our lives and protect ourselves from this

fireship which is on the point of setting us on fire.' I should have taken this discourse for a dream, if the words 'haul down the flag' had not wakened me up more than the appearance and approach of the fireship. I looked behind me and saw a circle formed round M. de Casamara, the Genoese, who, at the departure from Cadiz, had been flag captain on board the *Real*. On seeing the fireship, he had collected Captain Pendrichi, the Intendant Don Carlos Ratamosa, the Major St Just, and Lieutenant Don Pedro Sagardia, and had held forth this harangue to them. It is not difficult to influence people's spirits on such occasions, and it did not call for any eloquence to persuade them. However, without leaving my gun, but with a manner both haughty and scornful, I said to them: 'Gentlemen, no doubt you have forgotten that I am here and alive. I have told the King that His Majesty's flag shall never be given up to the enemy while I am alive. I shall not fail to-day in so glorious an engagement. Look then, gentlemen, to your courage for the means of destroying this fireship and think of nothing else. 'Go,' I said to the Intendant, 'to the lower deck and get the guns to bear; and promise a reward to him who shall sink the fireship.' I gave the same order, for another battery, to the Major Saint Just; I sent Captain Pendrichi to his quarters on the forecastle, and Lieutenant Sagardia in a boat to meet the fireship and tow her off. These orders were promptly executed and I added to Mr. Sagardia: 'Neglect no means of putting the bows of the fireship to leeward of the *Real*, even though she should be on fire; and see that you drive off the enemy's boat.' Enseigne de Vaisseau Don Pedro Arigoni and Don Juan Gaiosa, a garde-la-marine, placed themselves under the bows of the fireship with such intrepidity that the English crew was disconcerted.

Aboard the *Anne Galley*, as the British fireship was called, hatches and powder-kegs lay open and powder was strewn on the decks.[25] The crew sat waiting in the boat while Commander Mackie held the portfire in his hand, ready to set the ship afire at the right moment. At this ticklish juncture, he suddenly had to defend his ship against the threat of the Spanish boat which lay under his bow. The fireship fired a small cannon amidships, and it is believed that muzzle-flash from this set off the powder on deck causing an explosion. That at all events is the British version of the incident. De Lage's is as follows:

> They fired a light gun and some musketry at the boat, but could not hit it as the boat clung to her bows. The fireship's boat passed to larboard. Meanwhile the four Spanish ships which were to leeward and astern of the *Real* opened fire with all their guns on the fireship, without any of their shot hitting her. She came to within about fifteen yards of us. As soon as she was seen through the ports we fired three guns at her, the effect of which was so immediate and so lucky, that she would have sunk if the British had not made haste to set her on fire. In less than a minute she blew up. I was surprised, for a fireship ought to be much longer before exploding; but either they had no wish to burn us by a slow fire or else the cannon shot had upset their train. Wreckage of every sort fell on board our ship, but no damage was done by it. I myself was covered by burning fragments. Before the explosion of the fireship, I had seen two young officers dressed in blue and a third, somewhat older, in red and green, who, with five or six men, were doing all they could to grapple us. They were on the forecastle of their frigate and behaved with remarkable courage, regarding death with infinite scorn, so that I admired their gallantry. I heard them give

> the order for setting fire to the train; they could then have saved themselves by throwing themselves into the sea, if they had not determined to grapple the *Real*. I saw them blown up in the air and followed them with my eyes to the height of their foretop, without their clothes changing colour; but at that height they were enveloped in flames and reduced to a cinder; they all fell alongside the *Real*, light as corks and not two feet long. Their gallant behaviour made me suppose they were officers of the English admiral, and had promised him to burn the *Real* or die. They had kept their word, with courage worthy of everlasting fame.

When she sank, the fireship took with her to the bottom Master and Commander Mackie, a lieutenant, a mate, a gunner and two quartermasters.[26] Ten men got away in the escape-boat, but two of these were later shot by the Spaniards.[27]

On the flagship, in De Lage's words, 'those whom death had spared embraced one another, like people returned from the other world'. However, following the fireship attack, the *Real Felipe* was again attacked by the British, particularly by the *Namur*, and so badly hammered that she had to be towed clear of the battle. The number of dead and wounded reached 500.[28] Although he still had superiority of force, Mathews eventually broke off the attack because parts of his fleet had failed to obey the order to engage. He tried to re-form a line with the remaining ships but did not succeed, and the Franco-Spanish fleet was allowed to escape. This unsatisfactory performance resulted in a series of spectacular court-martials in England and the end of Mathews's career. It is interesting to speculate how a successful fireship attack might have changed the outcome, but in the event not only did it fail, but never again would such an attack be attempted in a fleet engagement at sea.

THE
LINE OF BATTLE DOMINATES:
THE THIRD ANGLO-DUTCH WAR
AND THE SCANIAN WAR

' ...it was inadvisable to attack a force such
as this, so much larger than our own and provided
with fire-ships, whilst we had not one.'

Michiel Adriaanszoon de Ruyter, 1652

After the second Anglo-Dutch War ended with the Treaty of Breda in 1667, the guns were silent at sea for a few short years. The roar of cannon was replaced by the noiseless struggle of mercantile competition, with vast fleets of merchantmen under the Dutch flag sailing unhindered on the world's oceans, demonstrating the reviving economic might of the United Provinces of the Netherlands. For her rivals, England and France, the only prospects of destroying this economic power seemed to be war. At sea her trade might be cut off, while on land there was the possibility of taking the rich Dutch cities and dismembering the union.

England's Charles II and France's Louis XIV daydreamed about these possibilities, but there was a treaty in the way. In 1668 England, Sweden and the United Netherlands under Johan de Witt (1625–1672) had concluded a 'triple alliance', the purpose of which was to check the aggressive expansionist policies of Louis, who was considering occupying the formerly Spanish southern Netherlands. However, from the Dutch point of view, Charles II seemed a far from trustworthy treaty partner. The humiliation following De Ruyter's total defeat of his fleet still rankled deeply, and while his ambassadors were publicly endorsing the peace he was beginning secret negotiations with Louis with the aim of engaging in joint operations against the hated United Netherlands. The prospects looked good.

France was the strongest land power in Europe at that time, and also had a splendid fleet, which had been built up by Colbert, the Minister of the Marine – who, as it happens, was a great proponent of fireships. Combining this fleet with the Royal Navy, which had been rebuilt following the Second Anglo-Dutch War, looked like an unbeatable strategy. Louis's land forces were poised to advance into the lowlands from the south and east, while the English king awaited the monetary rewards for falling in with the French plan – £1,000,000 for himself and the upkeep of his court, and £200,000 for his fleet.[1] It did not matter to him if these war plans were very unpopular with his subjects; the hoped-for spoils of victory would win over public opinion. And so the secret agreement was signed at Dover in 1670.

The next step was to persuade the English Parliament to approve a new war. Most of the members of the House considered any proposed war to be a financial venture, and it needed a provocation of some kind to inflame public opinion against the Dutch. The first attempt was made when the royal yacht *Merlin* sailed through an anchored Dutch fleet in August 1671 demanding the flag salute. The Dutch dipped their flags and struck their topsails, because they did not wish to provoke the English. So the yacht demanded a salute with cannon, but that really was too much. In response to this 'insult' Charles demanded a severe punishment for the Dutch admiral, but the Estates-General declined.

The next opportunity to whip up war fever arose on Monday 13 March the following year, about three in the afternoon, with an event that eventually developed into the Third Anglo-Dutch War. It started when the *Resolution* (successor to the ship burned in 1666) fired a broadside at a Dutch escort to the seventy-one-ship convoy of merchantmen that made up the annual 'Smyrna Fleet' as it sailed through the English Channel. Every year this richly laden fleet sailed from ports in the eastern Mediterranean towards home waters. The aggressor in this case was the seasoned captain Robert Holmes, who had already established himself as a provocateur in the Second Anglo-Dutch War. He led a squadron of six or seven well-armed ships of the line and worked zealously to serve the king when it came to '… the ruining of these people'.[2] But he had not reckoned on the determined resistance put up by the Dutch. Many of the merchantmen were armed with 20–30 guns, and they formed themselves into line like the English and carried on a running fight. Their captains and crews had much to lose, for they carried with them the private fortunes that they had built up through trade, and therefore had every incentive to fight. Although battered by English fire, they held their ground, and when the battle ended the next day few prizes had been taken. Instead, the English got a bitter foretaste of the war that the king was to to declare officially a few days later. Louis declared war a few days after that. Sweden was paid off with French gold, and kept out of the war. The Grand Pensionary's policy of building alliances was shattered, and only the Elector of Brandenburg and the Holy Roman Emperor stood with the United Provinces against England and France.[3]

In June 1672 French troops advanced, apparently inexorably, into the United Provinces, where the Dutch had little with which to oppose them. Panic set in, and as a last despairing measure the dykes were opened and the French were finally stopped by water and mud. At sea the Dutch were a little better prepared; despite difficulties in manning, they got their fleets to sea and sought out the enemy. In supreme command was the renowned Admiral de Ruyter, and serving under him were Admirals Adriaen Banckert, Aert Janszoon van Nes and Willem Joseph van Ghent. Altogether they had about eighty warships and at least thirty-six fireships; the 20,700 men aboard the ships manned almost 4,500 guns altogether.[4] De Ruyter's orders and tactics were simple and aggressive: find the enemy, attack him as vigorously as possible, and prevent the Allied fleets from linking up, thus preventing them from establishing a blockade of the Dutch ports.

The Allied forces that threatened the Dutch ships and bases with destruction had also put to sea early in the year. The French had about thirty warships and eight fireships under the command of Vice Admiral Count Jean d'Estrées (1624–1707), a general who had transferred to the sea service, while the English fleet comprised about fifty-five warships and twenty-two fireships. Thus the Dutch faced an almost unbelievable force of 6,000 guns and 34,500 men.

The commander-in-chief of the combined force was the Duke of York, who was bent on forcing the Dutch to their knees this time around. With him was the battle-hardened Edward Montagu, Earl of Sandwich, who had loyally put his talents and experience at his country's disposal, even though he felt that the king had picked an unwise fight with the Dutch. Samuel Pepys, who was distantly related to Sandwich and owed his post at the Admiralty to him,[5] often mentioned him in his diaries, once describing him as 'My Lord, my rich and raising cousin'. The aim of the Allied fleets was to destroy the Dutch battlefleet, to blockade their ports, and to landing troops in the northern part of the country. These operations, together with the French land forces advancing

from the south and east, would envelop the Dutch in a pincer movement.

The numbers of fireships in the three fleets are significant, and reflect the great belief in the fireship as a decisive weapon. The numbers of small craft and frigates had also risen, a consequence of the new distinction between ships suitable for fighting in the recently developed line-of-battle formation and the support craft, whose roles did not include involvement in the main gunnery duel. In previous decades, the ideal formation had consisted of three squadrons, with a vanguard, main force and rearguard (if they were sailing abreast, there was a centre with right and left wings), and in the mêlée that ensued small ships might be usefully embroiled in the fire-fight. However, for some years most commanders had been convinced of the advantages of sailing in line, and in this war these tactics became accepted as the norm.

The Dutch failed to pre-empt the combination of the enemy fleets, so when the two large naval forces first made visual contact on the morning of 29 May 1672, De Ruyter faced the combined fleet of the English and French. The captains were called aboard their respective flagships to receive their final instructions, and then began the manoeuvring to build a line and the struggle for the weather gage. Weather conditions were not favourable, and on 31 May the fleets lost sight of each other. The Duke of York received a report that the Dutch fleet was lying quietly at anchor off the island of Walcheren, which was a fair way off (about ninety sea miles, or 167 kilometres). Relying on this report, which later proved to be incorrect, and against the advice of Sandwich, he ordered the Allied squadrons to anchor in Sole Bay, off the Suffolk village of Southwold. Several ships needed maintenance and replenishment of victuals and water, and some men were even given shore-leave. But all these peaceful pursuits were interrupted dramatically on the night of 7 June, when a French frigate sailed in with the alarming news that the Dutch fleet was in sight to the north and would arrive in about two hours.

The day before, De Ruyter had learned that the enemy fleets had somewhat incautiously anchored on the English coast, and he immediately decided to make a surprise attack on the anchorage. The battle that followed, known as the battle of Sole Bay, took place on a pleasant day with light winds and quiet sea, and De Ruyter made his first approach with the wind from the north-east. The conditions were favourable for the use of fireships, which were given the important task of launching the first offensive.[6] Emerging out of the smoke of battle, they were to attack and throw the anchored fleet into panic and confusion, with the main force only later coming in to close-quarter action. De Ruyter delegated six warships for this purpose, each with its own fireship.

Admiral Willem Joseph van Ghent (1626–1672) commanded the van at the battle of Sole Bay (June 1672). As commander of the *Dolfijn*, he joined Jan van Brakel of the *Groot Hollandia* in an attack on the English flagship *Royal James*, and thus had a hand in setting up one of the most successful fireship attacks in maritime history. However, he paid for it with his life, being fatally wounded in the battle.

(FROM: DE JONGE 1858–62)

Such an attack, with as many fireships as regular warships, had never been attempted before, but the captains who had been chosen for the fireships were the boldest and most experienced in the fleet. However, wind, weather and the wishes of an admiral often go in different directions, and so it happened now. The breeze slackened and with it the momentum of the Dutch attack, giving the Allied ships time to weigh anchor and set sail. Then something quite unexpected happened: Admiral d'Estrées ordered the French fleet to make sail on a different tack from the English, causing the combination that was key to overwhelming the Dutch to drift apart. It may have been an error of communication, but many historians now believe that Louis XIV had given d'Estrées secret orders not to expose his new, untested and expensive warships

to serious battle damage. But the French did not get away altogether. De Ruyter ordered the Admiral of Zeeland, Adriaen Banckert, to pursue them with twenty ships. Banckert, who held the weather gage, offered battle to the enemy at some distance. Both sides ordered attacks by fireships. A Dutch fireship set course for the *Saint Philippe*, the flagship of Admiral d'Estrées, but the effort miscarried in classic fashion when the attacker was ignited prematurely by cannon-fire. An eyewitness saw the boat in which its crew tried to escape also being hit, and wrote, 'it is not believed that there were any survivors'.[7]

On the other side, the Dutch did sink a French fireship which had ventured too far out from the battle-line. Only in the late evening, well after his English allies had broken off the engagement, did d'Estrées rejoin them. The gamble of the English alliance had cost the King of France just a few masts and spars and 450 men, and he might well have been content with the way his flag officers had behaved. As an aside, the French attitude to fireships can be deduced from the high proportion of them in the fleet (in 1671 there were ninety-two regular warships and eleven fireships); perhaps appropriately, their names also suggested something perfidious, such as *Le Caché* (Hidden), *Le Déguisé* (Disguised), *Le Trompeur* (Betrayer) or *Le Perilleux* (Dangerous).[8] Most French fireships were relatively large, with over 20 guns, between five and seven officers and between twenty and twenty-eight men.

While the French had been withdrawing to the south, in the north De Ruyter enjoyed a numerical superiority over the English, who had no time to form a proper line. Their fireships and smaller vessels remained close inshore, with the big ships further to seaward. The flagships were left unsupported, while the ships with their specially selected captains, which were normally stationed immediately ahead or astern of the flagship, struggled to get into line, and the fireships which were supposed to attend the admiral closely had not yet closed up. At seven in the morning the Dutch first concentrated their attack on these 100-gun flagships – the Duke of York's *Royal Prince* (a newly rebuilt vessel, which in 1666 replaced its earlier namesake) and the Earl of Sandwich's *Royal James*.

The wind had dropped and the sea was quiet as the smoke of battle spread across the waters.

The two enemy fleets drew slowly closer together until they were within musket-shot of each other. The flagships of De Ruyter and Van Nes and those accompanying them, up to seven ships at one time, concentrated their fire on the *Prince*. However, the English ship defended herself vigorously, with the heavy guns of her lower battery firing with devastating effect. Shortly after 11am the *Prince* lost her main topmast, and as it came down it tore the mainsail and rendered several guns on the upper deck unusable. The Dutch musket-fire was so brisk than no one dared go aloft to clear away the wreckage, and the *Prince* could not take advantage of a breeze that sprang up to manoeuvre. Then, through the smoke, the crew glimpsed the silhouettes of two fireships being towed towards them by small craft.

One of the fireships was able to propel itself with sweeps, but the conditions for this attack were not good because the light wind meant a slow approach. The attackers were inevitably exposed to enemy fire for too long a period, and were brought under heavy fire by the *Prince*. One sank in a hail of shot, and the other had to luff up and break off the attack. The *Prince* then lost her fore topsail, and the only recourse was to use boats to tow her bow round, but the light breeze gave her enough steerage way to permit her escape, after which the Duke of York had to shift his flag to the *St Michael*.[9]

At the same time the English attempted their own fireship attack, in this case against one of De Ruyter's 'seconds', which had sustained damage to its rigging. Vice Admiral John Kempthorne ordered Captain Harris of the fireship *Anne and Judith* to attack, and he had managed to get very close to his target when his foreyard and its grappling-hook were shot away, preventing him from securing his target. De Ruyter sent a pinnace and a small frigate to cut off the escape of Harris's boat, and in the end the fireship burned out without effect, costing her brave crew five dead and five wounded.[10] It is likely that the great number of fireships available to flag officers on both sides of this encounter led to their being deployed extravagantly. For example, the *St Michael*, the second flagship of the Duke of York, saw through the smoke no fewer

than eight or nine fireships all aflame and drifting harmlessly past.

Sandwich's *Royal James* was also exposed to the concentrated fire of the Dutch ships in the early stages of the battle, partly because poor visibility made it difficult for her 'seconds' to assess the situation and partly because the Dutch attacked 'very smartly'. She had managed to sink two fireships with her guns, but it was Captain Jan van Brakel in the 62-gun *Groot Hollandia* who was to be her undoing. The Dutchman managed to get his ship across her bows and grapple, and raking fire the length of the English flagship caused horrifying

The admiral of Zeeland, Adriaen Banckert (*c*1615–1684), was an experienced battle-hardened sea-officer. At the battle of Sole Bay his division was ordered by De Ruyter to keep the allied French squadron (under d'Estrées) separated from the main English fleet. He fought his own battle some distance from the main fight, thus securing De Ruyter's numerical superiority over the English fleet under the Duke of York.

FROM: DE JONGE 1858–62)

slaughter. Sandwich thereupon ordered his men to repel boarders and cut the *Hollandia* loose, but his flag captain, Richard Haddock, dissuaded him, pointing out that the prospects of success were slim and emphasising that of the original 800 men, they had already lost 250 dead or wounded, while many of the upper deck guns were out of action. An attempt to board would cost so many more lives, and would reduce the number of men who were still serving the remaining guns. Their fire would slacken, causing the enemy to think she was finished, and encourage them to make a further attack.

So the *Royal James* drifted unmanoeuvrable and defended herself as best she might with the guns of the middle and lower batteries. The *Dolfijn*, a relatively big ship of 82 guns under Admiral Joseph van Ghent, approached and also considered boarding, but the wind did not permit this. The ships drifted slowly closer together, 'so close that a musket ball could easily have been tossed across' as one eyewitness described it in the *Dolfijn*'s logbook.[11] The *Dolfijn* fired broadsides from both decks, mostly double-shotted or canister-shot, with salvoes of musket-fire in addition:

> But they gave as good as they got … returning our fire with all their guns abaft the mainmast, shooting us to bits, dismounting our guns, tearing up the running rigging, and causing other harm. There were scores of dead and wounded, among them Admiral van Ghent. He was standing close to the mainmast, where he fell dead when a cannon-ball shot away his leg just above the knee, and he was hit with four or five musket-shots in upper body and abdomen. Also killed were Commander Jan Claaszoon van Oosthuizen and two or three seamen.

By noon the *Dolfijn* had so many holes between wind and water that the carpenters could not manage to plug them all, and with four pumps going she withdrew from the *Royal James*. The latter made use of the tide and dropped a stern anchor, and a boarding party managed to reach the deck of the *Hollandia*, which was still secured to the bow, and cut it free. A little while after midday, one of the last musket-shots fired from the *Dolfijn*'s maintop hit Captain Haddock in the foot. With blood oozing from his shoe, he was carried below for the ship's surgeon to cut away the torn flesh and tendons of a toe, and while he was off the deck the last chapter in the history of the *Royal James* began. Her crew were busy cutting the cable of the stern-anchor and setting the mainsail when a fireship suddenly appeared through the smoke, escorted almost to impact by another vessel. The fireship was the *Vrede*, with a crew of thirty-four men under the command of Jan Danielszoon van den Rijn of Rotterdam.

There was no time left for the *Royal James* to mount countermeasures, and the fireship drew inexorably closer until finally Van den Rijn laid his ship alongside and grappled securely with hooks and chains. Then thick black smoke poured from hatches and gunport, and almost immediately bright flames were seen in the tarred rigging of the English ship. She was firmly afire and her exhausted and decimated crew could not control the flames. Vainly they tried to fend off the fireship with firebooms, but it quickly became apparent that the *Royal James* was lost.

There are no eyewitness accounts of what exactly happened then, but the squadron of Admiral Sir Edward Spragge in the *London* passed the *Royal James* about two in the afternoon, and had to keep clear because she was enveloped in fierce flames. A little later, between three and four o'clock, Captain John Narborough in the *Prince Royal* saw the fire, and wrote in his log:

> … she being on a light fire and at anchor, for she rode with her head to the South by East and all the burnt yards and booms which dropped from her and the hull of the Dutch fireship which set her on fire drove astern of her to the northward as the tide set. There was four of our boats and small vessels taking up the men which saved themselves by swimming and on rafts.[12]

From the deck of the *Dolfijn*, the crew had seen the successful attack of the fireship on the Admiral of the Blue, and watched as the giant bonfire burned to the waterline. Her powder seems not to have exploded, and boats from English and Dutch ships pulled some of her people out of the water, including Captain Richard Haddock. Originally she had carried 800 men, but the majority of those who had survived the artillery battering perished by drowning. As to the fate of the Earl of Sandwich, there is no unanimous report. He was a heavily built man, so badly affected with gout that he had to be supported by two young men,[13] and had been lowered into a boat to transfer his flag, but the boat was probably capsized by desperate men in the water, causing Sandwich, one of England's finest admirals, to drown with the rest. His body washed ashore a week later together with several others, but was recognised from his clothing and an Order pinned to his chest.

Besides the death and injury, the loss of the ship herself was a bitter blow for the Royal Navy, because she had only been launched in the spring of 1671 and had in her short service proved herself

a good sailer. Her builder, Anthony Deane, had made use of iron knees and pillars in her construction, innovations that did not become widespread until a century later, but with her premature loss went the possibility of confirming the value of this method of construction.[14]

The battle raged on mercilessly all around the flagships. At first the English had difficulty in getting their ships out of the bay against unfavourable winds, and were unable to support one another. However, as the day wore on, the wind veered and it became easier to manoeuvre. Ships on both sides

that had sustained heavy damage to their rigging tried to withdraw from the field. On the few ships which had been boarded and captured, the prize crews struggled to get them back to their respective fleets, but often they could not manage it and the ships would be retaken. It was late in the afternoon, as the wind became unfavourable and fog rolled in, that the gunfire began to slacken. Lack of powder and exhaustion had their effect, and De Ruyter gradually distanced himself from the enemy; as dusk fell the fighting finally came to an end. It had involved 173 ships of the line and about

sixty-six fireships and frigates.[15]

Here and there on the horizon a ship still burned, but the thunder of the cannon had ceased, making it easier to hear the cries of the wounded. Both sides had sustained heavy losses, but the reports were contradictory and exact numbers difficult to estimate. On the two sides about 2,500 men in all had lost their lives. Aboard the *Prince* alone, there were fifty-one dead and fifty-two injured. About 800 wounded were landed in Southwold, and for days thereafter bodies continued to wash up on the shore.

The next morning the Duke of York, who had shifted his flag to three different vessels, decided not to continue the battle because of lack of ammunition and the miserable state of many of his ships, and ordered his fleet to run into the Thames. Nor did De Ruyter attempt to renew the attack, but withdrew his ships into Dutch home waters; he was later to describe the battle of Sole Bay as the longest, most heated and most desperate of his career.[16] The following day the *Dolfijn* landed the bodies of Admiral Van Ghent and ten of his men, along with about twenty-eight men who had lost a limb. Thirty others with lesser wounds remained on board.[17]

Both sides claimed victory, but neither of them could send ships to sea, as almost all were so badly damaged that they had to remain in port. Captain Narborough in the *Prince* reported seeing three English fireships burned out or sunk and fourteen Dutch fireships burned, sunk or boarded.[18] Although both fleets had tried to mount fireship attacks, there were no successes, apart from the one that led to the destruction of the *Royal James* – but that single event was so spectacular that it seems to have extinguished the memory of all the failures in contemporary minds. Nevertheless, it is striking that despite the use of an unprecedented number of fireships, this was the only attack to achieve its purpose, and perhaps this can be ascribed to the greater practical expertise that had been developed in countering this weapon. The greater effectiveness of line tactics must also have had an impact, with targets more difficult to isolate, and squadrons better handled; the line also placed more reliance on fast, accurate and sustained gunfire, which made fireship attacks more hazardous.

After Sole Bay the Anglo-French combined fleet was forced to abandon its plan to blockade the Dutch coast and land troops, but that year the Dutch were incapable of offensive action at sea, and limited themselves to the protection of their merchant fleet. On the Dogger Bank, the English did make an attempt to seize the returning East Indies Spice Fleet, but this miscarried and the convoy found shelter in the Ems estuary, from whence it was safely escorted home by De Ruyter.[19]

On land, the United Provinces were still threatened. At the beginning of June 1672 the French had crossed the lower Rhine, and in desperation the Dutch opened the sluices. As the polders slowly flooded and made progress difficult for the French, peace negotiations were initiated, but the conditions proposed by France and England were so severe that they actually provoked greater resistance. By 7 June the French had already occupied two-thirds of the country, but the flooding was now complete, stopping the French in their tracks and shattering Louis's dream of entering Amsterdam that year. He had hoped to starve the Dutch into submission, but after the battle of Sole Bay a solid blockade could not be maintained. There was no alternative way of forcing the Dutch Republic to submit, so now his troops waited for winter, when it would be possible to advance across the ice.

But time was no more on the Allies' side than on the Dutch. War was expensive, and Charles II, in particular, was chronically short of money. The Dutch began to recapture towns, and the French supply-lines were threatened by the Holy Roman Emperor, Leopold I, who was assembling troops to support the Dutch. In the winter of 1672–3 the French failed to use the ice to cross the 'Water-Line', and the land war bogged down, making a victory at sea now more necessary than ever. This was the Allied strategy for the New Year, the defeat of the Dutch battlefleet to be followed up by an effective blockade and the landing of troops in the north of the Netherlands.

In May 1673 the English and French fleets were at sea. De Ruyter based his outnumbered ships in the shallows at Schooneveld off the coast of Walcheren, at the mouth of the West Scheldt. His shallow-draught ships were designed for these

A Dutch sketch of the attack in March 1672 by Sir Robert Holmes's squadron on the Dutch 'Smyrna Fleet', a richly laden merchant convoy sailing homeward from the waters of the eastern Mediterranean. War had not been declared and it was a calculated act of provocation, but it was not the easy victory Holmes expected. The captains of the merchantmen, who had a great deal to lose, fought so bitterly that Holmes managed to take very few prizes. The vigour of the Dutch defence was a foretaste of what was to come in the Third Anglo-Dutch War once Charles II declared war a few days later.

(NATIONAL MARITIME MUSEUM PW5525)

waters, where they were almost unassailable, and yet at the same time capable of breaking out and attacking. In May his attempt to enter the Thames miscarried, and on 7 June the Allied fleet assembled off the mouth of the West Scheldt ready to exchange blows with him.[20] The Allies formed a line with the French in the centre. The new supreme commander, Prince Rupert, had fifty-four ships of the line and no fewer than twenty-four fireships besides his frigates. The French under Admiral Jean d'Estrées had twenty-seven ships of the line and between ten and eighteen fireships.

Edward Montagu, First Earl of Sandwich (1625–1672), had Charles II to thank for his title and his rank as admiral, both being rewards for his active participation in the Restoration of the monarchy in 1660. However, he was a talented and experienced fleet commander, and saw much action in the Second and Third Anglo-Dutch Wars. At the battle of Sole Bay in 1672 he was the victim of a fireship attack, becoming one of the most prominent casualties of this particular weapon.

(NATIONAL PORTRAIT GALLERY, LONDON, NPG 18634)

Against them, de Ruyter had only fifty-two ships of the line and twenty-five fireships. In his ketch sat Willem van de Velde the Elder, working now for the English, who sketched the panoramic view of the fleets drawn up for battle.[21]

Prince Rupert made the first move, attacking the Dutch with a group of his lighter ships of shallow draught, plus ten fireships. De Ruyter refused to rise to the bait: his ships did not scatter in panic before the fireships but held their positions, so Prince Rupert was forced to order his ships to retire. As a result, the intended confusion had the effect of disordering the Allied fleet and not the Dutch. Once again De Ruyter had made a cool-headed, competent – and unexpected – decision. In the course of the day he made skilful use of the shal-

lows, exploiting the edges of the banks and never giving the enemy a chance, and used local knowledge to compensate for his numerical inferiority. The encounter, which was labelled the first battle of Schooneveld, was intense, but the two sides kept at some distance from each other. By evening they had all fired their guns, but no ships had been lost and there was no decisive outcome.

Few ships were heavily damaged, and that made conditions unfavourable for fireship attack. Apparently one or two were attempted but were unsuccessful. An example is referred to in the logbook of the English *Royal Katherine* of about 80 guns, under Captain George Legge.[22] Like every capital ship, the *Royal Katherine* had her 'own' fireships, and Legge gave the order to attack the *Gouden Leeuw*, the flagship of Admiral Tromp, which was within range. The fireship obeyed the order but a Dutch 50-gun ship interposed, giving the fireship no choice but to grapple her. Instead of being set on fire, it then sank, having been so riddled with shot during the approach. This is a typical sequence of a failed attack. Legge was now unprotected and had another fireship brought up, but this proved to be unready. Its rigging was damaged and the firing-train was damp. From what Legge wrote it is apparent that he gave orders for it to be repaired and made ready for action as a matter of priority; it was both an indispensable weapon and Legge's life-insurance.

How much hope Prince Rupert, the supreme commander of the Allied force, had placed on the fireship as a weapon is apparent from a personal letter he wrote to the king. Both Dutch flagships would inevitably have been destroyed, he suggested, if the French fireships had been employed with more skill, and if the English ones had shown more courage.[23] Of course, he may not have been right, but the French certainly expended nine of their ten fireships, and six fireship captains had lost their lives, with three more wounded. The English had expended three or four and the Dutch five – all with no success by the ultimate yardstick, the destruction of an enemy capital ship.[24]

On 14 June De Ruyter attacked the Allies again, profiting from the fact that these shallow waters favoured the Dutch. This encounter became known as the second battle of Schooneveld, and was pri-

FORCER DES VAISSEAUX EMBOSSÉS

Forcer des Vaisseaux embossés, c'est rompre leur ligne, pour se faire un passage dans l'endroit qu'ils défendent, cette manœuvre est des plus hardies et depend en general de la disposition du lieu: s'il favorise l'action des brulots, on profite des nuits, ou brouillards obscurs pour en envoier s'acrocher à quelques Vaisseaux A, dont l'ennemi lui meme, coupe alors les amares, afin de sauver les autres Vaisseaux des accidents du feu; la ligne ainsi rompuë; les Vaisseaux B, entrent en se tenant au vent des Brulots, pour n'etre point exposés à leur feu.

Quand les precautions de l'ennemi, empechent de faire usage des brulots, on lui envoye des detachem.ᵗˢ de forts V.ᵃᵘˣ B, qui le prolongent, et rompent leur ligne, en enlevant à l'abordage, quelques Vaisseaux C; Cette manœuvre, est une des plus belles de la marine, on y brave le feu de toute l'armée ennemie, pour fondre sur elle, et rompre sa ligne avec fierté; on attaque encore des Vaisseaux embossés, en les bombardant, par des Batteries établies à terre ou par des Galiotes à bombes; c'est l'occasion qui décide, et à égal avantage, on prefere celles, qui epargnent plus les hommes, et les Vaisseaux.

Nicolas Ozanne in his *Marine Militaire* (1762) describes a situation favourable to a fireship attack. A squadron of five ships has formed a line to defend the entrance to a bay or harbour. If the attack is made at night, in poor visibility or in fog, there is a chance that the fireships will be able to get close to the defenders without being discovered, so there is no time left to take defensive measures. Again and again in the history of sea warfare, the threatened ships in this situation have cut their cables to avoid the fireship, leaving the way into the bay open for the attacker. The configuration shown here is reminiscent of the successful French fireship attack at the battle of Palermo in 1676.

(FROM: OZANNE 1762, PLATE 43)

marily a fairly long-range artillery duel, but again, despite their superiority in ordnance, the Allies could not achieve a decision: no ships were lost and there are no reports of the deployment of fire-ships.

At the beginning of August De Ruyter went to sea with seventy-five frigates and ships of the line and twenty-two fireships, his primary objective being the protection of a merchant fleet returning from the East Indies. The Allied fleet under Prince Rupert consisted of ninety ships of the line and frigates and twenty-eight fireships, and had a large contingent of soldiers aboard. It was also at sea, on the lookout for the enemy and hoping for a decisive stroke. On 20 August the two fleets made visual contact; both formed themselves into line and the struggle for the weather gage began. By the morning of 21 August De Ruyter had achieved this, and one after another the elements of his fleet, van, centre and rear, came into action. The battle that followed is known to the English as the battle of the Texel.[25]

As usual, the subsidiary squadron commanders went at it particularly fiercely, and on this occasion did not fire at a distance. Each of them knew that now was the time to strike decisively, and their chosen weapon was the fireship. Admiral Banckert's ships escaped destruction from a French fireship which attacked with great élan, and the failure of this assault is representative of many similar attempts. There are also references to other fireships whose task was to shield the flagship, their mere presence holding the enemy at a distance. It was about three in the afternoon when, as described by John Narborough, captain of the *St Michael*, 'Two Dutch fireships which followed Tromp endeavoured to lay the *Prince* on board. As they came along we plied them with shot, and the *Prince* bravely defending herself, they could not grapple, but set their ships on fire before they were fast, and burnt the fireships to no purpose astern of the *Prince*.'[26] Once again, this report reveals the usual way in which fireship attacks failed.

One of Van de Velde's panoramic sketches actually records this event. The *Prince* with its rigging in disorder is encircled by Dutch ships, defending itself against the fireships, and the artist notes on another sketch that two Dutch fireships chained

The dramatic loss of the splendid English three-decker *Royal James* at the battle of Sole Bay in 1672 – one of the highpoints of fireship warfare – proved a popular subject for marine painters. This is a version by Willem van de Velde the Younger, depicting the moment when the blazing *Vrede* struck the *Royal James* amidships. Although the ship was to burn for several hours, many of the crew can be seen already abandoning ship from the headrails and bowsprit. Most of the 800-man crew were lost, one of the victims being Admiral Montagu, who, ironically, was one of the Navy's strongest advocates of fireships.

together were set alight to block the way of the French squadron under d'Estrées.[27] It is obvious that Van de Velde had actually seen fireships in action, and he represents cannon-smoke as being lighter in colour than smoke from fireships, which rises in vertical or slanting clouds, lending his broad sketches of the battlefield more structure and drama.

Later in the afternoon the English tried to turn the tables. Christopher Billop, captain of the fireship *Prudent Mary*, attacked the *Olifant*, flagship of Isaac Sweers, one of Tromp's vice admirals. At first the attack went well, but then a Dutch fireship chained itself to the Englishman, and '… so the two fireships burnt both together'.[28] This was a form of victory for the Dutch fireship, since it cancelled out the potential success of the other. Yet another attack was attempted by two English fireships late in the evening: they attacked Dutch vessels from the weather position but, having come under fire, ignited before they were close enough and so burned out uselessly. It is a familiar story; Van de Velde noted on his sketchpad: 'English fireship on fire by accident or neglect.'[29]

As darkness fell, the firing ceased and the fleets, with many ships damaged, withdrew to their respective coasts. Both sides registered no losses of capital ships, but a lot of fireships had been wasted. Captain Narborough summed it up: 'In this day's fight we have not lost one ship, but spent some of our fireships to the number of six. The Dutch have spent about that number of their fireships in vain.'[30] Once again, the Allies had failed in their aim of blockading Dutch trade or landing troops on their territory. Nor had they beaten and destroyed De Ruyter's battlefleet, which meant that the immediate threat to the Republic was past, and Dutch merchant shipping could sail unhindered. In September 1673 the French fleet weighed anchor and headed for home, while in England Parliament was in an uproar about the high cost of the war.

Even the trade war had not paid off for the king. The enemy had captured more merchant vessels than the Allies, and the English Baltic trade was at a standstill, with the all-important timber, tar and naval stores no longer reaching Britain. In November Parliament declined to vote the king the money needed for the coming year. Louis XIV had not achieved his war aims either, having been forced to surrender one part of the occupied Netherlands after another. Besides taking the Dutch Netherlands, he had also intended to occupy the former Spanish Netherlands, where the withdrawal of Spain had resulted in a power-vacuum, but this would not have been in the interest of the English, who did not want a great power like France occupying that part of the Channel coast that lay directly opposite their own. Peace was signed between England and the United Provinces, and was ratified in February 1674 in the Treaty of Westminster. The Dutch promised to salute English warships, gave up New York (which they had reconquered the previous August), and paid an indemnity of two million guilders. However, a state of war continued to exist between France on the one side and the United Provinces and the Holy Roman Empire on the other, who were joined the following year by Spain.

In the Mediterranean, the Spaniards were having difficulty with their possessions in Sicily. Louis XIV, aspiring to be the major sea power in the region, used his large fleet to back the Sicilian rebels, who were fighting to gain independence for the island. At this juncture, for protection against the French navy, the Spanish turned for help to the *Stadhouder*, Willem, Prince of Orange. He responded by dispatching that seasoned campaigner De Ruyter (he was sixty-eight) to the Mediterranean with a squadron of eighteen ships of the line, beside some frigates and fireships, to support the Spanish. Their task was to hold the French fleet in check, and to assist in reanimating the Dutch Mediterranean trade, which had been adversely affected by the French. De Ruyter was up against an experienced and worthy foe, Admiral Abraham Duquesne (1610–1688), who had at his disposal twenty capital ships more powerful than those of De Ruyter.

On 8 January 1676 the opponents met for the first time at the battle of Stromboli, but despite the numerical superiority of the French, the encounter was not decisive. The Dutch maintained excellent fighting order and held their own, not just against the French ships of the line, but also against their fireships, which were mercilessly shot up as they

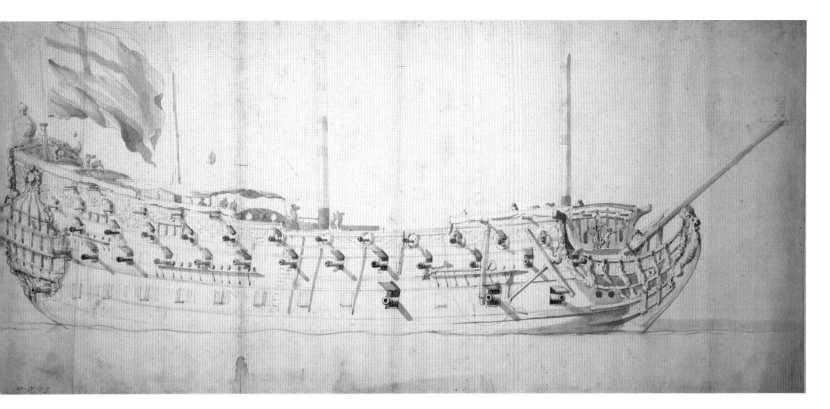

made their approach.[31] The second meeting, at the battle of Etna, occurred on 22 April, with the superior French fleet including twenty-nine ships of the line and nine fireships, and the Dutch-Spanish fleet nineteen big ships and five fireships. Again, despite the numerical imbalance, the result was inconclusive, and there are no reports of fireship attacks. However, the Dutch lost their beloved Admiral de Ruyter. Shortly after the onset of battle, a cannon-ball tore off his left foot and smashed his right leg, hurling him off the quarterdeck and on to the upper deck. He died in great pain some days later, on the evening of 29 April 1676.

From the beginning of April and right through May the Dutch and Spanish ships lay in the harbour of Palermo. The new supreme commander, Jan den Haen, was aware that the situation of his fleet was critical. Many of the ships remained unseaworthy following the last fight; the Spaniards were having difficulty supplying the spars, cordage and other material needed; and since De Ruyter's death the morale of the Dutch sailors had been wretched. De Haen made the decision that if obliged to accept battle, he would fight at anchor. This was not received with general approval, for the fairway was very narrow and left no room to manoeuvre, and the choice of offering battle in a

bay flew in the face of the principles laid down by De Ruyter. The embalmed body of the latter was now enclosed in a lead-lined chest in the great cabin of his former flagship, the *Eendracht*.

Without considering the ramifications, Den Haen constructed a crescent-shaped defensive line of twenty-seven warships in the Gulf of Palermo. They used warp-anchors to keep their broadside directed seaward, and between the ships of the line were stationed fireships and galleys, whose main task was to drive off enemy fireships. Both ends of the line were supported by shore batteries. The French reconnoitred the situation and, seeing their chance, approached the defenders early in the morning on 2 June 1676.[32] The ships were under the command of Louis-Victor de Mortemart, Duke of Vivonne, but the plan of attack had been drawn up by Vice Admiral Anne-Hilarion de Cotentin, Count of Tourville, someone who would make his mark on later naval history.

First a squadron of nine ships of the line, seven galleys and six fireships anchored near the Dutch right wing and opened fire. They were followed by a second group of ships, which anchored about a cable-length from the Dutch and fitted springs on the cables, allowing them to swing so that their broadsides faced the enemy. About 6.30 the French

The final moments of the burning *Royal James* at the battle of Sole Bay, in a painting by Peter Monamy. The listing wreck appears as a dark silhouette towards the right of the picture, while the battle continues to rage among both the big ships and (as shown in the foreground) the small craft.

fireships and their accompanying craft made their surprise attack through the almost impenetrable gunsmoke. They emerged so close to the defenders that they had no time to bring them effectively under fire, or to throw them off course. The threat drew ever closer and panic broke out among the men on the decks. The first to cut his cable was the Spanish vice admiral, and without offering any resistance his ship drifted towards the coast. One after another most of the ships, in total confusion, followed his example, and soon three Spanish ships and three galleys were aflame. The same thing happened at the other end of the defensive line, with a Dutch ship catching fire and in turn setting fire to two of its neighbours. All three ended with their powder-magazines blowing up violently.

The crew of the 64-gun Spanish flagship *La Nuestra Señora del Pilar* managed to fend off two French fireships, but then she was grappled at bow and stern by the third and fourth fireships, which somewhat ironically were named *Nôtre Dame de Lumière* (Our Lady of Light) and *Nôtre Dame de Bon Voyage* (Our Lady of the Good Voyage). The Spaniards were thrown into panic and many jumped overboard; this was how Admiral Diego d'Ybarra drowned. Shortly afterwards his ship exploded, and burning fragments falling on the *San Felipe* set it on fire; it too was destroyed. While four Dutch ships, having cut their cables, drifted towards the shore, most of the Spanish ships and all the galleys headed for the inner harbour at Palermo. Just a few Dutch ships under Admiral Jan den Haen stood and fought, and in the process the admiral's head was taken off by a cannon-ball. Driven almost ashore, four more Dutch ships defended themselves bravely, among them the *Eendracht* with Admiral de Ruyter's body in her great cabin. In this way the Admiral took part in his last battle.

With all his fireships expended, Admiral Vivonne broke off battle, with the French having suffered no losses other than their fireships, while on the Allied side seven capital ships and two galleys were destroyed in less than five hours. The number of dead, although not known exactly, was estimated at about 2,000. This one-sided affair is known as the battle of Palermo. It gave the French control of the Mediterranean, but they failed to take advan-

tage of it. Louis XIV, who had little grasp of the importance of sea power, became distracted by his other land campaigns and withdrew his fleet from the Mediterranean.

While this was going on, Dutch squadrons were operating in the waters of the West Indies and the Baltic, and the events in the latter area are worth mentioning because they show the potential of the fireship at its greatest. The conflict in the Baltic which lasted from 1675 to 1679 is known as the Scanian War because it nominally concerned the Swedish province of Skåne. Just as De Ruyter fought with the Spanish in the Mediterranean, Tromp was allied with the Danes in the Baltic against the rising power of the Swedish navy. Following the death of his Admiral of the Fleet, King Christian V of Denmark offered to make Admiral Tromp the supreme commander of this

In the Baltic, a Dutch fleet under Admiral Cornelis Tromp was engaged to support Denmark in countering the emergent sea power of Sweden. In June 1676 there was a pitched battle off the island of Öland between a Swedish fleet of forty-five ships of the line and eight fireships and the Danish-Dutch fleet of thirty-three capital ships and six fireships. It developed into a short-range passing battle, during which the Swedish flagship *Kronan*, a colossus with 134 bronze cannon and a crew of 800 men, capsized and blew up, as depicted here. During the battle a Dutch fireship attacked a surrendered Swedish flagship, contrary to orders, and the defenceless vessel became another total loss for the Swedish.

navy. With the approval of the Estates-General Tromp accepted, and he now led a combined fleet of Dutch and Danish vessels against Sweden.

After some indecisive preliminary skirmishes, the two fleets met finally came to blows on 11 June 1676 in what became known as the battle of Öland. The Swedes, led by Admiral Lorens Creutz, had forty-five ships of the line and eight fireships, and the Danish-Dutch fleet could counter with thirty-three ships and six fireships. However, the numerical disparity was compensated by the presence of Admiral Cornelis Tromp, and a series of catastrophes for the Swedish fleet now unfolded south of the island of Öland.[33]

Towards noon both fleets had formed up in line and commenced a series of passing duels at close range. Early in the process the Swedish flagship *Kronan*, a colossus armed with 134 bronze cannon,

was seen to heel over steeply, capsize and explode violently. The exact cause is uncertain, but it is suspected that the ship tacked after loosing off one broadside to fire the guns on the other side. The abrupt turn without a corresponding reduction of canvas made the ship list to one side, and perhaps the cannon on the weather side were not properly secured and rolled to leeward, increasing the angle of heel to the point where water flowed in through the lee gunports and caused the ship to overturn. As she lay on her beam ends, an explosion tore through her side, perhaps the result of a burning portfire coming into contact with powder supplies. So sank one of the mightiest warships of the day, taking 800 men down with her. Among them was Admiral Creutz, whose inexperience and poor seamanship had probably contributed to the disaster. One of the few survivors, Major Anders Sparrfeldt, claimed – in the best tradition of Baron Münchhausen stories – that the explosion blew him over two ships, and that he was saved by landing in the sail of another Swedish ship! Whatever the truth, he subsequently had a successful military career, and died peacefully in 1734 at the ripe old age of eighty-nine.[34]

After two passes in line, the catastrophe which had befallen the *Kronan* caused the Swedish fleet to withdraw in disorder. Tromp came within range of the 90-gun Swedish ship *Svärdet*, flying the flag of Admiral Uggla. For two hours she put up a brave defence against the fire of several Dutchmen, but eventually lost her mainmast. As Tromp approached, Uggla gave the order to strike his flag. Tromp accepted the surrender and had just sent a boat over to pick up Uggla when a Dutch fireship suddenly appeared, and, despite all orders to the contrary, its captain, Willem Willemsze of Amsterdam, refused to stop. He had come so far, and no one at the last moment was going to deprive him and his crew of their just premium! He ran his

ship alongside *Svärdet*, which was effectively defenceless, and set it on fire. Surprisingly quickly her powder exploded and only fifty-one of the 670-man complement escaped with their lives. Among the dead was the admiral.

All discipline evaporated in the Swedish fleet, as every ship tried by whatever means to escape, some falling into the hands of the enemy. On this disastrous day the Swedes lost eleven ships, including three of their biggest units, and their aspirations to sea power in the Baltic were finished. Many of the Swedish captains had obtained their posts by influence, and now they paid for their lack of competence with humiliation, court-martials and, in some cases, the gallows. On the Dutch side the fireship captain Willem Willemsze was held to have behaved in a manner both that was criminal and unprecedented. Tromp described him in a letter as a dastardly rogue,[35] but there is no certain record of how his case was disposed of, or whether he ever paid for the lives of so many people.

In June of the following year three big Swedish ships of the line, lying in the harbour of Malmö, were attacked by three Dutch warships and the fireship *Jacob and Anna*. The latter managed to destroy a battle-damaged Swedish ship which was already aground, with the loss of 150 lives.[36]

The favourable status quo for Dutch trade in the Baltic was restored after the battle of Öland, and negotiations between France and the United Provinces began in August 1678, with the various warring parties agreeing to end the conflict at Nijmegen in 1678–9. In essence Louis XIV was the winner, gaining some territory, but the Dutch got off relatively lightly. By agreeing to remain neutral in the ongoing conflict between France and Sweden, the Netherlands were given back those parts of the country which had been occupied by France; their overseas trading activities had survived once more.

CHAPTER SIXTEEN

PURPOSE-BUILT FIRESHIPS, MACHINE-VESSELS
AND OTHERS

'*It is hard to understand the use of fireships by civilised nations. In France they were used only rarely; Duquesne had some in his squadrons, but only because the English and Dutch had them, and it was necessary to have the same weapons as the enemy.*'

Le Marquis de Folin, 1892

THE TREATY OF NIJMEGEN IN 1679 DID nothing to restrain the expansionist policies of Louis XIV. France was the most powerful state in Europe, with a population twice that of England and ten times that of the United Provinces, and its battlefleet was the biggest in the world. Louis hoped to use this power to achieve victory over Spain and the Netherlands, and to secure his borders on 'natural' frontiers, like the Rhine or the Pyrenees, something which could be achieved only at the expense of his neighbours. Because France's economy was not primarily dependent on overseas trade, as was the case with the Spaniards and the Dutch, he was less concerned than they were with supporting the interests of his own merchants who did business abroad.[1]

The story was different in England and the Netherlands. To defend itself against the designs of France, the Dutch Republic had to look around for new allies, and by 1682 had forged alliances with Sweden and the Holy Roman Emperor Leopold I, leader of the German states. Leopold was a powerful ally, but his attention was focused on his struggles with the Turks on his eastern borders. In 1688 the Elector Palatine died and Louis XIV, despite his treaty obligations, decided to promote the claims of his sister-in-law to the Electorate, and he sent troops into the Palatinate and other territories on the left bank of the Rhine. Provoked by this, in 1689 the League of Augsburg, which included Sweden, the Netherlands and the Holy Roman Empire, was expanded to include Savoy and England under its new king, William III, who as Prince of Orange was also the Dutch *Stadhouder*. The aim of the league, now known as the Grand Alliance, was to protect the terms of the treaties of Westphalia and Nijmegen and ensure that they were observed.

The conflict that ensued was known variously as the War of Grand Alliance, the War of the League of Augsburg, the War of the Palatine Succession and the Nine Years' War. It began slowly, with the defence of the territories occupied by France being organised first. No decisive battle was fought before 1690.

The 'Glorious Revolution' of 1688 had changed the occupant of the English throne, and with it the diplomatic map of Europe. James II's pro-Catholic

After Barfleur, one large group of French ships fled to the small port of Saint-Vaast-la-Hougue, which offered some protection in the form of forts and gun batteries. However, an Allied division under Sir Cloudesley Shovell attacked the ships with the boats and small craft of the fleet, burning them all over two days. Fireships were sent in but were not needed, as the targets were not defended and could be boarded and set on fire by cheaper methods. This second painting by Adriaen van Diest gives a good general sense of the action, including the two widely spaced groups of French ships and the mass of Allied boats, but again the French ships would have been broached, broadside on, with their surviving canvas furled.

(NATIONAL MARITIME MUSEUM BHC0337)

The stern of the *Soleil Royal* – one of the most 'architectural' structures ever taken to sea. Designed by Jean Bérain and intended to reflect the magnificence of the Sun King, the work involved many of the leading artists of the French court. The interior was no less splendid and, according to reports circulated by the English, included a representation of the monarchs of Europe in chains at the feet of Louis XIV.

(DRAWING: AUTHOR AFTER ORIGINAL DRAUGHT)

The French fleet flagship *Soleil Royal* was the most impressive warship of her day, not only in terms of size and firepower but, especially, in the splendour of her decoration. She is shown here in the process of anchoring.

(DRAWING: AUTHOR AFTER ANTOINE LÉON MOREL-FATIO)

policies had stirred up so much fear and resentment among England's establishment that a caucus of nobles invited the king's daughter Mary and her fiercely Protestant husband William to invade the country on a mission of 'regime change'. Although he fled to France, James retained many supporters – known as Jacobites – in the country, and especially in Scotland and Ireland. He chose the latter for his attempt to regain the English throne with French help, and it was there that William's struggle to consolidate his grip on the country was first fought out.

The English and Dutch navies were now allies, and it needed their combined strength to match the huge French fleet. The first exchange of blows between the French and Anglo-Dutch squadrons occurred in 1689, brought on by a French operation to resupply and reinforce James's army as it fought in Ireland. The battle of Bantry Bay took place off the south-west coast of Ireland on 11 May 1689 and was indecisive, with both sides having fireships available but not deploying them. As a result of this encounter, the English Channel fleet was strengthened and its fitting-out accelerated.[2]

Although there had not been a spectacular fireship action for ten years, new fireships were constantly being brought into service. Favourable conditions for a successful attack had actually become fewer in number, because more rigorous line-of-battle tactics had diminished the opportunities for the deployment of fireships. Fleets were also operating further from home bases, and were staying at sea for longer periods and in more inclement weather conditions, throwing more strain on the fireships and their crews. However, no one wanted to do away with the weapons   not as long as everyone else had them – but if they were to be deployed successfully in the new conditions, it would no longer be adequate to use old merchantmen or captured vessels unfit for anything better. In 1689 the Royal Navy started to design and build vessels specifically as fireships, and by the end of 1690 twelve purpose-built 250-ton fireships were in service.

The intention was that these newly designed vessels would be better and more seaworthy than the fireships available up until then, and able to take on the modern French ships of the line. In design they basically resembled a small ship of the Fifth Rate. Being commercially built, they varied a little in dimensions, but a typical early example, the *Hawk*, of 288 tons, was 95ft long by 25ft in breadth (29m by 7.6m). They were of course more expensive than converted fireships, and they were contracted for at about £7 per ton, which was paid in four instalments of about £400 with the

final payment twenty days after delivery. This was a reasonable rate for ships of that size, but the builders were suspicious of the state of the Navy's credit and would only deliver once Parliament had guaranteed payment.[3]

However, the English shipbuilders did a good job. The new fireships were regarded as a success, and so contracts were signed for twelve further vessels. Their names give an unmistakable indication of their purpose, particularly in the 1691 and 1694 series, which included *Blaze, Etna, Flame, Vesuvius, Vulcan* and *Terrible*. The additional expense of these new ships actually paid off. At that time the average length of service for a fireship was two and a half years, but these specially built vessels ended up serving an average of seven years; twelve reached the astonishing age of ten years, and three lasted for over twenty.[4] By the end of 1689 the English fleet comprised fifty-four ships of the line, three frigates and seventeen fireships.

In the Netherlands too, the requirements for a successful fireship became more demanding. Defensive techniques in naval warfare had been improved in recent years, and apart from the threat of physical destruction that it posed, the ability of a fireship to throw an enemy squadron into disorder had diminished. In the 1680s, therefore, the Dutch began to build special-purpose fireships.[5] The money for their construction came from two sources: an extraordinary capital fund for rebuilding the fleet, and the budgets of the five regional admiralty boards. The details are unclear, but since each admiralty was independent it seems unlikely that the fireships were built to one particular design. This is confirmed by the number of guns carried, which might be anywhere from two to six, and the size of the crews, which ranged from twenty to thirty. Despite these building programmes, however, the total number of fireships declined. Gone were the days when the fleet included twenty or more fireships.

At the time of William III the Dutch fleet possessed no more than eight or nine fireships. A few were older vessels which had been converted – as was obvious from names like *Keurvorst van Brandenburg* (Elector of Brandenburg) or *Maagd van Enkhuizen* (Maid of Enkhuizen) – whereas the newer specially built fireships had names like those of their English counterparts: *Salamander* (a mythological creature of fire), *Etna* or *Stromboli*. They competed for such names with bomb-vessels, another type of special-purpose vessel coming into use at that time, which were fitted with heavy mortars firing explosive or incendiary shells. Between 1700 and 1706 the number of fireships in the Dutch fleet reached a low point, only two to four being listed, because it was assumed that in time of need more could readily be obtained by purchase, requisition or conversion.

The French Marine, too, seems to have had a few specially built fireships. In the National Archive (Marine) there is an entry for the year 1669 indicating that the administration of the Marine had ordered fireships built of fir or other inferior timber.[6] They evolved probably from the *frégate légère* (light frigate) and the *frégate vaisselle* (galley-frigate). These latter, which could be either rowed or sailed, appeared in the mid-seventeenth century and would have been similar to the few English Fourth Rates like the *Charles Galley* and *James Galley*, with two decks running the whole length fore and aft which made them suitable for conversion as fireships. The French fireships with frigate-type hull forms were fast sailers, and some names of French frigates between 1675 and 1758 suggest they were originally intended to be fireships, for example *La Trompeuse* (The Deceiver). Other light frigates were converted to fireships towards the end of their career, and were sometimes renamed to reflect this change of role; this was common practice from about 1670 until the mid-eighteenth century.[7] These were Fifth Rates, and hence too small for service in the line, and their captains and crews were paid accordingly.

The use of fireships spread beyond Western Europe when Russia established its first navy. On his visits to the Netherlands and England, Tsar Peter the Great learned much from the leading sea-powers, including the potential value of fireships. For his campaign against the Turks in the Sea of Azov, north-east of the Black Sea, in 1696, his new shipbuilding programme on the banks of the Don concentrated on smaller vessels – prams, galleasses, galleys and bomb-vessels – but it also included four fireships, built for the siege of the town of Azov, which was occupied by the Turks.

Unfortunately, they were hurriedly thrown together from unseasoned timber and quickly became unusable; by the time war was declared with Turkey in 1710, most were already rotten.[8]

Returning to the Nine Years' War, the next maritime clash was the battle of Beachy Head, which was fought on 10 July 1690 in the English Channel just off Eastbourne, with the French under the command of Anne-Hilarion de Cotentin, Count of Tourville (1642–1701), and the outnumbered Anglo-Dutch fleet under Arthur Herbert, Earl of Torrington (1648–1716). Both sides had a substantial number of fireships: over twenty for the French, and the Allies more than eleven. By any standards the battle was a defeat for the Allies.[9] No ship was sunk or captured during the actual encounter, but after the fleets drifted apart in the evening, the Allied fleet lost no fewer than fourteen ships burned or abandoned during the chaotic retreat, whereas the French lost none.

The Dutch van squadron under Vice Admiral Cornelis Evertsen the Youngest (1642–1706) had borne the brunt of the French onslaught. Caught in a period of calm by vastly superior numbers, the Dutch had taken heavy losses and managed to escape only by anchoring at the change of tide, while the less experienced French were carried away on the ebb. The Allies then withdrew into the mouth of the Thames, where by Evertsen's count no more than fourteen of his original twenty-two ships of the line remained battle-worthy. One of these was the 92-gun *Prinses Mary*, flagship of Rear Admiral Gillis Schey, which was just able to keep up with the disorganised fleet. For seven hours she had exchanged broadside after broadside with the ships of the French van under Vice Admiral Château-Renaud, and a contemporary pamphlet offers an impression of the critical state in which she found herself after the heavy fighting.[10] The enumeration may seem tedious, but it serves to underline just how fragile and susceptible to gunfire the rigging of the ships of that era was, and shows how vulnerable a ship became when its manoeuvrability was restricted by such damage.

Three quarters of the mizzen mast, mizzen topmast, crossjack yard, fore topgallant mast, spritsail topsail yard were shot away; mizzen yard, main mast, main yard, main topsail yard, fore topmast and fore topsail yard were unusable and would need replacing; the standing rigging had been shredded, with five of the mizzen shrouds, twelve of the main shrouds, and fifteen of the fore shrouds gone; all the mizzen topmast shrouds, five main topmast shrouds, and one of the fore topmast shrouds gone, along with all the main topmast backstays, mizzen stay, mainstay, main topmast stay and fore topmast stay; ties and chain slings of the main and fore yards, and preventers all gone; the sails were also totally ruined, eighty-one shot having pierced the main topsail, sixty-four the fore topsail, 130 the foresail; the mainsail and mizzen sail were shot away; and all stay- and studding-sails being shot down.

During the battle the ship had expended 24,800 pounds of powder, and twelve men were dead. Of the sixty wounded, forty were not fit for duty and able to help handle the ship; sixteen to eighteen men had lost a limb; and the ship's hull had taken 140 hits, some below the waterline. But the *Prinses Mary* had been lucky, for despite the numerous fireships available on both sides, there was no report of a successful fireship attack during this encounter. There are reports of burned and or stranded Dutch fireships,[11] but these were probably burned to avoid capture, like most of the other losses; the French intended a fireship attack on the beached 70-gun *Anne*, but her own crew burned her first.

The victory at Beachy Head or, as the Dutch called it, the battle of Bevesier, ensured the French command of the Channel for some weeks, but they did not have a follow-up plan which would have enabled them to exploit this advantage and alter the course of the war.

Scarcely two years after this triumph, Louis XIV planned another attempt to restore the English throne to James II by landing a force directly on English rather than Irish soil. An invasion force was assembled on the Cotentin peninsula, with its fleet of transports concentrated in the small harbour of Saint-Vaast-la-Hougue. Ever since Beachy Head Louis had believed that his fleet was invincible, and he now gave orders to the experienced commander the Comte de Tourville that he should sail from Brest on 25 April, seek out the enemy, engage them no matter how many ships they had

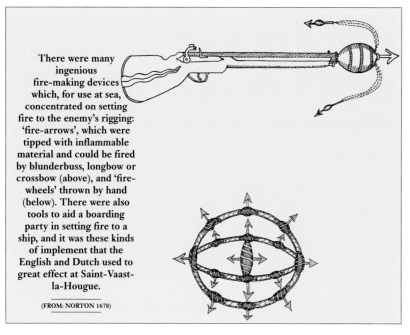

There were many ingenious fire-making devices which, for use at sea, concentrated on setting fire to the enemy's rigging: 'fire-arrows', which were tipped with inflammable material and could be fired by blunderbuss, longbow or crossbow (above), and 'fire-wheels' thrown by hand (below). There were also tools to aid a boarding party in setting fire to a ship, and it was these kinds of implement that the English and Dutch used to great effect at Saint-Vaast-la-Hougue.

(FROM: NORTON 1678)

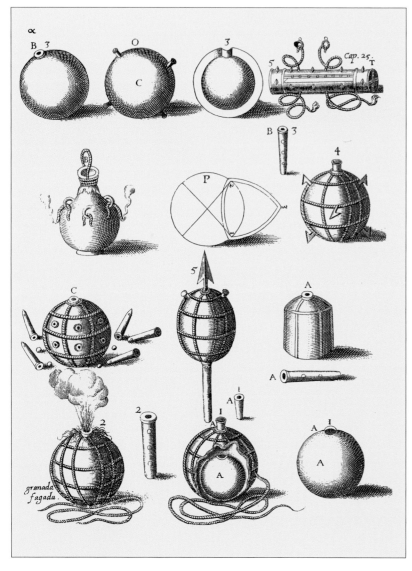

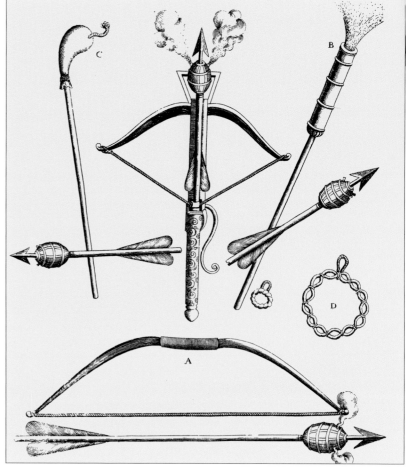

('fort ou faible'), and clear the way for the invasion force. It was admittedly a race against time, since Louis was counting on the inability of the English and Dutch fleets to unite before Tourville could offer battle. However, his initial intelligence was faulty, and when he heard that the enemy forces had already combined, he dispatched a fast-sailing vessel to countermand his earlier unconditional order. But it was too late, and the order did not reach Tourville before he sailed.[12]

Royal orders brook no delay, and the French admiral decided to take his fleet to sea, even before the expected reinforcements from Toulon and Rochefort had arrived (they had been delayed by a storm off Gibraltar and had lost two vessels). Commanded from Tourville's flagship, the magnificent but unwieldy 106-gun *Soleil Royal*, the fleet was buffeted by unfavourable winds, and by 29 May the French had got no further than Cap Barfleur, near Cherbourg, when they ran into the superior Anglo-Dutch fleet.[13] Their fleet of forty-five undermanned ships of the line and thirteen frigates

Various forms of fire-shot, carcasses and bombs which could be shot from mortars or hurled by hand. They were made of canvas, glass or pottery (designed to smash and explode when they hit the deck). In shape they might be round like shot, or like jugs with 'ears' to which burning fuses were attached and which ignited upon impact. A lantern shape was also possible (A). The cylindrical objects (B) were fuzes filled with slow-burning powder or with powder-filled cases containing musket-shot (C). The fire-shot were studded with these or with iron hooks, and were normally filled with an inflammable recipe of gunpowder, saltpetre, sulphur, turpentine and linseed-oil mixed together in various proportions.

(FROM: GALSCHUT 1692–1706)

In the early 1690s, such was the English interest in methods of attacking the French privateering ports that many schemes were considered. The well-known Dutch inventor Willem Meester was not the only man with such ideas, and this drawing is from an earlier proposal put to the Navy Board by the artilleryman Colonel Richards. The principal novelty of the concept is a stonework arch, constructed with variable resistance so that the powder-explosion would be directed either outwards (against ships and fortifications) or, if the ship was attacking a floating boom, downwards. Normally, the force of the explosion took the line of least resistance – through the decks or the hull bottom – so that the vessel had to be extremely close to its target to be effective, and Richards hoped that his 'directed' explosion would overcome this disadvantage. The Navy Board considered the proposal to be outside its area of expertise and recommended a practical test of its efficacy before seamen would have the confidence to man such a floating bomb. Richards's ideas were to be eclipsed by those of Meester, who enjoyed the patronage of the king, so it is unlikely that they were ever given a trial.

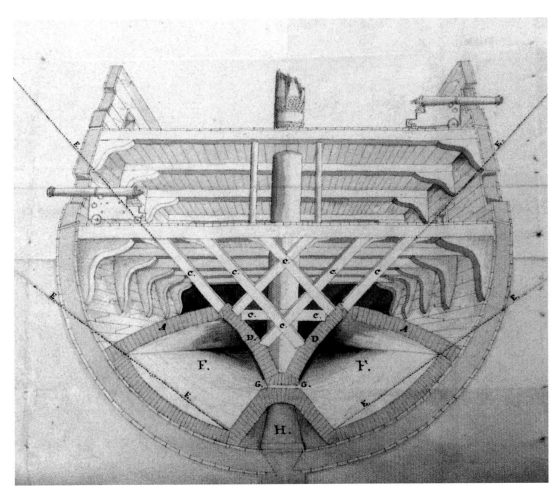

KEY

A Weakly constructed part of the double arch covering the powder and fireworks. Above it are piled heavy stones and scrap-iron

B Solid infill above the wooden braces

C The wooden braces strengthening the arch

D Reinforced part of the arch, to direct the force of the explosion outwards

E–E Theoretical direction of explosive force

F Interior of powder-vault

G Passage to allow the explosion to spread quickly

H Drainage to bilges and pump well

and fireships faced a combined Allied force of eighty-eight ships of the line, thirty frigates and nineteen fireships under the supreme command of Admiral Edward Russell (1653–1727) flying his flag in the *Britannia*; Philips van Almonde (1644–1711) led the Dutch contingent in his flagship *De Prins*.

About eleven o'clock in the morning, after the opposing fleets had cleared for action and formed into line-ahead, a heavy cannonade began. Many of the ships sustained significant damage and large numbers of casualties, but no ships were lost. In particular the *Soleil Royal*, the *Britannia* and the ships supporting them fought out a fierce broad-side duel at extremely close range that lasted for some ten hours. At one point, with the wind very slack, Tourville broke the English line, and as the wind freshened part of the English fleet 'doubled' him so that they were able to engage the French ships from both sides. But then the wind dropped again, and boats had to be used to swing the ships on to the correct heading to allow the fighting to continue.

About eight in the evening, in misty conditions, as the French were anchoring in scattered groups, the fireships' opportunity came. At the change of tide Vice Admiral Sir Cloudesley Shovell (1650–1707) ordered his fireships to attack, hoping to force the French ships to cut their cables and drift into range of the guns of a waiting English squadron. One of the fireships reached the *Perle*, but her crew managed to cut the attacker free; another closed the *Soleil Royal* and forced her to cut her cable, but when the fireship drifted past, she dropped anchor again. The attack cost Shovell four of his five fireships.

Thick fog descended about ten in the evening and the roar of the guns ceased. The men on the decks of the most heavily damaged ships dropped from exhaustion, and the ships scattered over a wide area. In the darkness only the flickering embers of the fireships were visible as they drifted and burned out. Tourville, who had defended himself brilliantly against a foe superior in numbers, now began the withdrawal towards Brest in the *Soleil Royal*, which was badly shot up and scarcely manoevrable.

The French ships were widely dispersed, and the Allies followed them in small groups. Each crew chose the course they felt would best lead them to safety, but because of the calms and unfavourable currents they had to anchor frequently. During the night some French ships tried to escape their pursuers by sailing through the dreaded Race of Alderney; the twenty that managed this eventually reached Brest, a notable feat celebrated in Robert Browning's poem 'Hervé Riel'. Another group sought sanctuary at Cherbourg, where the *Soleil Royal* was run aground. The proud three-decker was now a defenceless giant, dismasted and her hull riddled with shot-holes, the wreckage on her decks, splintered timbers and pools of blood attesting to the carnage of the day. Tourville hauled down his flag and transferred to another ship, while at the same time some of her 'seconds' were moved close to the *Soleil Royal* to protect her.

Another group of about twelve big ships made for Saint-Vaast-la-Hougue and assembled between the entrance to the port and the islet of Tatihou. The vessels with the most damage were run aground, in many cases because they had lost their anchors. They were pursued by the English and Dutch, who employed local pilots to guide them through these dangerous waters.

The Allies were well placed to exploit the desperate situation of the French fleet. Large deep-draught vessels could not get into Cherbourg, so now it was time to employ their numerous small craft. On 1 June, three days after the initial battle, Vice Admiral Sir Ralph Delavall ordered a flotilla of boats and fireships to reconnoitre the fairway into the harbour, but they came under heavy fire and had to withdraw. The next morning a second attack miscarried, but in the afternoon a force of three fireships and some boats managed, despite enemy fire, to get close to the *Soleil Royal*. This was exactly what a fireship captain, in this case Commander Thomas Heath in the *Blaze*, dreamed of. He waited until he was within pistol-shot of the French ship before he lit the train, and escaped with his men in the boat.

The French flagship had been designed to reflect the magnificence of France and its ruler, the 'Sun King'. The country's best artists and carvers had worked on the architectural features and the decorations, which consisted of representations of mythological characters. For the sculptures and carvings, the great draughtsman and engraver Jean Bérain (1637–1711) had submitted wax models to the king for his approval, and the work was then executed by the finest woodcarvers and sculptors in Paris.[14] The work did nothing for the ship's seakeeping or her military capabilities, but those who pointed this out during construction had been silenced. When the fireship crashed into her towering stern, the decorative work burned fiercely, and eventually she blew up violently. Thus perished one of the most splendid and powerful ships of the line that the world had ever seen.

The second fireship, *Wolf* commanded by James Greenaway, likewise got alongside the 74-gun two-decker *Le Triomphant* and set her afire. The *Hound* under Commander Thomas Foulis attacked the *Admirable*, but was subjected to such heavy fire that she caught fire prematurely. However, the *Admirable* did not escape her fate, for she was boarded by the crew of a small boat and successfully set on fire.

The ships that took refuge at Saint-Vaast-la-Hougue similarly offered a sitting target for fireships, but they lay so close onshore that the bigger English warships did not dare get too close to them. They were also protected by two forts, coastal batteries and 200 small craft and galleys, but despite this Vice Admiral Sir Edward Rooke launched an attack with Dutch and English boats and fireships on the evening of 2 June. When one of the fireships got alongside the 80-gun *Terrible*, the captain realised that the crew had fled, and he decided not to ignite his powder-train but instead to fire the *Terrible* by other means, thus saving his fireship for a second opportunity. The other French ships were attacked by the Anglo-Dutch flotilla through heavy defensive fire from the shore, and six were set alight.

Resistance on the ships themselves was minimal because their exhausted and demoralised crews had fled ashore the moment they grounded. That explains the ease with which the French ships in turn were boarded, plundered and set on fire using

Cross-section about midships of a 'Machine Vessel' or 'Infernal', probably intended to depict the *Vesuvius*, a converted fireship which was deployed in an attack on St Malo in November 1693. A is a load of old cannon and scrap-iron; B is sand ballast, over which about ten tons of powder in casks is stowed. This is covered by a 30cm layer of stonework, on top of which is a layer of bombs and old metal parts, D; another layer of stonework, covers this, with (at E) fifty powder-kegs and various fireworks. In the centre is a wooden channel which contains a fuze leading to the powder-charge. This infernal machine could be set off using fuzes or a clockwork detonator. The intention was to blast a huge hole in the harbour fortifications, but in the event it exploded prematurely, killing and wounding some of its crew. Undeterred, the English attacked the French Channel ports in the following years with explosion-ships of various kinds, most notably those invented by the Dutch engineer Willem Meester.

(FROM: DIDEROT/D'ALEMBERT 1803, *MARINE*, PAGE 6 AND PLATE XL)

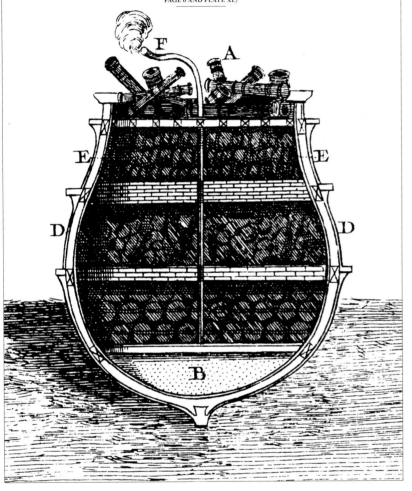

The extemporary implements were similar to those used in siege operations in land warfare. The fire-pike was a stave on the end of which was a canvas bag filled with inflammable material, which after igniting could be stuck in any available crack. Fire-arrows, with a wildfire tip, could be shot from a longbow or crossbow. Fire-balls were glass, clay or pottery containers, filled with incendiary material, but even a sturdy canvas bag stiffened with an iron cross, decorated with barbed hooks and filled with wildfire could be ignited with a fuze and hurled on to a ship's deck or into the rigging. A classic land warfare weapon was the fire-wheel, which consisted of old unravelled rope soaked in pitch and resin and formed into the shape of a wreath, perhaps incorporating a canvas tube filled with wildfire.[16]

The next day in Saint-Vaast-la-Hougue the evening was dead calm, and there was a further attack with boats and small craft to finish off the remaining French warships. Again the boat crews met almost no resistance from the abandoned ships, and they continued to destroy the final six enemy vessels by fire. To finish the job Rooke then attempted the more difficult task of attacking the transports inside the harbour itself. The fireships had to be towed in, but both went aground and had to be set on fire to no purpose; again any success was due to the small craft. In the Jacobite camp overlooking the bay, James II must have watched these bonfires with very mixed emotions – a residual pride in the achievements of the navy he had so fondly nurtured combined with the bitter realisation that his dream of regaining the English throne was literally going up in smoke.

At the battles of Barfleur and La Hogue (as the Royal Navy always spells it) the Allies expended eleven fireships[17] in return for a French loss of fifteen ships of the line and numerous transports and supply ships. Louis XIV managed to replace these over the next few years with newly built ships, but what he really lacked were well-trained experienced officers and crews and the resources to send them to sea. As a result the French navy gave up any ambition of dominating the ocean, and switched to commerce-raiding and privateering against Dutch and English trade, in which it enjoyed greater success.

whatever means were available – fire-pikes, fire-arrows, fire-balls. This encounter remains the classic example of the tactical use of fire using small craft equipped with a variety of extemporary implements – in effect a fireship substitute.[15] All of these fire-makers used a highly combustible material that the English called 'wildfire', which had no distinct recipe, but consisted of whatever the master-gunner and boatswain had at hand in their stores: fine priming-powder, pitch, naphtha, sulphur, resin, turpentine and flaxseed oil.

The centres of commerce-raiders and privateers were the Channel ports of St Malo, Dieppe, Le Havre and, especially, Dunkirk. The privateer fleets from the last-named were particularly renowned and inflicted enormous economic damage on the enemy. Commerce-raiding, or the *guerre de course* as it was known in France, was essentially a business, with investors, shipowners and captains running their own private enterprises. To set up a business a captain obtained a privateer licence or Letter of Marque, his crew were scrutinised, and a security bond was posted, after which he was free to capture enemy ships, or even enemy goods in neutral ships. He had to be careful to stay within the law, and if he stepped outside it could find himself declared a pirate. If he brought a captured enemy ship into port, the matter was examined, and if everything was in order the prize was sold and the money distributed to investors and crew. In modern terms, privateering was a way of 'privatising' the state monopoly of naval warfare, and while it could be very profitable, it was also a high-risk enterprise.

To protect themselves from commerce-raiding, merchantmen could adopt one of two basic defences: 'runners' sailed alone and relied on luck or good sailing qualities to avoid privateers; or ships bound in the same direction could assemble into a convoy, protected by warships. This latter was not the ideal solution, since it relied on providing an escort equal to the risk. As the men of the 400-ship outbound Smyrna Convoy discovered in June 1693, naval intelligence could be unreliable. When this vast fleet was eastward of Cape St Vincent off Lagos on the Portuguese coast, heading for the Mediterranean and the Levant, it was surprised by the combined French main fleets from Toulon and Brest. The threat from the French had been underestimated, and the Anglo-Dutch fleet covering the convoy had allowed it to sail into acute danger.

A heavy battle ensued, and despite a valiant rearguard action by the vastly outnumbered escort, a total of ninety merchantmen were captured. In the battle of Lagos, as it became known, fireships were available on both sides but none was sent into action. These captures caused disastrous financial losses in the City of London and Amsterdam. The

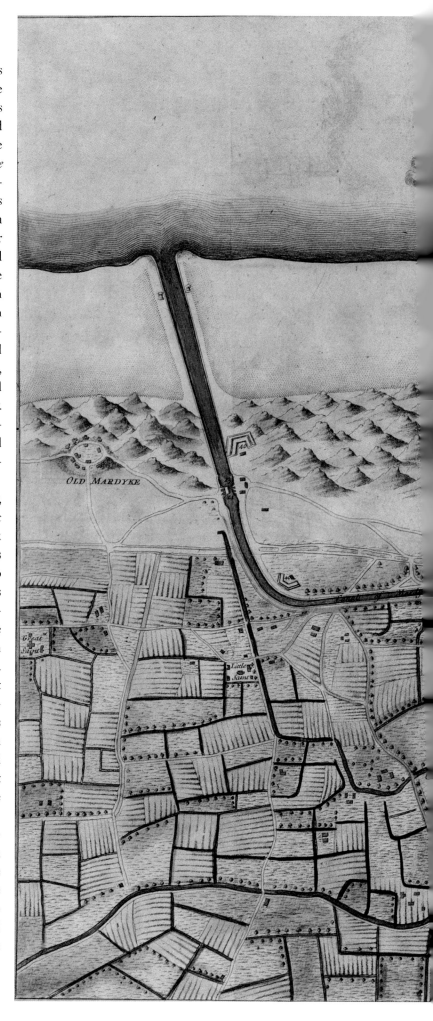

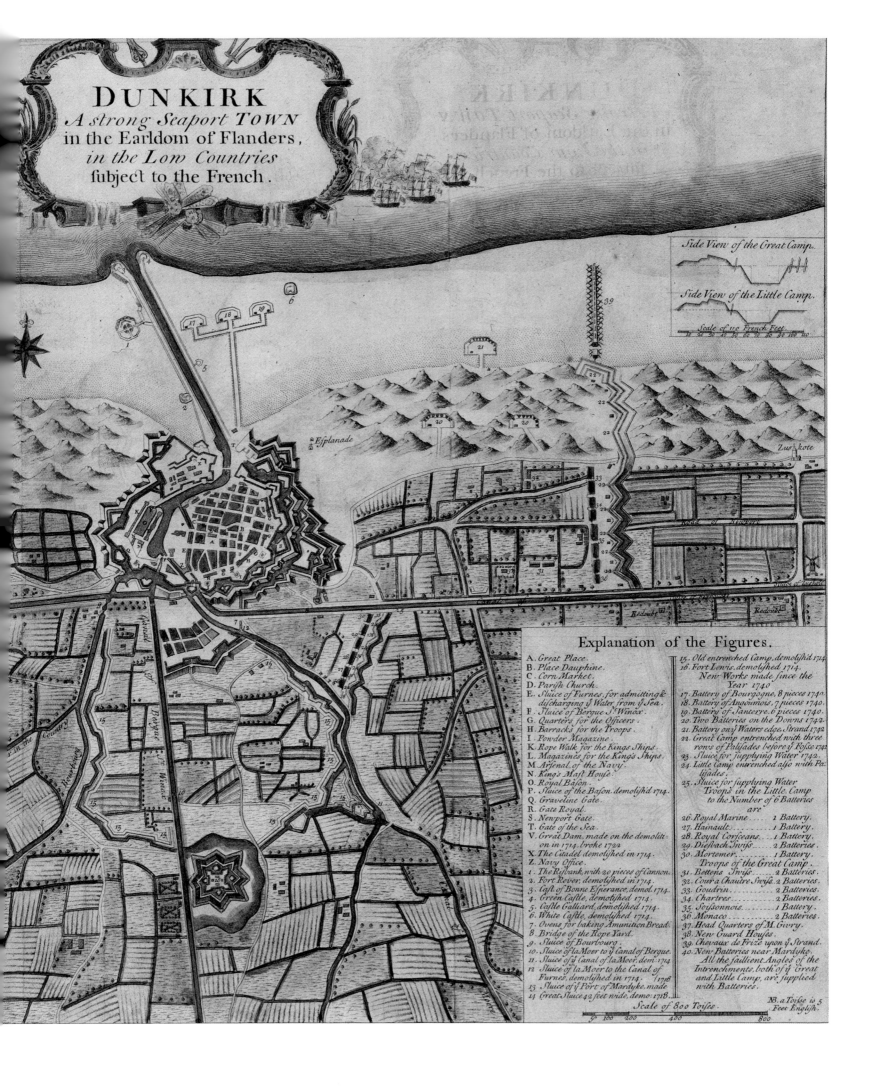

DUNKIRK

*A strong Seaport TOWN
in the Earldom of Flanders,
in the Low Countries
subject to the French.*

Side View of the Great Camp.

Side View of the Little Camp.

Scale of 110 French Feet.

Esplanade

Zuskote

Redoubt

Redoubt

Explanation of the Figures.

A. *Great Place.*
B. *Place Dauphine.*
C. *Corn Market.*
D. *Parish Church.*
E. *Sluice of Furnes, for admitting & discharging y Water from y Sea.*
F. *Sluice of Bergue St Winox.*
G. *Quarters for the Officers.*
H. *Barracks for the Troops.*
I. *Powder Magazine.*
K. *Rope Walk for the Kings Ships.*
L. *Magazines for the King's Ships.*
M. *Arsenal of the Navy.*
N. *King's Mast House.*
O. *Royal Bason.*
P. *Sluice of the Bason. demolish'd 1714.*
Q. *Graveline Gate.*
R. *Gate Royal.*
S. *Newport Gate.*
T. *Gate of the Sea.*
V. *Great Dam, made on the demolition in 1714. broke 1722.*
X. *The Citadel demolished in 1714.*
Z. *Navy Office.*
1. *The Risbank, with 20 pieces of Cannon.*
2. *Fort Rever, demolished in 1714.*
3. *Cast. of Bonne Esperance, demol. 1714.*
4. *Green Castle, demolished 1714.*
5. *Castle Galliard, demolished 1714.*
6. *White Castle, demolished 1714.*
7. *Ovens for baking Amunition Bread.*
8. *Bridge of the Rope Yard.*
9. *Sluice of Bourbourg.*
10. *Sluice of la Moer to y Canal of Bergue.*
11. *Sluice of y Canal of la Moer, dem 1714.*
12. *Sluice of la Moer to the Canal of Furnes, demolished in 1714. 1716.*
13. *Sluice of y Port of Mardyke, made.*
14. *Great Sluice 42 feet wide, demo: 1718.*

15. *Old entrenched Camp, demolish'd 1714.*
16. *Fort Lewis, demolished 1714.*
    New Works made since the Year 1740.
17. *Battery of Bourgogne, 8 pieces 1740.*
18. *Battery of Angoumois, 7 pieces 1740.*
19. *Battery of Santerre, 6 pieces 1740.*
20. *Two Batteries on the Downs 1742.*
21. *Battery on y Waters edge, Strand 1742.*
22. *Great Camp entrenched with three rows of Palisades before y Fosse 1742.*
23. *Sluice for supplying Water 1742.*
24. *Little Camp entrenched also with Palisades.*
25. *Sluice for supplying Water*
    Troops in the Little Camp
    to the Number of 6 Batteries
    are
26. *Royal Marine . . . . 1 Battery.*
27. *Hainault . . . . 1 Battery.*
28. *Royal Corsicans . . . 1 Battery.*
29. *Dieslach Swiss . . . . 2 Batteries.*
30. *Mortemer . . . . 1 Battery.*
    Troops of the Great Camp.
31. *Bettens Swiss . . . . 2 Batteries.*
32. *Cour a Chaultre Swiss. 2 Batteries.*
33. *Goudrin . . . . 2 Batteries.*
34. *Chartres . . . . 2 Batteries.*
35. *Soissonnois . . . . . . 1 Battery.*
36. *Monaco . . . . 2 Batteries.*
37. *Head Quarters of M. Givry.*
38. *New Guard Houses.*
39. *Chevaux de Frize upon y Strand.*
40. *New Batteries near Mardyke.*
    All the saillient Angles of the Intrenchments, both of y Great and Little Camp, are supplied with Batteries.

Scale of 800 Toises.

50   100   200   400   800

NB. a Toise is 5 Feet English.

French *guerre de course* had suddenly assumed threatening proportions, and the governments of the trading nations were going to have to do something about it. The question was what.

It was impossible to give all the myriad merchantmen adequate convoy, and hunting privateers at sea was the proverbial search for a needle in haystack, so it seemed logical to destroy their bases. However, the French Channel ports were hard to access and well fortified, and although the classic ships of the line with their bristling cannon were always the central players in any action at sea, these installations were beyond their reach. What was needed were smaller, lighter specially designed warships, like fireships, which could be sent in against wooden forts and guardships. But there was another new type of vessel that could destroy coastal fortifications: the bomb-vessel. These ships were small but very heavily built, with relatively full lines, and capable of carrying and firing a huge mortar.[19] The usual projectiles were hollow iron shells filled with a powder-charge, into which was fitted a wooden fuze filled with a slow-burning mixture, which was lit immediately before firing the mortar. However, it was a very uncertain and inaccurate weapon, and its handling demanded great skill and experience. As with fireships, a successful attack with bomb-vessels demanded that a great many factors all come together favourably – too many, in the eyes of many professionals.

Just at this moment of tactical uncertainty a man of many talents appeared on the scene. Besides his undoubted technical gifts, he was what we nowadays would call a promoter, possessing a talent for convincing a sceptical audience of the virtue of his ideas. The Dutchman Willem Meester (1643–1701), who had studied in Leiden, first came to the attention of the military as an inventor of specialist equipment. His design for easily transportable pontoon bridges earned him the favour of the *Stadhouder*, Willem of Orange, who named him commissioner of artillery, war machines and other inventions. When his patron became William III of England, he took Meester with him and promoted him to be Engineer and Keeper of the Artillery Arsenal in the Tower of London. Here he began secret experiments in the construction of a form of 'Hellburner'. These weapons were usually referred to in England as 'machine-vessels' or 'machines', but were more descriptively called *springers* (explosion-vessels) or 'infernals' by the Dutch.[20]

Meester's machine-vessels were based on an old idea, essentially a further development of the concept used by Gianibelli at the siege of Antwerp in May 1585. Nathaniel Boteler, writing in his *Dialogues* at the beginning of the seventeenth century, had been very sceptical about the practicality of this type of weapon, but perhaps Meester had never read this. Closer to home, Meester's countryman Cornelis Drebbel, like Boteler, had been present at the siege of La Rochelle in 1628 and had seen attempts to use such vessels miscarry. In any event, none of this negative evidence put Meester off.

Presumably for reasons of economy, the vessels that Meester acquired were small and decrepit, often old fishing craft such as Dutch herring-busses, and their poor condition was to hamper all his endeavours. They could not keep the sea for any length of time, and always seemed in need of refits. They were merely receptacles for his invention, which came in two versions, called the 'Great Machine' and the 'Small Machine'. Although the terms came to be applied to the vessels carrying them, strictly speaking, the 'machine' was the detonating mechanism, which like Gianibelli's was probably a piece of clockwork which fired a flintlock, giving the crew ample time to make their escape. Conventional barrels of gunpowder supplied the explosion.

The first time a vessel of this type was deployed was in November 1693, when an English fleet that included Fourth Rates, fireships, bomb-vessels and numerous small craft assembled off St Malo, one of the chief centres of French privateering. The bomb-vessels attacked first but could not get close enough to do significant damage, so during the night of 30 November a machine-vessel was prepared. As was to become the norm, Meester's vessels had not been ready, so one of the fleet's fireships, the *Vesuvius*, had been fitted out as an explosion vessel. It was really an experimental prototype, loaded with about four tonnes of powder and scrap metal, but since it was a conversion of one of the new purpose-built fireships, the sacrifice was obviously expected to be worthwhile.

As illustrated in Nicolas Ozanne's treatise *Marine Militaire* of 1762, a bomb-ketch fires its mortar at a floating timber barrier or boom (B), a task often given to fireships in the hope of destroying it by fire. Regarded as an alternative tactic, the bomb-ketch had the great weakness that it was never a precision weapon, and could achieve even reasonable accuracy only in calm seas. However, bomb-vessels were often given names similar to those of fireships, suggesting that both types were considered in the same light by naval authorities.

(FROM OZANNE 1762, PLATE 45)

ATTAQUE DE VAISSEAUX RETRANCHÉS.

On attaque autant qu'on le peut des Vaisseaux retranchés, par des galiottes à bombes A, ou des bat.res établies à terre, qui puissent rompre leur estacade B, ou du moins l'ébranler assés, pour que de forts V.aux achevent de la forcer, en courant dessus à pleines voiles; on profite aussi des nuits obscures, pour envoier des brulots, ou des chal.pes attacher des Chemises souffrées (g) à l'estacade, afin de la desunir, en rongeant par son feu, la partie qui est au dessus de l'eau; mais si ces premieres attaques, ne peuvent avoir lieu, on fait autant que l'on peut, canonner l'estacade par des V.aux C, qui courent ensuite dessus, pour achever de la rompre, et entrer dans le port; cette derniere manœuvre peut quelque fois devenir très dangereuse, particulierement, si les V.aux retranchés, sont amarés come les V.aux D, parcequ'on peut être retenu par l'estacade, et se trouver entre leur feu et celui des brulots, qu'ils pourroient avoir au vent.

Il y a des occasions, ou l'on prefere aux att.ques cy dessus, celle de combler l'entrée du port par des bâtiments lourdement chargés, que l'on coule à fond, afin d'en rendre l'usage plus difficile à l'ennemi, si on ne peut le detruire tout à fait.

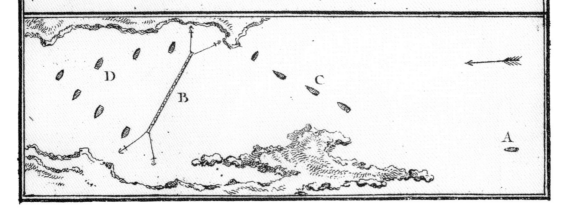

A later French account, which includes a drawing, describes the ship as ballasted with sand to improve its stability, with about ten tons of powder in kegs laid over it. These were covered in a layer of masonry about thirty centimetres thick, with 600 bombs and scrap metal on top, which were in turn covered with two layers of stonework. Over this bed and under the foredeck were laid fifty iron-bound powder-kegs with various sorts of fireworks. The halfdeck was covered with old cannon and other scrap metal, and in the middle of this infernal machine a vertical wooden channel led down to the first layer of powder-kegs, through which ran the fuzing that would ignite it.[21] This does not entirely tally with English descriptions, and it is not clear how such detail could have been gleaned in the first place, because *Vesuvius* got to within almost forty metres of the city wall before striking a rock and exploding prematurely, with the loss of the pilot and four men, knocking down part of the town wall and destroying the roofs and windows of about 300 houses in the town.[22]

Meester's own machine-vessels were to get their chance in the following year, 1694, when a number of assaults were launched against the fortified ports of Brest, St Malo, Dieppe and Dunkirk. Of these, the first was the least promising, because the attack on Brest came down to an attempted amphibious landing in Camaret Bay, where there were no suitable targets for machine-vessels. The English plan of attack had been betrayed, and then delays due to bad weather gave the renowned French fortification engineer Sébastien Le Prestre de Vauban (1633–1707) plenty of time to prepare the defences. The operation went tragically awry with the loss of 400 sailors and 800 soldiers, and the high expectations for Meester's machine went untested.

Meester's backers (first and foremost among them the king) continued to believe in his vision and to supply him with funds to build his special weapons, but a success was needed to convince the many sceptics, especially seamen, who knew how things could happen at sea. So many elements had to come together, many of them beyond human control, that success was always unlikely. Nevertheless, the authorities brushed all reservations aside. The relative failure of the first to be expended – at Dieppe in July – was obscured by

the conspicuous bravery of the captain of the *St Nicholas*, who reboarded the floating bomb when he noticed that the fuze had gone out. Meester himself was probably aware of his diminishing credibility, and during the rather half-hearted attack on Dunkirk in September 1694 he pushed for the deployment of two machines, claiming later in his defence that it was more of a demonstration of the technology than a serious attempt at destruction. One 'Great Machine', the *Abraham's Offering* containing ninety barrels of powder, and one 'Small Machine', the *William and Mary* with ten, were sent against one of the mole heads protecting the entrance to the harbour. The first got close to the target before being taken aback by a wind shift and drifting clear, but the second was hastily abandoned on the approach of some small craft. Both blew up without inflicting any serious damage.[23]

During 1695 more ambitious coastal assaults were planned, culminating in a far greater effort than any previously undertaken, this time for a second attack on Dunkirk. Meester had plenty of 'explanations' for the previous failures of his machines, and so the Dutch government made strenuous efforts to fulfil all of his demands. A force of about a hundred vessels was assembled, including frigates, bomb-vessels, fireships and machine-vessels, these last – as Meester had insisted – under his personal command.

A weak point of the machine-vessel, as with the fireship, was the problem of premature ignition or explosion occasioned by heavy defensive fire, which in this case would be from the French land batteries. To obscure the attackers, Meester, like his predecessor Cornelis Drebbel, had prepared a number of 'smoking-ships', whose purpose was to lay down a smoke-screen prior to the fireship attack. Drake had used a similar idea, and Meester imagined that it would be the key to a successful onslaught.

On Thursday 11 August, at five o'clock in the afternoon, the attack slowly unfolded. Success depended on keeping to an exact schedule. First the smaller frigates and bomb-vessels would bombard the forts protecting the port, and then, as the tide rose, the bigger ships would come into action. Two hours after the beginning of the action, Meester, still radiating optimism and energy, would get his chance to prove the worth of his invention.

First the smoke-ships would be sent in, emitting clouds of stinking fog, and following them, one after the other, would come the machine-vessels, which would drive up against the fortifications.

But once again the Dunkirkers had prepared themselves for the onslaught. At considerable expense they had strengthened the fortifications and defences, with the renowned privateer captain Jean Bart (1650–1702) commanding one of the forts, and many small craft with armed crews were in the water to defend the port against fireships and explosion-vessels. And then, as so often happens with a complex plan, it quickly began to unravel on contact with the enemy. The schedule could not be adhered to, the initial bombardment proved ineffective because the forts were too small a target, and the rough seas made the shelling inaccurate – of 1,200 bombs fired, only about ten hit their mark. When the smoke-ships were deployed the wind was so strong that the ships could not be positioned properly and their smoke was simply dispersed.

Because the bombardment had been so ineffective, the forts of Dunkirk were able to bring the smoke-ships under concentrated fire, and some crews were panicked into igniting them too early, while others were towed clear by defending small craft. That prevented the machine-vessels from getting close enough to do their job, so that any explosions would cause insufficient damage, and in the event Meester decided not to send them in. During the night, both he and the machine-vessels vanished, along with his reputation. His fame gone, he was accused of having done little except spend a lot of money, and even of diverting some of it 'to swell his accounts'. However, because of the protecting hand of the king he was never prosecuted, and he died poor and forgotten in 1701.[24]

The disappointing experience with machine-vessels encouraged a belief that the damage they could inflict on innocent civilians made them barbaric, a view widely promoted by French propaganda. Together with the fact that they had proved useless from a military point of view, this caused them to be rapidly abandoned. Had they enjoyed a spectacular success, they would perhaps have been seen differently. Bomb-vessels, however, which were similarly regarded as 'unchristian' when first introduced, proved too useful to give up.

The war that had begun with a dispute about the Palatine Electorship had escalated to involve many nations and even spread to the Caribbean and North America, where it was known as 'King William's War'. It was by no means confined to the sea, and in only a few of its sea-battles were fireships deployed, and then never decisively. As 1697 approached, both sides faced economic and financial exhaustion. French privateers had captured an estimated total of 6,700 prizes in the nine years of the war, but Louis's zest for war had trickled away with the emptying of his treasury. Finally in September 1697 the plenipotentiaries of the warring powers, France, England, Spain and the United Provinces, met to sign the Treaty of Rijswijk, with Leopold I belatedly following. Louis XIV retained possession of Alsace and Strasbourg, but was forced to renounce all his other objectives.

CHAPTER SEVENTEEN

FIRESHIPS
IN THE
EIGHTEENTH CENTURY

'...il est bon d'en avoir et de ne pas s'en servir.'

Diderot and D'Alembert, *Encyclopédie méthodique*, 1803

B Y THE END OF THE SEVENTEENTH CENTURY, fewer and fewer successes were being achieved with fireships in fleet battles. This was primarily the result of more disciplined tactics in sea warfare, and the trend continued into the early eighteenth century. Nonetheless, there was still some support for the tactical use of fireships among the sea powers, since they had occasional uses – and of course nobody would unilaterally abandon a weapon as long as the enemy possessed it.

The formalised fleet tactic of fighting in a 'line of battle' was well established by the beginning of the new century, and it remained true that a big ship could not be easily sunk or totally destroyed, even after taking heavy damage in an artillery duel lasting for hours. However, a ship of the line that could not manoeuvre properly (say, in confined waters), or one that found itself crippled and isolated, might be sunk using fireships, or perhaps in some cases bomb-vessels. Within this restricted scenario the occasional spectacular and significant fireship action still occurred, but with the exception of the *Real Felipe* in 1744 (discussed in Chapter 14) by the eighteenth century they were no longer being deployed on the high seas. The days of general mêlée fighting in the English Channel were long past.

The first conflict of the new century with a maritime dimension was the War of the Spanish Succession (1701–14), which arose from a dispute about who should succeed the last Spanish Habsburg ruler, Carlos II. At the time of Carlos's death Spain ruled parts of the West Indies, the Philippines, a large section of Italy, the Balearic Islands, Corsica, Sardinia and the Spanish Netherlands. The designated heir was Philip, Duke of Anjou (Philip V), a grandson of Louis XIV, and it was this prospect of an invincible alliance between France and Spain and their collective resources that proved intolerable to the other European powers. In particular, it brought Louis into conflict with the Holy Roman Emperor, Leopold I, who advanced the claim to the Spanish throne of his son Karl (who would then become Carlos III). Leopold enlisted England and the United Provinces as allies, and at sea the Anglo-Dutch and Franco-Spanish combined fleets faced each other, with the focal point of the naval conflict being the Mediterranean, especially the area off the coast of Spain.

In September 1702 the ships of the Anglo-Dutch fleet were off the north-west coast of Spain when they received the electrifying news that the Spanish Silver Fleet was at anchor in the harbour of Vigo. This prompted Admiral Sir George Rooke and his Dutch vice admiral Philips van Almonde to plan an immediate attack – this was obviously a rich prize, but as it later transpired it was the most valuable treasure fleet of all time. The Spanish galleons

This is how the engineer and engraver Nicolas-Marie Ozanne (1728–1811) represented a fireship of about 1760 in his *Marine Militaire*. His definition is a brief statement of conventional wisdom about the type. 'Fireships are vessels filled with readily inflammable materials and tasked with setting enemy ships on fire. On either side of the stern is a port through which the crew reach their launch after they have kindled a fire, and before the inflammable material, the fireship and the ship it has grappled are totally burned up. The fireship approaches the enemy from windward so that the fire will burn its rigging more vigorously. Grappling-irons 'A' at the yardarms hook themselves in the enemy's rigging, or grapnels are hurled across by hand. Older vessels are usually fitted out for this purpose. They are armed with cannon to destroy small craft or signal as the case may be. If a fireship is given the order to attack, other vessels are assigned to protect it and pick up its crew. Because of the chaos and panic which a fireship can elicit from the enemy, fireships often play a decisive role in battle.'

(FROM: OZANNE 1762)

were accordingly well protected, lying at anchor in a crescent formation with thirty French and Spanish escorting warships behind a wooden boom, covered by the guns of shore batteries. Rooke attacked with some smaller ships of the line and all his available fireships, and at the same time an out-flanking land force was sent to neutralise the forts.

The operation was an immense success, with the Spanish and French ships all being burned, driven aground or captured. Although the Anglo-Dutch fleet had ten fireships available, they were not needed, and the enemy ships that had been abandoned by their demoralised crews were fired in the time-tested fashion by the crews of small craft using extempore fire-balls, fire-arrows and pitch-wreaths, as at La Hougue. Powder was strewn on the decks of the victims and then set off with fuzes; in many cases, the ships blew up when the fire reached their magazines.[1]

Although this was achieved with practically no resistance, there was one episode involving a fire-ship which is of interest. A French fireship acting as a guardship attacked the English 80-gun ship *Torbay*. It was a classic attack which miscarried in the classic fashion. An eyewitness in the *Torbay* described it thus:

> … in the meanwhile a French fireship with its foresail and main topsail set, and all in flames from her masts aft came down before the wind and was very near us before we saw her. We vecred away cable, and I send my boat to endeavour to tow her off, but all in vain, for she clapped us aboard on the larboard bow and her sheer-hooks took hold of our foresail and set our quarter on fire. Thereupon many of the men went overboard and several were drowned.'[2]

The crew of the English ship managed to cut the fireship loose, so that she drifted away and exploded harmlessly while they managed to extinguish the fire aboard their own vessel.

The next engagement proved the greatest sea-battle of the War of the Spanish Succession. In August 1704 an Anglo-Dutch force under Admiral Rooke had taken Gibraltar, and a few days later a French fleet of fifty ships of the line under the

This is a crude but lively depiction of the capture of Barcelona in October 1705 by confederate forces (those supporting the claim of 'Carlos III' to the throne during the War of Spanish Succession). It clearly shows an English fireship being sent against a Spanish ship of the line, even though none was actually expended during this operation: apparently the fireship was so strongly associated with sea warfare by this time that the artist felt obliged to include one.

(BEVERLEY R ROBINSON COLLECTION, ANNAPOLIS)

command of Admirals d'Estrées and the Count of Toulouse met an Allied force of about the same strength. The French wanted to blockade Gibraltar and recapture it, and the ensuing battle of Malaga developed into a textbook line-of-battle encounter.

Neither side managed to destroy or capture any ships, but since the French did not renew battle the next day, it was a strategic victory for the English because they were then able to secure their conquest of Gibraltar. In terms of the history of the fireship it is highly significant that the French had between six and nine fireships, and the Anglo-Dutch fleet seven, but neither side deployed a single one. This battle marked the point at which the new fleet tactics had removed virtually all opportunity of fireship action. As a psychological weapon, in offence or defence, and as an active constituent of the battle fleet, closely following the flagship, the fireship had finally had its day.

When the War of the Spanish Succession ended

in 1713 with the signing of the Treaty of Utrecht, Louis XIV managed to hang on to his position of power, and he installed a Bourbon, Philip of Anjou, on the Spanish throne as Philip V. But the big winner was Great Britain, as it was now called following the Union of Scotland and England, which had won territories in the Mediterranean and North America. Now the largest navy in the world, the Royal Navy was on the way to becoming ruler of the seas.

With the reduction in the tactical possibilities of the fireship, numbers of the weapon declined steeply in comparison with its heyday in the mid-seventeenth century. In January 1639 the French fleet had nineteen fireships, and in the English service numbers reached twenty-six in each of the three Anglo-Dutch Wars (1652–64, 1665–7 and 1672–4). The highest point in the tally of fireships occurred in 1690 when, following Colbert's expansion of the French Marine, there were thirty

The National Maritime Museum has a very instructive model of the Sixth Rate *Dolphin* of 1732. The model is effectively divided down the centreline, the port side showing her appearance as a cruising ship with only oar ports and a midships ballast port on the lower deck. However, the starboard side depicts the vessel refitted as a fireship in 1746, with a row of bottom-hinged ports and a sally-port on the lower deck. In the waist two prominent features are the additional capstan (required because a fireship conversion could no longer work its cables on the lower deck) and the higher gallows required to keep the boats and spare spars clear of it.

(WIKIMEDIA COMMONS)

fireships in the French fleet.[3] In the relatively few years of peace the numbers dropped precipitously to around five or so in each of the major navies.

In the eighteenth century the maximum numbers were much more modest. At the time of the War of the Spanish Succession the Royal Navy reached ten or twelve, but in peacetime each fleet retained only about three fireships. They were essentially a wartime expedient: they needed constant attention, with their powder deteriorating over time and needing replacement,[4] so the cost of building and upkeep was a distinct disincentive in peacetime. Even in times of war, costs were high in proportion to the number of times they were used in their primary capacity, and in fact for most of their time in commission they were employed as small cruisers. There was also a human factor influencing the declining use of fireships: given the choice, a naval officer would find it much more lucrative to capture a prize than to reduce it to ashes.[5]

During the war with Spain that broke out in 1739 the number of Royal Navy fireships rose quickly to about nineteen; about fourteen served in the Seven Years' War (1756–63), and there was also an increase in fireships during the American War of Independence (1775–83). However, after the French Revolution and during the Napoleonic Wars the numbers decreased, with only four in service in 1800, and by 1805 (apart from a few exceptions that will be discussed below) hardly any remained.[6]

Even more modest than the numbers of fireships in the eighteenth century was the number of real successes with the weapon. However, the belief persisted that they might just have their uses in wartime, so it was worthwhile to keep a sufficient number available. In this spirit the Admiralty sent the following memorandum to the King in Council in October 1739: 'And in regard that your Majesty's fleets being employed in several parts of the world in carrying on the war against Spain, may require the service of a large number of fireships, we humbly desire your Majesty's directions for buying thirteen ships proper to be converted into fireships.'[7]

This Spanish war – the so-called 'War of Jenkins's Ear' – eventually flowed into the larger War of Austrian Succession, which lasted until 1748,

with the French joining in in 1744. Fireship attacks were not a major feature of the fighting at sea, but there were a couple of examples. In June 1742 five Spanish galleys which had transported troops to Spain were sailing along the French Mediterranean coast when they learned that a British squadron was approaching. They fled into the neutral French port of St Tropez, which was immediately blockaded by the British commander, Captain Richard Norris in the *Kingston*.

Then the Spanish made the mistake of firing at the British, and Commander Smith Callis of the fireship *Duke* was given the order to attack. It was the perfect scenario for a fireship – a stationary, almost defenceless target in a harbour – and the action succeeded, with the galleys burning to the water's edge so rapidly that the officers did not have time to rescue their possessions. Smith Callis was, as custom demanded, promptly rewarded with command of a bigger vessel.[8] The incident involving the *Real Felipe* at the Battle of Toulon is the other instance of a fireship attack in this war, although it was a vain one. It was probably the last example of a fireship sent against a warship which could defend itself, and in the open sea.

The next conflict of this century saw relatively few sea-battles in comparison to the number of battles on land. During the Seven Years' War (1756–63), which pitted England and Prussia against France, Austria and Russia, a total of ten fireships were purchased and four were converted from warships.[9] Some of these were local initiatives by commanders on foreign stations, and many had very short active careers, so the apparently high number is misleading. Despite the urgency of their acquisition, their real value was very limited: in two of the most important sea-battles of the war, the battle of Minorca in May 1756 and the battle of Quiberon Bay in November 1759, not one single fireship attack was attempted. Perhaps more significantly, at Lagos in 1759, when a superior British fleet drove ashore four French ships of the line, Admiral Boscawen sent in his boats to capture and burn the stranded vessels rather than use either of his two fireships.

Until the 1780s, in all parts of the world where Britain had maritime interests and wherever British fleets were found, there were never more than one or two fireships in company, and there are no instances of British fireships being deployed in anger. However, this was not the case everywhere, and there was a dramatic reminder of the horrendous potential of this weapon in naval warfare at the beginning of the 1770s.

Over a period of about 300 years there was a succession of wars between Russia and the Ottoman Empire, in the course of which Russia extended her territory to the east and south. The land campaigns are outside the scope of this book, but the powers involved also clashed at sea. In the summer and autumn of 1769 two Russian squadrons left Kronstadt, crossed the Baltic, and, after a short delay at Copenhagen due to bad weather, sailed out into the North Sea and down the western fringes of Europe before turning eastwards at Gibraltar. On 1 May they were in the eastern Mediterranean off the Ottoman coast, and once they had rendezvoused the two fleets began operations against the Turkish fleet.

The aim was to defeat the Turks before they could build up their fleet and attack the weak Russian fleet in the Black Sea. The commander-in-chief, Admiral Count Alexei Orlov (1737–1809), who was really a cavalryman, was something of a dashing adventurer and had been involved in the murder of Tsar Peter III and the succession of his wife as Catherine the Great. One squadron was commanded by Admiral Grigory Spiridov, while the other was under the command of Captain John Elphinstone of the Royal Navy (1722–1785), who had transferred to the Russian Imperial Navy with British approval and put his service and experience at Catherine's disposal.[10] In May 1770 his squadron brought part of the Turkish fleet to action off Nauplia; the Turks withdrew, but this gave Elphinstone a good chance to gauge the capabilities of the enemy. Early on the morning of 5 July the Russians sailed round the northern end of the Isle of Chios and sighted the enemy, who were anchored in the Straits of Chios, in the lee of the mainland north of the little port of Chesme (nowadays Çesme).

The Turkish commander, Kapudan Pasha Hosameddin, had anchored his fleet in two crescent-shaped lines, one behind the other. The first consisted of ten ships of the line about 200 metres

The Russian annihilation of a Turkish fleet at Chesme in 1770 was a triumph for the fireship, and gave a new lease of life to a moribund weapon. This is one of a series of prints engraved after the work of the well-known marine painter Richard Paton; it was popular in Britain and went through a number of editions. This view shows the climax of the battle, with most of the Turkish fleet on fire, exploding or already burned out and wrecked.

apart, and the second row had six ships, which were able to fire through the gaps in the first line. The Russian plan of attack can be quickly outlined. The nine Russian ships of the line were to sail parallel to the Turkish line and, when abreast their designated opposite numbers, luff and turn towards them. This would expose them to the broadside fire of the enemy during the approach, but Admiral Spiridov thought he could get away with minimal damage, given the indifferent training of the Turkish gunners. The plan had the advantage that it allowed the Russians to concentrate their fire on part of the enemy line, and so compensate for their numerical inferiority. However, it was a departure from textbook line-of-battle tactics of the day, which specified that none of the enemy line should be left unengaged.

Shortly before noon, when the Russians were about 650 metres from the defensive line, the Turks opened fire, without causing any great damage, and three-quarters of an hour later, when within ninety metres' distance, the Russians returned their first salvo from double-shotted guns. Admiral Spiridov's flagship, the 68-gun *Svyatoy Evstafiy* (St Eustachius), got within pistol-shot of the 84-gun Turkish flagship *Real Mustafa*, and tried to board. However, the mainmast of the Turk was on fire and crashed down on the Russian, starting a fire which the crew could not extinguish. First the magazine of the Russian ship blew up, quickly followed by a similar explosion of the Turkish vessel. Only sixty-nine out of the crew of 699 were rescued. About one o'clock the Turkish line began to falter, and the first ships cut their cables and withdrew into the Bay of Chesme, where they formed up in another defensive line across the harbour mouth.[11] The Russians spent the night of 6 July preparing for a renewed attack on the Turkish position, including fitting out extempore fireships from some auxiliary vessels (they had no designated fireships at this time). A bomb-vessel was sent in to shell the enemy fleet during the night and into the next day, and at the same time the Russian ships of the line opened fire on the coastal batteries and other seaward targets.

Under cover of darkness the following night, four Russian ships, two frigates and four fireships slipped into the Bay of Chesme and got within 500

metres of the Turkish line. The commander of the attack was Captain Samuel Greig RN (1736–1788), like his colleague Elphinstone a Scot who had transferred to the Russian service. About 11.30 the artillery attack on the closely packed Turkish ships began at a range of about 400 metres. Two hours later a lucky shot from the bomb vessel hit a Turkish warship and set the mainmast on fire, bringing it down and spreading the fire uncontrollably through the whole ship. The flames then leaped to the next ship anchored in the line, and just two hours later the powder-magazines of both burning ships exploded, with the result that other Turkish ships were set on fire by the burning debris which rained down.

In the midst of all the powder-smoke and fire, Greig now fired a rocket to signal his fireships into action. These vessels, which had been hurriedly converted from storeships, slipped out from behind the line and set course for the Turkish ships in a classic fireship attack. The Russians held their fire to avoid hitting their own ships, but the Turks aimed everything available at them as soon as they realised the danger. The crews of the Russian fireships were in large part Greeks from the nearby island of Psará, a population famous for their seafaring tradition.[12] Following the Greek rebellion against their Ottoman overlords in 1768, there was no love lost between them and the Turks, and their support for the Russians was a natural reaction.

In the first fireship were Greig and Lieutenant Drysdale, another British officer in Russian employ. It was attacked by two Turkish galleys and sunk, but officers and crew were able to make their escape by boat. The second fireship, which was commanded by a third British officer, Lieutenant Mackenzie, grappled a vessel which was already on fire. The third, under the command of Lieutenant Dimitriy Sergeyevich Ilyin, managed to get alongside an 84-gun ship and set it on fire, and he and his crew beat a successful retreat in their longboat. Lieutenant Gagarin in the fourth fireship came too late to inflict much damage. The 84-gun ship exploded a little later, and the falling debris set most of the remaining Turkish ships on fire. This turned the bay into one huge raging bonfire, and at the end of the day, out of fifteen ships of the line, six frigates and fifty auxiliary vessels, just one ship and five galleys escaped unscathed.[13] The battle of Chesme was a decisive triumph for the Russians, and for quite some time thereafter Orlov had naval supremacy in the Mediterranean.

The fireship captain Dimitriy Ilyin, who was descended from Russian minor nobility, could have been hailed as the native hero of Chesme, but in contrast to Captain Greig, who was promoted to admiral by Count Orlov after the annihilation of the Turks, he remained in command of a relatively small ship, the bomb-vessel *Molniya* (Lightning). It is true that he was decorated with the splendid Order of St George, and was promoted to captain before he retired in 1777, but he was only properly honoured on the 125th anniversary of the battle in 1895, when a memorial was erected over his grave. From 1887 until 2000 a series of mid-sized Russian ships in the Baltic Fleet carried his name, and in 2005 a street in the central city of Tver (Kalinin) was named after him.

To return to Western Europe, after the end of the Seven Years' War in 1763, the number of fireships in the Royal Navy had dropped to just one or two. At the beginning of the War of American Independence (1775–83) there was just one, and the first battle squadron sent to North America in 1778 had no fireships assigned to it.[14] In notes taken at a Cabinet meeting in March 1778 the Earl of Sandwich indicated there were seventy ships of all classes deployed in North America, just one of which was a fireship. However, the numbers were about to expand, partly as a result of new building. At the beginning of 1778 two vessels were purchased from merchant yards while on the stocks and completed as fireships.[15] The first purpose-built fireship was also laid down, and just a year later, in 1779, the Navy already possessed six fireships; by 1783 when the war ended the number had risen to seventeen.[16] At this time the number of fireships in the Dutch and French fleets also rose to six or seven. The British squadrons which sailed for North America or to protect trade in the West Indies after 1778 always had one or two fireships attached, although there are no reports of their being employed.[17]

This revival in the popularity of the fireship in the Royal Navy was partly a response to the adverse conditions of the war. By 1778 it was not just being fought against the colonial possessions, but also involved France and Spain, and the Netherlands would be dragged in later. The British fleet had worldwide commitments, from home waters to the Mediterranean and from North America and the Caribbean to the East Indies.[18] For the first time in the century the Royal Navy might have to face superior numbers wherever it fought. Despite the absence of recent successes, fireships remained – at least in the minds of fleet commanders – a potential 'equaliser', a counter-balance to superior firepower or larger numbers of enemy ships. To give one contemporary example, Rear Admiral James Gambier, writing from New York in July 1778, asked the First Lord of the Admiralty for permission to convert six transports into fireships. A superior French fleet was approaching, and Gambier was convinced that only fireships were in a position '… to make up the manifest inferiority in weight of ships'. He was beginning with a first transport as a 'temporary fireship' and estimated that it would take about four days to make the conversion.[19]

However, this practical reaction to wartime conditions was simply building on an existing revival of tactical interest in the gruesome old weapon among the Navy's higher echelons. The renewed enthusiasm for the fireship as a part of the battlefleet was largely based on the thinking of Captain Richard Kempenfelt and Admiral Lord Howe, the latter issuing *Fighting Instructions* in 1782 that gave special attention to the organisation of a fireship attack and in particular to how it should be backed up by supporting vessels.[20] The doctrine had never been laid down in such detail before, and Howe, who was all too aware that techniques of defence against fireships had become much more sophisticated, emphasised that the success of an attack depended on careful attention to starting position, weather conditions and adequate use of supporting vessels, and on making sure that all these factors were perfectly coordinated.

Having been a First Lord of the Admiralty, Howe was able to pass on his enthusiasm to a successor in the post, John Montagu, Fourth Earl of Sandwich (1717–1792). Sandwich – who gave his name to the famous snack as well as to the group of islands discovered by James Cook, nowadays

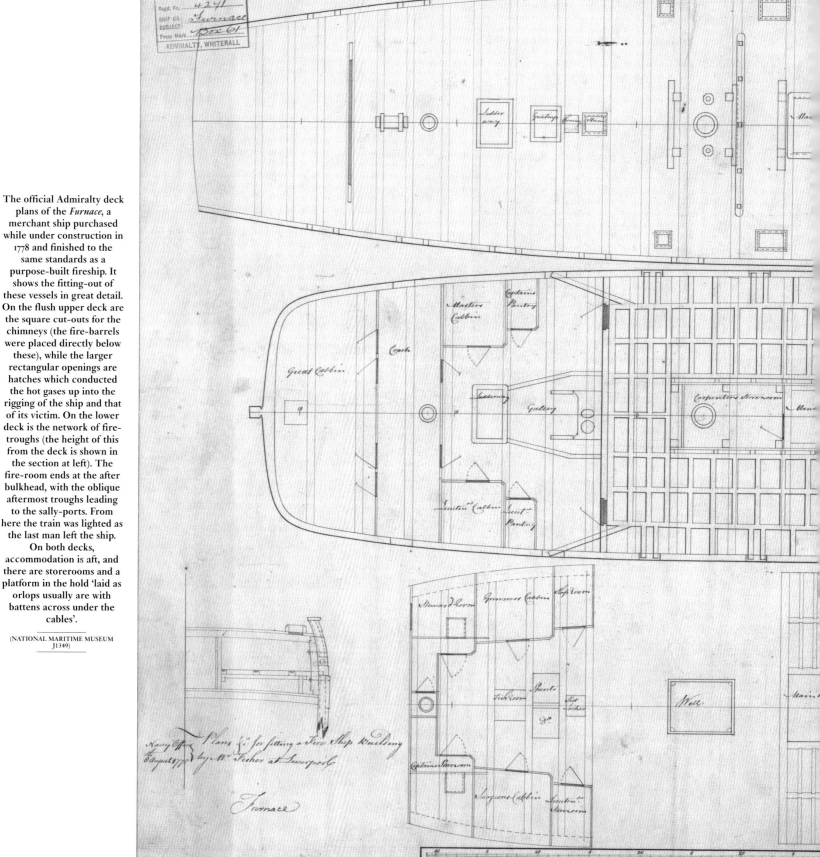

The official Admiralty deck plans of the *Furnace*, a merchant ship purchased while under construction in 1778 and finished to the same standards as a purpose-built fireship. It shows the fitting-out of these vessels in great detail. On the flush upper deck are the square cut-outs for the chimneys (the fire-barrels were placed directly below these), while the larger rectangular openings are hatches which conducted the hot gases up into the rigging of the ship and that of its victim. On the lower deck is the network of fire-troughs (the height of this from the deck is shown in the section at left). The fire-room ends at the after bulkhead, with the oblique aftermost troughs leading to the sally-ports. From here the train was lighted as the last man left the ship.

On both decks, accommodation is aft, and there are storerooms and a platform in the hold 'laid as orlops usually are with battens across under the cables'.

(NATIONAL MARITIME MUSEUM
J1349)

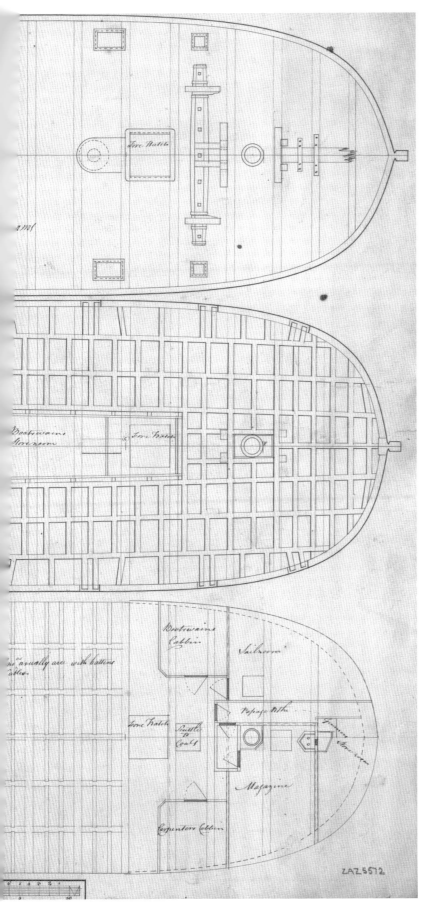

known as Hawaii – was a descendant of Edward Montagu, who had commanded part of the English fleet at the battle of Sole Bay and lost his life following a Dutch fireship attack. In a letter to Admiral Keppel, Sandwich wrote: 'I own I think that when great fleets are likely to meet, they [fireships] are a very useful engine of war. I should not be so confirmed in that idea had I not from reading and from conversation with many very able sea officers found them in the same sentiments, particularly Lord Howe, who, when he left England left it with me as a sort of legacy that that useful though horrid instrument might not be laid aside.'[21]

As First Lord, Sandwich decided that a new generation of fireships had to be built, and, as in 1689, these were to be designed as such from the outset. The battlefleet was in the process of being transformed by the introduction of copper sheathing, which retarded the growth of marine fouling, making ships faster; moreover, the newer ships of the line enjoyed better sea-keeping than their predecessors, so cruises tended to be longer. The new fireships were conceived with these requirements in mind: they were to have the performance of frigates and be coppered from launch. Sandwich felt that, although initially more expensive, this was a more long-lasting solution to the lack of fireships than the purchase and conversion of privateers or merchantmen.[22] The French were at a disadvantage in this respect: the British were so

Admiral Lord Howe (1726–1799) was a highly skilled tactician and a profound thinker on naval matters. In spite of the apparent decline of the fireship as a battlefleet weapon, Howe became a major exponent of its value, and his influence was probably responsible for the construction of new purpose-built fireships during the American Revolutionary War. Unfortunately, Howe's ideas were never clearly expounded so it is not certain what scenario he envisaged for the deployment of fireships, but they might, for example, have been useful against the huge Franco-Spanish fleet that seized control of the Channel in 1779. This was large in number, unwieldy and, since the ships had never previously exercised together, lacking in command and control – in earlier centuries it would have been ripe for fireship attack.

(AUTHOR)

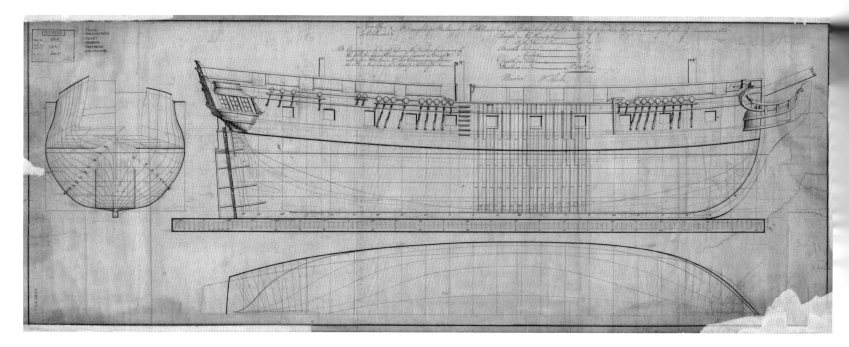

The Admiralty profile draught for the *Thais* class, the Royal Navy's last purpose-built fireships. The six vessels, ordered in October 1805, were very similar to the preceding *Tisiphone* class of 1781, both having a flush upper deck, the gunports in the waist distinguishing them from the sloops they otherwise resembled. They were fast sailers and spent most of their active careers as cruising ships.

(NATIONAL MARITIME MUSEUM J8048)

effective in blockading their ports that they had difficulty in obtaining enough rolled sheet-copper to follow suit. The fireships of the new *Tisiphone* (or *Pluto*) class of 1780 had a length on deck of 109 feet and a beam of thirty feet, and were quite large at around 422 tons; they carried a crew of fifty-five instead of the usual forty-five. Their hull-form followed the fine lines of the French frigate *Panthère*, which the British had captured in 1745.[23] Between 1780 and 1783 the British built nine examples of this class,[24] the first two entering service by the end of 1781. In addition to the usual purchases and conversions, there were then between eleven and thirteen fireships deployed on various stations stretching from home waters to the Leeward Islands in the West Indies. However, none of these vessels was ever expended in the traditional fireship role during the course of the war.[25]

Fireships were employed during the War of American Independence, but primarily by the Americans, who, faced with the vastly superior British fleet, improvised a number of such craft. An example was the night-time attack by two such extempore weapons against a small British flotilla comprising the 44-gun *Phoenix*, the 20-gun *Rose*, a schooner and two transports, which had been sent up the Hudson river to attack General Washington's flank in August 1776. The Americans countered with fire from shore batteries and an attack with small row-galleys, causing the British

to withdraw downriver. It was eleven o'clock on the night of the 16th when two dark shadows came out of the darkness, drifting towards the British vessels anchored in the stream. At first a renewed attack by a riverboat armed with an 18-pounder was expected, but then the ships revealed themselves as a schooner and a sloop, and the lookouts in the British vessels watched aghast as the oncoming craft suddenly blazed up while their crews made their escape. Frantically, the British cut their cables and tried to make sail. The first fireship hit one of the transports and set it on fire immediately. The second one, whose mainsail had caught fire prematurely, just missed the *Rose* and struck the bow of the *Phoenix*, her bowsprit lodging in her rigging. By the skin of their teeth her crew managed to fend off the fireship and rescue the *Phoenix*, but the next day they withdrew to the river mouth.[26] Having survived a potential man-made disaster, *Phoenix* succumbed four years later to the power of nature, being destroyed by an infamous hurricane in the West Indies in October 1780.[27]

After the Dutch had joined the French and Spaniards in supporting the Americans, the British declared war on them, and in August 1781 the battle of the Dogger Bank became the biggest encounter of the so-called Fourth Anglo-Dutch War. The British and Dutch fleets, of similar size and both convoying large numbers of merchantmen, ran across each other by accident. Neither

had any accompanying fireships, and the affair developed into a very formal line-of-battle encounter, in which both sides suffered considerable but not fatal damage to their hulls. After several hours, battle was broken off, and each fleet went on its way. But for Dutch trade, and especially the East Indiamen, this battle had devastating consequences. From then on the British imposed a blockade of the Dutch coast, preventing merchant convoys from getting in or out. Then in 1781 the British captured the Dutch Spice Fleet as it was returning from the East Indies, with a cargo worth ten million guilders, and the loss accelerated the downfall of the once-mighty Dutch East India Company.

This battle makes a telling comparison with what had occurred a century before in the last battle of the Third Anglo-Dutch War, the battle of the Texel (1673). At that time the Dutch fleet under De Ruyter had twenty-two fireships, and the English under Prince Rupert no fewer than twenty-eight. After the fight the English were in no position to enforce a lasting blockade of the Dutch coast, or to bring their trade to a standstill, and at the end of that war

the Dutch were once more able to revive their overseas trade. Now, a century later, it was entirely different. the economy of the United Netherlands failed to recover after the War of American Independence, and the once mighty Republic became no more than a second-class economic power. The glory days of the fireship had also passed, but as we shall see the concept still had life in it.

At the time of the Treaty of Paris, which brought the American War of Independence to an end, the Royal Navy comprised 468 vessels, including seventeen fireships.[28] But none of them had been deployed in the war, and in the peacetime that followed their numbers sank further until there were only nine when the French Revolution began in 1793. Numbers did not recover during the French Revolutionary War, although a dozen small craft were purchased in 1794 and rated as 'fire-vessels'. Active cruising fireships were few, and British squadrons blockading the French coast at this time usually had only one or two. From the list of fireship losses recorded by the Navy at this time, it appears that all were the result of accident rather

Although the fireship's credibility as a battlefleet weapon was in decline, it continued to find uses in what might be considered 'guerrilla' warfare. An example of this was the attack on the 44-gun *Phoenix* and 20-gun *Rose* in the confines of the Hudson river on 16 August 1776. Washington's army was being driven out of New York, but the British control of the waterways threatened to cut off his retreat, so he launched an attack to clear the Hudson. It very nearly succeeded in destroying the *Phoenix*, as depicted here, but the fireship was fended off.

(BEVERLEY R ROBINSON COLLECTION, ANNAPOLIS)

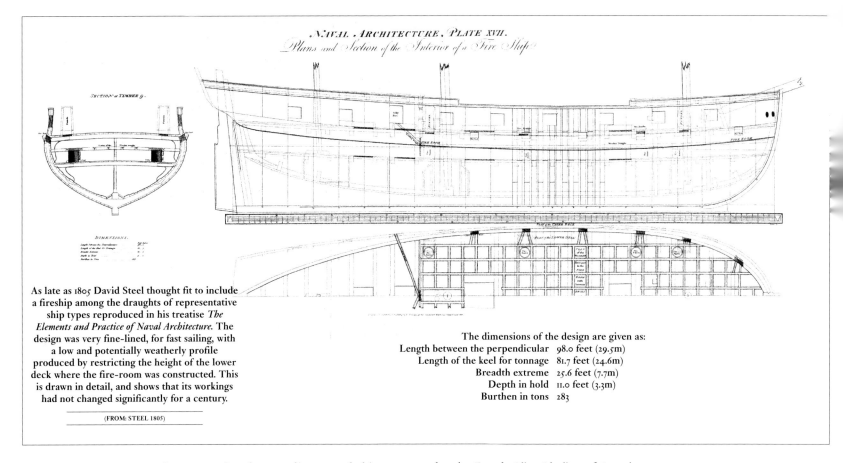

NAVAL ARCHITECTURE, PLATE XVII.
Plans and Section of the Interior of a Fire Ship

As late as 1805 David Steel thought fit to include a fireship among the draughts of representative ship types reproduced in his treatise *The Elements and Practice of Naval Architecture*. The design was very fine-lined, for fast sailing, with a low and potentially weatherly profile produced by restricting the height of the lower deck where the fire-room was constructed. This is drawn in detail, and shows that its workings had not changed significantly for a century.

(FROM: STEEL 1805)

The dimensions of the design are given as:

Length between the perpendicular	98.0 feet (29.5m)
Length of the keel for tonnage	81.7 feet (24.6m)
Breadth extreme	25.6 feet (7.7m)
Depth in hold	11.0 feet (3.3m)
Burthen in tons	283

than operational expenditure, and this was to remain the norm as long as such vessels were in existence.[29]

At the end of the eighteenth century, paradoxically, as the importance of the fireship as a weapon declined, increasing amounts of information about its design and operational use began to be published, and there are even some models. This was not conscious antiquarianism so much as the encyclopaedic curiosity about of all fields of knowledge and technology that characterised the Age of Enlightenment. Technical dictionaries of the time give many details about fireships, and all these books refer to the battle of Chesme in 1770. Clearly the battle made an immense impression on contemporary thought, causing strategists and tacticians to re-examine the usefulness of this old weapon.

An early example is Falconer's *An Universal Dictionary of the Marine* (1780), where the author devotes a section to a careful description of the interior of a fireship. The article 'Brûlot' in the 'Marine' section of Diderot and d'Alembert's immense compendium of the knowledge of the day, the *Encyclopédie méthodique* of 1803, gives an exact description of the 'fire-apparatus' of a fireship, even though the author, Honoré-Sébastien Vial du Clairbois (1733–1816), as Chief Constructor of the Marine at Brest, must have been aware of the dwindling importance of this weapon.[30] Significantly, he notes that 'The Russians destroyed the Turkish fleet thus [ie with fireships] in their last war.'[31] The same is true of the entry about fireships in the *Allgemeines Wörterbuch der Marine* (1793) by Johann Hinrich Röding, who would similarly have been aware of the events at Chesme. As late as 1805 David Steel in his *Elements and Practice of Naval Architecture* still carefully explains the function of a fireship as if it is a live issue. In a work of later date, *Dictionnaire da la Marine, à voiles* (1856), Bonnefoux and Paris move on to new experimental craft that can be used to set fire to a ship. There is again mention of a fireship attack, but in this case the reference is not to Chesme, but to some later use of fireships by the Greeks during their War of Independence against the Ottoman Empire (see Chapter 18).

In the first half of the nineteenth century, the fireship's dying days, many dictionary entries were

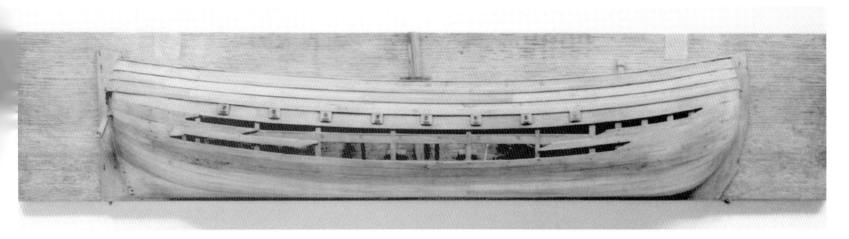

concerned with the moral aspect of this form of warfare. Still a fearsome weapon, it remained the only one which could totally annihilate a warship and its crew. The unease which many felt was not new: recall the anger of the Earl of Sandwich at the battle of Lowestoft in 1665, when an insubordinate captain set fire to three surrendered Dutch ships, slaughtering hundreds of men who were already out of the fight. Sandwich ordered that the captain be court-martialled, feeling that his conduct was unchristian and that the annihilation of a surrendered enemy violated the unwritten rules (see Chapter 11). The hard business of war allowed one to kill an enemy who was still fighting, but then as now, quarter was to be given if he surrendered. Seven years later, Sandwich's own fate would be sealed by a fireship when he refused to surrender.

A century later Vial du Clairbois in his *Encyclopédie méthodique* (1787) offered a somewhat nuanced opinion, namely that fireships should be used only as a deterrent. He excused their use by the Russians against the infidel Turks, but against fellow Christians, he believed, they should be used only as a threat: 'It is good to have some but not to make use of them.'[31] Likewise, Röding in his *Allgemeines Wörterbuch der Marine* agreed that the fireship was a dishonourable weapon to use against people.

In the nineteenth century, the use of fireships became ever rarer, but the number of voices demanding its repudiation increased, as did moral concerns about other more recently invented devices like underwater mines, which used delayed-detonation devices of various kinds. These were thought unmanly and brutal by many British commanders, an attitude for some that extended to fireships. When the Admiralty ordered a fireship attack on the French ships at the battle of Basque Roads off the western French coast in 1809, several officers declined to have anything to do with it. Even the admiral, the overtly religious Lord Gambier, could scarcely disguise his reluctance, so when Thomas Cochrane (1775–1860), a particularly determined commander and aggressive advocate of the fireship, took on the task he received less than whole-hearted support.

Besides the quarterdeck debate, the matter was discussed on the gun decks of the British ships off Basque Roads before the attack. The question was whether to attack the French in classic style by daylight, which would endanger numerous British ships, or to reduce the risk by using fireships. A contemporary opinion is offered by an eyewitness with the vivid *nom de plume* of Jack Nastyface:

> If that idea had been carried into effect to the full extent of its object, we should not only have burnt their shipping, but also the crews in them must have become sacrificed; and though it was an enemy, yet the thought is shuddering, that nearly ten thousand men, whilst they were harmlessly asleep in their cots and hammocks, might be roasted to death and perhaps without a moment to say Lord have mercy on me![32]

However, in the hope of totally annihilating the French fleet, Cochrane thrust aside all moral considerations and proceeded to attack with not just fireships but also explosion-vessels. This dramatic attack will be described in Chapter 18.

The Rijksmuseum in Amsterdam has a number of fireship models from the end of the eighteenth century. Most are of refitted fishing craft and show the alterations of the interiors. A central fire-gutter, which can be lit from two places, leads from the cockpit to the fore and after ends of the fire-room, where 'stoves' are built. The hold is packed with brushwood, and from the deck beams hang teardrop-shaped items that were probably filled with oil or other inflammable material. There are fire-barrels in the hold and also chain-bound chests filled with metal shot – presumably bombs set to explode with the heat of the fire so as to discourage the enemy from boarding the vessel. This makeshift form of fireship was designed to protect harbours and prevent access to the Zuiderzee after the British had neutralised the Dutch fleet during the era of the Batavian Republic in the Napoleonic Wars.

(RIJKSMUSEUM, AMSTERDAM, SK-A-307)

CHAPTER EIGHTEEN

THE LAST FIRESHIPS:
THE NINETEENTH CENTURY

*'It is a mode of warfare dreadful
to resort to and should not be practiced
by a civilized nation'*

Jack Nastyface, *Nautical Economy*, 1836

THE FIRST GREAT SEA-BATTLE OF THE French Revolutionary War took place, after three days of skirmishing, on 1 June 1794, a combat so far from any point of land that it was known simply as 'The Glorious First of June'. The British fleet was commanded by Richard, Earl Howe, and as would be expected from a life-long advocate of fireships, his order of battle included two such vessels, but his revolutionary French opponents had none. Howe was an innovative tactician, and in this battle he gave up the traditional broadside gunnery duel in parallel lines; instead he had his ships break the French line in several places and concentrate their fire on selected enemy ships. In a way this was a return to the naval tactics of 150 years earlier, bringing on a general mêlée, but by now the British did not need fireships to create the situation or to exploit it. The two fireships remained 'unexpended'.

If the days of the fireship in fleet battles were over, it still remained useful against trapped or immobilised ships. Two were used to help burn the abandoned French ships at Toulon when the British evacuated the surrendered port in December 1793. They were also useful in cutting out expeditions, which became more frequent as the outnumbered French navy increasingly refused to give battle in the traditional manner. In June 1800, for example, the *Dart*, a British sloop under Commander Patrick Campbell, led a flotilla of four fireships and boats in an attack on four French frigates that had taken refuge in Dunkirk Roads. Three frigates dodged the attackers and the fireships burned out fruitlessly, but Campbell managed to surprise and capture the French 38-gun frigate *Desirée*. The prize money more than compensated for any failure on the part of the fireships.[1]

A year later, in April 1801, two fireships accompanied the British fleet dispatched to Copenhagen, intended to pressure the Danes into abandoning the so-called League of Armed Neutrality, which included Russia and Sweden. The league was a clear threat to the Baltic trade, and particularly the naval stores on which Britain depended, and Admiral Sir Hyde Parker and his vice admiral Lord Nelson had orders to use force if the Danes failed to. However, the Danes made plans to resist the threat, building a defensive line of anchored ships of the line and floating batteries on the seaward side of Copenhagen. Nelson planned to attack and destroy this, and about 9.30 on the morning of 2 April 1801 his flagship the *Elephant* fired a signal gun, giving the order to weigh anchor. On the big British warships the crew began to break the anchors out of the ground. The plan of attack was simply to bring the British line abreast that of the Danes and anchor.

Much earlier, in the dawn twilight, the crews of the fireships *Otter* and *Zephyr* were also at the capstans, making their preparations for an exciting day. The guns and stores of powder had been lowered into the boats and transferred to the nearby *Bellona* and *Ganges*. As always, the fireship rule was to clear out any surplus powder prior to an attack for fear that it might cause a premature explosion and compromise the proper timing of ignition. Aboard the *Zephyr* the men made everything ready for the attack, and then, because any attack would be made at close range, thirty-five of the crew were sent off to other vessels, leaving Commander Clotworthy Upton and a skeleton crew of about ten.[2]

About 11.30 Nelson's ships took position abreast their opposite numbers in the Danish line, with an intervening distance of perhaps 220 metres, and the firing began. The next hours witnessed a brutal artillery duel between the anchored ships and floating batteries:[3] victory would depend on firepower alone. Behind the British line the fireships tried to maintain their position, while men in their fighting tops kept a sharp eye out for the signal from Nelson to attack. But Commander Upton and his men waited in vain. From about 2.30, the Danish ships, one after another, struck their flags, and British officers were rowed over in boats to accept their surrender. The fireships waited, but still there was no order to attack. At around four o'clock a burning Danish ship in the neighbourhood of the *Zephyr* blew up, and this caused one and then another Danish ship which had already surrendered to start firing again. They may have received fresh crews from shore, and Nelson, furious about this breach of the rules of war, now remembered his fireships. He sent a letter to the Danish Crown Prince warning that he would use them against the fractious vessels if they did not cease fire. This was

a classic use of the fireship as a threat, one which permitted a gentleman to surrender his vessel without losing his honour and reputation. Not long afterwards five hours of cannonade came to an end, the last Danish gun falling silent about four o'clock. On the evening of this dramatic day the men of the *Otter* and the *Zephyr*, who had never received the order to attack, were sent round in their cutters to the surrendered and abandoned Danish ships. Since these could not be removed, they were set on fire one after the other.[4]

In the years that followed Napoleon possessed the strongest land forces in Europe, but the British Royal Navy still ruled the oceans. The Navy's prime task in European waters was to blockade French warships in their individual ports, on no account letting them come out and unite to form a fleet strong enough to achieve control of the Channel, even for a limited period. For Napoleon the only way to deal with his one undefeated opponent was to conquer Britain itself, and in 1803 he began to assemble an invasion force at Boulogne that ultimately totalled 130,000 men. Besides the small craft already available, 2,300 oared gunboats were planned, which would be anchored in every Channel roadstead and estuary. Sooner or later, the weather would be favourable, the British fleet would be decoyed elsewhere, and his fleet would be able to cover the invasion. That was Napoleon's dream, and he waited for his chance.

Again and again the British tried to disrupt and delay these preparations. They watched the French coast closely, and in July 1804 they carried out an abortive assault on the port at Le Havre with sloops and bomb-vessels. Three months later they tried to destroy the invasion fleet at Boulogne, but it was difficult to get at the ships in these shallow waters, protected as they were by shore batteries. The attempt was made with a force of about twenty vessels, including brigs, luggers, gunboats and explosion-vessels. Besides these conventional craft, they employed a very modern weapon which they called a 'torpedo'.[5] This torpedo was the brainchild of the American inventor Robert Fulton (1765–1815), who, after attempting unsuccessfully to sell his ideas to Napoleon, decided to try his luck in Britain. Through the experiments of his friend and fellow inventor David Bushnell (1742–

Among the last uses found for fireships in major navies was in attacking blockaded or embayed ships that were restricted in their freedom to manoeuvre. The British launched one such attack on four frigates in Dunkirk Roads on 7 July 1800. As depicted in the foreground of this picture, the sloop *Dart* managed to surprise and capture the French frigate *Desirée*, but the four fireships set on the enemy failed to find targets, and can be seen in the background burning out to no effect. One of the fireships was the purpose-built *Comet* of 1783, the only one of the class to be expended in action.

1824), Fulton knew that it was possible to cause powder to explode under water, and he persuaded the British government that he could devise charges – or 'carcasses', 'coffers' or 'torpedoes', as he called them – that could float just below the surface and blow up enemy vessels. These were of various sizes and designs; the biggest 'carcasses' designed for the Boulogne expedition were eighteen feet long, weighed two tons, and were ballasted so that they floated just awash. They seemed to offer a solution to the particular problem of attacking the invasion flotilla, and Fulton was granted considerable funds and resources to make good his promises.

The other 'secret weapon' which was to be deployed on this occasion was called a 'catamaran'. This double-hulled craft was covered with tarred canvas, and ballasted with lead so that it sank almost to the water's surface. Between the hulls a crewman could sit with his lower body submerged propelling the craft with oars. He would be almost invisible in black guernsey clothing and with his face covered with a black balaclava. Each catamaran carried a pair of explosive charges connected by a hawser, the midpoint of which was secured to the vessel's cable, causing the two 'carcasses' to swing round with the current so that they lay on either side of the hull. A clockwork timing mechanism was set in motion, detonating after enough time had elapsed for the attackers to escape.[6] That was the theory, but as with all explosive vessels, a lot of factors – too many – had to come good.

On the night of 2–3 October 1804 some boats towed the conventional machine-vessels (which were converted fishing smacks) towards the French landing-craft and, once they came under fire, allowed them to drift through the anchored flotilla with a favourable tide and wind. The French artillery did their best to sink them, but in the end that was hardly necessary because they exploded one after another before they could wreak any damage. Catamarans and carcasses were also deployed, but they too achieved little. By sheer accident, a French boat collided with a black box floating deep in the water (a 'carcass'), an event that cost the lives of the coxswain and his crew of thirteen when it blew up.[7] Overall, the attack was an expensive fiasco, and confidence in Fulton's devices was severely dented.

However, Fulton later demonstrated the theoretical effectiveness of his weapons by blowing up the brig *Dorothea*, anchored in the Downs, using two of these 'torpedoes'. This gave a foretaste of what was to come in naval warfare, but like most inventions of that era, the weapons were deployed operationally before being adequately tested. In 1806 Fulton returned to America and continued his pioneering work on the development of the paddle-steamer.[8]

As it turned out, the attacks on the invasion craft by these methods did little to disrupt the French invasion plans, but in August the following year an attempt to unite Napoleon's naval forces in the English Channel miscarried, forcing him to realise that without local sea control the operation was doomed, and he postponed his invasion plans for good. Shortly afterwards, Nelson destroyed his high-seas fleet at Trafalgar, removing the threat for ever.

Nelson was the epitome of the battle-fleet admiral, but it seems that he was also interested in alternative methods of dealing with Napoleon's ships.[9] As far as he was concerned the fireship was peripheral to naval tactics, and like most of his colleagues he did not employ it. His ultimate weapon was a broadside battery manned by well-trained and highly motivated gun crews. However, a few weeks before he boarded the *Victory* to open the campaign that ended with Trafalgar, he attended a secret meeting in Downing Street. Present were the Prime Minister (William Pitt), the Minister for War, the engineer and artillery officer William Congreve (1772–1828), an exponent of military rockets, and Robert Fulton, who still retained some credibility with the government despite the failure of the catamarans.

The composition of this group invites speculation that its purpose was to explore new ideas or techniques that might be used to destroy the enemy, something beyond the classic fireship or machine-vessel. Perhaps Fulton and Congreve outlined plans and projects for rockets, mines and torpedoes that might meet the immediate threat, but at any other time that would have been morally questionable. Two months later Nelson's fleet annihilated the French fleet off Cape Trafalgar, leaving Britain the unchallenged masters of the ocean, with no further

The American engineer Robert Fulton (1765–1815), later famous as a steamship pioneer, tried to interest the Royal Navy in using underwater technology in its attempts to destroy Napoleon's invasion fleet in the Channel ports. The devices were secret at the time, and became the subject of rumour and disinformation, so it has always been difficult to determine the exact nature of the mysterious items variously called 'torpedoes', 'coffers' and 'catamarans'. However, the National Maritime Museum has a portfolio of very detailed plans drawn up by the French from examples recovered after the attacks. A selection of these demonstrates the main features.

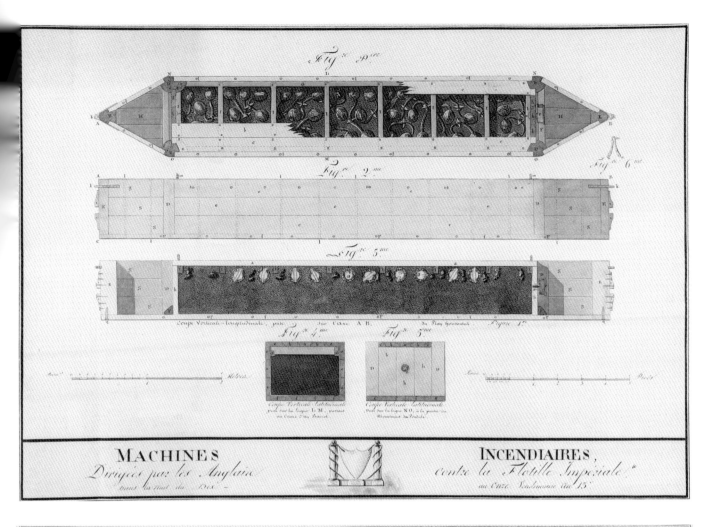

A large coffer, a twenty-one-foot-long just-buoyant wooden box filled with explosive, designed to be towed into a position from which the tide would set it against the target.

(NATIONAL MARITIME MUSEUM D9059-2)

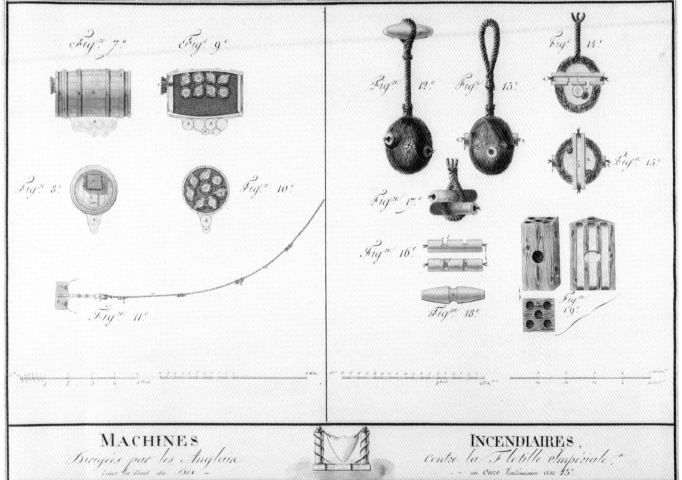

Explosive-filled 'hogshead', designed to be dropped in tethered pairs to drift down either side of an anchored ship. When the tether snagged the anchor cable, the tide would swing the hogsheads against each side of the ship. These were filled with gunpowder and 'combustible balls' (enlarged, right). Later replaced by more sophisticated copper cylinders known as small coffers, all these devices could be carried by boats or the famous 'catamarans'.

(NATIONAL MARITIME MUSEUM D9059-3)

need to bother with new and dubious methods of sea warfare. Naval orthodoxy reasserted itself, as was so trenchantly expressed by Admiral Earl St Vincent when commenting on Fulton's destruction of the *Dorothea*: 'Pitt was the greatest fool that ever existed, to encourage a mode of war which they who commanded the seas did not want, and which if successful would deprive them of it.'

Nevertheless, the last group of six specially built fireships for the Royal Navy went into service in 1806–7. The *Thais* class represented the highpoint in the development of this type of ship.[10] Like the *Tisiphone* class of the American War of Independence, their lines were based on those of the French corvette *Panthère*, and they were fine vessels. This is confirmed by the journal of Charles Chambers, ship's surgeon of the *Prometheus*, whose ship was at the second battle of Copenhagen in 1807 and who, like his predecessors in 1801, waited in vain for the order to attack.

> I was pleased to find the *Prometheus* sailed remarkably well, as she went upwards of 10 knots an hour with apparent facility, and would no doubt exceed that number under favourable and emergent circumstances. I cannot help regretting that a fine new ship like the *Prometheus* should be doomed to be burnt, should an advantageous opportunity present itself. Her accommodations in many respects are equivalent to several of our frigates, and she has more than once been mistaken for a vessel of that denomination. She carries 14 eighteen-pounder Carronades and 2 long Nines, and in case of demolishing the fire-room, is nearly capable of mounting nearly double that number.[11]

It is not clear why these fireships were built in the first place, since there was no obvious strategic need for them. Just five of them sailed as fireships for a year, with the others being re-rated as sloops and then being sold out of the Navy in 1808.[12]

———•———

After the battle of Trafalgar Napoleon did not give up on his navy, but tried to rebuild it gradually, which meant that many French ports contained well-found operational warships. Beyond the harbour, there was inevitably a British blockading squadron, but every so often small flotillas of French ships managed to break out and make a specific foray against British interests. One major breakout occurred in February 1809, but for the French it did not go as planned.

The Brest blockading squadron, under the command of Admiral Lord Gambier (1756–1833), was forced from its station for a few days by heavy weather. This was long enough to allow eight French ships of the line, under the command of Rear Admiral Jean Baptiste Philibert Willaumez (1763–1845), to slip out of the harbour of Brest at the break of dawn. His orders were to drive off the English squadron blockading Lorient, allowing the ships there to make their escape. They would then sail for the island of Oléron in the Bay of Biscay and pick up troops, supplies and any other ships at Rochefort before heading for the West Indies for a campaign of commerce-raiding. Once they had disappeared into the open seas of the Atlantic, they would pose a real problem for the British.

They got no further than the Pointe du Raz before the line of French ships was spotted by a British warship, and quickly all the squadrons of the Navy in the region were brought together. Visual contact was maintained with the French until the next day, and in the evening twilight they saw Willaumez and his ships sail into the Pertuis d'Antioche, the waters between the island of Oléron and the mainland, where they dropped anchor under the protection of the coastal batteries.[13] The British referred to these shallow waters as the Basque Roads or the Aix Roads.

The British fleet anchored further offshore, in the narrows just off the city of La Rochelle, and the positions of both fleets reawakened old ideas of what a fireship could do in this situation. Admiral Gambier took all possible precautions against a surprise fireship attack, ordering his ships to buoy their anchors and thus be ready to slip their cables at a moment's notice. Boats were kept in the water with poles, chains and grapnels to fend off approaching fireships. The apprehension of fireships was mutual. Gambier and his advisers vigorously discussed the best method of dealing

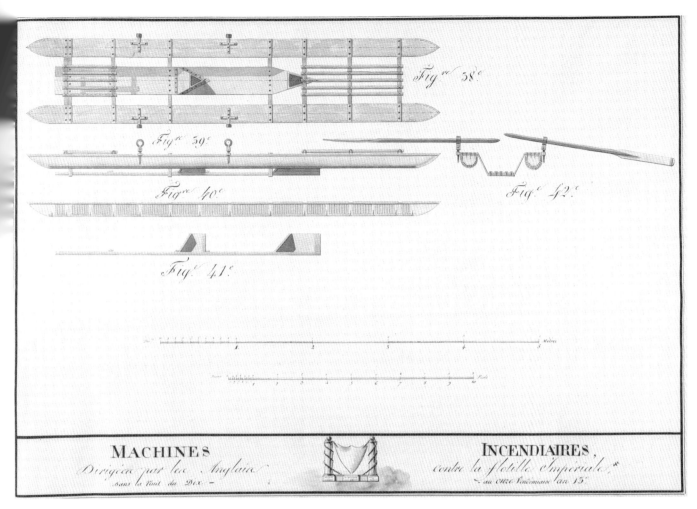

MACHINES

Dirigées par les Anglais

dans la Nuit du Dix —

INCENDIAIRES,

contre la flotille Impériale,

au Onze Vendémiaire an 15.

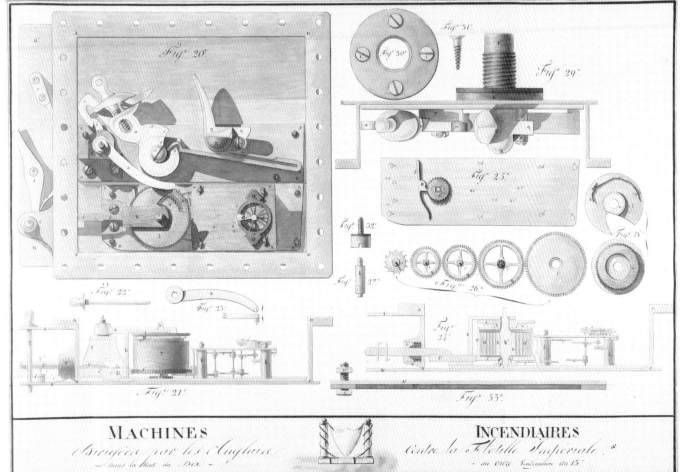

MACHINES

Dirigées par les Anglais

dans la Nuit du Dix —

INCENDIAIRES

contre la Flotille Impériale,

au Onze Vendémiaire an 15.

This plate from Nicolas Ozanne's *Marine Militaire* of 1762 shows a squadron which has barricaded itself behind a strong wooden boom. The baulks which form it have been bound by chains and secured by several anchors, and for extra security there are fireships to frighten off the enemy. The French believed that such barriers were impenetrable until Thomas Cochrane demonstrated otherwise at the battle of Basque Roads in 1809.

(FROM OZANNE 1762, PLATE 44)

VAISSEAUX RETRANCHÉS.

Retrancher des Vaisseaux c'est les defendre par une estacade A.B, formée de mats, ou fortes solives, solidement liées par des chaines de fer, et bien retenuës à des ancres C, ou amarages faits à terre; les Vaisseaux sont rangés derriere, sur un des cotés de la rade, ou partagés sur les deux, si l'endroit le demande pour empecher l'ennemi d'entrer, en rangeant la terre, de l'un ou de l'autre bord.

On place des brulots, dans les postes avancés D, d'où ils puissent fondre sur l'ennemi, en cas d'attaque; selon les occurrences, on fait croiser en dehors, des petits bâtiments E, pour découvrir les mouvements de l'ennemi.

Dans les circonstances imprevuës, et lorsqu'on n'a pas le tems de se retrancher, ou y suplée quelques fois, par des bâtiments que l'on coule à fond, dans le passage, afin d'arreter autant que l'on peut, les Vaisseaux qui tenteroient l'entrée, ces Bâtiments, se coulent de façon a pouvoir les relever, quand l'ennemi s'est retiré.

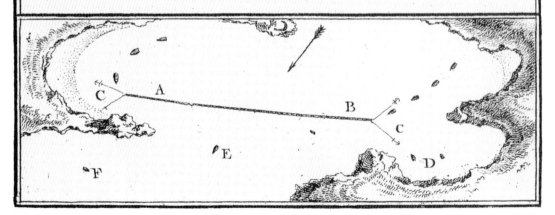

with the enemy. One camp suggested a quick force-ful Nelson-style assault, bearing down on the enemy with guns blazing. Against this, the navigation was known to be tricky, and the French ships were practically unreachable at the mouth of the Charente under the shelter of shore-batteries, so the losses in ships and men would be heavy. The other school of thought, which included Gambier himself, advocated a fireship attack, despite all the risks and imponderables this entailed.[14] But one way or another, something had to be done to neutralise the threat posed by the French force.

The First Lord of the Admiralty, Lord Mulgrave, had already outlined his position on 11 March, pointing out that the situation looked promising for a fireship and recommending this method. Gambier, however, was one of those naval officers of the time who were really uneasy about fireships, red-hot shot and explosive devices with time-delay fuzes, looking on these unorthodox methods as somehow unfair, unmanly and worthy of assassins rather than Christians. His profoundly religious, rather pedantic character was summed up by his nickname 'Dismal Jimmy'; 'It is a horrible mode of warfare', he wrote, 'and the attempt very hazardous, if not desperate.'[15] He wanted reassurance from the Admiralty, but in London the authorities had no qualms whatsoever and had already prepared for the enterprise. Twelve fireships and five explosion-vessels had already been dispatched to the Basque Roads.

Gambier learned also that William Congreve, an artillerist and engineer, was on his way, bringing a special invention and an operating crew. His apparatus, which had already proved successful on land and at sea, made use of black-powder rockets to set enemy ships on fire from a distance. It weighed about nineteen kilograms and had a range of 270 metres. Unlike a mortar, it had no recoil, so it could be fired from small boats, but on the other hand it was not particularly accurate.[16]

Then the British had a stroke of luck. On 19 March the frigate *Impérieuse* sailed into Plymouth. She had come from the Mediterranean and was under the command of Lord Thomas Cochrane, Tenth Earl of Dundonald (1775–1860). Scarcely had Cochrane landed than he was summoned by telegraph to the Admiralty, where Lord Mulgrave asked the daredevil captain what he thought about the potential

of a fireship attack at Basque Roads. The Admiralty knew that in Cochrane they had the right man – he was not only a brilliant and inventive warship commander, but also an unruly individualist, and as an independent member of Parliament he had been a vocal critic of Admiralty policy; better, therefore, to involve him in any controversial operation from the outset, so if things went awry he would be poorly placed to make trouble. Furthermore, as a frigate captain he had enjoyed a successful career as a raider up and down the French coast, so he was familiar with the region. His specialised knowledge and expertise would be essential.

Cochrane, unlike Mulgrave, did not favour a classic fireship attack. He thought it would almost certainly miscarry if the normal defensive measures were used to counter it, so he proposed that explosion-vessels be deployed as well. The Admiralty accepted the plan, and after some hesitation, Cochrane was persuaded to lead the attack, although he knew that this would lead to problems with some of the more senior officers under Gambier's command. Many were jealous of his reputation and some felt that the appointment of a mere post captain was a poor reflection on the competence of the fleet. But time was of the essence, and each day that passed increased the chance of a French breakout, so Cochrane's energy and enterprising spirit were invaluable. What the British did not know was that the French fleet had been divided by a power-struggle among the French senior officers, which was eventually resolved when Vice Admiral Zacharie Jacques Théodore Allemand prevailed over Rear Admiral Willaumez and took command of the fleet.

By 3 April Cochrane was with Gambier's ships and was finally was able to get a good look at the tactical situation east of the island of Oléron. For the moment there was not much more to do, since the explosion-vessels and rockets had not yet arrived. He started by converting a few available transports; using the materials found on board the ships of the line, the shipwrights were able to outfit a dozen conventional fireships, and the relatively large *Mediator* (a purchased merchantman serving as a Fifth Rate) was selected to smash through the floating boom, behind which lay the French fleet.[17] Three of the merchant ships were converted to

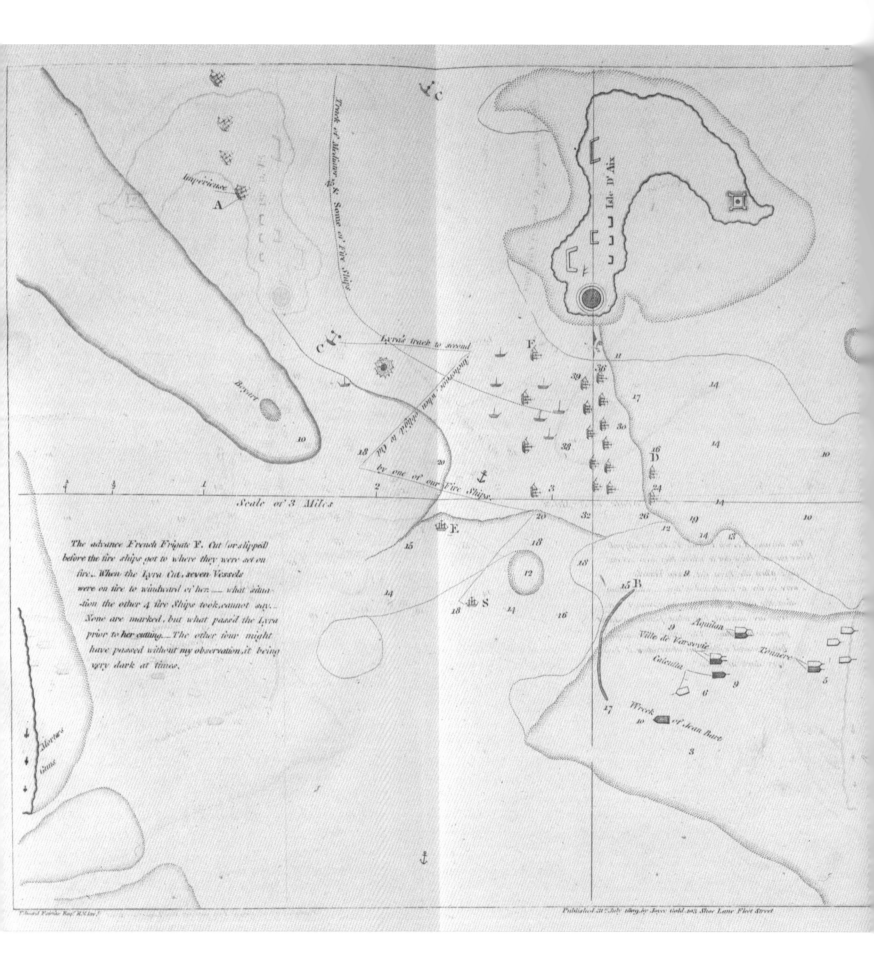

Impérieuse

A

Track of Malicare &c. Some of Fire ships

c

Lyra's track to second anchorage when obliged to Cut by one of our Fire Ships.

Boyart

Isle D'Aix

C

F

11

36

39

17

14

18

20

30

16

D

14

38

24

14

10

Scale of 3 Miles

E.

26

19

10

12

14

13

32

18

15

18

12

15 B

14

18

S

14

16

Aquilon

9

Ville de Varsovie

Tonnère

Calcutta

9

6

5

The advance French Frigate F. Cut (or slipped) before the fire ships got to where they were set on fire.. When the Lyra Cut, seven Vessels were on fire to windward of her... what situation the other 4 fire Ships took, cannot say... None are marked, but what pass'd the Lyra prior to her cutting...The other four might have passed without my observation, it being very dark at times.

Mortars

Guns

17

Wreck of Jean Bart

10

3

Edward Fairfax Esq. R.N. inv.ᵗ   Published 31.ˢᵗ July 1809 by Joyce Gold, 103 Shoe Lane Fleet Street

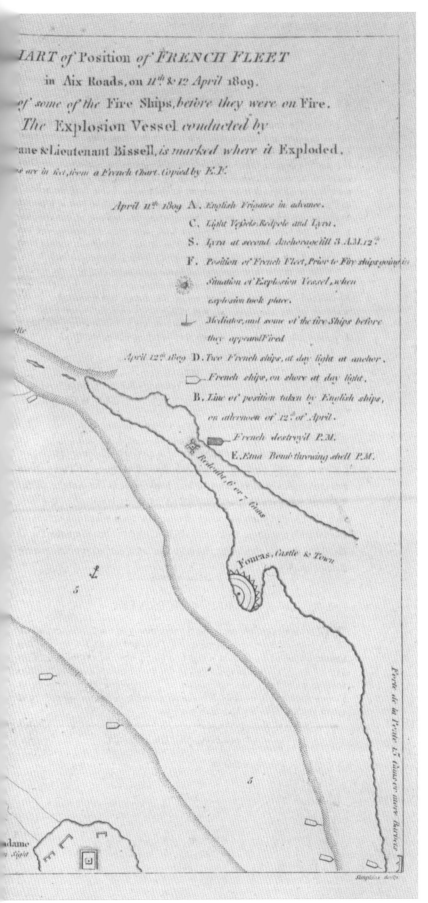

CHART of Position of FRENCH FLEET
in Aix Roads, on 11ᵗʰ & 12 April 1809.
of some of the Fire Ships, before they were on Fire.
The Explosion Vessel conducted by
rane & Lieutenant Bissell, is marked where it Exploded.
are in feet, from a French Chart. Copied by E. F.

April 11ᵗʰ 1809 A . English Frigates in advance.

C . Light Vessels Redpole and Lyra.

S . Lyra at second Anchorage till 3 A.M. 12ᵗʰ

F . Position of French Fleet, Prior to Fire ships going in

Situation of Explosion Vessel, when explosion took place.

Mediator, and some of the fire Ships before they appeared Fired

April 12ᵗʰ 1809 D . Two French ships, at day light at anchor.

French ships, on shore at day light.

B . Line of position taken by English ships, on afternoon of 12ᵗʰ of April.

French destroyd P.M.

E . Etna Bomb throwing shell P.M.

explosion-vessels. Their sides were strengthened to increase the violence of the explosion, and in each hold were packed 1,500 powder-kegs in big casks, with bomb shells secured on the covers and 3,000 hand-grenades packed around them. The whole thing would function like a gigantic mortar. A fuze was laid from the explosive to the stern so that the crew would have about twelve minutes to make their escape. Meanwhile, volunteers were called for throughout the fleet to serve as captains and crews of these vessels.[18]

For these crews there was not just the risk of premature explosion, but also the danger that if captured they would be brutally handled, if not shot out of hand. So they all had to have a prepared cover-story – for example, that they had fallen overboard or belonged to a merchant ship which had previously sunk.

On 10 April more fireships from England reached the Basque Roads, giving Cochrane a total of twenty. His force was now complete. Time was pressing, so the following evening, with a strong wind and high sea, the volunteer captains assembled aboard Lord Gambier's flagship. Cochrane gave them their final instructions, explaining that he himself would lead the attack in the first explosion-vessel. To this end, the *Impérieuse* had already sailed in the direction of the boom, with two explosion-vessels in tow. Cochrane would attempt to break the boom with one of them, and if that did not work the second one would follow. Once the way was clear, the fireship captains were to take advantage immediately of the flood tide, this second wave attacking the French ships themselves. Three other frigates would take up predetermined positions in order to pick up the escaping fireship crews.

It was dark as pitch when Cochrane, with a lieutenant and a crew of four men in one of the explosion-vessels, reached the area where they believed the boom to be. They could not see the French ships, and could only guess how far they were from the boom. Cochrane ordered the men into the boat and waited for the moment when he would light his portfire and set the fuze alight. Then he would spring into the boat and the men would pull for their lives against wind, waves and tide to ensure that they were as distant as possible

A chart of the attack by the British fleet on the French ships in Basque Roads in April 1809. The Isle d'Aix is shown at the top; the British attacked down the channel to its left, and the position of Cochrane's explosion-vessel is marked by a starburst. Cochrane broke the boom, leaving the way open for the fireships, which panicked the French ships into cutting their cables. The neat formation shown in the centre of the chart dissolved, and individual ships drifted into the shallows and on to the shoals (bottom), where they were damaged by English gunfire and some were forced to surrender. To Cochrane's disappointment and disgust Admiral Gambier was not prepared to risk the main fleet in order to destroy the French ships decisively.

(NATIONAL MARITIME MUSEUM D9264)

when the explosion occurred. There is something resembling an eyewitness account of this phase of the action; although, strictly, it is fiction, its representation of the explosion-vessel's approach to the boom and the following detonation is supported by factual reports. The author was Captain Frederick Marryat (1792–1848), who was to call on his experience of service with the Royal Navy for a series of authentic stories of the maritime world, producing heroes who were forerunners of C S Forester's Horatio Hornblower and Patrick O'Brian's Jack Aubrey. At this time he was a midshipman aboard the *Imperieuse* and a volunteer in one of the explosion-vessels. In his first book, *Frank Mildmay, or the Naval Officer*, he describes the attack:

The night was very dark, and it blew a strong breeze directly in upon the Isle d'Aix, and the enemy's fleet. Two of our frigates had been previously so placed as to serve as beacons to direct the course of the fire-ships. They each displayed a clear and brilliant light; the fire-ships were directed to pass between these; after which, their course up to the boom which guarded the anchorage was clear, and not easily to be mistaken.[19]

Marryat, in the persona of his hero Midshipman Frank Mildmay, recalls exactly what it was like to serve aboard an explosion-ship. 'They were filled with layers of shells and powder, heaped one upon

after I had lighted this port-fire, which was connected with the train. Until I was fairly in the boat, and out of the reach of the explosion – which was inevitable and might be instantaneous – the sensation was horrid. I was standing on a mine; any fault in the port-fire, which sometimes will happen; any trifling quantity of gunpowder lying in the interstices of the deck, would have exploded the whole in a moment. Only one minute and a half of port-fire was allowed. I had therefore no time to lose.

Finally, he lit the fuze and leaped into the boat, at which the men began to row as hard as they could to get as far away as possible … 'we were not two hundred yards from her when she exploded'.

Some distance away, the crews of the English ships perched in the rigging and stared tensely into the night, wondering when they would see the flashes of the explosion-vessels among the French ships. Many of them thought it 'a cruel substitute for a manly engagement'.

The French had been forewarned of a fireship attack and so had taken appropriate countermeasures. They imagined the boom to be unbreachable, constructed as it was out of hundreds of metres of stout spars, lashed together with chains and anchored to the sea-floor with large iron blocks.[20] Behind this, they felt secure, but as an additional precaution their boats were gathered along the boom.

The attack succeeded more quickly than Cochrane had expected, the first explosion ripping apart the quiet of the night. Shells, grenades and wreckage from the ships flew in all directions, at the same time setting off the Congreve rockets, which disappeared into the distance with a fearsome hissing like glowing snakes. An observer on the British side wrote later: 'Here was exhibited a grand display of fire-works at the expense of John Bull; no gala night at Ranelagh or Vauxhall could be compared to it.'[21] The boom was torn from its moorings, and the energy of 1,500 powder-kegs swept a violent wall of water before it. The boat with Cochrane's fleeing crew had not got far before the wreckage of their former vessel and the rest of its explosive cargo came down around them. The 'coffin' bobbed like a cork on the waves and then

another: the quantity on board of each vessel was enormous. We had a four-oared gig, a small, narrow thing (nicknamed by the sailors a 'coffin'), to make our escape in.'

Marryat describes how the strong wind drove the ship against the boom, and how the frigates remained in the darkness. Into Mildmay's head came a line from Dante: 'Abandon hope, all ye who enter here!' The ship crashed hard broadside into the boom, and the crew just managed to spring into their boat, while Mildmay seized his torch. Only later was he able to express the sentiments that came to him at that moment:

If ever I felt the sensation of fear, it was

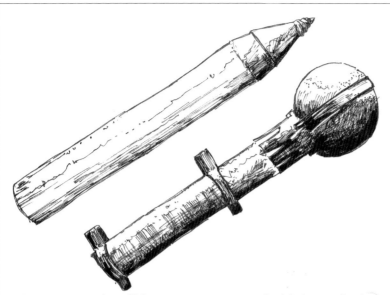

Two Congreve rockets which were deployed in 1807 at the bombardment of Copenhagen by the British fleet. They were named after their inventor, the artillery officer and engineer William Congreve (1772–1828). The tube was similar to that of a pyrotechnic rocket, powered by black-powder, and it carried either a pointed incendiary head or a rounded-off one filled with explosive. Each one weighed about 19kg and had a range of about 270 metres. An advantage of the weapon was that it had no recoil and so could be launched from small craft, but it was very inaccurate. The device was used for the first time on a large scale at Boulogne in 1806, and the following year at Copenhagen; it was used again during the British attack on the French fleet at Basque Roads in 1809. However, these days it is probably best remembered for being fired at the US Fort McHenry in 1814, since it is commemorated in a line of the American national anthem: 'the rockets' red glare'.

(DRAWING: AUTHOR AFTER TWO ITEMS IN THE CITY MUSEUM, COPENHAGEN)

French fleet arose because the men saw the fire-ships but could not be sure they were not more explosion-vessels, which would be more difficult to counter, and all discipline vanished. Later during his exile on St Helena, Napoleon, discussing this phenomenon with one of his English warders, concluded: 'They ought not to have been alarmed

by your *brûlots*, but fear deprived them of their senses, and they no longer knew how to act in their own defence.'[23]

In the morning light of 12 April the extent of the disaster suffered by the French fleet became visible. The tide had turned at midnight, and as it ebbed eleven of the great ships of the line had been left high and dry, keeled over at perilous angles, with their guns unable to bear. As long as the tide was out, they remained an easy target for a second attack, so Cochrane signalled Gambier to inform him of this unrivalled and very promising opportunity. Gambier, however, hesitated to launch an all-out attack.

Naval historians still disagree about the reason: was it timidity, or did he just resent the attempt by a junior captain to browbeat his admiral? However, faced with the commander's inaction, Cochrane decided on his own initiative to move on the enemy without delay, believing that a lot more destruction could be inflicted on the stranded ships. With

Captain Thomas Lord Cochrane (1775–1860), later Tenth Earl of Dundonald, was not only an extremely successful British sea officer but also an inventor who was involved with, among other things, the development of unconventional weapons. That led to his being given command of the attack on the French fleet at Basque Roads in 1809, at which he deployed fireships and explosion-ships of his own design. After being disgraced in a stock-market scandal, he left the Royal Navy and served in the navies of Chile and Brazil before taking command of the Greek fleet in the War of Independence against the Ottoman Empire. In all his commands he advocated the use of the steam power and the deployment of fireships and explosion-ships. After his rehabilitation, he was appointed commander of the British fleets in North America and the West Indies and rose to the rank of admiral, and was still promoting some of his innovative schemes as late as the Crimean War.

(WIKIMEDIA COMMONS)

was swamped, and they were rescued by the skin of their teeth. Ten minutes later the second vessel blew sky-high.[22]

Now the second phase of the attack got under way. First Cochrane sailed his frigate through the breach in the boom, followed by about twenty unlighted silhouettes. But the fireship flotilla quickly fell into disorder, with only four of them coming within striking distance of the French warships (their principal target was the flagship of Admiral Allemand, the *Océan*). In panic cables were slipped, guns and ammunition were thrown overboard, and the ships drifted uncontrollably towards shoals, ran aground or collided with each other. But none of the fireships caused direct damage, with most burning out in the darkness, far from any target. It was the centuries-old problem of fireship captains losing their nerve, setting their vessels on fire too early and abandoning them. Also demonstrated was the huge psychological effect these weapons could have. The disorder in the

the support of a small detachment from the main fleet, he did succeed in irreparably damaging one or two more before Gambier ordered him to break off the attack. Cochrane was furious, and eventually Gambier ordered him to return to England. Although this was not a case of total annihilation, the French had been forced to abandon their planned Caribbean expedition, and Napoleon later used the word 'imbécile' to describe the French admiral who had allowed his ships to get into this sad situation. However, things did not go well for the British admiral either.

At home, Cochrane was hailed as the hero and was made a Knight Commander of the Bath, an honour awarded only for outstanding achievement. This event marks the point at which honours and social accolades replaced the financial rewards and prospects of promotion that successful fireship captains of an earlier era had enjoyed.However, Gambier himself demanded credit, as commander-in-chief, for the success of the action, and this roused the enmity of Cochrane. As a Member of Parliament, Cochrane objected to a plan to offer a vote of thanks to the man who, in his view, had merely observed the battle from afar. Stung by the criticism, Gambier demanded a court-martial and,

not surprisingly, he was found not guilty by his colleagues. For Cochrane, things went downhill from then onwards, in part because his outspoken attitude made him many enemies in the Navy and the government. The senior naval authorities deemed him 'uncontrollable', and his career stalled. Later Cochrane was implicated in a stock market fraud, and was stripped of his honours, lost his seat in Parliament, and was thrown out of the Service. He remained a popular hero in Britain, with many admirers and supporters, but decided that if his native country did not appreciate his talents sufficiently he would take them abroad.

Throughout the rest of his long adventurous life, Cochrane continued to develop unconventional weapons for use against ships or coastal installations. He went on trying to improve explosion-vessels, one of his innovations being the addition of small metal particles – like the terrorist's nail-bomb – designed to maximise casualties. These were thought by his superiors to be 'effective but inhumane' and were not pursued. As the Duke of Wellington said in his inimitably succinct style, 'Two can play at that game.'[24] Some of Cochrane's schemes even presaged the use of poison gas in war; these were kept secret until 1908.[25] For attacking coastal fortresses he dreamed up a new version of the well-known 'smoke-ship' of Sir Francis Drake, known as the 'sulphur-vessel' and inspired by a visit to sulphur mines in Sicily in 1811. On the upper deck of a small vessel he planned to spread a layer of charcoal and lumps of sulphur. The burning charcoal would cause the sulphur to melt, emitting smoke which would cause coughing by irritating the airways. He envisaged these vessels being deployed with favourable wind and tide, emitting 'noxious effluvia' as they drifted towards shore installations and causing their garrisons to take to their heels to escape the stink. He also came up with idea of the 'temporary mortar' – a small vessel in which the decks were stripped out, and a bed of clay laid in its bottom planking. This was covered with scrap metal and gunpowder, and finally with a layer of animal carcasses and rows of shells. By appropriate ballasting, the whole vessel was heeled to one side to 'aim' it at its target, and it would then explode like a gigantic mortar.

The English naval officer and novelist Frederick Marryat (1792–1848) served as a midshipman under Cochrane in the *Impérieuse*, and survived the night attack by fireships on the French fleet at Basque Roads in 1809. In his first novel, *Frank Mildmay, or the Naval Officer* (1829), which is largely autobiographical, he describes his impression of that event.

(NATIONAL MARITIME MUSEUM PU3575)

Cochrane would get the opportunity to put some of these notions in to practice during the Greek War of Independence.

———•———

Following the Turkish occupation of the Peloponnese peninsula in 1715, the Greeks had responded with a series of revolts. For hundreds of years they had proved a thorn in the side of the Ottoman Empire, supporting the enemies of the Turks – Venetians, Emperor Charles V and, as fellow Orthodox Christians, the Russians. In the battle of Chesme (1770), for example, the Russian fireships that made a successful attack on the Turkish fleet had been crewed in part by Greeks.

The uprising that began in the spring of 1821 was particularly well planned. At that time there were colonies of Greek merchants and shipowners in all the trading centres of Europe and America, and from them arose secret societies whose aim was to establish an independent Greek state. The revolt spread quickly, first in the Peloponnese, and then to the offshore islands such as Hydra and Spetses (both centres of trade and shipping), and from Chios to Psara in the west. The Turks, who were not expecting a rebellion, were taken by surprise, and the Greeks quickly succeeded in many parts of the Peloponnese. Because the Ottoman army had been involved with a war in Persia, the number of troops stationed in Greece was small, their organisation poor, and their equipment outdated.[26] The Turks withdrew to their fortified cities, where they were besieged by the Greeks.

The strategic aim of both sides was to control the roads and supply routes between the strongpoints and the remainder of the Peloponnese. Many of these scattered bases and garrisons could be supplied only by sea, and consequently control of the Aegean was key to the success or failure of the rebellion. Opposing the Greeks was a substantial Ottoman battle-fleet, based in Constantinople (Istanbul) and commanded by a 'Captain Pasha' who was next in rank to the Sultan and Grand Vizier; at the beginning of the nineteenth century the Turkish fleet consisted of around twenty ships of the line, most of about 80 guns and seven or eight frigates of about 50 guns, with five corvettes and about forty brigs completing the list.

However, the Turkish fleet did not compare well with the navies of any of the Western European nations. The discipline and seamanship left much to be desired, while the obsolete guns and carriages made precision fire impossible. Traditionally there had been many Europeans among the crews, particularly Greeks from both mainland and islands doing their military service, who were responsible for seamanship and sail-handling, while the marines and gunners were mostly Turks. But with the outbreak of the rebellion most of the Greek seamen vanished, to be replaced by raw, inexperienced pressed men.[27] Tactical expertise in repelling fireships was simply nonexistent.

On the other side the Greek 'fleet' at the beginning of the uprising consisted of a flotilla of about forty lightly armed merchant vessels, noted for their handiness and speed, which mostly hailed from the islands of Hydra, Psara and Spetses. However, numbers quickly expanded to somewhere between sixty-five and ninety vessels. These small craft, from 200 to 300 tons, had at best 20 small guns for self-defence, so there was absolutely no thought of waging war in the traditional line-of-battle sense; not surprisingly in these circumstances, they turned to the tried and tested idea of fireships. The Greeks had not forgotten about what happened at Chesme, and although they had no purpose-built fireships, they quickly improvised a number from single-decked merchant brigs, on which they piled brushwood, black-powder, charcoal, naphtha, sulphur and alcohol on the decks to accelerate the spread of the fire. These vessels were purchased for a lump sum, and of course the crews were paid at a higher rate than those of other vessels, with premiums depending on the size of the enemy vessel destroyed.[28]

Until the spring of 1821 the Greeks had had the Aegean more or less to themselves, but in June a Turkish squadron under Admiral Kara Ali emerged from the Dardanelles and immediately became a prime target. The general inexperience of the Turkish sailors quickly demonstrated itself on 5 June when the Greeks managed to separate a Turkish ship of the line from the Ottoman fleet and made an attempt to destroy it with a fireship. This was unsuccessful, but a few days later, in the

first light of dawn on 8 June, two Greek fireships, accompanied by small craft from Spetses, attacked again. The Turks fired at them, but because of the poor state of the ships' gun carriages most of the shot went high, and as the fireships drew closer the Turkish ships cut their cables and began to drift. One of the fireships grappled and soon the fire spread everywhere. With some effort the Greeks were dissuaded from the completely unnecessary act of boarding, and finally the Turkish ship blew up in a huge cloud of black smoke. The rest of the Ottoman fleet withdrew temporarily to the security of the Dardanelles.[29]

The Greeks' joy at this victory quickly received a setback, however, for they soon learned just how unpredictable fireships really were. In July, near the island of Kos, a second attempt to use them miscarried, with three expended without effect and a fourth captured. In August another fireship was expended to no avail.[30] The rule that fireship attacks were rarely successful also obtained in the Aegean.

In May 1822 the Greeks mounted an attack on an Ottoman fleet cruising in the waters off the island of Chios. Three of the fifteen Greek vessels were fireships, but the Greeks withdrew after yet another unsuccessful attack and the vain expen-

diture of a fireship. The Ottoman fleet, consisting of six ships of the line and nine or ten frigates, besides small craft, anchored in the Strait of Chios just off the town of Chios itself.

The night of 18 June, which was dark with a little moonlight, found the Turks celebrating the end of Ramadan and the capture of Chios. The stern lanterns of the *Mansur El Liwa*, the flagship of Admiral Pasha Kara Ali, and those of his vice admiral could be seen from afar. The previous evening two harmless-looking Greek vessels had been sighted in the Strait of Chios, heading north as if for the Gulf of Smyrna. As darkness fell, they abruptly altered course and rapidly approached the Ottoman fleet from upwind. The captain of the first was Andreas Pipinos from Hydra, and the second was commanded by Konstantin Kanaris (1793–1877), who came from the island of Psara, to the west of Chios. Both ships were well prepared for their mission: besides a deck cargo of brushwood and inflammable liquids, they had their hulls strapped with copper bands, intended to hold the wooden structure together and prevent it from disintegrating too rapidly once it had caught fire.[31] The idea was to make sure that once their victim was grappled, the fire would last longer and be harder to extinguish.

In the National Historical Museum, Athens, Greece, there is a somewhat battered model showing the longitudinal section of a two-masted Greek merchantman as converted to a fireship. It has two complete decks, between which is the fire-room, but some traditional fireship characteristics are absent. The fire-gutters are laid directly on the deck, but the fire-barrels in the form of troughs are readily identifiable, presumably with apertures in the deck above them. Forward of the foremast on the deck there is a bowl-shaped barrel with a chimney above. Below the forecastle is a big fire-barrel which is fitted with a tapered siphon, designed to aim the fire in a specific direction.

(NATIONAL HISTORICAL MUSEUM, ATHENS)

At the beginning of the Greek War of Independence the crews of Turkish warships underestimated the danger posed by fireships and failed to take sufficient precautions. This resulted in some spectacular fireship successes for the Greeks, although these would become rarer during the course of the war. This picture by Constantinos Volanakis celebrates one such night attack on an anchored Turkish frigate. The small fireship is grappled fast to the side of the target, with the fireship crews escaping in their boats.

(NATIONAL HISTORICAL MUSEUM, ATHENS)

Towards midnight, both vessels were abreast the carelessly guarded Ottoman warships. First of all Kanaris rammed his fireship into the bow of the 84-gun *Mansur El Liwa*, his bowsprit pushing through an open bow port. He then ignited his vessel and escaped with his crew. Within a few minutes the wind had fanned the fire throughout the Turkish ship, and it burned so violently that the glare was visible as a red glow in the sky as far away as Smyrna, eighty kilometres away. Panic ensued, and the Turkish crew fled in overfilled boats, accompanied by the shrieks of the numerous Greek slaves who were trapped in the inferno aboard the *Mansur El Liwa*. Kara Ali in one of the boats was struck by burning rigging and severely wounded; he was brought ashore but died the following day.

Less than an hour after the attack, fire reached the powder-magazine, and the floating bonfire burst apart in a gigantic explosion.

Pipinos, the other fireship captain, took the Turkish vice admiral as his target, but had less luck than Kanaris. He tried to grapple, but the defenders cut away the chains before the fire had spread out of control and the fireship burned out without causing damage.[32]

The Greek naval forces, whose captains were often at odds with each other, failed to exploit the disorder into which the Ottoman fleet had been cast, and once again the Turks withdrew into the waters of the Dardanelles. In the late summer of that year the new commander of the Ottoman fleet, Kapudan Mehmet Pasha, again ventured into the

escape.[33] Even today, this event is celebrated on the island of Spetses with an annual festival called 'armata', in which there is a splendid fireworks display and a big model ship is symbolically burned.

By the following year, 1823, the Turks had learned from their mistakes, and for fear of fireship attack they no longer sent ships of the line into the Aegean, but only frigates, brigs and small craft. These tactics were rewarded with fewer losses to fireships, although the Greeks continued to keep one or two fireships with their squadrons. These continued to exert a deterrent effect, keeping the Turks with their vastly superior firepower at a distance.

Konstantin Kanaris (1793–1877), who came from the Greek island of Psará, was a merchant master at the beginning of the Greek War of Independence. Between 1822 and 1827, as a fireship captain, he achieved a series of great successes against Turkish warships in the Aegean, earning himself the nickname 'the Terror of the Turks'. When independence was won, the war hero was elected to the National Assembly, and he went on to become Commander of Squadrons and Forts, then Navy Minister and finally President of the newly founded Kingdom of Greece.

Aegean in an attempt to keep the supply lines open and relieve the Turkish garrisons. In September the fleet totalled eighty-four units, including seven ships of the line and fifteen frigates, while the Greeks had about sixty brigs and schooners and ten fireships – a relatively large number of fireships, reminiscent of the fleets of the seventeenth century.

Whenever the Turkish ships were sailing in narrow waters between the islands, the Greeks tried to attack with fireships, with mixed results. They had some success in the autumn when Kanaris attacked the Ottoman fleet off Tenedos and managed to destroy the flagship of the Turkish vice admiral, although the flagship of the supreme commander-in-chief, Mehmet Pasha, just managed to

The situation changed dramatically a year later, when a new power entered the fray. Making little progress against the revolt, Sultan Mahmud II (ruled 1808–39) turned for help to his powerful vassal Mehmet Ali, Pasha and Viceroy of Egypt. The effectively independent Mehmet Ali had reorganised his forces, with French technical assistance, to produce a modern army and fleet. The commander of the fleet was his son, Ibrahim Pasha, and in July a force of fifty-four warships, with infantry and cavalry aboard, sailed from the harbour at Alexandria.[34] The position of the Greeks in the Aegean now deteriorated rapidly. The Turks and their allies landed in the Peloponnese and laid waste to the countryside. They also successfully attacked many Greek islands, destroying the towns

and enslaving their inhabitants.

These events strengthened sympathy through-out Europe for the Greek cause, and many people offered help, but in the short term the Greeks had to rely on their own endeavours. In August 1824, in an encounter in the waters off Samos, Kanaris, the fireship captain, renewed the offensive, setting fire to one of the finest Turkish ships, a 54-gun frigate. The blaze soon reached the powder-room and the ship blew up.[35] By the end of the maritime campaign that year, the Greeks, in expending twenty-one fireships, had succeeded in destroy-ing six Turkish warships along with their entire crews. But once again the Turks had learned from their defeats, and they became increasingly watch-

ful. The Greek fireshipmen had to give up on night attacks because these were too easily detected, and during the day flotillas of small craft kept watch for any vessel which came suspiciously close to the Turkish-Egyptian fleet. The situation became so discouraging that some Greek fireship crews hes-itated, despite the higher pay, to take their ships into action if the prospects were too unfavourable.[36]

Throughout 1825 the Egyptian fleet transported reinforcements to the Peloponnese from Alexandria. This made it an obvious target, but an attempt by the Greeks to attack the fleet in Alexandria harbour with fireships camouflaged as merchantmen miscarried. Significantly, in 1825 there is mention for the first time of ten fireships in the

Egyptian fleet sailing out of Alexandria, and in December the Egyptians used fireships against a Greek squadron. The Turks had also learned how to respond to fireship attack, by bringing the approaching vessel under such heavy fire that it was bound to catch fire prematurely.[37] Greek fireship successes diminished in number as a result.

Against this trend, in May the redoubtable Captain Kanaris struck lucky again. Employing six fireships, he managed to destroy a British-built 44-gun frigate, along with two brigs and several transports. In any case, the decline in the success rate was relative: during the whole war, the Greeks launched fifty-nine fireship attacks, of which thirty-nine were successful[38] – a ratio that compares very favourably with the achievements of centuries past. However, in general these years saw the Greeks losing ground by both land and by sea. At this critical moment, however, the Greek navy took on a new commander – Lord Cochrane.

After his expulsion from the Royal Navy, Cochrane had fought against Spain, at first on the side of its colonies Chile and Peru, and then from 1823 to 1825 in the Brazilian service. To some extent his achievements depended on his being able to inspire and draw experienced British officers and crews to his cause, and during his time in South America he continued to show his penchant for explosion-vessels and fireship attack by night. Most of his success had been achieved by more conventional means, but he regularly fell out with his employers over money and his general reluctance to follow orders.

Then he accepted an invitation from the Greeks to outfit and modernise their navy, using steam vessels built in Britain and frigates built on the American pattern. Getting these vessels ready proved a slow business, because he could not find enough experienced crews to man them. Greek seafarers were more interested in plunder than in naval discipline, and he lacked professionals with the technological expertise to run the temperamental steam engines.[39]

In May 1827, as First Admiral of Greece, Cochrane was in the Aegean, once again living up to his reputation as an ingenious and innovative man. He planned attacks using fireships which would be towed into position by a steam vessel,

but the attack he made in June on the Egyptian fleet in the harbour of Alexandria was quite conventional. He sailed his fleet (which included eight fireships) across the Aegean, and made ready an explosion-vessel, but he was disappointed when on asking for volunteers he found crews for only two of his fireships. One of these did get into the harbour, grappling and destroying an Egyptian brig-of-war. This was a decent success, but the well-known psychological effect of fireships was even more apparent, for the inhabitants of Alexandria fled, fearing a bombardment of the city. As to what happened next, reports vary. According to Greek accounts, the Egyptian ships fled from the harbour in all directions, but the Egyptian version is that the Greeks imagined that the fleeing ships were coming out to attack them and withdrew. Whatever the truth, the scattering of the Greek fleet tarnished Cochrane's glory somewhat.[40]

Despite Cochrane's presence, the Greeks' struggle for independence was not going well. They were short of money, their leadership divided by political in-fighting, and everywhere the Turkish-Egyptian forces were gaining ground. The Western powers were worried about the reviving strength of the Ottoman Empire, and in July 1827 Britain, France and Russia signed a treaty calling for a cease-fire which appeared to guarantee self-determination for the Greeks. Their reasons for doing so were complex and varied, but grounded in concern for what each power regarded as its traditional interests in the Levant. Britain at that time had control of the Ionian Islands, which they had taken over from France in 1815 (only in 1864 did they revert to Greek sovereignty), and in both England and France Philhellene sentiments were rampant, with many influential people sympathising with the Greeks. The Russians were traditional enemies of the Turks, but their attempts at territorial aggrandisement at the expense of the Ottoman Empire were not welcomed by the other powers. On top of the political instability cause by the war, the merchantmen of all countries trading in the Aegean had suffered from the activities of Greek privateers and pirates, who had taken advantage of the political disorder. Therefore, the re-establishment of security in the region became a priority, and a coalition squadron made up of ships from

the three signatory nations was dispatched into the eastern Mediterranean, under the command of the very experienced Admiral Sir Edward Codrington (1770–1851).[41]

Codrington tried in vain to establish a cease-fire between the Greeks and Ibrahim Pasha. In negotiations he threatened to blockade the Ottoman fleet, and hinted at active intervention by the Allied forces, but the Turks continued their brutal massacres of Greek civilians in the Peloponnese. The Sultan, perhaps not understanding the political realities, was unwilling to make the slightest compromise.[42] While the negotiations were proceeding, the ships of the Ottoman fleet had gathered at their main naval base, the Bay of Navarino (nowadays the Bay of Pylos), a natural harbour on the southwest coast of the Peloponnese. The Allied fleet waited outside the bay, hoping to hold Ibrahim Pasha in check, and to prevent Turkish-Egyptian ships from making a foray out of the bay, until a truce had been arranged.

Besides many small craft, Ibraham Pasha's fleet included three ships of the line and seven two-decked frigates. They were anchored in three lines, in a horse-shoe formation, their broadsides directed towards the entrance to the roadstead, with five or six fireships positioned at the extremities of the horse-shoe. The Allied force consisted of ten British ships under Codrington; seven French ships commanded by Count Henri de Rigny and eight Russian ships commanded by Count Login Petrovich Heyden; ten of these were ships of the line. The official intention was to intimidate the Turks into agreeing a cease-fire, not to engage in open warfare, and Codrington was under orders to use force only if absolutely necessary.

Aboard the Allied ships, there was little trust or belief in the Turks' good intentions; some wondered if they were too cowardly to fight, and on the British ships there was fierce discussion about the prospects of conflict, a matter on which there were mixed opinions. Most of the men felt that the tension could only result in violence, and on the evening of 19 October many of the crew on board the 76-gun *Genoa* drew up their wills, while others wrote letters to their loved ones at home. Among those seamen who could write was the Scotsman Charles M'Pherson, who had entered the Navy,

The climax of the battle of Navarino, 20 October 1827: the explosion of a Turkish frigate. The young Scottish seaman Charles M'Pherson left an eyewitness account of the role played by Turkish fireships at the beginning of the battle. This print is one of a series engraved after paintings by George Philip Reinagle, who was himself present during the battle.

(NATIONAL MARITIME MUSEUM PW4820)

contrary to his parents' wishes, when he was seventeen. For his friends, who could not write, he scribbled a few lines, and he later penned a vivid description of the battle, to which the following account is indebted.[43]

Before sunrise on 20 October the Allied ships cleared for action. By the light of a few lanterns, a human chain, standing on decks and companionways, brought up shot and cartridges to the gun decks from the *Genoa*'s magazine. Then every man repaired to his battle station. At dawn they made sail, and the whole squadron glided with a light breeze into the Bay of Navarino, astern of Codrington's flagship the 84-gun *Asia* and followed in the course of the next hours by the Russian and French contingents. At eleven o'clock it was 'Up Spirits!' but when the *Genoa*'s crew mustered for the daily issue of grog, no one was in a cheerful mood, the old witticisms and jokes falling flat. Instead, they toasted each other with the words 'May we all meet again tomorrow!', knowing that if things turned out badly, there would be many empty places. If there were to be fighting, the *Asia*, *Genoa* and *Albion* would be in the thick of it. At noon they were piped to dinner.

Now Admiral Codrington brought his ship to anchor abreast the Turkish line, at a distance which only increased the nervousness that both sides had been experiencing for days.[44] The gun captains sighted along the barrels of their double-shotted guns. Over in the Turkish ships, which were at point-blank range, everything looked quiet and peaceful, but they knew that their opposite numbers were doing the same thing. Canvas was furled and M'Pherson, who was fore topman, had a splendid view of the whole Bay of Pylos and the opposing fleets. He could see what a tremendous risk Codrington was taking, and how exposed the *Genoa* was, since she lay directly abreast two enemy ships of the line, with a double-banked frigate a little further away off to starboard, and three big frigates a gunshot off the bow and another one off the stern.

M'Pherson was distracted from observing the panorama by the sudden roar of a cannon and the crackle of musketry. The frigate *Dartmouth* had been designated by Codrington to keep watch on one of the Egyptian fireships, which was anchored close by, and the captain sent a cutter with a lieutenant and eight strong men to investigate what looked like preparations to fire it. Once they were alongside, while one man held on with a boat-hook, another, cutlass in hand, scrambled over the main channel on to its deck. At that moment he received a pistol-shot to the head and the boat's crew were greeted with a salvo of musketry. The lieutenant was killed and four of the crew wounded. Naturally the others returned the fire, but the fireship's crew sheltering behind the bulwarks were not hurt. The cutter withdrew to the *Dartmouth*, and as the boat reached safety, the fireship began to smoke. It had been ignited, and its crew had abandoned it. A second attempt to reach the fireship also went awry, with the loss of several more men.

About the same time Codrington sent a boat with the master of the *Asia* on board to the Turkish flagship, the 84-gun *Ghiuh Rewan*, to inform Ibrahim Pasha that he would not open fire unless he was fired upon. The master, who was also acting as Codrington's interpreter, gave the message, and the boat cast off to return to the *Asia*. At that point, as the master sat in the sternsheets, he was killed by a musket shot, and the boat's crew pointed to the flag of truce they carried, only to be met with a salvo of small-arms fire. They withdrew towards the *Asia*, and when they were within safe distance Codrington answered the Ottoman misconduct with a broadside, of such force that it caused the *Ghiuh Rewan* to heel over. The other ships then started to fire at each other and the fighting became general. The battle of Navarino, the last fleet engagement of the age of sail, began in confusion, and afterwards it was difficult to say just who fired the first shot.

On board the *Genoa*, which lay just astern of the *Asia*, M'Pherson was on his way down from the foretop and heading for his station on the lower gun deck when the Turkish ships opened fire. The cry went up: 'Stand clear of the gun! Fire!' The gun crews went about their business, and M'Pherson describes the shocking and terrible scene that played itself out on the decks of his ship for the next hours. The *Genoa* was a stationary target and in the line of fire from several enemy ships, and M'Pherson saw many of his messmates horribly dismembered, and the bloody decks strewn with wood splinters. He witnessed the fearsome sight of the surgeon and his mates dealing with the wounded, and saw hundreds of Turks everywhere in the water trying to avoid drowning as they clung to floating wreckage. Towards the end of the battle, twenty-six of the *Genoa*'s 460-man crew were dead, and thirty-three wounded; every time the powder of a burning enemy ship exploded she felt the thump under her keel.

M'Pherson recognised that the Turkish crews had fought bravely, with none surrendering and all of them firing as long as they could from their blazing vessels. But all this heroism was in vain. The Egyptian fireships were deployed but without success. A French ship of the line, *Scipion*, was threatened by one of them, but at the last moment her boats were able to tow it clear, and likewise the frigate *Sirène* was attacked but managed to escape.[45] M'Pherson's captain, Walter Bathurst, who did not survive the battle, was ordered to send a boat with a hawser over to *Asia*'s stern in order to swing the huge ship round as a fireship drifted towards her. The manoeuvre succeeded, and despite being dismasted and incapable of moving on her own, she avoided contact. The sun had already set when, about six o'clock, firing finally ceased.

Everywhere in the Bay of Navarino, the wrecks of the once-powerful Ottoman fleet remained visible as they burned out in the darkness. At the hatchways of the *Genoa*, a boatswain's mate using a megaphone bellowed the order to the exhausted crew to cease fire. The last great sea-battle involving only sailing ships was finally over, and with it the last attack of a fireship against a sailing warship. The next morning only twenty-nine of Ibrahim Pasha's eighty-two ships were still afloat,

and none of them was battle-worthy.

The victory over the Ottoman fleet effectively secured Greek Independence, but the war dragged on for a couple of years until in 1829 the Convention of Constantinople agreed an armistice. Formal peace came in 1832 with the signing of the Treaty of Constantinople, which established the boundaries of the new Kingdom of Greece. Konstantin Kanaris, 'the Terror of the Turks' as he was admiringly called, was elected to the Greek National Assembly in 1827, the year of Navarino. Later he commanded a division of the Greek navy and became a senator, Minister of the Navy and in 1862 President of Greece.

With the annihilation of the Ottoman fleet, Lord Cochrane found himself without an enemy to fight and essentially out of a job. After the term of his contract expired he returned to England, where his inventive spirit remained active. He promoted the development of the marine steam engine, and as mentioned earlier he continued to work on terror weapons. Following a change of government in England, he was pardoned by the king and restored to his seniority in the Royal Navy. With the rank of admiral he commanded the North American and West Indies Squadron, and from 1848 to 1851 he was Admiral of the Atlantic Fleet. He was still promoting his unconventional weapons during the Crimean War, but after a most eventful and adventurous life he died in 1860.

The Greek War of Independence brought to an end the story of the fireship in the age of sail, but far from undergoing a decline into decrepitude, the weapon saw a remarkable resurgence in its use and effectiveness. Indeed, in terms of its success rate, the fireship's last war may be considered its best.

AFTERWORD:
OPERATION CHARIOT

ON THE CORNISH COAST 26 MARCH 1942 was a sunny day with a light breeze from the east-north-east. Between two and three o'clock in the afternoon a flotilla of sixteen coastal-forces craft sporting a strange-looking violet camouflage (known as 'Mountbatten pink') sailed out of Falmouth. It looked like a routine anti-submarine patrol, but a sharp observer would have noted something unusual about these mahogany-built craft, in that the crew numbers were larger than usual and extra drums of fuel were lashed on their decks. An hour later three destroyers in the harbour cast off their moorings and steamed out into the Channel.[1]

Once in open water, the group took up the usual anti-submarine V-formation and set a course for the south-west, and then about seven o'clock altered course to the south. Undetected by the enemy, they passed the coast at Finisterre and the entrance to Brest harbour about eighty-eight kilometres away. Two of the destroyers detached themselves from the group and returned to the English coast. About seven o'clock the next morning, the remainder altered course to east-south-east, and in the evening they steered to the north-east towards the mouth of the Loire and the harbour of St- Nazaire. At 22.00 they passed a buoy which a British submarine had laid for them, and they knew they were on course and in the right time-frame for the operation to be a success.

It was an action which had been planned in the spirit of the old fireship or explosion-vessel attack, and like its antecedents it depended on surprise and unconventional tactics. As in earlier days too, it required the co-operation of supporting craft, which were to clear the way for the weapon itself, and one of the vessels was in reality something different from its outward appearance. As in times

Campbeltown in the process of being refitted for the St Nazaire Raid. The after funnels have been removed and the forward pair raked to resemble the profile of a German torpedo boat.

(WIKIMEDIA COMMONS)

past, its armament had been reduced to a minimum, and it was manned by a skeleton crew. Also as in the machine-vessels of old, an explosive charge had been walled up, and there was a plan to use a smoke-screen to make targetting difficult for the enemy guns. And finally, as in the past, any survivors of this near-suicide mission would be rewarded with high honours.

The boats approached in two line-ahead columns, with the destroyer between them. The centrepiece was HMS *Campbeltown*, an old ex-American 'four-stacker' with her original funnels reduced to two and cut back so that at first glance she could pass for a German torpedo-boat of the *Möwe* class. The bridge and decks were protected with heavy steel plates, behind which a number of dark shadows were crouching. The *Campbeltown* reduced her speed to five knots, for she was not approaching by the usual deep fairway that led into St Nazaire harbour, but was entering the Loire estuary from the south-west, through relatively shallow water. She touched bottom a couple of times, but slid off: during the conversion every bit of inessential weight had been removed, so that her draught would be at an absolute minimum.

A flight of aircraft roared over the group, coming from the sea towards St Nazaire. Over the town searchlight beams reached up into the sky. The townspeople heard anti-aircraft fire and the explosions of a few bombs; although it was a surprisingly short raid, it put the German troops in the town and in the port on the alert. Something strange was brewing.

At 01.15 the destroyer and her escort were discovered, and the signal-lamps began to blink and searchlights swept the water's surface – friend or foe? The destroyer flew the Kriegsmarine ensign and replied to the recognition signals in the German fashion, but it took five minutes for the gun crews manning the shore batteries to realise that it was not a German destroyer, and that this was no ordinary formation.

The reason for this old-style operation went back to the commissioning in February 1941 of the battleship *Tirpitz*, sister-ship of the *Bismarck*, which was intended to be deployed as a commerce-raider but, on Hitler's orders, was first sent to Norway. She was the most modern battleship in the world, and mindful of the difficulty it had had in sinking her sister-ship the previous year, the Royal Navy was anxious to prevent her from operating against the Atlantic life-line. But sheer size can be a problem as well as an advantage. There was only one facility on the German-controlled French Atlantic coast which could dock and repair such a big ship, and that was the Normandie Dock at St Nazaire, which had been specially built to handle the French luxury liner *Normandie* (79,280 tons gross), the world's first ship with a length exceeding 300 metres. It was in fact the biggest drydock in the world, at 350m long and 50m wide. The dock gates were huge water-filled steel caissons, 51m long and 11m thick.

If the *Tirpitz* were damaged in the Atlantic, she could only be repaired here at St Nazaire. The damaged *Bismarck* had been heading for St Nazaire for that purpose when she was sunk the previous year. It followed that if there was no functioning dock on the Atlantic coast, the *Tirpitz* would not venture out into the Atlantic, since she could hardly expect to reach home waters without coming within range of the British Home Fleet and the planes of the RAF.

After Brest, St Nazaire was the most heavily defended place in western France. The occupying troops had installed a whole arsenal of defensive guns, although this had been done less for the sake

The bridge of the *Campbeltown* as prepared for Operation Chariot with additional plating and splinter-mattress protection.

(WIKIMEDIA COMMONS)

of the Normandie Dock than for the U-boat pens, or bunkers, which were impervious to air attack. Altogether there was a garrison of 5,000 men in the town, besides 1,000 more manning guns of every calibre, the radar stations and the searchlight crews. Attacks of the conventional type just would not work against a fortress like this, and bombing was too inaccurate to destroy the dock gates entirely. The only way to put the dock out of action was to make a surprise attack – that is to say, something resembling the attacks on the Channel ports during the Napoleonic Wars, something that the enemy would consider completely impossible.

This idea was heavily dependent on the use of a special military force, the Commandos, which had recently been set up at Churchill's instigation. These highly trained elite units were instructed in unusual techniques and unconventional tactics, and included many skilled specialists. Their role was to make surprise raids into enemy territory, reconnoitre, destroy some special target, and disappear again. The St Nazaire plan was developed by Lieutenant Colonel A C Newman and featured all these tasks.

The success of the plan also assumed close co-operation between the Royal Navy and the commandos. The *Campbeltown* and the coastal forces would try to remain undetected for as long as possible as they approached the port. Each boat had, in addition to its regular crew of twelve, a party of fifteen commandos on board, comprising demolition and security teams who were to land and carry out specially assigned tasks. Their targets were the pump-houses and the dock gates at the north or inshore end of the dock.

Campbeltown herself was a US-built flushdeck destroyer of 1918 vintage, originally the USS *Buchanan*, which had been transferred to Britain under the 'Lend-Lease' agreement of 1940. Immediately under and abaft the position where the *Buchanan*'s forward gun had been mounted, there was now a large steel tank, in part formed by steel bulkheads constructed in the bow. This held twenty-seven depth-charges, containing altogether about four and a half tons of the explosive Amatol encased in concrete. No doubt Gianibelli, Meesters and Cochrane would have been pleased by that detail.

The captain of the *Campbeltown*, Commander Stephen Halden Beattie RN, was to steer his vessel straight at the dock gates and ram them at full speed. Then the sea-cocks were to be opened, and the seventy-five-man crew and commandos would land. About five hours later, the explosive charge would blow up, and once the landing parties had done their job, they would regroup on the mole, from whence the motor-launches would take them off. That, at least, was the plan.

On the night of 27–28 March 1942 the *Campbeltown*, flanked on each side by a line of motor-launches, was travelling at full speed, about one and a half kilometres from the entrance to the harbour, when at 01.27 the German guns opened fire on the unknown vessel. The destroyer was the primary target, and despite the sheltering steel plates there were casualties, but she imperturbably held her course. The Kriegsmarine battle-flag was hauled down and the White Ensign hoisted. In the

Norman Wilkinson's dramatic painting of Operation Chariot showing *Campbeltown* approaching her target under a hail of fire. In the left foreground the commandos aboard one of the coastal craft prepare for landing.

steel tank, a specialist armed the detonators for the depth charges, and a few minutes later, at 01.34, the *Campbeltown* struck the south gate at twenty knots. The bow rose up at a steep angle and the hull was compressed by about twelve metres. Immediately the sea-cocks were opened to sink the stern and prevent its being towed clear, and seven commando teams jumped ashore, carrying demolition charges, axes and sledgehammers.

For the motor-launches things did not go to plan.

A famous image of *Campbeltown* rammed into the gates of the Normandie Dock. Minutes later the ship blew up, destroying the gates and putting the drydock out of action. The raid was a great success but came at a terrible cost: those killed, wounded and captured totalled 96 per cent of the personnel involved.

They were not so badly shot up as the destroyer, but it took only a few hits to set them on fire. These 112ft-long craft were lightly built and carried no armour plating. Because of their very limited radius of action, they had to carry drums of high-octane fuel on their decks, and these doomed them. Eight of them were destroyed in the first few minutes, and the only option for their crews was to jump into the water and cling to the rafts. Many of them drowned or burned to death from the fuel-fires on the surface of the water. Only a few of the accompanying commando teams made it ashore, but, together with the troops from the *Campbeltown* they managed to destroy the pumping installations and pump-houses of the dock gates beyond repair.

About an hour after the ramming, the returning commandos began to assemble on the Old Mole, in hope of recovery, however risky. The few remaining motor-launches tried to make themselves invisible by laying down a smoke-screen, in effect recreating the conditions of traditional fireship warfare, before pulling the survivors from the water. But they were still under fire, and there was not enough space for all the commandos, so about a hundred of them were left ashore with no chance of rescue by sea.

During the retreat downriver the boats remained under fire, and two of them, carrying the wounded and the crew of the *Campbeltown*, were lost. About 04.30 four of the original sixteen boats reached the rendezvous point, forty-six kilometres off the dock entrance; here they met a destroyer escort, which took off their crews. Three more boats reached the point later and made their own way back to Falmouth.

About 02.00 the commandos who had been left in the dock area came under intense fire from shock troops and had to withdraw into the town. They hoped to head south to the Spanish border, and so reach Gibraltar, but many of them fell during the attempt. The town was sealed off, a systematic house-to-house search was made, and by 10.00 it was all over. The surviving commandos, about 200 of them, had expended all their ammunition and were taken prisoner. Only five men managed, with the help of French civilians, to reach Gibraltar.

Some of the prisoners were among the many curious bystanders who gaped at the beached *Campbeltown*. For the Germans, it was absolutely unbelievable that so small a force, and such an inferior vessel, had dared to attack a strongly fortified U-boat base, and the soldiers swarmed over the destroyer, while souvenir-hunters unscrewed fittings to keep as mementoes. Nick Burn, one of the commandos, described how at one point he was standing fairly close to the ship, surrounded by German soldiers. He knew that although the intended hour for the detonation had passed, it might go sky-high at any moment, and noted with some satisfaction that many soldiers remained aboard the wreck, while also realising that he himself was too close for comfort.

In a nearby hut, an English-speaking officer was interrogating Commander Beattie, and when he learned that he had been aboard the *Campbeltown*, it gave him pause for thought: could this man really believe that the mighty dock gates could be destroyed by simply ramming them with a ship? Beattie began to feel rather uncomfortable, but 'At that moment there was a bang!', and when the smoke cleared, the bow of the *Campbeltown*, and the men on it, had vanished. The south dock gates were

Cole under tow off Aden. In October 2000 the American destroyer was the victim of an attack by an explosion-ship in the old style, carried out by two suicide-bombers. The explosion tore a huge hole in the side of the ship, killing seventeen sailors. Despite the fact that the ship was taken unawares, efficient damage control kept the ship afloat and eventually it was towed out of the harbour and transported to a US dockyard aboard a semi-submersible.

(WIKIMEDIA COMMONS)

shattered, and water swept into the Normandie Dock, carrying the rest of the destroyer's hull with it. Any possibility of using St Nazaire as an Atlantic base for the *Tirpitz* was gone, and the mighty battleship would never leave northern waters. Being within striking range from Britain, she was regularly attacked from the air and by midget submarine until November 1944, when she was finished off by special 'Tallboy' bombs dropped by RAF Lancaster bombers.

Of the 630 men who took part in Operation Chariot, only twenty-seven came back. The rest were taken into captivity or killed. Five members of the team were awarded the Victoria Cross, Britain's highest honour for bravery.

———•———

In its use of a small sacrificial vessel manned with near-suicidal commitment, Operation Chariot may be seen as the final manifestation of the mind-set behind so many attacks by fireships and 'infernals' in the age of sail. However, the employ-ment of such 'terror' weapons has received a new twist in the modern world, where the possibility of a fatal conclusion to the operation has been replaced by certainty. For much of its history, the fireship was a weapon of the weaker party, a relatively cheap method of redressing an imbalance of military power; but because it was nevertheless deployed by conventional navies, there was a limit to the risk that the state could call upon its personnel to accept. The attack on the American destroyer USS *Cole* while refuelling at Aden on 12 October 2000 was different: the suicide-bombers owed no allegiance to any national government and were driven by fanatical beliefs actively to seek 'martyrdom'. In terms of the resources 'expended', the result was spectacular: the ship nearly sank and cost $220 million to repair. The event proved that even sophisticated modern warships are still vulnerable to surprise, and that, now that cheap but deadly weapons are driven by those with no concern for their own lives, it would become even more difficult to defend them. It is an old idea revived with a vengeance.

NOTES

INTRODUCTION

[1] William Richardson, *A Mariner of England*, 1908, quoted in Gautier 1973, note 30.

[2] Dassié 1695, 114.

[3] Corbett 1909, 130.

CHAPTER 1

[1] Höckmann 1985, 90–1.

[2] Stenzel 1907–11, part I, 270.

[3] Viereck 1975, 118.

[4] Casson 1971, 152–3; Landström 1961, 84.

[5] Romocki 1895, 8.

[6] Haldon 2007, 41–3. See also Pryor and Jeffreys, 2006.

[7] Romocki 1895, 30.

[8] Rodgers 1967, 44.

[0] Oudendijk 1941, 132.

[10] www. The NAVIS project/ ships/ Haithabu.

[11] Feldhaus 1914, 940.

CHAPTER 2

[1] In this and following chapters dates are expressed in the New Style, using the Gregorian Calendar introduced in most of Continental Europe in 1582. However, until 1752 England and its colonies continued to use Old Style dating based on the earlier Julian Calendar, which lagged behind New Style dates by ten days.

[2] Meteren 1640, 480.

[3] Meteren 1640, 482.

[4] Quoted in Parker 1979, 265.

[5] The Flanders or Flemish *pleit* is a long obsolete boat type somewhat resembling a *tjalk*. It is believed that those involved here would have been about six metres long, having little sheer and a gently curving high stem, and drawing very little water. Petrejus 1978, 59; Sopers *c*1930, 72; Van Beylen 1970, 170–1.

[6] Schiller 1966, 338.

[7] Meteren 1640, 495.

[8] Stettner 2000.

[9] Meteren 1640, 495.

[10] Wislicenus 1910, 64–5.

[11] Witsen 1690, 185.

[12] De Jonge 1858–62, vol I, 133.

[13] Feldhaus 1914, 941 and 1240. A 'Mass' is measure of volume of between 1.1 and 1.7 litres.

[14] Romocki 1895, 242 and 253.

[15] Meteren 1640, 496.

[16] Schiller 1966, 344.

[17] Duffy 1979, 78.

[18] Meteren 1640, 497.

[19] Israel 1995, 219.

CHAPTER 3

[1] Corbett 1899, vol I, 77 ff.

[2] Lewis 1969, 94.

[3] On Hawkins's third slave-dealing voyage see David 1981, 397 ff; Corbett 1899, vol I, 87 ff; Hampden 1981, 27 ff; and Lewis 1969, 100 ff.

[4] At that time, the tonnage of a ship was a measure of its cargo-carrying capacity, allowing comparison with other vessels of similar build. It was not a measure of displacement. See Kirsch 1990, 25.

[5] Quoted in Lewis 1969, 100.

[6] Quoted in Hampden 1981, 38.

[7] Lewis 1937.

[8] Kirsch 1990, 18 ff.

CHAPTER 4

[1] On Francis Drake see Hampden 1981 and Rodgers 1967.

[2] The planning for and lead-up to the Spanish Armada are described in Rodriguez-Salgado 1988; Rodgers 1967; and Rowse 1955.

[3] Rodriguez-Salgado 1988, 23–4.

[4] On the development of the Armada campaign see Rodriguez-Salgado 1988, 233 ff; Rodgers 1967, 240 ff; Mattingly 1959; Fernández-Armesto 1988; Waters 1975; and Rowse 1955.

[5] Rodgers 1967, 240 ff.

[6] Laughton 1895, vol II, 7.

[7] Laughton 1895, vol II, 8.

[8] Oppenheim 1902–14, vol V, 151.

[9] Rodgers 1967, 261.

[10] Rodriguez-Salgado 1988, 120.

[11] Rodgers 1967, 309.

[12] Quoted in Oppenheim 1902–14, vol II, 306.

[13] Quoted in Oppenheim 1902–14, vol IV, 205.

[14] The English fireship attack is described in Rodriguez-Salgado 1988; Laughton 1895, vol II, 240 ff; Rodgers 1967, 309; and Fernández-Armesto 1988, 185.

[15] Rodgers 1967, 309.

[16] Quoted in Rodriguez-Salgado 1988, 242, 260.

[17] Rodriguez-Salgado 1988, 32.

[18] Lewis 1969, 157.

[19] Corbett 1919, 179, Clowes 1897–1903, vol I, 490.

[20] Quoted in Usherwood 1983, 18.

[21] Oppenheim 1902–14, vol I, 219.

[22] Clowes 1897–1903, vol I.

[23] Quoted in Wernham 1985, 131.

[24] Corbett 1919, 164.

CHAPTER 5

[1] Coggeshall 1997, 11.

[2] Butler 1929.

[3] Kemp 1976, article 'Mainwaring'.

[4] Butler 1929, 311.

[5] Gardiner/Atkinson 1899–1906, vol III, 33.

[6] Butler 1929, 319–20.

[7] Fyers 1925.

[8] Fyers 1925.

[9] Warnsinck 1940, 88 ff; Romocki 1895, 357–8.

[10] Romocki 1895, 359.

[11] Warnsinck 1940, 92.

[12] Anderson 1969–70.

[13] Anderson 1969–70.

[14] Padfield 1979–82, vol I, 170–1.

CHAPTER 6

[1] Worcester 1971, 335.

[2] Scheuring 1987, 9.

[3] Scheuring 1987, 289.

[4] Scheuring 1987, 320–1.

[5] Scheuring 1987, 322–3. Translated from the Chinese by H L Scheuring.

[6] Boxer 1969, 49 and 63.

[7] Groeneveldt 1898, 45.

[8] Groeneveldt 1889, 127 ff.

[9] Groeneveldt 1889, 132.

[10] Mundy 1905–36, vol III, part I, 227 ff.

[11] Mundy 1905–36, vol III, part I, 229.

[12] Mundy 1905–36, vol III, part I, 231.

CHAPTER 7

[1] Warnsinck 1940, 103 ff.

[2] Boxer 1930, 16.

[3] Quoted in Boxer 1930, 12.

[4] The events leading up to the battle are described in Boxer 1930 and Padfield 1979–82, vol I, 171 ff.

[5] Quoted in Boxer 1930, 211.

[6] Mundy 1905–36, vol III, part I, 37–8.

[7] Boxer 1930, 193.

[8] Mundy 1905–36, vol III, part I, 40.

[9] Boxer 1930, 167, 184.

[10] Boxer 1930, 51.

[11] Israel 1995, 269.

[12] Boxer 1930, 60 ff.

[13] Warnsinck 1940, III.

[14] Anderson 1969–70.

[15] Anderson 1969–70; Roncière 1920, 86 ff.

CHAPTER 8

[1] Gardiner/Atkinson 1899–1906, vol II, 237.

[2] Gardiner/Atkinson 1899–1906, vol II, 246.

[3] De Jonge 1858–62, vol I, 647.

[4] Coggeshall 1997, 32.

[5] Tanner 1903–9, vol IV, 227 ff.

[6] Macgregor 1973, 15 and 34.

[7] On fitting out a fireship see Vreughdenhill 1951, 68 ff; Witsen 1690, 184 ff; Falconer 1780, article 'Fire-Ship'; Röding 1793, article 'Brander'; Diderot/d'Alembert 1803, vol I, 201; Steel 1805, 397 ff; Korth 1826, 436 ff; Howarth 1979, 116 ff; De Jonge 1858–62, vol I, 647.

[8] Powell/Timings 1969, 136.

[9] De Jonge 1858–62, vol I, 647.

[10] Witsen 1690 gives the composition as one part gunpowder, half a part saltpetre, a quarter part resin and a quarter part sulphur.

[11] Falconer 1780, article 'Fire-Ship'.

[12] Falconer 1780, article 'Fire-Ship'.

[13] Coggeshall 1997, 26.

[14] Perrin 1928, 441.

[15] Fox 1996, 256.

[16] Powell/Timings 1969, 144.

CHAPTER 9

[1] Coggeshall 1997, 2.

[2] Perrin 1928, 372.

[3] The National Archives, Kew, PRO Adm 1/3557, 12 February 1689.

[4] Baynham 1970, 51.

[5] Coggeshall 1997, 79.

[6] Thomas 2004, 160.

[7] Coggeshall 1997, 45.

[8] Coggeshall 1997, 44; Kemp 1976, article 'Myngs'; Fox 1996, 323.

[9] Gardiner/Atkinson 1899–1906, vol II, 180.

[10] Powell/Timings 1969, 79.

[11] Coggeshall 1997, 38.

[12] Fox 1996, 76.

[13] Powell/Timings 1969, 65 and 79.

[14] Corbett 1905, 149–50.

[15] Powell/Timings 1969, 126.

[16] Coggeshall 1997, 49.

[17] Tanner 1903–9, vol IV, 103.

[18] HMC Finch IV, 299, 7 July 1692.

[19] Coggeshall 1997, 51.

[20] Voorbeytel Cannenburg 1950.

[21] See the printed report in the Scheepvaartmuseum, Amsterdam, Ref B-I-558(20)/A.1373 (1), and also Haverkorn 1899.

[22] Clowes 1897–1903, vol II, 197.

[23] Coggeshall 1997, 40.

[24] Coggeshall 1997, 43.

[25] Vergé-Franceschi 1996, 197.

[26] De Jonge 1858–62, vol I, 646.

[27] Warnsinck 1934, 119.

[28] Quoted in Coggeshall 1997, 58.

[29] Coggeshall 1997, 45.

[30] Clowes 1897–1903, vol II, 297.

[31] Coggeshall 1997, 45.

CHAPTER 10

[1] Oppenheim 1902–14, vol IV, 119 ff.

[2] Butler 1929, 267.

[3] Oppenheim 1902–14, vol III, 45.

[4] Padfield 1979–82, vol I, 183.

[5] On the causes of the First Anglo-Dutch War see Israel 1995, 714 ff; Padfield 1979–82, vol I, 181 ff; and Junge 1980, 143 ff.

[6] Israel 1995, 715.

[7] Hainsworth/Churches 1998, 3–4.

[8] De Jonge 1858–62, vol I, 415.

[9] The outbreak of the First Anglo-Dutch War is described in Hainsworth/Churches 1998, 4 ff; Ballhausen 1923, 36; and Clowes 1897–1903, vol II, 144 ff.

[10] Israel 1995, 715–16.

[11] Padfield 1979–82, vol I, 188.

[12] Israel 1995, 716.

[13] Padfield 1979–82, vol I, 194; Weber 1987.

[14] Corbett 1917, 576.

[15] Corbett 1917, 576.

[16] Gardiner/Atkinson 1899–1906, vol I, 265 ff.

[17] Corbett 1905, 89–90.

[18] Gardiner/Atkinson 1899/1906, vol II, 64–5.

[19] Padfield 1979–82, vol I, 202 ff; Ballhausen 1923, 370.

[20] Gardiner/Atkinson 1899–1906, vol II, 142.

[21] Quoted in Atkinson 1912, 47.

[22] Padfield 1979–82, vol I, 228; Ballhausen 1923, 592.

[23] Quoted in Atkinson 1910, 202 ff.

[24] Padfield 1979–82, vol I, 221; Atkinson 1910, 202 ff.

[25] On the economic consequences of the First Anglo-Dutch War see Israel 1995, 716 ff and Ballhausen 1923, 89.

[26] Ballhausen 1923, 627.

[27] Ballhausen 1923, 477.

[28] Padfield 1979–82, vol I, 232. Another source (Israel 1995) cites eleven ships and 4,000 men.

[29] Ballhausen 1923, 477.

[30] Rittmeyer 1907–11, vol I, 188.

[31] Clowes 1897–1903, vol II, 197.

[32] Ballhausen 1923, 646 ff.

CHAPTER 11

[1] National Maritime Museum 1967, 7.

[2] Warnsinck 1921, 242–300.

[3] Clowes 1897–1903, vol II, 256.

[4] Padfield 1979–82, vol II, 35.

[5] Anderson 1929, 223; Fox 1996, 109.

[6] The Battle of Lowestoft is described in Warnsinck 1921; Hainsworth/Churches 1998, 116 ff; Padfield 1979–82, vol II, 36 ff; Clowes 1897–1903, vol II, 262 ff.

[7] National Maritime Museum 1967, 8.

[8] Anderson 1929, 225; Fox 1996, 113.

[9] Warnsinck 1921.

[10] Anderson 1929, 228.

[11] Coggeshall 1997, 61; Fox 1996, 121.

[12] Warnsinck 1929.

[13] Padfield 1979–82, vol II, 47.

[14] Padfield 1979–82, vol II, 48; Shelley 1939.

[15] On the Four Days' Battle see National Maritime Museum 1967; Padfield 1979–82, vol II, 50 ff; Fox 1996; Dik 1993, 148–210; De Jonge 1858–62, vol II, 68 ff.

CHAPTER 12

[1] Warnsinck 1940, 392.

[2] De Graaf 1930, 85.

[3] Fox 1996, 241.

[4] Fox 1996, 250.

[5] On preparing a fireship see Coggeshall 1997, 29.

[6] The fireship attack on the *Henry* is described in Powell/Timings 1969, 234; Fox 1996, 237 ff; and Clowes 1897–1903, vol II, 272.

[7] Falconer 1780, 128.

[8] The second day is described in Fox 1996, 259 ff.

[9] The third day is described in Fox 1996, 277 ff.

[10] Dik 1993, 194.

[11] De Jonge 1858–62, vol II, 77.

[12] The fourth day is described in Fox 1996, 295 ff; Kitson 1998, 194 ff; and National Maritime Museum 1967, 16 ff.

[13] Fox 1996, 298.

[14] De Jonge 1858–62, vol II, 81.

[15] National Maritime Museum 1967, 24.

[16] De Jonge 1858–62, vol II, 83.

[17] Fox 1996, 317.

[18] Fox 1996, 325.

[19] Fox 1996, 318.

[20] Fox 1996, 321.

CHAPTER 13

[1] On the St James's Day Battle see Fox 1996, 331 ff.

[2] Anderson 1928, 13.

[3] Fox 1996, 335.

[4] 'Holmes's Bonfire' is described in National Maritime Museum 1967, 30–1; Anderson 1928, 18 ff; and Powell/Timings 1969, 278 ff.

[5] Powell/Timings 1969, 131.

[6] Powell/Timings 1969, 134.

[7] Padfield 1979–82, vol II, 57

[8] Sources for the Dutch attack on the Medway include Rogers 1970; National Maritime Museum 1967, 38; De Jonge 1858–62, vol II, 193 ff; and Padfield 1979–82, vol II, 61.

[9] Clowes 1897–1903, vol II, 424.

[10] De Jonge 1858–62, vol II, 188.

[11] National Maritime Museum 1967, 38.

[12] De Jonge 1858–62, vol II, 198.

[13] De Jonge 1858–62, vol II, 201.

[14] De Jonge 1858–62, vol II, 206–7; Rittmeyer 1907–11, 296.

[15] De Jonge 1858–62, vol II, 206–7; Warnsinck, 1921.

[16] See Röding 1793, article 'Spring auf dem Ankertau'.

[17] Lambertus van den Bos, "T Leeven en Daden van Michiel Adriensz. De Ruyter', in Van den Bos 1676, quoted in Dik 1993, 200.

[18] Coggeshall 1997, 59.

[19] Clowes 1897–1903, vol II, 297.

CHAPTER 14

[1] Powell/Timings 1969, 192.

[2] Gardiner/Atkinson 1899–1906, vol III, 38.

[3] Jal 1970, article 'Brûlot'.

[4] On defences against fireships see Laughton 1902, vol I, 15 and Harland 1984, 310.

[5] De Jonge 1858–62, vol II, 787.

[6] Oppenheim 1902–14, vol IV, 8–9.

[7] Fox 1996, 286.

[8] Diderot/d'Alembert 1803, vol I, 202.

[9] Gardiner/Lavery 1992, 30, 182–3; Corbett 1917, 'Origin of the Line of Battle'.

[10] Nicholas Tracy, 'Naval Tactics', in Gardiner/Lavery 1992, 182–6; Tunstall/Tracy 1990, 17–20.

[11] Potter 1968, 42–3.

[12] Kitson 1990, 156.

[13] De Jonge 1858–62, vol III, 724.

[14] Corbett 1905, 239 ff; Corbett 1909, 166 ff.

[15] Witsen 1690, 185.

[16] Gardiner/Lavery 1992, 28–9.

[17] Gardiner/Lavery 1992,

[18] Powell/Timings 1969, 246.

[19] Hayward 1655, 33.

[20] Blanckley 1750, article 'Fire Boom'.

[21] De Jonge 1858–62, vol. II, 206 ff.

[22] Meurer 1925.

[23] Laughton 1902, II, 209 ff.

[24] The Battle of Toulon (Cap Sicié) and the fight of the *Real Felipe* are described in 'The Journal of M. de Lage de Cueilly – Captain in the Spanish Navy during the campaign of 1744. Translated from the French by Lieutenant Thomas G. Carter, R.N.', in Laughton 1902, 208–88 (comments in square brackets by the author); and Clowes 1897–1903, vol III, 95 ff. On the character of Juan José Navarro de Viana y Búfalo see Novi 1997.

[25] Clowes 1897–1903, III, 100.

[26] Clowes 1897–1903, III, 100.

[27] Coggeshall 1997–1903, 70.

[28] Clowes, 1897–1903, III, 100.

CHAPTER 15

[1] Padfield 1979–82, vol II, 75.

[2] Ollard 1969, 174 ff.

[3] Padfield 1979–82, vol II, 79.

[4] De Jonge 1858–62, vol II, 774.

[5] Ollard 1969, 25.

[6] The Battle of Sole Bay is described in Padfield 1979– 82, vol II, 81 ff; De Jonge 1858–62, vol II, 282 ff; and Anderson 1946, 14. See also www.ship-wrecks.co.uk/BattleofSOLEBAY.htm.

[7] Anderson 1946, 176.

[8] Dassié 1695, 104 ff.

[9] Anderson 1946, 97.

[10] Anderson 1946, 174–5.

[11] Warnsinck 1940, 349–50.

[12] Anderson 1946, 98.

[13] Hainsworth/Churches 1998

[14] Fox 1980, 110.

[15] Clowes 1897–1903, vol II, 301.

[16] Padfield 1979–82, vol II, 88.

[17] Warnsinck 1940, 351.

[18] Anderson 1946, 101.

[19] Anderson 1946, 23.

[20] On the First Battle of Schooneveld see Warnsinck 1940, 354–5 and Rittmeyer 1907–11, 334 ff.

[21] Van de Velde 1958–74, vol I, 137.

[22] Anderson 1946, 300.

[23] Kitson 1998, 270.

[24] Anderson 1946, 35.

[25] Rittmeyer 1907–11, 341 ff; Anderson 1946, 356 ff.

[26] Anderson 1946, 359.

[27] Van de Velde 1958–74, vol I, 140.

[28] Anderson 1946, 360.

[29] Van de Velde 1958–74, vol I, 139.

[30] Anderson 1946, 361.

[31] Stenzel 1907–11, 234.

[32] On the Battle of Palermo see Rittmeyer 1907–11, 385 ff and Roncière 1920, 637 ff.

[33] Anderson 1969, 105 ff; www.marine.nl/historie/marinemuseum/Webspecials/heldendaden/1675-1678/Oland; De Jonge 1858–62, vol II, 518 ff.

[34] www.axelnelson.com/skepp/kronan.html.

[35] De Jonge 1858–62, vol II, 528.

[36] De Jonge 1858–62, vol II, 538.

CHAPTER 16

[1] Lambert 2000, 80–1.

[2] Padfield 1979–82, vol II, 123–4.

[3] Coggeshall 1997, 35.

[4] Coggeshall 1997, 36.

[5] De Jonge 1858–62, vol III, 730 ff.

[6] Quoted in Jal 1970, article 'Brûlot'.

[7] Boudriot/Berti 1992, 61 ff.

[8] www.gatchina3000.ru/brockhaus-and-efron-

encyclopedic-dictionary (in Russian).

9 Warnsinck 1934, 90 ff.

10 Quoted in Warnsinck 1934, 117–18.

11 Warnsinck 1934, n. 116.

12 www.marine.nl/historie/marinemuseum/
Webspecials/heldendaden/Negenjarigeoorlog/La_
Hougue/.

13 The Battle of La Hougue is described in Meurer
1925, 174–5; Lambert 2000, 80–1; Clowes 1897–1903, vol
II, 348 ff; and De Jonge 1858–62, vol III, 300 ff.

14 Lemineur 1996, 76 ff.

15 Gardiner/Lavery 1992, 87.

16 Oppenheim 1902–14, vol II, n. 44; Norton 1678, 156.

17 Clowes 1897–1903, vol II, n. 256.

18 Padfield 1979–82, vol II, 143–4.

19 Röding 1793, article 'Bombardiergaliote'.

20 Warnsinck 1940, 422.

21 Diderot/d'Alembert 1803, vol 00, 000.

22 Fyers 1925; Rittmeyer 1907–11, 459.

23 CSPD: W&M 5, 306: letter from Sir Martin Beckman
to Duke of Shrewsbury, 14 September 1695,

24 Warnsinck 1940, 423–4; Fyers 1925.

CHAPTER 17

1 De Jonge 1858–62, vol III, 594

2 Quoted in Padfield 1979–82, vol II, 162. See Owen 1938,
84 (Hopson's Journal) and
www.eudocs.lib.byu.edu/index.php/The_Battle_of_
Vigo,_Spain,_during_the_War_of_Spanish_Successi
on.

3 Numbers of contemporary fireships are given in
Gardiner/Atkinson 1899–1906; Fox 1980.
Powell/Timings 1969; Dassié 1695; Warnsinck 1934;
and De Jonge 1858–62, vol III.

4 Coggeshall 1997, 77.

5 Gardiner/Lavery 1992, 87.

6 Baugh 1977; Pâris 1886; Fincham 1851; Corbett 1905.

7 Baugh 1977, 217.

8 Clowes 1897–1903, vol III, 84 and 237.

9 Figures from Winfield 2007

10 'John Elphinston Papers Relating to the Russo-
Turkish War', 1769–1850 (bulk 1769–1771), Princeton
University Library, Department of Rare Books and
Special Collections, Manuscripts Division, C0951.

11 On the Battle of Chesme see Anderson 1952, 278 ff
and www.hronos.km.ru/sobyt/chesmen 1770.html
(translation from Russian: Gerhild Kirsch).

12 Brewer 2001, 94.

13 www.hronos.km.ru/sobyt/chesmen 1770.html
(translation from Russian: Gerhild Kirsch); Anderson
1952, 278 ff.

14 Clowes 1897–1903, vol III, 406.

15 Sandwich 1771–80, vol I, 362, 422.

16 Fincham 1851, 102–3; Corbett 1905, 248.

17 Clowes 1897–1903, vol III, 406 ff.

18 Mahan 1890, vol I, 517.

19 Sandwich 1771–80, vol II, 304–5. Ironically, James
Gambier was the uncle of Lord Gambier (1756–1833),
the British commander so reluctant to use fireships
at the Battle of Basque Roads in 1809.

20 Corbett 1905, 248.

21 Sandwich 1771–80, vol II, 177.

22 Sandwich 1771–80, vol III, 176.

23 Coggeshall 1997, 36.

24 Coggeshall 1997, 36.

25 Sandwich 1771–80, vol IV, 428–9.

26 Sandwich 1771–80, vol I, 153.

27 Clowes 1897–1903, vol III, 479.

28 Corbett 1905, 248.

29 Clowes 1897–1903, vols III, IV.

30 Diderot/d'Alembert 1803, vol I, article 'Brûlot'.

31 Diderot/d'Alembert 1803, vol I, article 'Brûlot'.

32 Nastyface 1836, quoted in Baynham 1970, p. 49 ff.

CHAPTER 18

1 Clowes 1897–1903, IV, 531.

2 Jackson 1900, II, 135.

3 The Battle of Copenhagen (1801) is described in
Clowes 1897, vol IV, 532.

4 Jackson 1900, vol II, 135.

5 Clowes 1897–1903, vol V, 69–70.

6 Schubert 2006, 15. Drawings of these devices, made
by the French from unexploded examples, are
reproduced in Gardiner 1997, 82–4.

7 Clowes 1897–1903, vol V, 70.

8 Hennig 2007.

9 Crossland, 2005.

10 Coggeshall 1997, 37 and 98.

11 Perrin 1928, 367 ff.

12 Coggeshall 1997, 37.

13 Clowes 1897–1903, vol V, 252 ff.

14 Nastyface 1836, in Baynham 1970, 50.

15 Clowes 1897–1903, vol V, 256.

16 Gardiner/Lavery 1992, 154; Perrin 1928, 392.

17 Nastyface 1836, in Baynham 1970, 51.

18 Thomas 2004, 157.

19 Marryat nd.

20 Thomas 2004, 159.

21 Nastyface 1836, in Baynham 1970, 51.

22 The Battle of Basque Roads is described in Clowes
1897–1903, vol V, 255 ff; Thomas 2004, 157 ff; and Vale
2002, 'The Basque Roads Affair'.

23 Barry O'Meara, Napoleon in Exile, 1822, vol II, 291,
quoted in Thomas 2004, 188.

24 Lloyd 1946.

25 Lord Cochrane's Secret War. www.everything2.com/
e2node/The%2520Lord%2520Cochrane%2527s%252
0Secret%2520War%2520Plan

26 Aridas 1982, Introduction.

27 Brewer 2001, 91 ff.

28 Brewer 2001, 95.

29 Anderson 1952, 484.

30 Anderson 1952, 485.

31 Brewer 2001, 164.

32 The Greek fireship attack on 18 June 1822 is described
in Brewer 2001, 163 ff and Anderson 1952, 487–8.

33 Anderson 1952, 489.

34 Brewer 2001, 236.

35 Anderson 1952, 495.

36 Brewer 2001, 236.

37 Anderson 1952, 503–4.

38 Tsoulios nd, vol II, 507.

39 Thomas 2004, 297 ff.

40 Thomas 2004, 309; Anderson 1952, 513–14.

41 Anderson 1952, 508.

42 Thomas 2004, 310.

43 Charles M'Pherson (1826–1828). Extracts from Life on
Board a Man-of-War with a description of the Battle
of Navarino in Baynham 1970, 144 ff.

44 On the Battle of Navarino see Brewer 2001, 330 ff;
Thomas 2004, 312; Anderson 1952, 523 ff; and
Baynham 1970, 148 ff.

45 Brewer 2001, 332.

AFTERWORD

1 Operation Chariot is described in Phillips 2000;
www.combinedops.com/St%20Nazaire.htm; and
www.war-
experience.org/history/keyaspects/stnazaire/default
.asp.

BIBLIOGRAPHY

Short references such as 'Anderson 1928' are as cited in the notes. For further information on many topics see Wikipedia at www.en.wikipedia.org.

Anderson 1928 = ANDERSON, R C (ed), 'Naval Operations in the Latter Part of the Year 1666', in Perrin 1928, 3–47.

Anderson 1929 = ANDERSON, R C (ed), *The Journal of Edward Montagu, First Earl of Sandwich: Admiral and General at Sea 1659–1665*. Navy Records Society, London 1929.

Anderson 1946 = ANDERSON, R C, *Journals and Narratives of the Third Dutch War*. Navy Records Society, London 1946.

Anderson 1952 = ANDERSON, R C, *Naval Wars in the Levant 1559–1853*. Liverpool 1952.

Anderson 1969 = ANDERSON, R C, *Naval Wars in the Baltic 1522–1850*. London 1969 (reprint of 1910 edition).

Anderson 1969–70 = ANDERSON, R C, 'The Thirty Years' War in the Mediterranean', *The Mariner's Mirror* 55 (1969), 435–451; and 56 (1970), 41–57.

Aridas 1982 = ARIDAS, KARIN (ed), *Freiheit oder Tod: Bilder des Panagiotis Zografos über den Kampf der Griechen gegen die türkische Fremdherrschaft 1821 bis 1830. Mit Auszügen aus den Memoiren des Generals Makrygiannis*. Leipzig and Weimar 1982.

Atkinson 1910 = ATKINSON, C T (ed), *Letters and Papers Relating to the First Dutch War 1652–1654*, vol IV. Navy Records Society, London 1910.

Atkinson 1912 = ATKINSON, C T (ed), *Letters and Papers Relating to the First Dutch War 1652–1654*, vol V. Navy Records Society, London 1912.

Ballhausen 1923 = BALLHAUSEN, CARL, *Der erste englisch-holländische Seekrieg 1652–1654 sowie der schwedisch-holländische Seekrieg 1658–1659*, vol I. The Hague 1923.

Baugh 1977 = BAUGH, DANIEL A (ed), *Naval Administration 1715–1750*. Navy Records Society, 1977.

Baynham 1970 = BAYNHAM, HENRY, *From the Lower Deck: The Royal Navy 1780–1840*. Barre, Massachusetts, 1970.

Blanckley 1750 = BLANCKLEY, THOMAS RILEY, *A Naval Expositor, Shewing and Explaining The Words and Therms of Art belonging to the Parts, Qualities, and Proportions of Building, Rigging, Furnishing, & Fitting a Ship for Sea* etc. London 1750 (reprinted Rotherfield 1988).

Boudriot/Berti 1992 = BOUDRIOT, JEAN and BERTI, HUBERT, *La frégate: Étude historique 1650–1850*. Collection Archéologie Navale Française, Paris 1992.

Boxer 1930 = BOXER, C R, *The Journal of Maarten Harpertszoon Tromp anno 1639*. Cambridge 1930.

Boxer 1969 = BOXER, C R, *The Portuguese Seaborne Empire 1415–1825*. London 1969.

Brenton 1823 = BRENTON, E P, *Naval History of Great Britain*. London 1823.

Brewer 2001 = BREWER, DAVID, *The Flame of Freedom: The Greek War of Independence 1821–1833*. London 2001.

Bruns 2004 = BRUNS, WERNER, 'Geschichte und Rekonstruktion der *Eendracht* von 1654', *Das Logbuch* 3 (2004), 92–7.

Butler 1929 = BUTLER, NATHANIEL, *Boteler´s Dialogues*, ed W G Perrin. Navy Records Society, London 1929.

Casson 1971 = CASSON, LIONEL, *Ships and Seamanship in the Ancient World*. Princeton 1971.

Clowes 1897–1903 = CLOWES, W. LAIRD, *The Royal Navy: A History from the Earliest Times to the Present*, 7 vols. London 1897–1903 (reprinted London 1996–7)

Coggeshall 1997 = COGGESHALL, JAMES LOWELL, 'The Fireship and its Role in the Royal Navy'. Unpublished dissertation, Texas A&M University 1997.

Corbett 1899 = CORBETT, JULIAN S, *Drake and the Tudor Navy: With a History of the Rise of England as a Maritime Power*, 2 vols. London 1899.

Corbett 1905 = CORBETT, JULIAN S, *Fighting Instructions 1530–1816*. Navy Records Society, London 1905 (reprinted London 1971).

Corbett 1909 = CORBETT, JULIAN S, *Signals and Instructions 1776–1794*. Navy Records Society, London 1909 (reprinted London 1971).

Corbett 1917 = CORBETT, JULIAN S, *England in the Mediterranean: A Study of the Rise and Influence of British Power within the Straits 1603–1713*, 2 vols. London 1917. Vol II Appendix, 'Origin of the Line of Battle', pp 569–80.

Corbett 1919 = CORBETT, JULIAN S, *The Successors of Drake*. London 1919.

Crossland 2005 = CROSSLAND, JOHN, 'Nelson Planned to Use Submarines and Mines', *The Sunday Times*, 16 October 2005.

CSPD: W&M 5 = *Calendar of State Papers Domestic: William & Mary 5, 1694–1695*. London 1906.

Dassié 1695 = DASSIÉ, F, *L'Architecture Navale, contenant la Maniere de construire les Navires, Galeres, Chaloupes & autres especes de Vaisseaux; l'Explication des Termes de la Marine; & les Définitions & proportions de toutes sortes de Bâtimens de Mer*. Paris 1695 (reprinted San Remo 1994).

David 1981 = DAVID, RICHARD (ed), *Hakluyt's Voyages: A Selection*. Boston 1981.

Davidson 1973 = DAVIDSON, H R E, 'The Secret Weapon of Byzantium', *Byzantinische Zeitschrift* 66 (1973), 61–74.

De Graaf 1930 = *Reisen van Nicolaus de Graaff. Gedaan naar alle gewesten des werelds beginnende 1639 tot 1687 incluis*, ed J C M Warnsinck. Linschoten Society XXXIII, The Hague 1930.

De Jonge 1858–62 = DE JONGE, J C, *Geschiedenis van het Nederlandsche Zeewezen*, 5 vols and index. Haarlem 1858–62.

Dickinson 1913 = DICKINSON, H W, *Robert Fulton: Engineer and Artist*. London 1913. Chapter 8 at http://www.history.rochester.edu/steam/dickinson/chapter8.html.

Diderot nd = DIDEROT and D'ALEMBERT (eds), *Recueil de Planches sur les Sciences, les Arts Libéraux, et les Arts Méchaniques, avec leur Explication – Arts Militaires*. Paris nd.

Diderot/d'Alembert 1803 = DIDEROT and D'ALEMBERT (eds), *Encyclopédie méthodique, ou par ordre de matières; par une société de gens de lettres, et savans et d'artistes etc. Marine*. Paris 1803 (reprinted Nice 1987), 3 vols.

Dik 1993 = DIK, G C, *De Zeven Provintiën: Een poging tot reconstructie, mede aan de hand van de nog bestaande Van de Velde-Tekeningen, van 's lands schip de Zeven Provinciën van 80–86 stukken, gebouwd voor de Admiraliteit van de Maze in 1665.* Franeker 1993.

Duffy 1979 = DUFFY, CHRISTOPHER, *Siege Warfare: The Fortress in the Early Modern World 1494–1660.* London 1979.

Falconer 1780 = FALCONER, WILLIAM, *An Universal Dictionary of the Marine etc.* London 1780 (reprinted Newton Abbot 1970).

Feldhaus 1914 = FELDHAUS, F M, *Die Technik: Ein Lexikon der Vorzeit, der geschichtlichen Zeit und der Naturvölker.* 1914 (reprinted Munich 1970).

Fernández-Armesto 1988 = FERNÁNDEZ-ARMESTO, FELIPE, *The Spanish Armada: The Experience of War in 1588.* Oxford 1988.

Fincham 1851 = FINCHAM, JOHN, *A History of Naval Architecture.* London 1851 (reprinted London 1979).

Folin 1892 = FOLIN, LE MARQUIS DE, *Bateaux et Navires: Progrés de la Construction navale a tous les Ages et dans tous les Pays.* Paris 1892 (reprinted Grenoble 1978).

Fox 1980 = FOX, FRANK, *Great Ships: The Battlefleet of King Charles II.* London 1980.

Fox 1996 = FOX, FRANK L, *A Distant Storm: The Four Days' Battle of 1666, the Greatest Sea Fight of the Age of Sail.* Rotherfield 1969.

Fyers 1925 = FYERS, EVAN W H, 'The Story of the Machine Vessels', *The Mariner's Mirror* 11 (1925), 50–90.

Galschut 1997 = GALSCHUT, D, *Pyrotechnia of konst in 't vuurwerken geschreven op 't schip Huijs Ter Lo.* 1692–1706. Delft 1997.

Gardiner 1997 = GARDINER, ROBERT (ed), *The Campaign of Trafalgar 1803–1805.* London 1997.

Gardiner/Atkinson 1899–1906 = GARDINER, SAMUEL RAWSON and ATKINSON, C T (eds), *Letters and Papers Relating to the First Dutch War 1652–1654,* 3 vols. Navy Records Society, London 1899, 1900, 1906.

Gardiner/Lavery 1992 = GARDINER, ROBERT and LAVERY, BRIAN (eds), *The Line of Battle: The Sailing Warship 1650–1840.* Conway's History of the Ship, London 1992.

Gautier 1973 = GAUTIER, MAURICE-PAUL, *Captain Frederick Marryat: L'homme et l'oeuvre.* Paris 1973.

Groeneveldt 1898 = GROENEVELDT, W P, *De Nederlanders in China: De eerste bemoiingen om den handel in China en de vestiging in de Pescadores (1601–1624),* Bijdragen tot de Taal-, Land- en Volkenkunde van Nederlandsch Indië, The Hague 1898.

Hainsworth/Churches 1998 = HAINSWORTH, ROGER and CHURCHES, CHRISTINE, *The Anglo-Dutch Naval Wars 1652–1674.* Stroud 1998.

Haldon 2007 = HALDON, JOHN, 'Greek Fire: A Medieval Weapon of Terror', *Minerva: The International Review of Ancient Art & Archaeology* (July–August 2007), 41–3.

Haldon/Byrne 1977 = HALDON, J and BYRNE, M, 'A Possible Solution to the Problem of Greek Fire', *Byzantinische Zeitschrift* 70 (1977), 91–9.

Hampden 1981 = HAMPDEN, JOHN (ed), *Sir Francis Drake, Pirat im Dienst der Queen: Berichte, Dokumente und Zeugnisse des Seehelden und seiner Zeitgenossen 1567–1596.* Munich 1981. First published in English as *Francis Drake Privateer: Contemporary Narratives and Documents,* London 1972.

Harland 1984 = HARLAND, JOHN, *Seamanship in the Age of Sail: An Account of the Shiphandling of the Sailing Man-of-War 1600–1860, Based on Contemporary Sources.* London 1984.

Haverkorn 1899 = HAVERKORN VAN RIJSEWIJK, P, 'De eerste oorlog met England en W. van de Velde de oude', *Oud Holland* 17 (1899), 33–46.

Hayward 1655 = HAYWARD, EDWARD, *The Sizes and Lengths of Riggings etc (1655) and the Hayward–Kendal Pamphlet Controversy, 1656* (reprinted London 1967).

Hennig 2007 = HENNIG, KLAUS J, 'Ein Mann macht Dampf', *Die Zeit,* 33 (9 August 2007).

HMC Finch IV = HISTORICAL MANUSCRIPTS COMMISSION, *Report on the Manuscripts of the Late Allan George Finch, Esq of Burley-on-the-Hill, Rutland,* vol IV. London 1965.

Höckmann 1985 = HÖCKMANN, OLAF, *Antike Seefahrt.* Munich 1985.

Howarth 1979 = HOWARTH, DAVID, *Die Kriegsschiffe.* Amsterdam 1979. First published in English as *The Men-of-War,* Time-Life Seafarers series, London 1978.

Israel 1995 = ISRAEL, JONATHAN I, *The Dutch Republic: Its Rise, Greatness and Fall, 1477–1806.* Oxford 1995.

Jackson 1900 = JACKSON, T STURGES, *Logs of the Great Sea Fights 1794–1805,* 2 vols. Navy Records Society, London 1899 and 1900 (reprinted by the Society 1981).

Jal 1970 = JAL, AUGUSTIN, *Nouveau glossaire nautique d'Augustin Jal: Révision de l'édition publieé en 1848.* Paris 1970–89.

Junge 1980 = JUNGE, HANS-CHRISTOPH, *Flottenpolitik und Revolution: Die Entstehung der englischen Seemacht während der Herrschaft Cromwells.* Stuttgart 1980.

Kemp 1976 = KEMP, PETER (ed), *The Oxford Companion to Ships and the Sea.* London 1976.

Kirchhoff 1910 = KIRCHHOFF, HERMANN, *Seehelden und Admirale.* Leipzig 1910.

Kirsch 1990 = KIRSCH, PETER, *The Galleon: The Great Ships of the Armada Era.* London 1990.

Kitson 1998 = KITSON, FRANK, *Prince Rupert: Admiral and General-at-Sea.* London 1998.

Korth 1826 = KORTH, J T D, *Die Schiffbaukunst, oder die Kunst, den Bau der Kriegs-, Kauffahrtey- und anderer Schiffe nach theoretischen und praktischen Regeln auszuführen.* Berlin 1826 (reprinted Kassel 1980).

Lambert 2000 = LAMBERT, ANDREW, *War at Sea in the Age of Sail 1650–1850.* London 2000.

Landström 1961 = LANDSTRÖM, BJÖRN, *Das Schiff: Vom Einbaum zum Atomboot.* Gütersloh 1961. Also published in English as *The Ship,* London 1961.

Laughton 1895 = LAUGHTON, JOHN KNOX (ed), *State Papers Relating to the Defeat of the Spanish Armada anno 1588,* 2 vols. Navy Records Society, London 1895 (reprinted by the Society 1981).

Laughton 1902 = LAUGHTON, JOHN KNOX, *The Naval Miscellany II.* Navy Records Society, London 1912.

Lemineur 1996 = LEMINEUR, JEAN-CLAUDE, *Les vaisseux du Roi Soleil.* Nice 1996.

Lewis 1937 = LEWIS, MICHAEL, 'Fresh Light on San Juan de Ulua', *The Mariner's Mirror* 23/3 (1937), 295–315.

Lewis 1969 = LEWIS, MICHAEL, *The Hawkins Dynasty: Three Generations of a Tudor Family.* London 1969.

Lloyd 1946 = LLOYD, CHRISTOPHER,

'Dundonald's Crimean War Plans', *The Mariner's Mirror* 32 (1946), 147–54.

Macgregor 1973 = MACGREGOR, DAVID R, *Fast Sailing Ships. Their Design and Construction 1775–1875*. Lymington, Hampshire 1973.

Mahan 1890 = MAHAN, ALFRED THAYER, *Der Einfluß der Seemacht auf die Geschichte*, 2 vols. Berlin 1890 (reprinted Kassel 1974). First published in English as *The Influence of Sea Power upon History*, London 1890.

Mattingly 1959 = MATTINGLY, GARRETT, *The Armada*. Boston 1959.

Marryat nd = MARRYAT, CAPTAIN FREDERICK, *Frank Mildmay or the Naval Officer*. London nd (Kessinger Publishing reprint).

Meteren 1640 = METEREN, EMANUEL VAN, *Meteranus Novus, Das ist: Wahrhafftige Beschreibung Dess Niederländischen Krieges etc.*, vol I. Amsterdam 1640.

Meurer 1925 = MEURER, ALEXANDER, *Seekriegsgeschichte in Umrissen: Seemacht und Seekriege vornehmlich vom 16. Jahrhundert ab*. Berlin 1925.

Mountaine 1756 = MOUNTAINE, WILLIAM, *The Seaman's Vade-Mecum and Defensive War by Sea etc.* London 1756 (reprinted London 1971).

Mundy 1905–36 = MUNDY, PETER, *The Travels of Peter Mundy in Europe and Asia 1608–1667*, ed Richard Carnac Temple, 6 vols. Hakluyt Society, Second Series, London 1905–36.

Nassau-Siegen 1973 = NASSAU-SIEGEN, GRAF JOHANN VON, *Das Kriegsbuch*. Wiesbaden 1973.

Nastyface 1836 = NASTYFACE, JACK (alias William Robinson), *Nautical Economy or Forecastle Reflections of Events during the Last War*. London 1836 (reprinted London 1973).

National Maritime Museum 1967 = *The Second Dutch War 1665–1667, Described in Pictures & Manuscripts of the Time*. National Maritime Museum, London 1967.

Norton 1678 = NORTON, ROBERT, *The Gunner: The Making of Fire Works*. London 1678 (reprinted Amsterdam and New York 1973).

Novi 1997 = NOVI, CARLOS, 'The Marqués de la Victoria and the Advancement of Naval Lexicography in Eighteenth-Century Spain', *The Mariner's Mirror* 83 (1997), 136–49.

Ollard 1969 = OLLARD, RICHARD, *Man of War: Sir Robert Holmes and the Restoration Navy*. London 1969.

Oppenheim 1902–14 = OPPENHEIM, M (ed), *The Naval Tracts of Sir William Monson*. Navy Records Society, London 1902 (vols I and II), 1912 (vol III), 1913 (vol IV), 1914 (vol V).

Oudendijk 1941 = OUDENDIJK, JOHANNA K, *Een bourgondisch ridder over den oorlog ter zee. Philips van Kleef als leermeester van Karel V.* Amsterdam 1941.

Owen 1938 = OWEN, J H, *War at Sea under Queen Anne*. Cambridge 1938.

Ozanne 1762 = OZANNE, NICOLAS-MARIE, *Marine Militaire ou Recueil des differens Vaisseaux qui servent a la Guerre. Suivis des Manoeuvres qui ont le plus de Raport au Combat ainsi qua l'Ataque et la Defense des Ports*. Paris 1762.

Padfield 1979–82 = PADFIELD, PETER, *Tide of Empires: Decisive Naval Campaigns in the Rise of the West.* Vol I: *1481–1654*, London 1979. Vol II, *1654–1763*, London 1982.

Pâris 1886 = PÂRIS, EDMOND, *Collection de plans ou dessins de navires bateaux anciens ou modernes existant ou disparus avec leur éléments numériques nécessaires a leur construction*, part III. Paris 1886 (reprinted Hamburg 1984).

Parker 1979 = PARKER, GEOFFREY, *Der Aufstand der Niederlande: Von der Herrschaft der Spanier zur Gründung der niederländischen Republik 1549–1609*. Munich 1979. First published in English as *Spain and the Netherlands 1549–1609*, London 1979.

Pemsel 1985 = PEMSEL, HELMUT, *Biographisches Lexikon zur Seekriegsgeschichte: Seehelden von der Antike bis zur Gegenwart*. Koblenz 1985.

Perrin 1928 = PERRIN, WILLIAM GORDON (ed), *The Naval Miscellany III*. Navy Records Society, London 1928 .

Petrejus 1978 = PETREJUS, E W, *Oude zeilschepen en hun modellen: Binnenschepen jachten en visscherschepen*. Bussum 1978.

Phillips 2000 = PHILLIPS, C E LUCAS, *The Greatest Raid of All*. London 2000.

Potter 1968 = POTTER, ELMAR B and NIMITZ, CHESTER W, *Seemacht: Eine Seekriegsgeschichte von der Antike bis zur Gegenwart*. Herrsching 1968. First published in English as *Sea Power: A Naval History*, New York and London 1960.

Powell/Timings 1969 = POWELL, J R, and TIMINGS, E K (eds), *The Rupert and Monk Letter Book 1666*. Navy Records Society, London 1969

Pryor/Jeffreys 2006 = PRYOR, J H and JEFFREYS, E M, Appendix, 'Greek Fire', in *The Age of the Dromon*. Leiden 2006.

Rittmeyer 1907–11 = RITTMEYER, RUDOLPH, *Seekriege und Seekriegswesen in ihrer weltgeschichtlichen Entwicklung. Mit besonderer Berücksichtigung der großen Sekriege des XVII. und XVIII. Jahrhunderts.* Vol I: *Von den Anfängen bis 1740*, Berlin 1907. Vol II: *Von 1739–1793*, Berlin 1911.

Rodgers 1967 = RODGERS, WILLIAM LEYARD, *Naval Warfare under Oars, 4th to 16th Centuries: A Study of Strategy, Tactics and Ship Design*. Annapolis 1967.

Röding 1793 = RÖDING, JOHANN HINRICH, *Allgemeines Wörterbuch der Marine in allen europäischen Seesprachen nebst vollständigen Erklaerungen*, 3 vols text, 1 vol plates. Hamburg and Halle 1793 (reprinted Amsterdam nd).

Rodriguez-Salgado 1988 = RODRIGUEZ-SALGADO, M J et al, *An International Exhibition to Commemorate the Spanish Armada*. Exhibition catalogue, London 1988.

Rogers 1970 = ROGERS, P G, *The Dutch in the Medway*. London 1970.

Rogers 1971 = ROGERS, HENRY HUDDLESTON, *Collection of Ship Models: United States Naval Academy Museum*. Annapolis 1971.

Romocki 1895 = ROMOCKI, S J VON, *Geschichte der Explosivstoffe*, vol I: *Geschichte der Sprengstoffchemie, der Sprengtechnik und des Torpedowesens bis zum Beginn der neuesten Zeit*. Berlin 1895.

Roncière 1920 = RONCIÈRE, CHARLES DE LA, *Histoire de la Marine Française*, vol V: *La Guerre de Trente Ans: Colbert*. Paris 1920.

Rowse 1955 = ROWSE, A L, *The Expansion of Elizabethan England*. London 1955.

Sandwich 1771–80 = *The Private Papers of John, Earl of Sandwich, First Lord of the Admiralty 1771–1782*, ed G R Barnes and H J Owen, 4 vols, Navy Records Society. Vol. I: *August 1770 – March 1778*, London 1932. Vol. II: *March 1778 – May 1779*,

London 1933. Vol. III: *May 1779 – December 1780*, London 1936. Vol. IV: *1781–1782*, London 1938.

Schenkel 1998 = SCHENKEL, RONALD, 'Feuer! Feuer an Bord! Brennende Schiffe dienten in Seeschlachten als Waffen – und wurden zu einem Motiv in der Malerei', *Mare* 9 (August–September 1998).

Scheuring 1987 = SCHEURING, HANS LOTHAR, *Die Drachenfluß-Werft von Nanking: Das Lung-chiang ch'uan-ch'ang chih, eine Ming-zeitliche Quelle zur Geschichte des chinesischen Schiffbaus*. Frankfurt 1987.

Schiller 1966 = SCHILLER, FRIEDRICH, *Sämtliche Werke, vol IV: Historische Schriften*. Munich 1966.

Schubert 2006 = SCHUBERT, P, SOHST, H et al, *Die deutschen Marinen im Minenkrieg*, Vol I. BoD, Rostock 2006.

Shelley 1939 = Shelley, Roland J A, 'The Division of the English Fleet in 1666', *The Mariner's Mirror* 25 (1939), 178–96.

Sopers c1930 = SOPERS, P V M, *Schepen die Verdwijnen*. Amsterdam c1930

Steel 1805 = STEEL, DAVID, *The Elements and Practice of Naval Architecture illustrated with a Series of Thirty-Eight Large Draughts and Numerous Smaller Engravings*. London 1805 (reprinted London 1977).

Stenzel 1907–11 = STENZEL, ALFRED, *Seekriegsgeschichte in ihren wichtigsten Abschnitten mit Berücksichtigung der Seetaktik*, 4 parts. Hanover and Leipzig 1907–11.

Stettner 2000 = STETTNER, HEINRICH, 'Brander contra Schiffbrücke: Die Sperrung der Schelde und der Fall Antwerpens 1584/85 – auch ein Stück Quellen- und Literaturgeschichte', *Deutsches Schiffahrtsarchiv* 23 (2000), 251–70.

Tanner 1903–9 = TANNER, J R (ed), *Naval Manuscripts in the Pepysian Library at Magdalene College, Cambridge*, 4 vols. Navy Records Society, [London] 1903–9.

Thomas 2004 = THOMAS, DONALD, *Cochrane: Britannia's Sea Wolf*. London 2004.

Tsoulios nd = TSOULIOS, GEORGE. *Historical Album of the Greek War of Independence 1821*, 2 vols. Athens nd.

Tunstall/Tracy 1990 = TUNSTALL, BRIAN, *Naval Warfare in the Age of Sail: The Evolution of Fighting Tactics 1650–1815*, ed Nicholas Tracy. London, 1990.

Usherwood 1983 = USHERWOOD, STEPHEN and ELIZABETH, *The Counter-Armada, 1596: The Journal of the 'Mary Rose'*. London, Sydney and Toronto 1983.

Vale 2002 = VALE, BRIAN, *The Audacious Admiral Cochrane: The True Life of a Naval Legend*. London 2004.

Van Beylen 1970 = VAN BEYLEN, J, *Schepen van de Nederlanden*. Amsterdam, 1970.

Van den Bos 1676 = VAN DEN BOS, LAMBERTUS, *Leeven en Daden der Doorluchtighste Zee-Helden en Ontdeckers van Landen deser eeuwen*. 1676.

Van de Velde 1958–74 = *Van De Velde Drawings: A Catalogue of Drawings in the National Maritime Museum Made by the Elder and the Younger Willem van de Velde*, ed M S Robinson. Vol I : *A Catalogue of Drawings in the National Maritime Museum Made by the Elder and the Younger Willem van de Velde*, Cambridge 1958. Vol II: *The Ingram Volume*, Cambridge 1974.

Van de Veldes 1982 = *The Art of the Van de Veldes: Paintings and Drawings by the Great Dutch Marine Artists and their English Followers*. Exhibition catalogue, National Maritime Museum, London 1982.

Vassilios 1998 = CHRISTIDES, VASSILIOS, 'Fireproofing of War Machines, Ships and Garments', in *Sailing Ships of the Mediterranean Sea and the Arabian Gulf*, vol. I, ed Christos G Makrypoulias, Graeco-Arabica Supplement I, 11–17. Athens 1998.

Vergé-Franceschi 1996 = VERGÉ-FRANCESCHI, MICHEL, *La Marine française au XVIIIe siècle: Guerres-administration-exploration*. Paris 1996.

Vichot 1971 = VICHOT, JAQUES, *Les gravures des sièges de Ré & La Rochelle (1625–1628): Deux chefs-d'oevre de Jaques Callot: Étude historique et descriptive*. Paris 1971.

Viereck 1975 = VIERECK, H D L, *Die römische Flotte: Classis Romana*. Herford 1975.

Voorbeytel Cannenburg 1950 = VOORBEYTEL CANNENBURG, W, 'The Van de Veldes', *The Mariners Mirror* 36/3 (1950), 185–204.

Vreughdenhill 1951 = VREUGHDENHILL, A, *Koningen scheepsbowers en zeevaarders*. Amsterdam 1951. Includes a description of a fireship by Willem Claesz. van Utrecht, *Arithmetische en Geometrische Pracktycke der Bosschieterye*, 1641.

Warnsinck 1921 = WARNSINCK, J C M, 'De laaste tocht van Van Wassenauer van Obdam: Voorjaar 1665' (1921), in Warnsinck 1940, 242–300.

Warnsinck 1929 = WARNSINCK, J C M, *De retourvloot van Pieter de Bitter (Kerstmis 1664–Najaar 1665)*. The Hague 1929.

Warnsinck 1934 = WARNSINCK, J C M, *De vloot van de koning-stadhouder 1689–1690*. Amsterdam 1934.

Warnsinck 1940 = WARNSINCK, J C M, *Van vlootvoogden en zeeslagen*. Amsterdam 1940.

Waters 1975 = WATERS, D W, *The Elizabethan Navy and the Armada of Spain*. National Maritime Museum, Maritime Monographs and Reports 17 (1975).

Weber 1987 = WEBER, R E J, 'The Introduction of the Single Line Ahead as a Battle Formation by the Dutch 1665–1666', *The Mariner's Mirror* 73 (1987), 5–19.

Wernham 1985 = WERNHAM, R B, *After the Armada: Elizabethan England and the Struggle for Western Europe 1588–1595*. Oxford 1985.

Winfield 2007 = WINFIELD, RIF, *British Warships in the Age of Sail 1714–1792*. Barnsley 2007.

Wislicenus 1910 = WISLICENUS, GEORG, *Die Entwicklung der Seekriegswaffen*. Berlin 1910.

Witsen 1690 = WITSEN, NICOLAES, *Architectura Navalis et Regimen Nauticum ofte Aaloude en Hedendaagsche Scheeps-Bouw en Bestie etc*. Amsterdam 1690 (reprinted Amsterdam nd).

Worcester 1971 = WORCESTER, G R G, *The Junks and Sampans of the Yangtze*. Annapolis 1971.

INDEX